CW01011182

Heir Island
Inis Uí Drisceoil

Its History and People

AERIAL PICTURE OF HEIR ISLAND
Also showing the Skeams, East Calf Island, Cunnamore Point, Whitehall harbour, Ardagh, Turkhead,
Quarantine and Sandy islands, the Catalogues
and the north east corner of Sherkin Island (part of Farrancoush townland)

Based on Ordnance Survey Ireland Permit No. 7904
© Ordnance Survey Ireland and Government of Ireland

Aerial picture on cover taken by Daphne Pouchin Mould
© Sherkin Island Marine Station

Heir Island
Inis Uí Drisceoil

Its History and People

EUGENE DALY

Heron's Way Press
2004

First published in 2004 by Heron's Way Press,
c/o Eugene Daly,
Curraheen, Leap,
Co. Cork, Ireland

British Library Cataloguing in Publication Data
A CIP catalogue record for this book is available from
the British Library

ISBN 0-9548662-0-7

Typeset and Printed by Inspire Design and Print, Skibbereen, Co. Cork
The author acknowledges funding by The Heritage Council

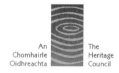

An
Chomhairle
Oidhreachta

The
Heritage
Council

The Author

Eugene Daly is a native of Turkhead, Church Cross, Skibbereen, situated on the shores
of Roaringwater Bay. His father, Micheál O'Dálaigh was a native of Cape Clear and his
mother, Mary Pyburn, a native of Heir Island. Eugene lived in Heir Island in his grand-
parents' house in *Paris* in his early youth and started his schooling in the island.

Eugene has a lifelong love of the islands in Roaringwater Bay and in particular of Heir
Island. The sea and the islands are in his blood from his Pyburn and Cahalane ancestors
on his mother's side and the Dalys and O'Driscolls from Cape Clear on his father's side.
He has a keen interest in local history and has contributed articles to the *Mizen Journal*,
The *Southern Star* and *Rosscarbery Past and Present*. He is also a poet and has written
many poems about Heir Island.

Eugene has been very much influenced by his uncle, Jack Pyburn, and never tires of
listening to stories of the old days and of life under the "towel" in the old lobster boats.
During his college days Eugene spent one summer lobster fishing off Kinsale with the
late Neilly O'Donovan of Heir and the late Timothy John Cadogan, Ardagh, Aughadown, in the *Pride of Toe Head*.

Eugene is a retired national school teacher and lives near Leap in West Cork.

This book is dedicated to my wife, Kathleen, who has come to love Heir Island as much as I do. Without her support, enthusiasm, advice and expertise with a computer, this book would never have been published. Many of the photographs have been taken by her. This book is as much Kathleen's as mine.

Also for all the kind, big-hearted people of Heir Island, especially my late mother, Mary Daly, (nee Pyburn), and my grandmother, Lou Pyburn (nee Cahalane)

Heir Island

At the highest point
A lichened boulder,
Where Mass was prayed.

The long finger of the Reen
Extends towards Sherkin.
The sea breaks in endless moans.

Between Heir and Cape
Skerries surface with the ebb,
Hags that fisherman avoid.

In the west a salmon sun
Eases into the sea,
Beyond known and fabled islands.

The sea rocks with a lullaby
Lilt under the bridge.
Three herons rise from the reeds.

Eugene Daly

The above poem was first published in a Sense of Cork in 2001.

Introduction

Islands are enchanted places. Heir Island, in the centre of the archipelago of islands in Roaringwater Bay, is, for me, the jewel in the crown. Wide vistas of sea, islands and rocks, sandy strands, a profusion of colour when the flowers bloom, a mosaic of heather and furze in late summer, the rugged heath and high cliffs in the Dún, all contribute to its beauty. For generations, little yawls went out to catch lobster and crayfish, to net mackerel and herring, to long-line for cod, ling and gurnet. The same men, at plough time and harvest, had to turn their backs on the dangerous, provident sea to consider the urgencies of the land. They had to cut and draw seaweed to enrich the land, to fashion lobster pots in winter, to flail the corn.

Women kept fires going, drew water from the wells, milked the cows, made butter, baked bastable cakes, reared large families. They knew hardship and poverty, mourned exiled children and siblings. They had to pick periwinkles in bare feet on cold winter days. Young men went to sea or emigrated to England, U.S.A. or Australia. Sometimes the younger members of a family never met an older brother or sister because of emigration. But there was great community spirit. Neighbour helped neighbour. They were poor but happy, as one islander put it. On winter nights they went scoruíochting; the old stories were told and retold. They danced and sang, listened to stories, played cards.

They knew the vagaries and changes of the weather in all seasons. Their livelihoods and sometimes their lives depended on a good reading of the weather. Many things had to be taken into consideration: the phases and appearance of the moon, the ebb, flow and sound of the seas, the habits of birds and animals plus a hundred intangibles the urban dweller knew nothing about.

An old man or woman dies, and a store of unique experience is lost forever. The ethos and outlook of the islanders has changed since I was a child. But Heir retains its unique ambience, its peace and a lifestyle in tune with the rhythm of nature. People are more prosperous and more independent now. But the sea and strand, hills and rocks are still there and I am thankful that I saw those everlasting things with a child's eye and the vivid people who lived among them and their benign rituals.

This is their story.

Eugene Daly, July, 2004

Note: The correct spelling for Heir Island is Heir. In olden days it was usually spelled Hare. In the text, direct quotes are spelled Hare, where it is spelled as such in documents, newspapers, etc.

Location

If you want to visit Heir Island, follow the N71 from Cork to Skibbereen. As you leave Skibbereen, still on the N71, you will have the Ilen River – Eibhile (sparkling river) on your left. As you leave the town you will see Abbeystrowery graveyard on your right, just beyond the old bridge. Here thousands of victims of the Famine are buried. The Skibbereen area and the Mizen peninsula were very badly affected in those awful years.

About four miles west of Skibbereen, you pass the church and graveyard of St. Matthew on your right at a bend. Just beyond the church, turn left and follow the road. After passing St. Comghall's Church at Lisheen, you will reach the height of Lisheen at Minihan's pub. From here there is a panoramic view of Roaringwater Bay from Baltimore to Schull. If the day is clear you will see the two biggest islands, Sherkin and Cape Clear to the southwest and right in the middle of the bay is Heir, its white cottages sparkling in the sunshine. If you look across the bay to the Iveagh (Mizen) peninsula you cannot miss the reconstructed McCarthy castle at Kilcoe, or the peak of Mount Gabriel, the highest hill in the peninsula.

If you follow the narrow winding road from Lisheen, you will see on your right the partly-ruined Rincolisky castle of the O'Driscolls, also called Rincor. At the bottom of the Pound Hill you will see high-walled Whitehall House, for long the home of the Townsend family, former landlords of the townland and some of the islands, East Calf Island and the Skeams. Finally you will reach land's end, Cunnamore Point. There are two ferries serving the island; timetables are well displayed.

Heir Island is less dramatic visually than Sherkin or Cape Clear. It is mostly low-lying with the highest land, a coastal heath, at the western end, and running through the middle of the island a ridge of rocky land. It has much to offer: peace and solitude, shining sandy beaches, a profusion of wild flowers especially in early summer, dramatic cliffs at the western end and from the higher points of the island, panoramic views. Here the lark still sings, butterflies flutter on fine days and seals cry on the rocks. A sense of undisturbed tranquility, a slow pace of life and the sea everywhere. The sounds are all natural – the eternal movement of wind, the ocean's roar or waves lapping against the rocks, seabirds' cries, choughs swirling over the Dún, the piping of oystercatchers, the haunting call of the curlew, the raven's croak – and the occasional engine noise of old cars, tractor or motor boat.

Acknowledgements

My research into *Heir Island, Its History and People* has been greatly facilitated by the many island people, those still living on Heir and those who have settled on the mainland, who shared with me their knowledge of the island: the boats, the fishing, the land, the placenames, the characters, the stories. Those people, a few, alas, no longer with us, gave generously of their time and were always extremely hospitable. They were generous with information, stories, photographs. Without their assistance this book could not have been written. I feel privileged to record in print their stories and memories of Heir. I am sincerely thankful to the following, who still reside on Heir:

My uncle Jack Pyburn and his family, Jimmy (Poulnacalee), John (Whitehall), Richie (Heir) and Dan (Cork), Lizzie Minihane, Dan McCarthy, John and Rose Harte, Danny Murphy, the late Neilly O'Donovan, Heir Island.

My gratitude also to the following Heir Islanders who now live on the mainland: Eddie Pyburn, Schull, John Fitzgerald and his wife Bridie (nee O'Driscoll), Skibbereen, Mary O'Flynn (nee Cotter), Bantry, Margaret O'Sullivan, (nee Murphy), Clonakilty, Kathleen McSweeney (nee Murphy), Skibbereen, Francis Fitzgerald, Hollyhill, Aughadown, Kathleen Griffin (nee Burke), Schull, Christy Burke, Schull, Finbarr Harte and his wife Mary Ellen (nee O'Driscoll), Skeagh, Aughadown, Michael Harte, Mohonagh, Nelly Healy, (nee Fitzgerald), Old Head of Kinsale, Brenda O'Neill, Dublin, Marie Leonard (nee Harte) Kilkilleen, Michael Minihane, Garrettstown, Peter and Dan Joe Murphy, Cunnamore, Katie O'Driscoll (nee O'Donovan), Kilkilleen, Tadhg O'Driscoll, Kilkilleen, Michael John Harte, Cloughboola, Skibbereen and Heir, Margaret and Peggy O'Donovan, Skibbereen, Michael John O'Neill, Whitehall, Mary Falvey, (nee McCarthy), Enniskeane, Lizzie O'Connor (nee Cahalane), Cork, Neil McCarthy, Velvetstown, Buttevant, Mary and Denis McCarthy, Cork.

Special thanks to Willie O'Regan, West Skeam and Whitehall, who shared with me his immense knowledge of island history and lore; also Mary Dwyer (nee Harte) Collatrum and East Skeam.

Many thanks also to those with island connections: Cliffy and Mary Minihane, Cunnamore, Michael and Nancy Minihane, Cunnamore and Skibbereen, Breda Harte, Lahertanavally, Aughadown, James Cadogan, Ardagh, Church Cross, Mary McCarthy, Coolanuller, Hannah Minihane, Kinsale, Timmy Joe, Rose and Jerome Whooley, Lisheen, Maureen Davis (nee Cadogan), Lissaree, John Paul Healy, Cashelane, Durrus, Mary McCarthy, Tragumna, whose father came from

Heir, Connie and Paddy McCarthy, Ballycumisk, Ballydehob, whose grandfather was Ricky O'Regan, West Skeam, Mary and Stevie Lynch, Kilbrinogue, Ballydehob, Kieran and Eileen Daly, Hollyhill, John Merwick, N.T., Kilcoe, Molly Cadogan, Ardagh (deceased), Mary Sheehan (nee Desmond), Leap, whose father came from East Skeam, Kevin O'Regan, Aughadown and Liam O'Regan, Southern Star, whose grandfather came from East Calf, Connie Desmond, Whitehall, Donal Hurley, Aughadown, whose ancestors lived on East Calf; Denis O'Driscoll, Kilkilleen, Alfie O'Mahony, Skibbereen, Denis Shanahan, Union Hall.

I am grateful to the following:- Seamus Ryan, North St., Skibbereen, Adrian Healy, Leap, John Thulier, Kinsale, Carol Gilbert, Castlehaven, Séamus Ó Máille, Beaufort, Killarney, George Bush, Crosshaven and Baltimore, Eleanor Calnan, Leap, Richard Posgate, Whitehall, Danny Allen, Toormore.

I am grateful to the following whose ancestors came from Heir: Karen Linden, Boston and Baltimore, Steve Cesareo, Hillsdale, New Jersey, Betty and Bruce Pimmentel, New Jersey, Dan Murphy, Colorado, John Henderson, New York, Catherine O'Connor, Isle of Wight and London, Con Harte, Australia and East Skeam, Marion Haughey, New York, Mary Kacin, Teaneck, New Jersey, (deceased) Eileen Fagan (nee Murphy) New York; Denis Scanlon, New York; Gen Dunworth, Florida;

I am grateful to the following who have made Heir Island their home and assisted me in my research; Percy Hall, John and Patricia Moore, Don and Mary O'Connor, Frank and Gene Dawe, Professor Gunter Glebe, John Desmond and Elmary Fenton, Gubby Williams and Christine Thery, Bill and Liz Morris.

I am grateful to Ted O'Driscoll, Baltimore for copy of the line plans of the *Hanorah;* to Mary Jordan and Colm Ó Cuileannáin for photograph of the *Fionn.* Thanks also to Peggy Townend, Turkhead, for photographs. I am grateful to Pierce Hickey for photographs, Fr Augustine Keating for a picture of West Skeam and Mrs Maureen Fahy, Glandore, for a copy of a map of West Skeam.

I owe a debt of gratitude to Dr. Éamon Lankford, for his generous assistance with source material and encouragement, also to Matt Murphy of Sherkin Island Marine Centre for advice and encouragement and for permission to use aerial photographs.

I am grateful to John Finn, Registrar of Fishing for the Port of Registry of Skibbereen, for facilitating access to the Register of Fishing Boats and to Laurence Connolly for access to his own personal records. School Folklore Manuscript has been reproduced with the kind permission of the head of the Department of Irish Folklore, University College, Dublin.

Many thanks to Tim Cadogan of Cork County Library for his assistance in sourcing material and also to his colleagues in the library, Kieran Wyse and Niamh Cronin. I would also like to thank personnel at Cork City Library, Cork County Archives, staff at *Southern Star*, Daphne Pouchin Mould, Mary Mackey, editor of the Mizen Journal, staff at National Library and National Archives, Dublin, Boole Library, U.C.C., Central Statistics Office, Dublin, Ordnance Survey Office, Dublin, and to the archivist in Department of Agriculture for source material.

I want to thank also Professor Pádraig De Brún and his wife, Margaret, for generous assistance with source material and encouragement at all stages, Professor Roibeárd Ó hÚrdail and Fr. Patrick Hickey.

Special thanks to Fr. Cahill, Adm. Aughadown for permission to check island entries in the parish records. Many thanks to Paul and Elizabeth Coppinger, Ayrshire, Scotland, for information on the Coppinger family.

I wish to thank Marianne Cosgrave, Congregational Archivist, Mercy Order, for access to Annals of Skibbereen Convent of Mercy. I wish to thank Dungarvan Museum for permission to reproduce picture of Dungarvan Quay, Dept of Folklore for permission to use picture of donkey with toploads, and National Library for permission to use picture from Spillane Collection. I am grateful to Fr Pat Codd, OSA, for help in obtaining information on Fr Charles O'Driscoll.

I wish to thank my wife, Kathleen, for typing the manuscript, scanning photographs, proof-reading and overall enthusiasm for this project; my family for their support and encouragement, my cousin, Karen Linden, for her professional expertise in getting my written maps onto the computer.
To understand the present we must know the past. I regret that I did not start my research earlier before so many of the older generation passed on. If I have omitted anybody who helped me it is not intentional and I apologise.

To my late father, Micheál Ó Dálaigh, I owe my love of the Irish language and folklore, and to both my father and my mother, Mary Daly (nee Pyburn) my love of islands, in particular the islands of Roaringwater Bay.

Special thanks to Michael Minihane, who, with his camera, depicted life in West Cork over a long period. His pictures depict Island people and their life on land and sea. Michael was more than generous in giving me access to his photographs.

Special thanks to Fr Patrick Hickey for permission to quote from his scholarly book *Famine in West Cork* which gives a detailed account of life in West Cork in the early nineteenth century.

Eugene Daly
July 2004

Contents

Appendices

List of Maps

AN OLD PICTURE OF HEIR ISLAND TAKEN BY MRS FOY OF BALTIMORE

The photo was taken between 1909, when the bridge was built, and 1928 when the new houses were built. Note Cadogan's house in the foreground which no longer exists. The narrow causeway was only wide enough for a donkey cart. Note the two lines of posts on either side of the bridge, which were later replaced by concrete walls. (© Pierce Hickey)

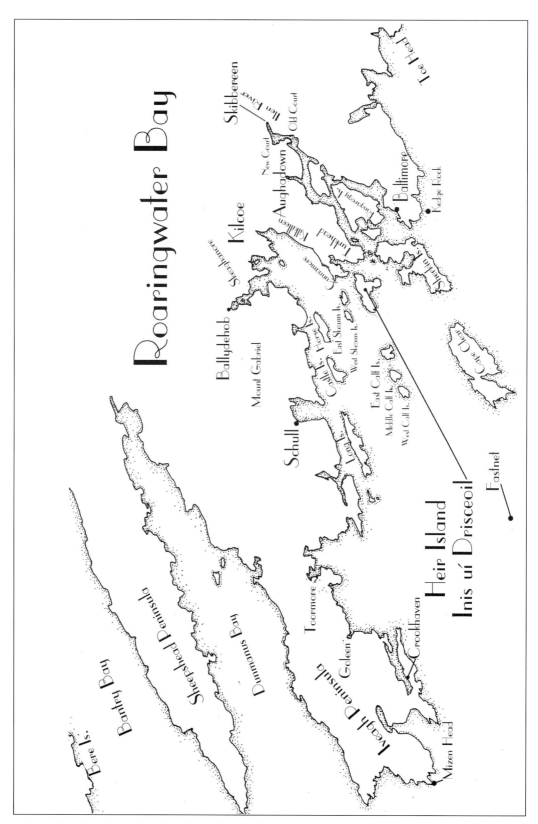

Roaringwater Bay

Toe Head

Skibbereen

Ilen River

New Court

Old Court

Aughadown

Ringarogy I.

Ballimore

Ledge Rock

Kilcoe

Turkhead

Lullhead

Kilfillen

Sherkin

Creaghmore

Mannin

Ballydehob

Stouke

Mount Gabriel

Castle Is.

Horse Is.

East Skeams Is.

West Skeams Is.

East Calf Is.

Middle Calf Is.

West Calf Is.

Cape Clear

Schull

Long Is.

Toormore

Goleen

Crookhaven

Fastnet

Heir Island

Inis uí Drisceoil

Bere Is.

Bantry Bay

Sheepshead Peninsula

Dunmanus Bay

Ivcagh Peninsula

Mizen Head

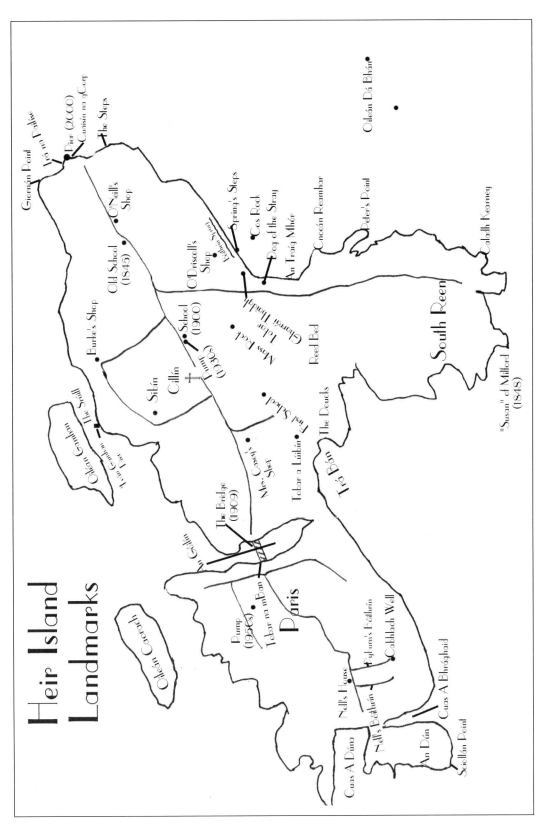

Heir Island Landmarks

JIM CON McCARTHY AND HIS MOTHER KATE OUTSIDE THEIR HOUSE IN 'PARIS'

—1—

Heir Island

The summer sun is falling soft on Carbery's Hundred Isles
'The Sack of Baltimore', Thomas Davis

Situation

Heir Island, often incorrectly spelled Hare Island, is the third largest of an archipelago of islands in Roaringwater Bay, off the south-west coast of County Cork. The name of the bay is apt because of its wild appearance during Atlantic gales. In Irish the bay is called Loch Trasna[1]. The coastline is rugged, with many rocky outcrops; the bay, dotted with islands, rocks and skerries, is often referred to as 'Carbery's Hundred Isles', as the area is part of the barony of Carbery.[2]

The islands are the heights of what was once a land mass lost to the ocean. Like the other inlets of Cork and Kerry, it is a drowned valley or ria.[3] In fact the bay consists of several drowned valleys, evident from the fact that the islands and rocks are placed in a linear fashion, the rock strata lying in a north-east – south-west direction. The most southerly line consists of Sherkin – (Inis Arcáin)[4] and Cape Clear, (Oileán Chléire) which lie immediately west of Baltimore. The most northerly line consists of Horse Island, Castle Island, Long Island and Goat Island, which lie close to and parallel to the Mizen Peninsula. Coolum, Bird Island, East Skeam and West Skeam comprise another line south westwards from Cunnamore on the mainland. Parallel to this is another line westwards from the townlands of Ardagh and Turkhead, namely Heir Island and the three Calf Islands, East, Middle and West. Another distinct line of islands and rocks consists of Ringaroga, Spanish, Quarantine, Sandy and the Catalogues.

Indeed it is obvious that the whole bay was once a complete land mass. During the Pleistocene era,[5] that ended only 10,000 years ago, huge ice-sheets moved down from the north, sundering the bay into many islands and rocks. The soil of the islands has developed from the extensive brown or grey glacial drift deposits of silt, sand, pebbles and small boulders.[6] Most of the soil is acid and poor in lime, a feature accentuated by the leaching of lime and other minerals in the wet climate.

The main focus of this book is Heir Island and its nearest neighbours, East and West Skeam and East Calf, all of which are part of the parish of Aughadown. The northern islands and the Middle and West Calf belong to Schull parish, while the southern islands are part of the parish of Rath and the Islands. All the islands are interconnected by proximity to each other, a shared commercial and social contact and bonds of marriage and friendship.

Heir Island is mostly low-lying; the highest ground, 92 metres, is at the western end. The area is approximately 380 acres.[7] At the north side are Oileán

Gamhan, *Island of the Calves,* consisting of eight acres, and Oileán Caorach, *Island of the Sheep,* area two acres. Heir is separated from the mainland of Aughadown by a narrow stretch of water; the nearest point on the mainland is Cunnamore.

There is a very gentle rise from the pier at the eastern end. In the middle of the island there is a small hill, then a gradual descent to the Bridge, which spans a long inlet called the Góilín, the southern part of which is often called 'The Bog'. West of the bridge and sheltered by higher land to the west, is the most populated part of the island, usually called Paris.[8] There is another gentle rise to the Dún headland. The Dún consists of coastal heath, surrounded by high cliffs and is almost cut-off from the rest of the island by two deep inlets opposite each other, Cuas a Bhrághaid and Cuas a Dúna. A road leads from the pier almost the full length of the island, dwindling to a track and then a boreen as you approach the Dún. From the Dún there is a splendid view of the bay with its islands, rocks and reefs. There are no townlands but the island is divided into four areas, Heir Island East, Middle, West (Paris) and the Reen peninsula, which projects southwards towards Sherkin.

The most interesting habitat is heathland which dominates the western end of the island. Heathy ridges, following the SW-NE direction of the rocks, extend eastwards from here. There is some deep fertile soil, mainly north of the central ridge, together with deep pockets between the rocky ridges. On the northern side of the Reen is an extensive marsh, dominated by reeds, which were once used for thatching the houses.[9]

In his *History of Cork*, published in 1750, Smith describes Heir Island thus:

> To the N.W. of Inisharcan (Sherkin) lies Hare Island, a large fruitful spot; and near it are four (sic) small islands called the Schemes, not expressed in any former chart. All these islands, together with the adjacent coast, produce large crops of fine English barley by means of sea sand which is the manure mostly used .... From it (Mount Gabriel) is a noble prospect of a vast extent of a rude uncultivated country, from the Mizen Head to Ross, with an infinite number, as the poet, John Milton says 'of sea-girth islands that, like to rich and various gems inlay, the unadorned bosom of the deep.'[10]

Topography

The rocks that make up most of Roaringwater Bay are old Red Sandstone of the Devonian Age, laid down some 350 million years ago. Running SW-NE from the Fastnet Rock to Rosscarbery, they are extensively folded. The erosion of the rocks in the Bay has produced rugged scenery, jagged rock outcrops, submerged rocks and reefs. There is serious erosion in parts of Heir island, especially on the south side, which faces the Atlantic, on Leán Caorach and on both Skeams. If the Lochán, which is south of the inlet at Paris, continues to be eroded, the island will be split in two. Cork County Council are endeavouring to stop the erosion by placing large boulders here to absorb the force of the sea.

The lowest and thickest part of the Devonian sandstone rocks is the Sherkin formation, at least 1,050 metres thick on the east side of Cape Clear. This is overlaid by the Castlehaven formation, dominated by fine-grained purple sandstone, which forms most of the islands north of Sherkin and Cape Clear. A distinctive stratum of this is the Kiltorcan Beds of yellowish sandstone that out-crop on Turkhead and Heir Island. These rocks erode to produce the more gently rounded landscape of the islands north of Sherkin and Cape Clear. The soil of the islands consists of four main categories. The Rosscarbery series con-sists of brown podzols[11] derived from shale and sandstone of good depth and drainage but low mineral content. This soil type, traditionally used for grazing and cultivation, covers Sherkin, Heir, the Skeams and the adjacent mainland to the east. For generations lime-rich sea sand was spread over the land in the is-lands to improve the lime and mineral content.[12]

Human Habitation

The Roaringwater Bay area has been inhabited for at least 4000 years and pos-sibly up to 6000 years. In the Middle Stone Age (pre 4000 B.C.) our ancestors were nomadic hunter-gatherers. They were constantly on the move from season to season, hunting wild animals, such as deer and wild boar, and fishing along the coast and in the rivers. They gathered sea-shells and picked fruit and berries in season. Shell middens were found on the south side of Castle Island, which date probably from the Middle Stone Age.

Roaringwater Bay, its islands and adjacent countryside, reveal evidence from all eras of human occupation, from the earliest times to the present day. West Cork has a complex history of human settlement and invasion. From the Neo-lithic (New Stone Age) era (4000–2000 B.C.) we have, for example, Arderawinny Portal Dolmen[13] near Toormore Bay, west of Schull and Cape Clear Passage Tomb, excavated in 1984, and most likely from the same era. The discovery of farming and the domestication of animals took place in Mesopotamia, present day Iraq, about 6500 B.C. and gradually spread westwards through Europe re-sulting in a population explosion. The settled lifestyle, a regular plentiful supply of food and the increased child-bearing capacity of women living a sedentary life, was the reason for the population increase. Primitive farming technology reached Ireland about 4000 B.C.[14]

From the Bronze Age (2000 B.C. to 500 B.C.) we have Mount Gabriel Cop-per Mines, the oldest in north-west Europe. Copper began to be used as tools and weapons in Ireland about 2000 B.C. When tin was added to copper to make bronze, another stride forward was made, as bronze is much stronger than cop-per. Among the archaeological remains from this period are the Wedge Tombs at Altar and Toormore, west of Schull, a Boulder Tomb in Lisheen, parish of Augh-adown, standing stones in Comillane, Cape Clear and Celtic Art Stone near North Harbour, Cape Clear.[15]

About 500 B.C. iron was introduced to Ireland by the Celts, who with their iron weapons, easily defeated the Bronze Age peoples who were here before them, iron being far superior to bronze as a tool or weapon. The culture of the Celts was dominant until 1200 A.D. From the Celtic Iron Age (500 B.C. to 500 A.D.) we have many coastal promontory forts along the coast, including

Sherkin and Cape Clear. It is possible that there was a promontory fort, prob-ably a temporary one, on the Dún headland of Heir, although there is no visual evidence of such. The name Dún means a fort or fortress. West of Heir is East Calf Island, off which is a little island, called Dooneen *Little Fort*.

From the early Christian era, (500–1100 A.D.) we find West Skeam Church and graveyard, several ringforts such as those at Rathruane and Meenvane near Schull, and Cove Church, Cell and Children's Burial Ground on the eastern side of Toormore Bay.

From the Medieval Period (1100 to 1700 A.D.) we have many castles, more correctly called tower houses, such as Kilcoe, Rincolisky (Whitehall), Baltimore (Dún na Séad), Sherkin (Dún na long) Cape Clear (Dún an Óir). All the castles from Castlehaven to Rincolisky were built by the O'Driscolls. The O'Mahonys built all the castles in the Mizen Peninsula, with the exception of Kilcoe, which was a McCarthy stronghold. There are medieval churches on Sherkin (The Abbey) and on Cape Clear (Cill Chiaráin) by North Harbour. We can be cer-tain, therefore, that the Roaringwater area has been inhabited certainly from the Bronze Age, 4,000 years ago, and probably from the New Stone Age 6,000 years ago, with the possibility that there were people here from the Middle Stone Age more than 6,000 years ago.[16]

KILCOE CASTLE IN ROARINGWATER BAY *(Photo: Kathleen Daly)*

Kilcoe Castle was the last stronghold in West Cork to surrender to English forces after the defeat of the Irish chieftains at the Battle of Kinsale (1601). The garri-son in the castle was under the command of Conor O'Driscoll, eldest son of Sir Fineen O'Driscoll. It was built by a branch of the McCarthys, Clan Dermod McCarthy, on a small island, Mannin Beag, connected to the mainland by a causeway.

— 2 —

History of O'Driscolls

In Irish, Heir Island is Inis Uí Drisceoil, O'Driscoll's Island. The O'Driscolls were one of the great sea-faring clans of Ireland. 'The O'Driscolls, the scourge of the Sasannach (English) sailor' were the ruling family in West Cork before other powerful Irish families, the O'Mahonys, McCarthys, O'Donovans, O'Sullivans and the Norman families came to the territory that was later to be called Carbery.[1] The O'Driscolls were the strongest family of the Corca Laoidhe (pronounced Corcalee) long before the coming of Christianity, indeed, before the coming of the Celts. Corcalee means the tribe or territory of Laoidhe; the Irish word corca signifying the land or territory, and *Laoidhe*, the person who gave his name to the territory.[2]

The family name O'Driscoll comes from Eiderscel (or Eidersceoil), son of Finn, who lived in the tenth century, or from an earlier Eiderscel, grandson of Aenghus Bolg, great-great-grandson of Lughaidh Laoidhe. According to the 'Genealogy of Corcalee', edited by the Gaelic scholar, Dr. John O'Donovan, in 1849, Eiderscel was 16th in descent from Lughaidh MacCon, High King of Ireland in the 3rd century A.D. This Lughaidh was the grandson of Lughaidh Laidhe from whom the tribal name of Corca Laidhe was taken. Through Lughaidh Laidhe, the O'Driscolls and their relatives claim descent from Ith, the uncle of Milesius, who led the Celts or Milesians when they conquered Ireland[3] The practice of using surnames didn't begin until the 11th century; the family name was often based on a famous ancestor. When surnames were adopted, the family was called Ó Eidersceoil, which, in time, was shortened to ODrisceoil.

Lughaidh Mac Con became the most powerful leader in the country and was High King of Ireland for several years in the 3rd century A.D. Like many kings he was dethroned and had to return to his native Corcalee. He was later killed near Enniskeane and his remains were cremated. His ashes were put in an urn and placed in a tomb on top of Corran Hill near Leap. The tomb was looted in 1840 and his ashes scattered to the winds. Mac Con (pronounced Mikun) was a personal name used in Cape Clear into the mid twentieth century, where there was a very strong man, named MacCon Mór ODrisceoil.

Genealogists have tried to prove that the O'Driscoll clan is descended directly from the leaders of the Celts, who invaded Ireland about 500 B.C. However, it is more likely that the O'Driscolls were pre-Celtic Erainn[4] people, usually known as the Fir Bolg and had settled in West Cork before 500 B.C. The Genealogy of Corcalee describes the different tuatha (territories) of Corcalee, each tuath ruled by a sub chief. A grandson of Eidersceoil, from whom the name O'Driscoll is derived, Mac Raith Ua hEitersceoil is credited with founding the cathedral in Rosscarbery. The first of the clan to receive mention of first name and surname was Conchobhar Ua Etersceoil, who died in Rosscarbery in 1103.[5] Today his name in English would be Connor or Cornelius O'Driscoll. Eidersceoil is derived from two Irish words: *idir*, between and *scéal*, a story, so eidersceoil means an interpreter or a go-between (ambassador). There are various spellings: Eiderscel, Eidersceoil, O hEdriscoll, OhEdriskell, Etersceoil.

The O'Driscolls were the most powerful sept of the Corcalee tribe. Other modern family surnames who were part of the tribe include O'Hayes, O'Leary, O'Cronin, O'Duggan, O'Hennessy, O'Flynn, O'Lynch, Murray, Shelly, Cullinane, Calnan, O'Fehily or Field, Nolan, Hamilton, O'Deasy etc.

A tuath was a political unit over which a chieftain ruled. If it was a large area (mórthuath) its ruler was a king. Each tuath was virtually independent and the land was the common property of the clan inhabiting it. The land belonged to the clan, not to the chieftain or king. The chieftain, (in Irish, Taoiseach) was elected by the clan; the tánaiste, or designated successor, was second to the chieftain in power. By the Irish law of Tánistry the new chieftain could be elected from a wide range of relatives of the old chieftain, sons, brothers, uncles. This was different to the Norman law of primogeniture, when the first born son automatically succeeded his father.

Compression

At one time the O'Driscolls ruled all the coastal territory from Kinsale to Kenmare. Before the coming of the Normans in 1169, the O'Driscolls and the other families of Corcalee were attacked and much of their territory taken by the Eoghanacht families – O'Mahony, McCarthy, O'Sullivan and O'Donovan principally – so called because they were descended from Eoghan Mór, King of Munster in the third century A.D. The Eoghanacht, in turn, were pressurised and driven south from their homelands in Limerick and Tipperary by the Dál Cais, Brian Ború's clan, the O'Briens, the most powerful clan in Ireland at the time. The O'Driscolls had complete power over their extensive territory until they were defeated by the O'Mahonys at the Battle of Morrahin, near Kilcoe, in 747 A.D. The chief Eoghanacht family, the McCarthys, became Kings of Desmond, (South Munster), and had large tracts of land in Cork and Kerry. In 1232 Domhnall Gat McCarthy, with help from the O'Driscolls, defeated the O'Mahonys and made himself Lord of Carbery. From then until the late 16th century, it was customary for the chieftain-elect of the O'Driscolls to receive his rod of office from McCarthy of Carbery, who was their overlord.[6]

The O'Sullivans wrested the Beara peninsula from the O'Driscolls, moving south from their territory in Tipperary. The O'Mahonys settled around Bandon and later took hold of all the Iveagh (Mizen) and Muintirveara (Sheep's Head) peninsulas. The O'Donovans with their kinsmen, Collins and Connolly, cut a swathe southwards from Drimoleague into the Leap, Glandore and Myross areas.[7]

With the coming of the Normans, (Barrys, Barretts, Hodnetts, Slineys, etc) O'Driscoll's territory was further compressed. The Barrys acquired large tracts of land and built castles in Ibane and Barryroe, the Hodnetts in Courtmacsherry, the Arundels in Ring near Clonakilty, the Slineys in Baltimore and the Barretts in Glandore. The O'Driscoll territory at the time of Elizabeth I's reign (1558 to

1603) had been reduced to three areas, namely Collymore, Colleybeg and Gleann Bearracháin (Castlehaven). Colley is thought to be Cothluighe, a contraction of Corca Laidhe.[8] Their territory in 1590 was roughly coterminous with the Diocese of Ross.

The name Heir Island is derived from Inis an Oidhre (the island of the Heir)

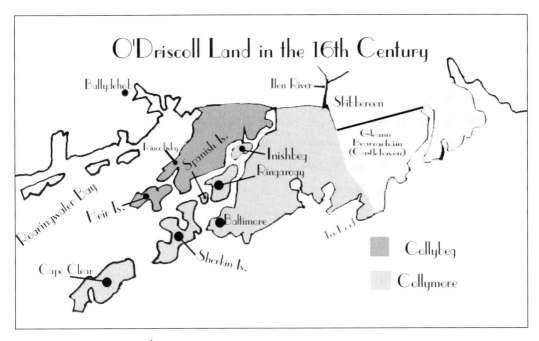

because O'Driscoll Óg, who ruled Collybeg, was heir to the leadership of the clan.[9]

Collymore consisted of 65 ploughlands,[10] comprising the civil parishes of Tullagh, Creagh and parts of Castlehaven, with the large islands of Cape Clear and Sherkin and the islands near the mouth of the Ilen river, Ringaroga, Inisbeg, Spanish Is. etc. It was bounded on the north by the Ilen river and the eastern boundary was a line from the Ilen, near Skibbereen, to the sea near Toe Head. Baltimore, *Dún na Sead*,[11] became the principal seat of the chieftain, O'Driscoll Mór. They built many other castles: Dún na Long[12] on Sherkin, Dún an Óir[13] on Cape Clear, Dún na nGall on Ringaroga, Inisbeg, Oldcourt and Cloghane in Lough Ine Island.

Collybeg, with an area of 34 ploughlands, was on the northern side of the Ilen, consisting of the civil parishes of Aughadown and Kilcoe, a few outside townlands, and included Heir Island, the two Skeams, and East Calf Island. The main castle was at Rinn Cúl Uisce[14] *Rincolisky,* or as it is called today, Whitehall, pictured overleaf. This was the territory of the heir or Tánaiste, O'Driscoll Óg. O'Driscoll Mór was the taoiseach or leader, while O'Driscoll Óg, the tánaiste, was second in power and heir to the leadership. There are references to O'Driscoll castles at Aughadown, later Aughadown House, and one in the townland of Ardagh[15] but no trace remains of either castle. Gleann Bearracháin (Castlehaven), consisting of 5½ ploughlands, was ruled by Sliocht Thaidhg

RINCOLISKY CASTLE

(Tadhg's sept), descended from Tadhg O'Driscoll, who died in 1472. Their headquarters was Castlehaven Castle, no longer standing.[16]

At the beginning of the 16th century, the O'Driscolls, although their territory was much reduced, were still the premier maritime lords of southwest Ireland. A century later, practically all of their lands had been taken, their power broken, and Baltimore, the traditional seat of their power, colonised by English settlers. Whatever vestiges of power and possessions they retained after the defeat of the Irish chieftains in the crucial battle of Kinsale in 1601 disappeared in the wars of the 17th century.

Most of the O'Driscoll wealth and power had come from their dominance of the sea from Cape Clear to Kinsale. The richest fishing grounds in Europe were on their doorstep. Foreign captains paid for facilities to extract 'train' oil from pilchards, for pilotage, anchorage, boat repairs, provisioning, hides, wool, linen and timber.

Fishermen paid them an annual fee of nineteen shillings, a barrel of salt, a barrel of beer and a barrel of flour for the right to fish, the chieftain also taking a share of the catch. Salt was imported from France and wine from France and Spain. Records show that large quantities of dried and salted fish were exported to mainland Europe from the 15th to the 18th century. Fleets from Britain, Spain, France, Portugal and Norway came to harvest the large shoals of pilchards, herring and other fish. Because herring and pilchards are soft oily fish, they had to be salted within 24 hours to retain their flavour. The O'Driscolls grew very wealthy on the dues paid to them by the fishermen for the use of their harbours and bays for refitting, revictualing and landing their catch. This was known as the Black Rent. [17]

An Inquisition held in Rosscarbery in 1609 gives a clear insight into

O'Driscoll's income, prior to the Battle of Kinsale. According to the records of the inquisition, every ship and barque that came into Baltimore Harbour paid the chief lord, O'Driscoll Mór, four pence sterling to anchor there. If they came to fish, O'Driscoll was paid nineteen shillings and two pence, a barrel of flour, a barrel of salt, a hogshead (54 gallons) of beer and a dish of fish three times a week, on Wednesdays, Fridays and Saturdays. If the fishermen dried their fish in any part of O'Driscoll's territory they were obliged to pay thirteen shillings for the use of the rock. In addition, if any fishing boat was to sell fish in Baltimore or its environs, O'Driscoll 'was to receive six shillings and eight pence for every hundredweight (8 stone in old measurement)of white fish and every barrel of pilchards or herrings sold.' [18]

To put this in perspective, three cows could be bought for £1 at that time. Since fishing boats might spend weeks in the area, fishing and drying their catch, there was also a great demand for fresh meat which was was taxed by the O'Driscolls. Wine was in great demand in medieval Ireland. O'Driscoll was to receive four gallons of every butt (63 gallons) landed in his territory. To protect his valuable resources, it was forbidden for any pilot to conduct any ship or barque over ten tons out of Baltimore, without first obtaining a licence from O'Driscoll Mór or his bailiff. Presumably this was to ensure that all dues had been paid; all the piloting was carried out by O'Driscoll's men.

All wrecks and all goods and materials washed ashore also belonged to O'Driscoll Mór. To enforce his will, O'Driscoll had constables and bailiffs employed, as well as a chief galley of 30 oars and several other vessels, who patrolled the fishing grounds. Clerks regulated the market in Baltimore. Altogether, these fees added up to quite a considerable sum, with the large fleet of fishing boats and trading vessels visiting the area. In 1569, for example, it was reported that 200 Spanish vessels were fishing off the south-west coast, as well as carrying away beef, hides and tallow. O'Sullivan of Ardee, near Kenmare, Co. Kerry, was paid £300 annually by foreign captains for the right to fish in the early 16th century. Since Baltimore is nearer to Spain and since O'Driscoll ruled over a greater area of coast, it is almost certain that he was earning much more than the amount collected by O'Sullivan.[19] Payment was made in réals and testas, money, which became the local currency. The words réal (6 pence) and toistiún (four penny piece), names in old Irish currency, had their origins in West Cork's coastal commerce.[20]

It must have been the O'Driscolls' demand for black rent and their dominance of the sea that brought them into conflict with the merchants of Waterford city. The O'Driscolls allied themselves with the Powers of County Waterford and kept up a running feud with the merchants and burgesses of that city for two centuries. According to the Carew manuscripts, in 1368 a pitched battle took place between the Waterford merchants and the Powers in Glenoradmore, Co. Waterford, the Powers being aided by 'Raymond O hEidriscoll with his galley and men. The Mayor, Sheriff and Justice of the Peace with about 100 men were slain and on the other side, Power, the baron of Dunhill with divers (several) of the Powers and of the Ohedriscolls'.[21]

In 1413 another Mayor of Waterford, Simon Wicker, sailed to Baltimore where he landed at supper time on Christmas Day and gained entrance to O'Driscoll's great castle by pretending he had come 'more to daunce and drinke and so to departe'. However, they made prisoners of O'Driscoll, his son and other relatives, saying to them that they should go with him to Waterford to 'syng their carroll'. (sing their carol) The Annals of Connacht record their fate: 'A.D. 1414. Ó hEitirsceoil Mór was craftily killed by the crew of a merchant ship.'[22]

In 1450, the O'Driscoll chieftain, Fineen, was outlawed as a result of the number of the king's subjects being killed in the area. It was this Fineen who was responsible for the building of Sherkin Abbey for the Franciscans, about 1460, after having previously gone on pilgrimage to the monastery of St. James at Compostella in Spain. In 1461 the O'Driscolls, again allied with the Powers, fought another battle against the citizens of Waterford at Ballinmacadam, County Waterford. The Carew manuscripts give victory to the Waterford men who made prisoners of 'O hEdriskoll Oge with 6 of his sonnes, who were then brought to Waterford with three of their Gailiges.' (gallies).[23] O hEdriskoll Óge (O'Driscoll Óg) was chieftain of Collybeg.

In 1537 the final clash between the O'Driscolls and the Waterford men occurred; it was catastrophic for the O'Driscolls and marked the beginning of the end of their power. In February of that year three Portuguese ships, carrying wine and other merchandise from Spain to Waterford, were driven by storms towards the Baltimore area. One of the ships, the *Las Sancta Maria de Soci,* was driven towards Baltimore. There, Fineen O'Driscoll, his son Conor and his illegitimate son Gilly Duff, agreed to pilot the ship into the harbour for three pipes of wine (one pipe equalled 126 gallons). Having tasted the wine, the O'Driscolls captured the ship, imprisoned the crew and began to distribute the 72 tons of wine among their neighbours (1 ton equals 252 gallons).[24]

On March 3rd news of the incident reached Waterford. Piers Doben Mayor of that city set off with 24 men in a pickard,[25] that was well armed with artillery pieces. They recaptured the vessel, bombarded the great hall of Dún na Long castle on Sherkin with cannon and then sailed for home. Later that month, they exacted full revenge. Led by their Mayor, four hundred men sailed in three vessels to Baltimore Harbour. On April 1st they proceeded to shell Dún na Long castle, the bombardment continuing all night. When the garrison fled in the morning, the Waterford men landed on the island. They spent five days there, destroying all the villages on the Island, all the boats of the O'Driscolls, the Franciscan Abbey and the mill. They sailed to Cape Clear, where they again proceeded to destroy all the homes. Then they landed in Baltimore, burned O'Driscoll's Castle, ravaged Inisbeg and destroyed the O'Driscoll castle there. They then ravaged the island of Inishpite *Spanish Island* 'where Fineen had his most pleasant seat in a castle, adjoining to a hall, with an orchard and grove.' As a result of this attack, the power of the O'Driscolls was effectively broken. Although the boats were replaced and the castles repaired, there is no record of the O'Driscolls ever attacking Waterford or merchant vessels again. The bombardment of Dún na Long castle was probably the first artillery attack in the South West of Ireland.[26] A couple of centuries later, the O'Driscoll castle on Ringaroga, was knocked and the stone used to build the Cathedral in Skibbereen.

Sir Fineen O'Driscoll

The last and most famous of the O'Driscoll chieftains was Fineen O'Driscoll, who became chieftain in 1573, with the title O'Driscoll Mór. With Elizabeth I determined to subdue Ireland completely, Sir Peter Carew took over large sections of Munster and Leinster in the late 16th century. This involved the O'Driscolls. On Carew's list were 'Collymore, Colleybeg; O'Driscollmore and O'Driscoll oge (Rincolisky) holdeth 2 horsemen, 40 footmen'.[27] A worried Fineen travelled to London in 1573 to make a surrender of his lands and obtain a regrant from the Queen. Three years later he swore allegiance to Sir Henry Sydney, the Lord Deputy, and in 1583 called upon the Privy Council in London. As a reward for his loyalty he was knighted, being henceforth known as Sir Fineen, surrendering his Irish title Taoiseach. Agreeing with the English policy of Surrender and Regrant[28] didn't mean the loss of his lands but it was a rejection of the Irish law of Tánistry. The lands were really the property of the clan and were not his to surrender, but from now on, according to English law, they were his and his heirs. This policy made it much easier for the English to capture the clan's territory, because if the chieftain didn't remain loyal to the throne, he could be declared a traitor and have his lands confiscated. Sir Fineen remained loyal to the English until the Spaniards landed in Kinsale and Castlehaven in 1601, coming to the aid of Hugh O'Neill and Hugh O'Donnell, chieftains of Tyrone and Donegal respectively, who had defeated British forces in Ulster and driven them out of Ulster in what is known as the 'Nine Years War' (1592–1601). With an increased possibility of the Northern chieftains, with Spanish aid, being successful in the war, practically all of the West Cork chieftains came to support O'Neill. Rather reluctantly O'Driscoll joined O'Sullivan, O'Mahony, McCarthy and O'Donovan in the rebellion. His two eldest sons, Fineen and Conor, went to the Spanish commander in Kinsale, Don Juan del Aquila, to offer assistance.[29] Sir Fineen handed over his castles in Baltimore and Sherkin to the Spanish.

Part of the Spanish fleet, under Pedro de Zubiar, was blown off course and landed in Castlehaven. An English fleet, under Sir Richard Leverson, attacked Castlehaven but was driven off with heavy losses. However, things went badly wrong at Kinsale. After the defeat of the Northern Earls there, O'Neill retreated back to Ulster, Hugh O'Donnell sailed out of Castlehaven to go to Spain to seek further aid. The English recaptured Castlehaven and Sir Fineen handed over his castles in Baltimore and Sherkin to the English without resistance. Dún an Óir castle on Cape Clear was taken after bombardment. Carew, the President of Munster, devastated the countryside as he marched westwards after Kinsale to exact revenge on the West Cork clans who had rebelled. O'Sullivan Beara was the last to resist. After taking all the O'Driscoll and O'Mahony strongholds, Carew attacked Dunboy Castle, near Castletownbere, O'Sullivan's main castle. O'Sullivan had put some of his clan on Dursey Island, but they were forced to surrender and 300 men, women and children were massacred there. After the fall of Dunboy and the subsequent massacre, Donal O'Sullivan Beara, with 1000 of his tribe, decided to retreat to Ulster. Of the 1000 that set out only a handful survived.[30] This journey, undertaken in the heart of winter, has come to be known as 'The Retreat of O'Sullivan Beara'.

Sir Fineen O'Driscoll was pardoned. Carew wrote of him 'the poor old man was overruled by his son and hath no disposition to be a traitor but his son and heir, called Conor O'Driscoll, is a malicious rebel.'[31]

Conor O'Driscoll did much to retrieve the honour of the O'Driscolls. He helped O'Sullivan Beara defend Dursey Island. He later put a garrison into Kilcoe Castle, to help Clan McCarthy, which Carew hadn't captured on his march to Dunboy. Kilcoe was the last castle in West Cork to fall to the English.[32]

In 1602, the chieftains of West Cork, aware that their cause was lost, decided to emigrate – the Flight of the West Cork Earls as Fr. Patrick Hickey, historian, calls it. Conor O'Driscoll, Conor O'Mahony of Leamcon and Dermot McCarthy of Kilcoe sailed for Spain with the Jesuit priest Fr. Archer, a staunch supporter of O'Neill.[33] Five years later the northern Earls, O'Neill, O'Donnell, O'Rourke and Maguire fled to Spain and Italy since known as 'The Flight of the Earls'. With them went Donal O'Sullivan Beara. The loss at Kinsale is a major watershed in Irish history, marking the beginning of the end of Gaelic Ireland.[34]

Sir Fineen was back in favour with the English; his castles were restored to him on condition of his paying £500. He had to borrow this and made a fateful deal with two planters,[35] William Coppinger and Thomas Crooke, to whom he mortgaged his land. Financially ruined by the Nine Years War and no longer able to charge vessels for fishing off the coast of Baltimore, he granted a 21 year lease of the town and a great part of his territory of Collymore to a Londoner, Thomas Crooke. A wealthy man, Crooke soon established an English colony in Baltimore. By 1608 the whole area around Baltimore was occupied by newcomers.

During this period, Sir Fineen was also borrowing money from Walter Coppinger, descendant of an old Danish Catholic family from Cork city. Over a period Fineen borrowed £1,700 and in return mortgaged 16 ploughlands to him – the same lands that were leased to Crooke. Since O'Driscoll was unable to pay, Coppinger, by 1629, had gained control of most of the O'Driscoll land in Collymore and Collybeg, except that owned by Crooke. Sir Fineen died, a broken old man, in his castle on Castle Island on Lough Ine about 1631.[36]

The O'Driscolls attacked the English planters again during the rebellion of 1641. After this came the Cromwellian wars and what little land was left to the O'Driscolls and the other chieftains, was forfeited.

In 1643, seven of the O'Driscolls were outlawed for supporting Charles I against the Cromwellians. In 1690 any of the O'Driscolls still in possession of their lands lost them. The O'Driscolls of Collybeg lost all their lands to the Coppingers, who, in turn, lost them to the Beechers principally.

The most common first names for males in the O'Driscoll clan include Finn (later Finín), Aodh (Hugh), Tadhg, Conchubhar (Connor, Cornelius), Éireamháin (anglicised Herman), MacCon (pronounced Miocan). There was a Cape Clear giant named Conchubhar Ac Éireamháin (Conor, son of Herman), who was about eight feet in height, stout in proportion and possessing incredible strength.

— 3 —

Early Christianity

The Corcalee (O'Driscolls) gave Ireland its first born saint, Ciarán (Kieran) of Cape Clear. Trá Chiaráin *Kieran's Strand*, North Harbour, Cape Clear is now the name of Fintrá Cléire[1] where Ciarán built his Church, quite likely the first in West Cork. Ciarán was born about 352 A.D. According to the Genealogy of Corca Laidhe, one of the sons of Aenghus Bolg was Aenghus Maine who had a daughter Liadhain, or Liedania, who married a prince from Ossory, named Lughaidh. Their son was Ciarán, the early Christian saint of Cape Clear and of Seir Ossory.[2] Some of the Corcalee tribe were initially based in the midland counties, but were driven southward to West Cork. This explains how a princess of Corcalee married a prince from Ossory, Co. Offaly. Ciaran is sixth in descent, through his mother, from Lughaidh Mac Con, High King of Ireland. Ninth in descent was St. Fachtna, the founder of the monastery and school of Ros Ailithir (Ross of the Pilgrims) at Rosscarbery, who established the diocese of Ross, becoming its first bishop and patron saint. His feast-day is August 14th.

It is generally accepted by historians that Ciarán preached Christianity in West Cork before St. Patrick came to Ireland. The first Mass in Ireland is said to have been celebrated in Cill Chiaráin near North Harbour, where the ruins of a medieval church still stand. In Cape, his feastday, March 5th was a holy day; the whole population gathered at Tobar Chiaráin *Kieran's Well* on the eve. The people did the 'rounds' from the well to the graveyard, reciting the Rosary and other prayers. Bottles of the sacred water were blessed at Mass on the morning of his feastday and it was sprinkled in the homes and in the outhouses to bless and protect the people and their animals. No Cape Clear boat ever went to sea without a bottle of the water, at least up to the middle of the last century.[3] Water from Tobar Chiaráin was regarded as having sacred and healing properties; it was considered a great cure for sea-sickness and for a variety of diseases and ailments.

After preaching in Corca Laidhe, Ciarán preached in Ossory, from where his father had come, becoming Bishop of Seir, near Birr, Co. Offaly and patron saint of the diocese of Ossory. He is alluded to as 'the holy Bishop Ciarán, the first-born of Irish saints.' To distinguish him from other holy men of the same name, he is usually called Ciarán the Elder of Seir.

Ciarán is also remembered in places outside of Ireland, in Brittany, in parts of Scotland, but particularly in Cornwall, where he is known as St. Piran. In Cornwall he is credited with introducing the art of smelting tin. As a result of this, the Cornish flag is a white cross on a black background, representing the white metal, that flows out of the black mass when it is heated, and so is a metaphor for the emergence of truth and light from darkness.[4]

Cornwall and West Cork have had close connections going back to the Bronze

Age. Copper was mined at Mount Gabriel and other parts of West Cork, tin in Cornwall, the two of which combined, constituted the alloy, bronze (nine parts copper to one part tin), used to make tools and weapons.

Tradition has it that Ciarán had a brother Kame or *Céim*, who built a wooden church on West Skeam Island, *Inis Céim, Céim's island*. This wooden structure was replaced by a stone built church, dating back to the 9th or 10th century. There is no written reference to Céim's existence but the people of Cape Clear, Heir and Skeams had a firm belief in Céim's existence. There was a saying in Cape Clear: 'Níor tháinig Pádraig thar Léim anoir; bhí Ré na Críostaíochta bunaithe ann cheana fein ag Ciarán agus a dheartháir, Céim.' – *Patrick never came west of Leap. The Christian era had already been established there by Ciarán and his brother Céim*.[5] It is also claimed that Ciarán had a sister who founded a nunnery in the townland of Ardnagroghery,[6] Aughadown, on the site of an old disused burial ground called the Bonnavaun.[7]

Twenty seven bishops of Corcalee (O'Driscoll) succeeded Fachtna as Bishop of Ross, showing the strength of the tribal system. St. Conall, who succeeded Fachtna as Bishop of Ross, gives his name to Tobarconnell (Conall's well) in the townland of Glebe, Aughadown parish. Some of the O'Driscoll Bishops of Ross were: Donal O'Driscoll (1047–57), Fineen O'Driscoll (1096–1125), Laurence O'Driscoll (1412–18), Hugh O'Driscoll (1490–96) to name a few.[8]

Placenames referring to St. Ciarán on the mainland of West Cork include Kilkieran (St. Kieran's Church) in Rathbarry parish. In Kilmoe parish there is a townland named Killeane (Cill Liadhain, Liadhain's church), where Ciarán is credited with building a church for his mother, Liadhain.[9]

In early Christian times, the Corcalee territory became synonymous with the Catholic diocese of Ross, established in the 6th century. The Corcalee tuath (territory) gradually diminished in size due to attacks from other Irish clans and Norman English, resulting in Ross becoming one of the smallest diocese in Ireland.

— 4 —

Coppingers, Townsends, Beechers

Coppingers

The Coppingers were early Danish merchants who settled in Cork and acquired much land in County Cork following the Battle of Kinsale in 1601. Sir Walter Coppinger gained large tracts of land all over West Cork. He succeeded in annexing most of Collymore from the O'Driscolls through unpaid debts which Sir Fineen O'Driscoll could not honour. He also acquired the lands of O'Driscoll Óg, which comprised most of Aughadown Parish, with Heir Island and Skeams. In the townland of Ballyvireen, between Glandore and Rosscarbery stands the ruins of Coppinger's Court, the largest house in Carbery, built in the early 17th century by him.

As we have seen in Chapter Two, the main beneficiaries of the Rebellion of 1601–02 in the area were the Coppingers. Among the lands granted to Sir Walter Coppinger in 1614 were the following: 'half of the castle, town and half of Rinecoolecusky containing 3 plowlands, half of the island, town and lands of Inish driskell, containing 3¾ plowlands; half of the island or town of East Inishcame, 2/3 plowland'. (Rincolisky, Heir Island and Skeams.) Part of the will of James Coppinger, made in 1665, mentions 'the three plowlands[1] of Rinecowluskie, the three plowlands and nine gneeves[2] of Inishdriscoll, the nine gneeves of Iniscame. (Rincolisky, Heir Island and East Skeam).[3]

A grant of 1626 gave him possession of the rest of Collybeg. Thus, bit by bit, the ancestral lands of the O'Driscolls, on both sides of the Ilen River, passed from their hands.

In the 1640s, the Coppingers, who were Royalists, supported Charles I in his war with the Parliamentarians, led by Cromwell. With the execution of Charles and Cromwell's subjugation of Ireland, the Coppingers lost their lands, but mostly to other members of the family, who had managed to remain in favour with the Cromwellians. Some Coppinger lands passed to Colonel Richard Townsend, who had been sent to Ireland by the English Parliament. This Townsend was the ancestor of the Townsend family that soon gained large tracts of land, their principal seat being at Castlehaven, renamed Castletownshend. They also had estates in Rosscarbery, Myross and Aughadown.

The Coppingers were forgiven for their part in the War of the 1640s, but they lost all their lands after supporting the Stuarts against William of Orange in the War of the Two Kings (1689–1691). James Coppinger was outlawed for high treason. Ironically he was a grandson of Colonel Townsend, to whom his lands at Whitehall passed. Samuel Townsend, grandson of the Cromwellian Colonel, obtained the castle and the lands around it, on which he built the Georgian house, which he called Whitehall. The house and the remains of the walls that surrounded it, still stand.[4]

Affadowne Parish

(A page from the 'Book of Survey and Distribution', reproduced as a handwritten table listing proprietors, denominations of lands, acres, profitable and unprofitable lands for Affadowne Parish. The totals shown at the foot read 4545-0-0 / 4263-0-32 / 281-3-8, and "Whereof Gleabe & Bishops Land" 1645-0-0 / 1370-0-0 / 275-0-0.)

Above is a copy of a page from 'Book of Survey and Distribution,' compiled in 1659, which shows ownership of 'Hare Island als Inisodriscoll by Dominick Coppinger of Rincolusky, area 196 acres, all profitable.' This survey was undertaken to help the re-distribution of lands. All who were considered anti-Cromwell, had their estates taken and given to 'planters' from England.

Affadowne Parish is bounded on the North with the Parish of Abbyshrewry, on the East with the Harbour of Baltimore, on the south with the Maine Sea and on the west with the harbour of Maine and Parish of Kilcoe.

In this parish belongs several islandes as Inisodrisoll als Hare Island with the Kames and Inispike Island which lieth in the Bay of Baltimore and the three former on the south of this Parish.

The quality of the soyle of this Parish is generally very good arable meadow and pasture the most whereof belongs to the Bishop of Rosse, on the Glebe Land of this Parish stands the walls of a Church. In Inispike als Clare Island is a house, at Rincolisky a castle, with many cabins in several places of the parish being pretty well inhabited; it is divided into the several denominations viz East Eniscame, West Eniscame, Ardragh, Callatrumore etc as shown on the following page.

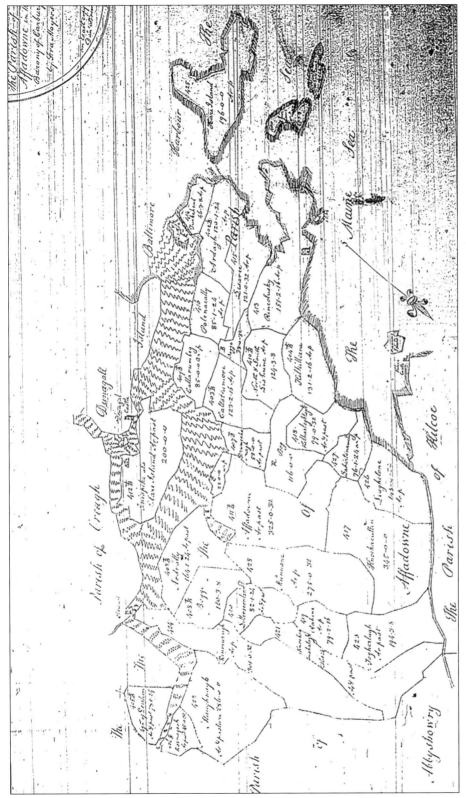

DOWN SURVEY MAP OF THE PARISH OF AFFADOWNE (c.1655–59)
Courtesy of Boole Library, UCC

	Number in plott	Proprietors Names	Denomt of Lands	No of Acres by Admeasmt	Landes Profitable	Landes Unprofitable
	400	James Coppinger	East Eniscame	025-3-8	Ar & past 025-3-8	
	401	Bishop of Ross	West Eniscame	016-1-24	The same 016-1-24	
	402	The Same	Ardagh	120-1-24	The same 120-1-24	
	403	The Same	Callatrinmore	123-2-16	The same 123-2-16	
	404	The Same	Killkilleene	131-2-16	The same 131-2-16	
	405	The Same	Drishine 4 gneeves	078-1-24	The same 078-1-24	
	406	The Same	Rosnagosh	045-0-32	The same 045-0-32	
	407	The Same	Drumnacaharagh	058-0-0	The same 058-0-0	
	408	The Same	Ardralyes	164-1-24	The same 164-1-24	
	408	The Same	part of the same	120-3-8		Bog 120-3-8
	409	The Same	Callatrumbegg	085-0-0	The same 085-0-0	
	410	The Same 3 gneeves Donimick Coppinger 3 gneeve	South and North Lisheene	124-3-8	124-3-8	
B		Common to the adjacent towns		38-0-32		Bog 038-0-32
	411	The afores. Bishop	Aaffadowne 2 plough	325-0-32	The same 325-0-32	
C		Glebe Land	of the same	022-0-0	The same 022-0-0	
R		Belonging to the adjacent townes		116-0-0		Bog 116-0-0
	412	The afores. Bishop	Inispike als Clare Island	200-0-0	The same 200-0-0	
	413	Dominick Coppinger	Rincolisky	151-2-16	The same 151-2-16	
	414	The Same	Turkehead	046-3-8	The same 046-3-8	
V		The Same	a small island nearby) to the same)	006-3-8		Rocky 006-3-8
	415	The Same	Lisaree	121-0-32	The same 121-0-32	
	416	The Same	Polenacally	085-1-24	The same 085-1-24	
	417	The Same	Knockacullen	345-0-0	The same 345-0-0	
	418	The Same	Killharlaghta	099-0-32	The same 099-0-32	
	419	The Same	Rahine six gneeves	079-2-16	The same 079-2-16	
	420	The Same	Lettirshanlane	082-1-24	The same 082-1-24	
	421	The Same	Knocknamahalla	256-1-24	The same 256-1-24	
	422	The Same	Mughanagh	286-0-0	The same 286-0-0	
	423	The Same	Togherlagh	194-3-8	The same 194-3-8	
	424	The Same	Rinnmurragh	301-0-32	The same 301-0-32	
	425	The Same	Hare Island als) Inisodriscoll)	196-0-0	The same 196-0-0	
	426	Thomas Coppinger	Leaghclone	145-0-32	The same 145-0-32	
	427	The Same	Lahartanavally	076-1-24	The same 076-1-24	
	428	The Same	Munnane	275-0-32	The same 275-0-32	
	The Totall			4545-0-0	4263-0-32	281-3-8
	Whereof Glebe & Bishops Land.			1645-0-0	1370-0-0	275-0-0

The spelling above is as in original document. Modern spelling of townlands: East Skeam, West Skeam, Ardagh, Collatrum More, Kilkilleen, Drisheen, Rosnagoose, Dromnacaheragh, Ardralla, Collatrum Beg, South and North Lisheen, Aughadown; Inishbeg, Rincolisky, (Whitehall) Turkhead, Lissaree, Poulnacallee, Hollyhill, Kilsarlaght, Rahine, Letterscanlan, Knocknamohalagh, Mohonagh, Foherlagh, Reenmurragha, Leighcloon, Laheratanavally and Munnane. Turkhead – the small island nearby is Inisleigh. Knockacullen, Cnoc a Chuilinn, hill of the holly, is today called Hollyhill.

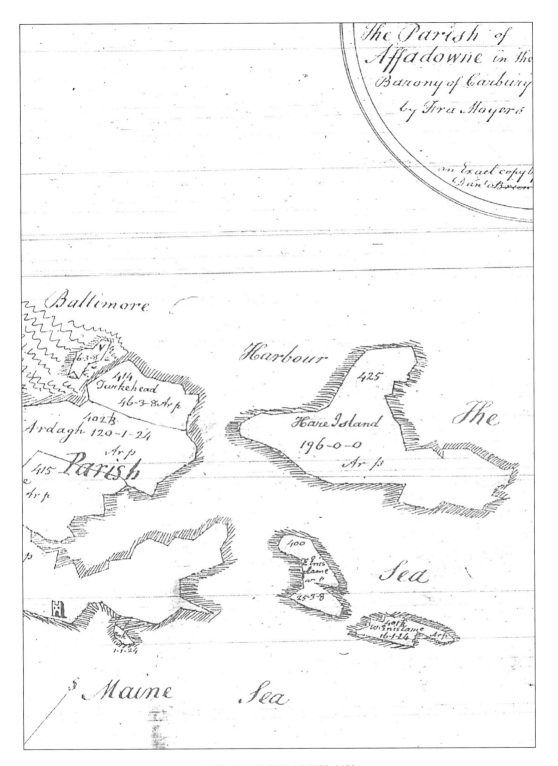

The Parish of
Affadowne in the
Barony of Carbury
by Fra Moyer:

an Exact copy
Dan.O'Brien

Baltimore

Turkehead
46-3-8 Ar p

Ardagh 120-1-24
Ar p

Parish

Ar p

Harbour

425

Hare Island
196-0-0
Ar p

The

400
Ennis
lame
ar p
25-3-8

North
Ennislame
16-1-24 Ar p

Sea

Maine   Sea

DOWN SURVEY MAP 1655–1659
Courtesy of Boole Library, UCC

Townsends

Samuel Townsend (1689–1759), fifth son of Bryan Townsend, settled at Rincolisky. (Whitehall today). On the hillside nearby are the remains of O'Driscoll Óg's

castle, which had passed into the hands of the Coppingers early in the 17th century. Rincolisky was one of the estates forfeited by the unlucky James Coppinger in the 1690s for supporting the Jacobites against William. Samuel Townsend built Whitehall House, using stone from the old O'Driscoll Castle of Rincolisky. It was built in the Italian style with a double staircase and pilasters painted in imitation marble. His son, Edward Mansell Townsend, who inherited the estate, was known as 'Splendid Ned'. When his son, Samuel, married, he assigned all the estate to him. This Samuel, Oxford educated, was a very gifted man and a noted musician.

During his lifetime nothing was done to improve the house or estate. He divided his time between England and Dublin, only coming to Whitehall for short periods. He was a grand juror in Cork and in 1798 he was High Sheriff of County Cork.

1798 was the year of the United Irishmen rebellion and there was much unrest in the country. Wolfe Tone had brought a large fleet of French ships into Bantry Bay in 1796. However, they ran into a storm and some of the ships were blown off course and those that came into Bantry were unable to land. If the French had landed with their large force, it is very possible that they would have defeated the English forces. The English were very disturbed; large numbers of troops and militia dragoons were placed at Townsend's disposal. These were usually quartered on the inhabitants, beating them into subjection. To avoid disturbance and the possible ruin of his tenants, many of whom were Cromwellian soldiers' descendants, Townsend, together with the Parish Priest and Protestant Rector, decided to guarantee the peace of the parish. No troops were sent into Aughadown and there was no disturbance.

Samuel retired to London for a long period, leaving his wife and ten children in Whitehall. The house was old, square and uncomfortable. His wife hired an architect and Whitehall was transformed. The Townsends held splendid Balls; members of the Aristocracy visited – the Earl of Bantry, Lord Audley, and sometimes the Earl of Shannon. He had yachts built, the 30 ton *Blonde* and the 48 ton *Medina*. Denis Minihane, of Heir Island and Cunnamore, was in charge of the Townsend yachts. The Townsends kept a large kennel of hounds for hunting. After his wife's death, Samuel Townsend let the mansion for a while to Lord Audley.[5]

Daniel Donovan, in *Sketches in Carbery,* describes Whitehall as an elegant white house, with a fine horseshoe staircase and tall windows dropping down on to lawns which lead to the water's edge. Until they left, early in the 20th century, the Townsends lived in some grandeur, entertaining elaborately in the stately dining room, the table laid with superb silver and Cork glass. There were endless balls and parties and trips around the bay and out to Cape Clear in the jolly boat.[6]

Writing in the *The Irish Country House*, Peter Somerville Large, a distant cousin of the Townsends, describes Whitehall House as follows

> Whitehall, originally built from stones of a neighbouring O'Driscoll tower, was enlarged in 1816 to keep up with houses in the neighbourhood, a move which, as so often happened, sank the family into irrevocable debt. Whitehall had a ghost who went around in chains, a dungeon under the breakfast-room table and a secret passageway, leading to the O'Driscoll castle. In the eighteenth century, a page, was sent down the passage to investigate and never returned. There was no trace of him when they explored a century later; all they found were stone bottles and a heap of rusty swords for arming tenants against Whiteboys.
>
> The new drawing room with its long windows overlooking the sea was a focus for balls and house parties to which Cork society was invited … … At Christmas the table groaned beneath the weight of good things. Priceless deeply cut old Cork glass, beautiful ware and old china, and quantities of exquisite old silver, to say nothing of the rounds of spiced beef, turkeys, hams, Christmas pudding, apple pies, far more than could ever be eaten.

The Townsends were landlords of the Skeams and East Calf islands. A three storey summer house was built on East Skeam, which was later occupied by the Barry family, who reduced it to two storeys. The three families who inhabited East Skeam into the twentieth century were all employees of Townsend: Barry, Desmond and Cadogan.

The Townsends and Coppingers give their names to places in Skibbereen: Townsend Street and Coppinger's Lane, off Townsend Street.

Beechers

By the end of the 17th century, the Beechers and Townsends monopolised the area previously known as Corcalee. The Beechers owned about 19,000 acres in the parishes of Aughadown, Abbeystrewery, Tullagh, Creagh and most of the islands of Roaringwater Bay – Sherkin, Cape Clear and Heir.

The defeat of the Irish chieftains at Kinsale, opened the way for many English planters to come into West Cork, the most powerful being the Beechers. Phane Beecher from Kent was granted 14,000 acres in Co. Cork in 1568 after the unsuccessful Desmond rebellion. He brought a band of followers with him and settled them on estates. With Richard Boyle, the great Earl of Cork, he established the town of Bandon as an English stronghold. They had so much land in County Cork that it was said that one could travel from Baltimore to Bandon, without leaving Beecher territory. Phane's eldest son, Henry, who had married Mary Lyon, daughter of the first Protestant Bishop of Cork, inherited the estate. Their eldest son, Major Henry Beecher, married Elizabeth Notte, daughter of

Thomas Notte, who had an estate at Aughadown and so, by marriage, the Beechers came to settle in Aughadown, about 1640.[7] The Census of Ireland in 1659 describes Affadowne (Aughadown): 'two ploughlands in Affadowns, containing 11 English and 33 Irish persons and having as Tituladoes Henry Beecher Esquire, Thomas Beecher, Susan Beecher, John Godfrey and Richard Tonson, Esquire.' It also gives Ballmore (Baltimore): 'three plowlands in Tullagh Parish, containing 14 English and 43 Irish persons with Tituladoes Lyonell Beecher and John Selby.' Aughadown house was built about 1670. The townland of Paddock was formerly part of Hollyhill; the name was altered by Beecher, owner of Aughadown House.

Henry Beecher's only son, Colonel Thomas Beecher, who was aide-de-camp to William III at the Battle of the Boyne in 1690, during which the King gave him his gold watch, is described as 'of Sherkin Island and Aughadown'. He was governor of the barracks in Sherkin afterwards, for which he received 10 shillings a day. His widow's will was made in Aughadown in 1720, so it is certain that the Beechers were established in Aughadown before 1700; it was now their principal residence. The Beechers, who built Aughadown House, laid out an estate around it by clearing the tenants off a 400 acre area. There were 50 acres adjacent to the house for orchards and pleasure grounds and an area north of the house adjoining the main road, now the N.71, was a deer park. The Beechers were the principal landlords of Heir Island until 1854 and much of Aughadown until the late 19th century.

John Beecher, who married about 1740, built Hollybrook House near Skibbereen in 1751 and that became their principal residence. Aughadown and its lands were let to tenants. A Hutchinson family, and through marriage to them, the Lawtons, became the principal tenants. The Lawton family is remembered in a placename, Lawton's Height, between Lisheen School and Church Cross.

A generation later, Henry Owen (Harry) Beecher married Catherine Jermyn of Aughadown, whose family owned several townlands, including Kilsarlaught and Laheratanavally, and he returned to live in Aughadown. There is a tradition that he accidentally shot his son while they were out hunting, but this is not certain. His wife's estates, which she had retained in her own name, passed out of Beecher hands again after her death. Harry Beecher left Aughadown House about 1840 and retired to Lough Ine House. Aughadown House was never occupied after his departure. It fell into disrepair after 1900 and no longer stands.[7] The land is now owned by the Hurley family.

Writing in 1972, Peter Somerville-Large found 'Aughadown House in ruins, its deer park divided into fields'. Daniel Donovan, in *Sketches of Carbery,* published in 1876, described it as, a 'strong castellated mansion, entered by a drawbridge, surrounded by beautiful ground and having a gazebo on one of the heights behind.' The gazebo was approached by a ramp along which the 'gentry' used to drive their carriage in order to enjoy the magnificent view out over Roaringwater Bay.

— 5 —
The Eighteenth Century

By 1700 practically all Ireland was in the hands of English settlers. There was peace in the country for the most part, the peace of a defeated subject race. In the era of the so-called Penal Laws, Catholics had little access to education and they were practically forbidden to practice their religion. The only schools were the 'hedge' schools, where travelling teachers taught the poor in some disused building, or in fine weather, in a sheltered area outside, hence the name Hedge Schools. The teachers were paid small contributions by the parents on a quarterly basis, varying between one shilling and four shillings per quarter. Children of the very poor had little chance of getting any education. Reading, writing, arithmetic and Christian Doctrine were the subjects usually taught.

Some of these hedge schoolmasters were very learned men. Perhaps, the most famous in West Cork was Seán Ó Coileáin, who had a hedge school in Myross, near Union Hall. Known as' the silver tongue of Munster' he wrote some great poems in Irish, the most famous being his *Lament for Timoleague Abbey*. (Tig Molaga)

This was the century of the Mass Rocks, when Catholics often had to hear Mass in private houses or in the open, out of sight of the authorities.

The Great Frost of 1739–40 led to Famine in most of West Cork in the winter of 1740–41. However, the area seems to have recovered quickly from this calamity. Richard Pococke, an English clergyman and famous traveller, toured the area in 1758. He found 'every spot sown with oats, English barley or potatoes, which they are forced to cultivate for their support'. This is the first written reference to the potato in West Cork. He saw a mill working in Kilcoe, and in Roaringwater Bay, he watched boats laden with turf on their way to markets in Kinsale and Cork.[1] Despite political and religious disputes, there was a definite economic improvement towards the end of the 18th century. It was not only Protestants who prospered; some Catholics began to share in it as well. This resulted in the emergence of a Catholic Middle Class, especially in the towns and cities.

In the countryside, the small farmers were deprived of their ancient grazing rights to common land, a right that went back to Gaelic Ireland, when the land was the property of the clan and not the chieftain. In the 1760s and 1770s groups of men assembled at night to level fences which had been erected on commons. They were called 'Levellers' or 'Whiteboys' from the white shirts they wore so that they could identify one another in the dark. They resisted the landlords on questions of rent and tenure and took measures, including murder, to prevent people taking land once held by evicted tenants. They were described as 'a vast trade union for the protection of the Irish peasant.'[2]

The Whiteboys wanted to regulate the relationship with priest, parson and landlord to the small farmers' benefit. In post-Reformation Ireland the Catholic majority was forced to pay tithes[3] to the Protestant Church. The Catholics naturally were unwilling to pay; as they also had to pay dues to their own priests. As well as opposing the payment of tithes to Protestant clergymen, the Whiteboys also opposed Catholic priests who, they felt, were overcharging their flock. They were an organised, oath-bound secret society. Some Whiteboys were hanged. In one case, a priest, Nicholas Sheehy, from County Tipperary, who was accused of involvement in one of their conspiracies, was hanged, with two others, in Clonmel in 1776. Arthur Young, who was travelling in the south of Ireland at the time, noted that the hangings of Whiteboys made the country more peaceful but the evils connected with the tithe system continued.

Another wave of Whiteboy violence broke out in 1785. The priests preached against the violent measures sometimes taken by the Whiteboys. They drove the Parish Priest of Caheragh out of his parish. They broke into the house of the Parish Priest of Rath, near Baltimore, 'brought him out naked in the midst of wind and rain,' and compelled him to take the Whiteboy oath.[4]

In the summer of 1786 'the delegated of the Munster peasantry met and protested against the avarice of the priesthood and the intolerable exactions of the tithe-farmers'. They decided not to pay priest or tithe-proctor any more than certain fixed rates. Finn's *Leinster Journal* reported that, in July 1786, Whiteboys 'assembled in the parish of Aughadown and proceeded to the glebe house, and pursued the Popish priest, Daniel Burke, who fled for refuge to a neighbour's house and on reaching him, broke his windows and doors and almost tore down his house'. The Whiteboys of the period 1760–1790 had their origins mainly in economic grievance and were also anti-clerical, against both Catholic and Protestant clergy alike.[5]

The French Revolution, which started in 1789 and which saw the overthrow of the monarchy, made the English rulers very nervous as the Revolutionaries offered to aid other nations to win liberty from oppressors. Revolutionary ideas spread and, in Ireland, led to the foundation of the United Irishmen, founded in Belfast in 1791, by Wolfe Tone, Samuel Russell and others, whose aim was to unite Catholics and Protestants in a Republic, forcing the English out by use of force if necessary.

— 6 —

Early 19th Century Records

A more detailed picture of Heir Island life emerges from the 1820s onwards, with the availability of various official documents, containing information on population, landholding and housing. The genealogy of the islanders can be accurately traced from 1822, with the start of Catholic Church registers of baptisms and marriages in Aughadown parish.

Tithe Applotment Lists

Between the years 1823 and 1838, approximately 2,500 parishes in Ireland, were surveyed under the Tithe Composition Acts. Commissioners were appointed by the Lord Lieutenant to list all titheable land in each parish. Those appointed for Aughadown were Richard Long, and Thomas Evans.

The imposition of tithes on Catholic tenant families was the cause of much unrest. The tithe was one tenth of the produce of the land, payable in kind, to support the Church of Ireland clergy, so the poor Catholic farmer had to pay not only to support his own priests but also those of another religion. There were many skirmishes between farmers and tithe proctors,[1] who sometimes had to get the constabulary to protect them. A description of one such skirmish is to be found in the 'Humble Memorial of Swanton's Town (Ballydehob), near Skibbereen' to the Duke of Richmond, Lt. General and General Governor of Ireland, dated 30th September, 1812.

William Swanton stated that he had been for some years the collector of tithes in a part of the parish of Aughadown, leased to him by Lord Riversdale. He said he had received every possible opposition from the inhabitants of the parish in collecting tithes by the people rising in large bodies and mobs, armed, beating the persons who went on behalf of the Petitioner to value the tithes. On the 14th September, 1812, two people from the Petitioner went to the lands of Rinco (Rincolisky) in order to value the tithes for that year. A 'mob' (according to Swanton) of about 100 people, armed with guns, pikes, scythes, swords and bayonets screwed on long poles, assembled together and fired several shots in the air. They threatened 'to cut and destroy' the Petitioner's men if they attempted to value the tithes or remained in the parish. Because of the strong opposition they had to withdraw.[2]

The following day he sent the tithe assessors to Aughadown again. This time, he applied for assistance from the magistrate, the Rev. Richard Townsend, who sent with him three sub-constables together with some soldiers, 12 privates and a corporal. They were met by a party of people upwards to 200, mostly armed as the previous day, who formed in line of battle and hoisted a flag. They continually threw stones at the party, who had to return, without assessing the tithes[3]

The tithe system had been in existence before the dissolution of the monasteries by Henry V111 in the mid 16th century. The Composition Act of 1823 specified that tithes due to the Established Church, (the Church of Ireland), which had hitherto been payable in kind, (potatoes, grain etc,) should now be paid in money. As a result it was necessary to carry out a valuation of the entire country, civil parish by civil parish, to determine how much would be payable by each landowner. Not surprisingly, tithes were fiercely resented by those who were not members of the Church of Ireland and all the more because the tax was not payable on all land. In Munster, for example, tithes were payable on potato patches but not on grassland, with the result that the poorest had to pay most.

The tax was based on the average price of wheat and oats over the seven year period up to 1823 and was levied at a different rate depending on the quality of the land. An organized campaign of resistance to the payment of tithes, the so called 'Tithe War' culminated in 1831 in large-scale refusals to pay the tax.

One of the Commissioners, Richard Long, is listed as owning five acres in Heir Island Middle. The total valuation of Heir Island in the Tithes Composition, on which the tithe levy was based, was £274.00. with a total tithe of £28.2.0. for the whole island. This was almost a hundred pounds higher than the later Griffith Valuation, (1852) which valued the land at £169-1s-0d and the buildings at £15-3s-0d, giving a total of £184-4s-0d. For each household the document lists by name the occupier of every holding, the acreage of each holding and the tithe due per annum. On Heir Island, the holdings varied in acreage from 3 to 18 acres; in East Skeam the highest acreage was 20 acres, on West Skeam, 16 acres, and on Calf East 50. The survey has one major fault, from a historical view point, in that it listed only the names of landowners; landless persons, such as farm labourers, fishermen, servants, any family without land, and certain categories of land were not mentioned. Because of this the survey cannot be regarded as being as important as a Census, but it was the first list of land occupancy in Ireland, together with an accurate surveying of the land. Even though the tithe lists are not a full list of householders, nevertheless, they are valuable in that they constitute the only country-wide survey for the period and are valuable precisely because the heaviest burden of the Tithes fell on the poor for whom few other records survive.

Tithe Applotment Book

Valuation of the parish of Aughadown made by Thomas Evans and Richard Long esq., Commissioners under the Tithe Act of George 4th. The tithe was valued at the following scale of prices per land produce:

Wheat   30 shillings per bag.
Oats   30 shillings per barrel
Butter   4 pounds per cwt. (hundredweight = 112 pounds)

Thomas Evans had 40 acres in Poundlick, civil parish of Creagh. Richard Long had a large farm in the Paddock, Hollyhill area of Aughadown Parish.

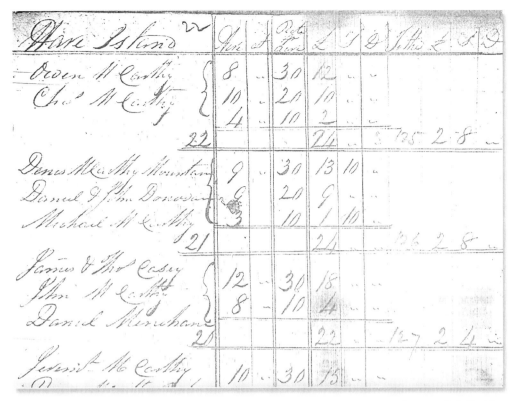

The above is a copy of the first page of the original Tithe List for Heir Island.

	ACRES	TITHE PER ANNUM
Heir Island		
Owen McCarthy	8	
Chas. McCarthy	10	
	4	
	22	£2-8-0
Denis McCarthy Mountain	9	
Daniel & John Donovan	9	
Michael McCarthy	3	
	21	£2-8-0
James & Thomas Casey	12	
John McCarthy	8	
Daniel Minihane	—	
	20	£2-4-0
Jeremiah McCarthy	10	
Denis McCarthy Rabagh	9	
Charles McCarthy Rabagh	—	
	19	£2-8-0

Corn. & Michael Cadegan &		
John Minahan	13½	
Denis & Dan Shanahan)	18	
John & Denis Driscoll)	7½	
	39	£4-4-0
Michael & Pat Driscoll	11	
Timothy Mahony	7	
Batt & Garrett Cotter	4	
	22	£2-11-0
Denis Shanahan	3	
Daniel Murphy	15	
Cors & Patrick Burke &		
Cors Driscoll & Jer McCarthy	17½	
Richard Long Esq	5	
	40½	£4-16-0
Thomas Kearney	6	
Cornelius Harte	6	
Denis Collins	3	
	15	£1-13-0
Flor & Denis Neill	10	
Daniel Harrington	13	
No Name	4	
	27	£3-0-0
Timothy Regan	6	
Batt Cotter	8	
	2	
	16	£1.16.0
TOTAL TITHE FOR ISLAND	274	£27-8-0

East Skeam

Timothy Desmond	9	
	10	
	1	
	20	£2-8-0
Denis Horrigan)	8	
Catherine Cadogan	11½	
	1	
	20½	£2-7-6
TOTAL TITHE FOR ISLAND	40½	£4-15-6

West Skeam

Thomas Regan	16	
Timothy Regan	14	
	30	£3-16-0

East Calf

Sam. Townsend Esq.	20	
	20	
	<u>10</u>	
	50 acres	£5-15-0

The tithe payable by three families who inhabited East Skeam was £4.15.6. for its 40½ acres, while the two families on West Skeam (30 acres) paid £3.16.0. The tithe for East Calf, (50 acres), was £5.15.0. Names are given as written in original document.

Griffiths Evaluation

Richard Griffith, born in Dublin in 1784, had already established himself as a distinguished geologist and inspector of Irish mines when, in 1825, he was chosen to be Ireland's Boundary Surveyor. Griffith's appointment coincided with the government's determination to achieve a uniform system of land measuring and valuing for the purpose of eliminating various inequities in levying the two main forms of local taxation in Ireland, the tithe and the county cess,[4] at the townland level. As the head of the Boundary Department of Ireland, he spent forty years supervising land valuation and in particular the great Ordnance Survey of Irish townlands, which fixed local boundaries throughout the nation.

In the Griffith evaluation of 1852 the following householders in Heir Island, Skeams and East Calf island are listed with a list of their immediate lessors, description of tenement and the rateable annual valuation. The occupiers are listed in groups. The old houses were built very close to each other, in little villages, in the more sheltered parts of the island.

NO. 18: INISHODRISCOL OR HARE ISLAND.

IMMEDIATE LESSORS

Group A – Heir Island West

1.	Timothy Donovan	Edw. And Geo. Becher.
2.	Michael McCarthy	"
3.	J. McCarthy (Mountain)	"
4.	Jeremiah Murphy	"
5.	Jeremiah Minaghan (Minihane)	"
6.	Jeremiah Donovan (O'Donovan)	"
7	Margaret McCarthy	"
8	Timothy McCarthy	"
9	John McCarthy	"
10	Charles McCarthy	"
	Honoria McCarthy	"
11	Unoccupied	Michael McCarthy
12	Denis McCarthy	Honoria McCarthy
13	Andrew Hurley	Edw. And Geo Becher

14	Henry Casey	Jeremiah Donovan.
15	Richard Pyburn	Honoria Driscoll.
16	James McCarthy	Charles McCarthy

Group B – Heir Island Middle

1	Cornelius Burke	Edw and Geo. Becher
2	Michael Foley	"
3	Michael Burke	"
4	Daniel Murphy	"
5	Honoria McCarthy	"
6	Denis Shannahan	'
7	Catherine Minaghan (Minihane)	"
8	John Shannahan	"
	Denis Shannahan	"
	John Shannahan	"
9	Daniel Foley	Michael Foley
10	unoccupied	Daniel Murphy
11	John Hart	Edw and Geo Becher
12	Daniel Shannahan	same
13	unoccupied	Daniel Shanahan
14	Eleanor Shannahan	Cornelius Burke
15	Mary Regan	Edw and Geo Becher
16	Thomas Young – National School House	"

Group C – Heir Island East

1	John Neale (O'Neill)	"
2	Denis Neale (O'Neill)	"
3	Jeremiah Neale (O'Neill)	"
4	Florence Neale (O'Neill)	"
5	Michael Neale (O'Neill)	"
6	Rev. Edward Spring	"
7	Patrick Driscoll	"
8	Daniel Casey	Denis Neale
9	Unoccupied	Florence Neale
10	Daniel McCarthy	Rev. Edward Spring
11	John Fitzgerald	Catherine Driscoll
12	Thomas Regan	Rev. Edward Spring
13	Island Society	Edw and Geo Becher
14	Miles McSweeney Teacher.	Island Society.

Group D – North Reen.

1	Patrick Driscoll	Edw and Geo Becher
2	Michael Coghlin (Coughlan or Cahalane?)	"
3	Catherine Driscoll	"
4	Richard Cotter	"
5	Daniel McCarthy	"
6	Florence Neale (O'Neill)	"
7	Patrick Driscoll	"

Group E – South Reen

1	Cornelius Hart & Daniel Hart	Edw and Geo Becher
2	John Hart	"
3	Michael Hart	"
4	Unoccupied	Cornelius & Daniel Hart
5	Unoccupied	same

Exemptions.
1. Thomas Young – National School House
2. Island Society School House.

Illaungawna: (Oileán Gamhan) Cornelius Burke. Sir Hy.W.Becher, Bt
Illaunkearagh: (Oileán Caorach) Rev. Edward Spring.   "

East Skeam

1.	Denis Horrigan (Horgan)	Samuel Levis
2.	Denis Cadigan	"
3.	Timothy Desmond	"
4.	Timothy Mahony	"

West Skeam

1	Richard Regan	Samuel Townsend.
2	Mary Regan	"

Calf Island East

1	Samuel Townsend	in fee
2	Daniel Minihane	Samuel Townsend.

All surnames spelled as in original document

Four families, O'Mahony, Kearney, Collins and Harrington, listed in the Tithe Applotment List are not in the Griffiths Evaluation List of 1852. Three other families, Hurley, Casey and Foley, listed in Griffith Evaluation, are gone from Heir Island in the 1901 Census.

Distribution of Houses in Griffiths Evaluation Map

Houses were built in little villages or collections in the most sheltered parts of the island. The same was true of Cape Clear, where they called each congregation of houses a bloiscín. The largest group of houses was situated in the lower part of Heir Island West, commonly called Paris. This village was in the low area west of the Bridge, sheltered from all westerly points by the rising ground to the west. Here there were 17 houses, one unoccupied, in 1852, stretching from the 'Rock', the area west of the bridge to where the Maier family live today. The occupants were McCarthy (9), Minaghan (Minihane) 1, O'Donovan (2). Murphy (1), Hurley (1), Casey (1), Pyburn (1). The dominant name was McCarthy. The immediate lessors of practically all the island houses were Edward and George Beecher.

The houses in Heir Island Middle can be divided into two groups, the first of which consisted of three houses in the Midlands, just opposite 'Leán Gamhan, occupied by Burkes (2) and Foley (1).

The second group in the Midlands had high ground to the south so it was fairly sheltered. It consisted of fifteen houses, two of which were unoccupied. The names of the owners were Shanahan (6), Minaghan (Minihan) (1) Murphy (1). McCarthy (1), Foley (1), Harte (1) O'Regan (1). Thomas Young occupied the National School House in the Doucks.

Heir Island East is the area stretching approximately from the old school to the eastern pier, again the Beechers being the immediate lessors of most. It consisted of fourteen houses, one unoccupied. The occupants were Neale (O'Neill) (5), O'Driscoll (1), Casey (1), McCarthy (1) Fitzgerald (1), O'Regan (1). The Rev. Edward Spring, Rector of Kilcoe, zealous proselytizer on Cape Clear and Heir, occupied one house and the Island Society was in possession of the School House. Miles McSweeney, teacher, occupied a house, leased to him by the Island Society. Thomas Regan and Daniel McCarthy had houses leased from Edward Spring. We note that the Barry family were not on East Skeam in 1852, so they settled there sometime between 1852 and 1901. The Mahony family on East Skeam are gone by 1901. The Minihane family on East Calf are probably the predecessors of the Minihanes of Paris, Heir, although previously it is believed they moved from Cape to Heir.

The houses in the North Reen were situated on south-facing land near where the O'Connor family lives today. It consisted of seven houses occupied by the following families: O'Driscoll (3), Neale (O'Neill) (1). Coghlin (Cahalane) (1), Cotter (1), McCarthy (1)

There was another 'village' of houses on south Reen near where Seán and Rose Harte live today. Here there were six houses, two of which were unoccupied, the other four, all inhabited by Hartes.

— 7 —

Famine

IRISH EMIGRANT'S LEAVING HOME – THE PRIEST'S BLESSING
Illustrated London News

There were recurrent famines in Ireland before the Gorta Mór (The Great Famine) of 1845–1849. The year 1741 is remembered as Bliain an Áir (The Year of the Slaughter). This was caused by the Great Frost of 1740–41, which resulted in poor grain and potato crops. In 1816 the summer and autumn were extremely wet and cold and the crops suffered badly, which caused great distress among the poor. A typhus epidemic killed a great number of people.

The weather was remarkably severe in the early months of 1820. The River Lee was frozen over. Bad weather continued into 1821, when May and June were dry, cold and frosty and rain fell in torrents in the autumn. The potatoes rotted in the fields. The years 1820–22 were very hard on small tenant farmers and labourers. They had to deal with high rents, tithes, depressed agricultural prices, a rising population and rotting potatoes. The famine in 1822 was only a summer famine, not as severe as the Great Famine. The English government seemed to have taken prompt action as Fr. Michael Collins, Administrator of Skibbereen, and later Bishop of Ross said 'ample, timely supplies came from England.'[1]

To provide employment for the poor in remote areas, the English government sent Richard Griffith, to take charge of road-building, which was necessary for

33

trade. The main project for West Cork was a new road connecting Skibbereen and Crookhaven, which started in 1823.[2]

After Catholic Emancipation in 1829, achieved mainly through the efforts of the Liberator, Daniel O'Connell, the penal laws were ended. Roman Catholics wanted better churches than the old ones. In 1832 a new chapel was completed in Lisheen, the site being donated by local landlord, Samuel Townsend, to the parish priest, Fr. James Mulcahy.[3]

The population of West Cork rose dramatically, as in Ireland generally, in the years 1800–1845. Landholders divided their farms between their sons, so that the holdings got smaller and smaller. The population depended almost entirely on potatoes which gave the best return per acre.

On the islands, and indeed in most parts of Ireland, people lived in little villages, the houses very close to each other. The houses were small, smoky, stuffy, unhealthy. In 1833, W.W. Beecher of Creagh divided the 649 acres of Cape Clear into holdings of about five acres each.[4] On Heir Island, as elsewhere, the houses were built in sheltered spots. The arrangement and the poor quality of the housing was very unhealthy and contributed to the spread of fever.

The Great Famine

The years of the Great Famine are seared into the subconscious of every Irish person. Millions of words have been written about the Famine, its causes, the million people dying of starvation and fever, the flood of emigration, the injustice reflected in the fact that food, in the form of wheat, meat, dairy produce was exported while thousands were dying, the belated efforts by the English government to provide relief works so that people could work long hours to enable them to buy yellow meal (Indian corn), the sense of wrong and hatred of the English which it engendered. It is well documented that West Cork in general was one of the worst hit areas during the Famine, with Skibbereen and the Mizen peninsula in particular, suffering terribly.

Thomas Swanton, of Scrahanyleary, Ballydehob, a Protestant landlord, wrote a letter to the editor of the *Nation* newspaper which was published on the 13th March, 1847. This is part of the letter

> What I now desire, in the bitterness of my soul, to represent, is the famished, diseased, helpless perishing state of the people of this district. We have no landlords in fee resident, no medical man resident, no hospital, no refuge, no asylum. The pangs of dysentery and the agonies of death are suffered without shelter, without attendance, without comfort. I see no laws enacted, no plans proposed by those in authority, calculated to revive prosperity in our peculiarly depressed circumstances. The horrors of famine and pestilence are before us and the black clouds of despair hang over us . . . .

Blight struck the potato crop in Aughadown and the islands in Roaringwater Bay in 1846–47. Relics of former ridges, called lazy beds, can be seen in several places; towards the western end of Long Island the ridges extend right down to the rocks. The population of the Bay was once so dense that even small windswept islands held human communities. Some of these, like the Calf islands were unpleasant places in which to live, especially in winter, when bad weather often prevented the inhabitants from leaving the islands for weeks. Yet several of the settlements on the Calf islands and Skeams survived until the middle of the twentieth century. West Skeam was abandoned in 1940 and East Skeam in 1958.

In assessing the direct effects of the Famine on the people, it is revealing to compare the census returns for 1841 and 1851, bearing in mind that potato blight struck first in 1845, that the famine reached its worst in 1847 but continued until 1849. Therefore, in 1851, the people would have been just recovering from the worst years of the Famine.

In the Aughadown Parish Records, the parish priest, Rev. Fr. Troy, has an entry for the month of August 1847 – 'A dreadful year of famine' and for the month of November 1947, he wrote, 'All dying of starvation, no Baptisms' The following tables shows a dramatic decline in both baptisms and marriages in Aughadown at the height of the famine.[5]

CATHOLIC MARRIAGES 1845–1852		CATHOLIC BAPTISMS 1845–1852	
Year	Aughadown	Year	Aughadown
1845	60	1845	331
1846	29	1846	301
1847	7	1847	119
1848	9	1848	105
1849	6	1849	100
1850	24	1850	87
1851	19	1851	65
1852	13	1852	88

The people of Aughadown parish suffered greatly during the famine. Tradition has it that Kilcoe Church was built on the site occupied in 1847 by a fever shed. In six healthy months in 1845, 117 children were baptised in the parish but in

EMIGRANTS ARRIVAL AT CORK – A SCENE ON THE QUAY

six dreadful months in 1847, there were only 9. Sixty marriages took place in the parish in 1845 but in 1847 there were only seven.[6]

The following reflects the population decline on Heir, East Skeam, West Skeam, East Calf, Cape Clear, Sherkin and townlands in Aughadown South, adjacent to Heir.

	1841	1851	% REDUCTION
Heir Island	358	288	20%
West Skeam	22	14	36%
East Skeam	29	27	7%
East Calf	19	8	58%
Cape Clear	1052	819	22%
Sherkin	1126	696	38%
Turkhead	45	35	22%
Ardagh	121	61	50%
Fasagh	97	53	45%
Lisheen Lower	83	27	67%
Lisheen Upper	132	87	34%
Lisaree	73	58	20%
Laheratanavally	135	36	73%
Poulnacallee	82	29	64%
Kilkilleen	161	162	1 person incr.
Cunnamore	134	52	61%
Whitehall	103	61	41%
Ardnagrohery	77	31	60%

The population of the civil parish of Aughadown fell from 5,757 in 1841 to 3,329 in 1851, that is a decrease of 42%. The populaton of the civil parish of Kilcoe fell from 2,339 in 1841 to 1,238 in 1851, a decline of 47%. Kilcoe had a low mortality rate, so the fall was due mainly to emigration.

It is clearly illustrated in the table above that the Famine had a worse effect on the mainland than on the islands. The population of Heir Island fell by one fifth, slightly less than Cape Clear and much less than Sherkin. While accepting that other factors rather than death or emigration, could have affected the numbers, it is clear that the Famine struck very hard in Cunnamore, Whitehall, Ardnagrohery, Laheratanavally, Lisheen and Poulnacallee. There was a similar decline in all the other townlands of Aughadown not shown on table. Killkilleen is the only townland which actually increased in population in that terrible decade 1841–1851.

Writing about Cape Clear and Sherkin, Father Charles Davis P.P. Rath and the Islands wrote:

> Their staple food entirely disappeared. Indian meal of the coarsest and cheapest kind was brought to the island. To purchase that ready money was necessary. With the food disappeared their fishing gear, their clothes, nay even the beds they lay on, pledged in pawn offices never to return. The hunger and want in the most aggravated and hopeless form pervaded the island.[7]

The story was similar in Heir and the other islands. The women and children were surviving on edible seaweeds and shellfish, while most of the 'yellow meal' was given to the father if he was able to get work in the various relief works – building roads, piers, etc. so that he would have the strength to continue working. A letter in the *Southern Reporter* in January 1847 describes the appalling living conditions and lack of adequate relief work on Sherkin and Cape Clear; the same story applied to all the other islands. The writer stated that he knew of an able bodied man on Sherkin, who lived six days on two meals, and that when he got a piece of bread on the sixth day, he took it home to his starving father without even touching it. On Cape Clear the labourers were so weak that when they met a hill or leaca (slope), they had to go down on all fours and walk like an animal.

Dear Old Skibbereen is one of the best-known and most poignant songs about the Famine. In the second verse, the unknown writer describes the coming of the blight on the potatoes and the rent that the tenants had to pay.

> *My son, I loved my native land with energy and pride*
> *'Till the blight came over all my crops, my sheep and cattle died.*
> *My rent and taxes were to pay, I could not them redeem*
> *And that's the cruel reason why I left old Skibbereen.*

Many of the starving people had to go to the workhouse in Skibbereen. Built in 1839, to take 800 inmates, by January, 1847, it held 1169, of whom 332 had a fever. In the workhouses, there was a section for men, a section for women, for boys and for girls so that when a family entered they were separated from each other. The workhouses were dreadful places and families entered only as a last resort. Because of overcrowding, fever spread rapidly in them.[8]

Soup kitchens were set up to feed those who were starving. In Aughadown parish, the vicar, Archdeacon Stuart, was chairman of the relief committee; in January 1847, he appealed to the Cork Ladies' Association for money, food and clothing. He stated that he had a list of 1,900 persons who were in need of aid (of whom $1/5$ were working on the roads). He stated that death from starvation was rare, but that fever was killing hundreds. The soup kitchen was giving out 1,440 pints of soup daily, which was nearly sufficient, but they had insufficient subscriptions to buy more.[9]

There were two soup kitchens in Aughadown, one at Newcourt where Lionel Fleming lived and the other at the glebe house under Archdeacon Stuart. Earlier a soup kitchen was established in Kilcoe, run by the vicar, Rev. James Freke and J.M. Swanton of Ballydehob.

Jeremiah O'Callaghan, a reporter with the *Cork Examiner*, did much to highlight the awful conditions people were reduced to. He visited Kilbrinogue, between Ballydehob and Schull, and described it as 'a charnel house' with a corpse in every cabin. He concluded that all the people would die within weeks. He was correct; the village disappeared completely, as did the village of Meenies, north of Drimoleague.[10]

Fr. Troy, P.P. of Aughadown found people dead in many of the cabins of the parish. He took a coffin to one of them to bury a man who had been dead for six days but discovered that his wife and three children were too weak to help him to coffin the putrid corpse so he had to call his curate, Fr. Walsh.[11]

There were countless deeds of heroism and self-sarifice. Dr. Robert Traill,

Vicar of Schull, who was chairman of Schull relief committee, opened a soup kitchen and helped the starving and the fever-ridden people of all denominations in the Schull area. He contracted fever himself and died. Many of the Catholic clergy and dispensary doctors, like Dr. Daniel Donovan in Skibbereen, did their utmost to help. The Gaelic scholar and Protestant landlord, Thomas Swanton of Crannliath, Ballydehob, protested that 'murder was going on' for the sake of profits of English merchants.[12]

Strong farmers collaborated with landlords to clear the land of cottiers. Farmers as well as landlords gained from the export of corn and cattle. Some land-grabbing went on; some families are ashamed of what their ancestors did in those years.

The Government's response to the crisis was to establish committees who organised road-building and quay-construction, on which the men could work, to earn money for food. Many of the workers died on these projects as they were too weak to work and often had to walk long distances to their place of work. The pay was usually 8 pence a day; Indian meal cost up to two shillings (24 pence) a stone. In December 1846, up to a thousand workers from Caheragh Parish marched into Skibbereen demanding food. In Aughadown Parish it was decided to build a road from Whitehall to Cunnamore, about 1¾ miles and a road to Turkhead, about 2 miles. The Turkhead road was built but the Whitehall to Cunnamore road was not built until the early 1920s.

Fatal Shooting

At the height of the Famine, on Christmas Eve 1848, a vessel, named the *Susan*, of Milford, laden with wheat, was wrecked on the Reen of Heir Island. A rock off the headland is called *Oileán Topmast*, Topmast Island, where she was wrecked. For the starving people of the island it must have been a God-send. The attitude of people along the coast and on the islands to shipwrecks was that every effort should be made to rescue the crew of shipwrecks. We see in Chapter 14 that the Heir islanders risked life and limb in saving people in several shipwrecks. However, it was felt that any 'wrack' washed ashore became the property of the finder. Tomás Ó Criomhtain, of the Great Blasket Island, in his masterpiece, *An tOileánach* (The Island Man), wrote that the people of the Blaskets would have starved in the Famine years only for the food obtained from shipwrecks on the island. The press used the phrase 'depredations of the country people' to describe plundering of wrecks.

In Heir Island five coastguards from Baltimore Station and a policeman were placed on guard at the wreck site. It is hardly surprising that the starving people made forays to snatch some of the cargo or wreckage which was washed up at some distance from the main wreck. However, this had fatal consequences for John Murphy, a Heir Islander, shot by a coastguard named George Moore. Moore was placed under arrest by the policeman after the shooting. At Murphy's inquest, a coastguard officer explained, 'that the cargo being foreign wheat, was subject to a duty and that it would be the duty of the waterguards, when in charge of it to use all care and diligence to prevent plunder.'[13]

On Saturday, December 30th, an enquiry was held at the Police Barracks,

Aughadown, concerning the shooting dead of John Murphy on Wednesday 27th. The jury failed to agree on a verdict, and after being locked up for six hours, they were discharged on the advice of Dr. Donovan of Skibbereen, who stated that one of the jurors had become ill. The investigation continued on Monday, January 1st, 1849. The jury heard evidence from Captain Boileau, Henry Higgins Esq. and from Lieutenant John Harrison, commander of Baltimore Lifeguard Station, who had gone with the other coastguards to the island on the 24th, who then returned to Baltimore and had been unable to return until Wednesday because of severe weather. The coastguards erected a tent near the scene so that they could guard the wreck and its cargo.[14]

Michael Harte, in evidence, stated that he was a brother-in-law of the deceased. On the morning of the 27th, he heard a shot while in bed, got up, and went towards the wreck, where he was accosted by the prisoner (Moore), who said that he would shoot him if he did not come back. He returned to where Moore stood and saw him take up his gun. Harte told him not to fire because he would shoot some person, but Moore didn't heed his warning. Harte saw Moore put the gun to his shoulder, take aim and fire. Murphy fell immediately. There were two persons with Murphy at the time and about fifty to sixty people scattered about the headland. Murphy was doing nothing wrong at the time and there could not be any plundering going on without his seeing it. When his brother-in-law was shot, all was confusion. The corn that was saved was then carried off by the people. Four other witnesses, Daniel Murphy (brother of the deceased), John McCarthy, Timothy McCarthy and John Dawley (probably Daly) were called and all gave similar testimony except that they were not near enough to hear the conversation between the witness, Harte and the prisoner, Moore.

Thomas Dowlan, the policeman with the lifeguards, stated, in evidence, that he was in the tent when the shot was fired and did not see the man fall. Moore immediately came into the tent and said that he had discharged his carbine and that the people said that a man had been killed. Dowlan said that he was aware that plundering had been going on during the night but that he saw no plundering on the Wednesday morning. He had fired shots in the air during the night for the purpose of intimidating the people; he stated that he made a prisoner of Moore for the purpose of quieting the excitement and anger, which was very great after the man was shot.

John Donovan, boatman for the lifeguards, said he was near the tent when the shot was fired, but did not see the deceased hit. He said that Murphy was about 100 yards from Moore, but could not see distinctly as the morning was hazy. He had fired himself during the night and it was he who had put in the fatal charge. He had seen a man and a woman carry off two pieces of stick that morning but had seen no other plundering until after the man was shot.

Timothy Daly, 'extra man' at Baltimore Coastguard Station, stated that he was near the tent when deceased was shot but did not see the occurrence; he judged that the distance between Moore and Murphy was about forty to fifty yards. He said that there were about one hundred and fifty people on the rocks and hills about but he saw no plundering except two people carrying off sticks. He saw no stones being thrown. Cornelius Harrington, Chief lifeguard boatman, said that he was not present when the shot was fired, but he saw the area after the shooting and thought that the dead man was about four hundred yards from where the shot was fired.

Dr. Donovan was next examined and sworn in. He told the inquiry that he was with Murphy when he died and subsequently carried out a post mortem on his body. He stated that his death was caused by a gun shot wound in the right side.

> The ball entered between the lower rib and the hip on the right side and escaped in the same position on the left side, wounding the intestines on its way and causing a considerable protusion of the bowels.

The ball took a direct course and could not, in his opinion, be discharged from a firearm, the muzzle of which was elevated at the time. In other words, the shot was not fired into the air to warn people; it was a low shot meant to cause injury or death.

After hearing the evidence, the jury retired, but when they returned, they stated that they could not agree on a verdict. The following verdict was, however, returned by the majority,

> That the deceased, John Murphy, on the 28th of December, 1848, in Hare Island in the County of Cork came by his death from a gun shot wound inflicted by George Moore, Coastguard at Baltimore whilst in the discharge of his duty protecting a wreck.

They concluded that due caution had not been used in firing the shot, but that it had been fired without malice. The proceedings then terminated and Moore was discharged from custody.[15]

— 8 —

Edward Spring

And The Island and Coast Society

Edward Spring was born in 1808 in Killarney, Co. Kerry. A graduate of Trinity College, Dublin, he was ordained a priest in 1835. He was appointed curate of Tullagh parish (Baltimore) in 1843 and resident curate of Cape Clear in December, 1849. In 1852, he was promoted, becoming Rector of Kilcoe and Cape Clear, which were united in one Mission at the time.[1]

The Island Society was established in 1833 in order to provide scriptural education for the children of the islands and other coastal areas of Ireland. It was renamed 'The Island Coast Society for Ireland' in 1847. The following is an extract from the Yearly Statement of Missionary Progress of the Islands and Coast Society 1850

> Along the coast of Cork, of Kerry, on Donegal and Mayo, the Schools and Readers of the Islands and Coast Society present themselves like green oasis in the surrounding wilderness. They are still indeed in the wilderness; for it is quite true that the Society cannot extend the blessings of education to all or half the places where, if more largely aided, it might with the greatest propriety, labour; and miles of country, without either Reader or Schoolmaster are yet to be found along the Coast, while many a fair Isle raised its picturesque head above the waves of the Atlantic, the natives of which have never yet had the opportunity of hearing the glad sound of the Gospel.

The society had its own ministers, churches, schools, teachers, scripture readers and agents in each missionary station.[2] The Island Society issued annual reports, starting in 1839.

After arriving in Baltimore, Rev. Edward Spring, threw himself, with great energy, into the new spiritual movement and decided to focus most of his attention on Cape Clear. When Spring arrived in Cape Clear, the Famine was raging all over West Cork, the islanders in severe distress. He was given a farm, from which an islander had been evicted by the landlord. The Old Coastguard Station was converted into the Cape Clear Parsonage at Inbhear (South Harbour). A school was established at An Cúm in Gleann townland. Food, blankets and a little medicine were distributed among those who sent their children to the school. Tenants at Glebe were dispossessed and the land given to 'imported Protestants' and converts. A fluent Irish speaker, he insisted on teachers, readers and agents having knowledge of the Irish language. Seventy children were said to be attending the Island & Coast Society School.[3] A Protestant Church, built of Cornish granite, was completed in 1849. Fr. Holland, in his history of

41

West Cork, claimed that 'Proselytism under every form was carried on.'[4]

The Island and Coast Society (also called Church Education Society) estab-lished a school on Heir Island early in 1848 with 73 pupils on roll.[5] In the 10th annual report (for 1850) Charles Donovan of Ballydehob, who was co-ordinator of the West Carbery Branch of the Island Society, reported that in 1848 in West Carbery there were 134 scripture writers, 334 spellers, 124 translators of the Bible and 810 pupils in 25 different schools. The Society claimed that people were turning to Protestantism to escape 'the iniquity of the Catholic priests' while the Catholics claimed that they turned for 'soup'. A new word entered the English language- 'souper', a person who converted to Protestantism to get food/soup.

In the Griffith's Evaluation of 1852, the following had houses leased in Heir Is-land East.

a. Island Society, from the landlords, George and Edward Beecher.
b. Rev. Edward Spring, from the landlords   '
c. Miles McSweeney, teacher, from Island Society. The teacher lived in the house adjoining the schoolhouse.

Thomas Regan and Daniel McCarthy had houses leased from the Rev. Ed-ward Spring, who also had Oileán Caorach leased from the Beechers. The school house was exempt from rent.

An Island Society Inspector, Daniel Foley, visited West Cork in 1849. He found on Cape Clear ninety five persons assembled in prayer, of whom all but eight, had originally been Catholic. He visited Heir Island, where he described the fifty pupils as 'Edward Springs'.[6]

Miles McSweeney was appointed Island Coast Society schoolmaster and Scripture reader on Heir Island on February 2nd 1848.[7] In the minutes for Jan-uary 6th, 1852 we read:

> Rev. Edward Spring has an English school there, fifty children attended, who could give as Mr. McSweeney, the teacher, declared a literal definition of geography and what was still better, were able to answer well in the Holy Scriptures.[8]

Unlike Cape Clear, Heir Islanders don't refer to any building being used for education and proselytising but reports by the Island Society, corroborated by newspaper reports, indicate that they were active on the island. The 'old schooleen' and the teacher's residence adjoining it (still standing) must have been the centre of Spring's mission to the Island.[9] It would appear that any is-landers 'who took the soup' reverted quickly to their own religion once conditions improved after the Famine.

The following list compares the numbers of pupils, claimed to be attending the Island Society School and the National School from 1846–1852.

	1846	1847	1848	1849	1850	1851	1852
Island Society School	–	69	73	39	26	55	16
National School	61	50	73	50	42	49	72

Obviously either one school or both exaggerated the numbers attending. In 1851, when the census population of the island was 288, the total number of pupils claimed, 55 and 49, totalled 104. This would mean that 36% of the population were of school going age, which is highly unlikely. Spring became the Vicar of Aughadown in 1864. When the worst of the Famine was over, the numbers attending the Island Society schools on Cape Clear and Heir Island fell rapidly. When he moved to Inchigeelagh in 1867, there were no pupils attending the Island Society School on Heir. In 1854, we find the following report 'All our schools I regret to say have been reduced in numbers lately, from many causes but one is the great increase of national schools which are got up for this purpose, not so much of educating the young as to prevent them from being instructed in the Bible'. The report also refers to trips made to the Skeams and Calf Islands by Island Society personnel, attempting to extend their proselytising activities.[10]

One of Spring's converts in Baltimore, later returned to the Catholic Church, and made the following recantation in Rath church.

> I solemnly declare in the presence of the Almighty and this congregation that it was hunger and hunger alone made me go to church for I expected that Mr. Spring would support me as he supported others who turned with him. He was good to me since I commenced going there …. I was always a Catholic in my heart, but I pretended to be a Protestant for the support I was getting from Mr. Spring …. My mind was very uneasy for I was going against my conscience …. I am now very sorry I ever went to church and I will never go there again.[11]

Spring denied that he used famine relief in this manner and asserted that he had actually turned one prospective convert away from his Church warning him of the sin of professing one religion on his lips while he had another in his heart.

Rev. Spring used to come to Heir Island from Baltimore and land on the North Reen. Steps were chiselled out of the rock for him in the Leacain just inside Cos rock. Leacain is the Irish word for a sloping hillside, which describes exactly the terrain, now overgrown with furze and brambles. The path along the hillside is still known as Bóithrín Spring (Spring's little road). Apparently he used to go for walks along the path. It is believed he distributed Indian meal and soup in the flat area west of the 'steps', where Mike Cahalane and Neilus Cahalane lived later.

One day Spring went to visit Lizzie Minihane's great grandfather, Peter Cotter, in the Reen. Peter was setting potatoes when Spring came and promptly told him to clear off. Apparently he had his best crop ever that year. According to folklore, Spring left a boat for the islanders when he departed.[12]

Rev. Daniel Foley, in his report on his visit to West Cork in 1849, wrote,

> We set out this morning (12th) for Cape Island, with considerable doubt that we should be able to reach it, as the wind was high and the sea rough but we resolved, at all events, on going as far as Hare Island, and are just returned from it, thoroughly drenched, being unable to proceed farther, the weather

became so severe …. I was greatly delighted with the School on Hare. The children answered remarkably well; and the sight of a large pot of stirabout boiling in the Teacher's house for their breakfast, was a truly gratifying one, many of the poor little creatures looked so famishing. This is a branch of our operations that must be supported. The consequences of a cessation of this re-lief would be truly awful.[13]

From a Report in 1861–62 we read

On the East Calf island resides but one family, who though bigoted Romanist, are very friendly. The people on the West Calf Island are particularly kind, and enter freely into conversation with me. These islands, together with the East Skeam form a fine field of missionary labour. On the latter, which I have visited most frequently, I am met with 'We are very glad to see you!' When visiting Calf islands on one occasion, during the planting season, amongst oth-er matters, I spoke of the resurrection; the men looked at me quite surprised and dropped their work to listen. They could hardly credit what I said, until I repeated in Irish that portion of the creed in which we assert our belief in the resurrection of the body. Hare Island appears of a different stamp altogether, so that one would imagine you were in some far-off spot, where Popery reigns undisturbed.'[14]

From the last sentence we can gather that whatever impact Spring had made initially, with regard to education and bible reading, had evaporated completely by 1861.

Edward Spring is also remembered in the School Folklore manuscripts of 1938[15]

About ninety years ago the people of this Island were very very poor. A good number of families were also almost starving. At the time a 'Minister' by the name of Spring came to the Island. He was a Kerryman and he had plenty of money. He built a school on the Island – 'no trace of this building today, but the site on which 'twas built is still pointed out by the old people'. – He also built a house which he used as a Church. He went around among the people, and offered them money and food, if they would send their children to his school, and attend service in his church on Sundays. Most of the inhabitants were forced through poverty to accept the money and food. Those who at-tended his church got plenty money and food and clothes. Others would not take either food or money and many of them died of hunger. He gave em-ployment too, to those who were willing to work, and a rough road on the Midland is still known as *Bóithrín Spring* There was a song made about him, but I have only a couple of verses of it.

Spring was a Kerryman born
He took his departure of late;
He steered his course for Baltimore Harbour,
And bid adieu to his old mother Kate.

Twas hard to blame the old people for turning with him, as God only knows how badly off they were, and 'twas hunger and nothing else made them do it. But plenty food came after to them.[16]

In a report in the *Skibbereen Eagle* in August, 1890, the reporter refers to the advantageous position of the people of Cape Clear, Sherkin, Heir Island and the other islands with regard to fishing. He writes

> Proselytism would again be rampant and the deserted Protestant Church in Hare Island might again be occupied with worshippers, the sight of whose starving families had effected what centuries of persecution had been unable to accomplish. There is no chance of such an occurrence now. The men are busy preparing for the autumn mackerel fishing. The fish cured in this season are principally cured for the American market and for the past two years considerable employment has been afforded.[17]

The following week he continued,

> The attachment of the Irish peasant to his religion is a historical fact and great must be the strain which could sever the strong chain which convictions and custom and the example of his persecuted forefathers has wrought and which binds him to Catholicity as to a safe and secure anchorage and shelter from the storms of the world. But the cry of a starving infant is a sudden powerful shock which often times tears the strength of old associations and custom out of a man's heart and he drifts against his will away. In the famine years the Hare islanders were in desperate need and their children were in need of bread which they could not obtain unless they sacrificed what they held most dear. At that awful time many of the islanders took 'the minister's food', which was then equivalent to a renunciation of their religion, and several attended the services of the Protestant Church which was erected on the island. A story is told at that time and has been made the subject of a pathetic ballad, which tells of the action of an old man who in his desperate want had gone over to the minister. The first Sunday when he was on his way to church, whole in body, for he was well supplied with good food, but sick in mind, for he felt keenly the degradation to which he had been exposed, he had to pass the Catholic Church. Suddenly he was seized by an uncontrollable impulse and disregarding inquisitive and prying eyes, he threw himself down on his knees before the sacred edifice in which he had attended divine worship from his cradle, and cried bitterly 'I'm leaving you; I'm leaving you till the praties grow'. It was the same way with the Hare Islanders. They renounced their religion to live but they returned to die in it. When the praties grew, the minister's church knew them no more and they turned back to the old faith.[18]

Edward Spring died on the 20th April, 1880 and the following obituary was printed in the *Eagle* and *Cork County Advertiser*.

> Many of our readers will regret to learn of the death of Rev. Edward Spring on the 20th April at Mangourney Rectory, after a few days illness, from bronchitis. In or about 46, he was a curate at Baltimore and subsequently took charge of the Aughadown parish as Rector. The deceased clergyman was highly gifted and a man of great literary attainments. It was whilst he lived in Baltimore he made his name famous in a religious controversy that fiercely raged between himself and the now Canon Fitzpatrick, of Midleton. Notwithstanding that he held strong and decided episcoparian opinions he

was highly respected by all classes and by none was he held in greater respect than by the Catholic community, who esteemed him for his sincerity, courtesy and gentlemanly demeanour. As a total abstainer he was also renowned, having earnestly devoted his whole life to the cause of temperance and worked faithfully with the immortal Fr. Mathew in battling against the evils of drink.[19]

MRS MARGARET MINIHANE WITH MRS KATE
BURKE AND HER SON, PAT

CATHERINE WHOOLEY (McCARTHY) WITH
HER HUSBAND PATRICK AND SON

JOHN J. MINIHANE, 'BIG JOHNNIE',
SUMMER 1927

PATRICK MURPHY,
HEIR ISLAND WEST

— 9 —

Emigration

With good reason Ireland has been called a nation of exiles. In 1841 before the Great Famine, the population of Ireland had reached an all time high of over eight million. During the decade 1845-1855, up to two million people, a quarter of the population, emigrated to Britain, to British North America (Canada today) and to the United States. The flow of emigration continued unabated for over a century, up to the 1960s. The exodus from Ireland was a result of poverty, famine, fever, the land system and the lack of opportunity. In later years most went in search of work, others in search of freedom and a better quality of life.

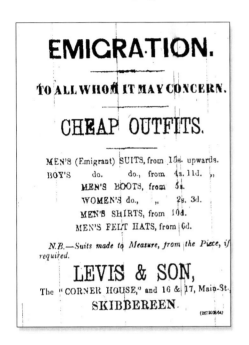

During the Famine many went initially to Canada as the fares were lower, but the majority subsequently crossed the border into the United States. The emigrants always travelled in Steerage Class.[1] In the early part of the nineteenth century, the fare to America was £12, but by the 1830s, the fare for steerage passengers, due to the competition between ship owners, was down to £3.10s for a journey that took from four to six weeks. Steerage passage to Canada in 1846 ranged from 50s to 60shillings and from 70s to £5 to the United States, with the Atlantic crossing taking about six weeks.

The failure of the potato crop during the Famine changed people's attitude to emigration. Previously they left reluctantly but the offspring of small farmers, labourers and fishermen, who had regarded 'emigration as the most terrible of all fates', now wanted to get out of Ireland.

Ships trading out of Crookhaven, Schull and Castletownbere, but especially Bantry and Baltimore, transported passengers to the New World. William J. Dealy of Bantry placed the following advertisement in the press:

> The Dealy of Bantry, 400 tons, is now ready. She is fitted out in a very comfortable manner for the reception of passengers, and wind and weather permitting, she will sail for St. John, New Brunswick about March 25th 1847. For freight passengers, apply to the owner, W.J. Dealy, Bantry.[2]

Cornelius Harrington of Castletownbere, owner of the *Govenor Douglas*, 1000 tons, and the *Ocean*, 400 tons, placed a similar advertisement in the same paper in March 1847.[3] Their destination, also, was St. John, New Brunswick, 'convenient to Boston'. All three ships were 'timber ships', bringing west their human cargo and returning with timber. On May 23rd an emigrant agent reported that all three ships were in quarantine in Partridge Island, in the port of St. John. The *Dealy* had sailed from Bantry with one hundred and sixty nine passengers, of whom twenty two died at sea. The *Governor Douglas* carried two hundred and thirty one passengers and the *Ocean* eighty nine, nobody from either ship dying en route.[4]

Comparing the *Dealy* and the *Ocean*, both 400 tons, we find that the former transported almost twice as many passengers as the latter. The *Ocean* was one of the ships whose passengers were satisfied with food, water and general conditions. Many, however, were more like the *Dealy* or worse, overcrowded, with unsatisfactory supplies of water and food. Many were indeed 'coffin ships.' The Malvina left Baltimore with one hundred and eighty three passengers, arriving in St. John on May 9th, only one man having died on board; the Leviathan left Baltimore with one hundred and thirty one passengers on July 6th 1847, arriving with two persons dead.[5] The schooner, Margaret Huges, was built in 1842 for William Hughes, whose family had come from Wales to Sherkin. She was probably named after his daughter. She was a class 'E1, 107 tons, registered schooner, rigged with standing bowsprit, carvel built, no galley and female figurehead.' She left Sherkin and sailed to Liverpool with emigrating islanders; she left Liverpool for Newfoundland on May 6th 1847, arriving in St. Johns on August 9th.[6]

Cornelius Harrington, in his advertisement, stated that St. John was convenient to Boston. He understood that for most people the U.S.A. was the 'promised land'. Most of the passengers who landed in St. John later crossed into the United Stated. An idea of the impact of the population movement can be gauged when it is considered that 37,000 Irish emigrants joined the 115,000 citizens of Boston in 1847 alone.[7] Boston became the most 'Irish' of the large American cities. There was very little welcome for them in the beginning; many Americans wanted to know nothing of the Irish 'fever-ridden Papist paupers'. The emigrants to the U.S.A. and Canada had, in those early years, to accept low wages and appalling living conditions. For years, being Irish and particularly being Irish and Catholic, was a stigma in American society. Gradually, however, the Irish became established and prominent in business, labour, politics and religious and cultural life. The need for labour in America, with the expansion of the American farming frontier, the construction of canals, roads, cities and industry, prompted American industries to actively recruit labourers in Ireland. The early emigrants saved their meagre wages to send passage money to family members left behind in Ireland. This system of 'chain emigration' continued until the 1960s. The Irish economy could not support most of Ireland's young people, who had come to expect more than grinding poverty. Emigration became an everyday feature of Irish life.

Even healthy people found the trans-Atlantic voyage arduous in those early days. For those weakened by malnutrition, it was a nightmare. Thousands died after landing. The quarantine facilities on Partridge Island St. John, on Grosse Isle in the St. Lawrence river and on Ellis Island in New York, were unable to cope with the flood of sick immigrants.

The bereavement, up-rooting and scattering of families caused by famine and emigration is well illustrated in the case of Jeremiah O'Donovan Rossa. His father died on the road works in 1847 and the family were evicted from their home soon afterwards. In 1848, an uncle, who had emigrated to Philadelphia, sent tickets for the passage of Rossa's mother, his brother and sister, leaving him alone in Ireland. He describes their departure in poignant terms.

> At Reenascreena Cross we parted … Five or six other families were going away and there were five or six carts to carry them …. to the Cove of Cork. The cry of weeping and wailing that day rings in my ears still …. That time it was a cry heard every day at every cross roads in Ireland'.[8]

He could have added every quay or pier, Baltimore, Trá Chiaráin, Heir Island, Schull, Crookhaven; indeed every little port from Kinsale to Killybegs from where ships sailed in the Famine years.

In a report in the *Skibbereen Eagle* of April, 9th 1892, headed 'Still They Go', we read,

> Last week 1,108 Irish emigrants left Queenstown for America, The previous week 715 departed for the great Republic of the West. So the emigration craze has set in once again with a vengeance. Moreover, these 1826 persons are all young, able-bodied, respectable and industrious people.

He continues

> The emigrants can't be prevented from departing, nor would it be fair to in-duce them to wait with patience in the old land till better times arrive. The live horse till you get grass policy is not sound …. Some say that Home Rule will settle the matter. But it will not of itself. … If the Home Rulers strike out on a truly democratic policy, under which the land would be nationalised as well as the laws, then the emigration would cease, but not till then.

Although many people who left Ireland looked forward to their new lives and opportunities, it was not without deep regret and heart-breaking sadness that people left their homes. Emigrants often felt that they were being driven from their homes and this attitude contributed to the natural bond between them once they landed in their new country.

After arriving in America, emigrants began to search for homes and a liveli-hood, settling in different parts of the United States and lending a distinctively

Irish flavour to the communities they joined and founded. It was understood that America was not the place to go if you were looking for an easy life. It was a difficult place for those unwilling to do menial jobs, as there was no welcome for the lazy. The emigrant was not asked what he was, but what he could do – if you can work with your hands, you will succeed.

No family was untouched by emigration and there are Heir Island descendants in many parts of the United States. Most of them settled on the East Coast of America, particularly in New Jersey, Maine and Massachusetts. Englewood, New Jersey was often called 'Little Heir Island,' on account of the number of island families living there. Some Heir islanders remember aunts and uncles who emigrated in the 1800s and were never heard from again. We must remember at this time that many people were unable to read and write and would not have been able to keep in touch with home. In other families, members who emigrated, aged around seventeen or eighteen, never knew or met their brothers or sisters who were born after they left.

It is not surprising that in the circumstances of this period that many people went missing. Relatives placed advertisements in the *Boston Pilot* in an attempt to locate them. In the *Boston Pilot* of 13th August, 1887 in the 'Missing Friends' column, we read:

> Information wanted of Daniel Driscoll, born in Hare Island, County Cork, Ireland, who came to this country about 30 years ago. When last heard from, about 18 years ago, was in some part of Pennsylvania. If yet living, will hear of something to his advantage by writing to his nephew, Daniel F. Driscoll, 143 North State Street, Concord, New Hampshire.[9]

Lawrence, Massachusetts, was itself an infant when it became the birthplace of a boy, who was destined to have one of the most notable careers ever achieved by a native of Lawrence. Six years prior to the birth of Charles Driscoll, Lawrence had been granted, on 20 April 1853, a city charter by the state legislature of Massachusetts. The same legislature had incorporated Lawrence as a town six years earlier, giving legal recognition to the rapidly growing community that has settled, beginning in 1845, on the banks of the Merrimack River at a spot called Deer Jump Falls. Charles Driscoll, son of Timothy and Bridget (Foley) Driscoll was born on 18th June, 1859, the two hundred and tenth child to be entered in the birth records of the fledgling textile city. The same records indicate that his parents were both natives of Ireland and that his father was a labourer. The author of Timothy's death notice in a local paper thirty years later indicated that Mr. Driscoll first came to Lawrence to work on the construction of the dam across the Merrimack at Deer Jump Falls. Upon completion of the dam, which was for years the longest in the world, Mr. Driscoll apparently worked as a labourer for the Boston and Maine Railroad. His later years of employment were spent upon various enterprises that eventually helped to make Lawrence a city. At one time he was employed upon the horse railroad, under his son, Daniel, who for a long time was overseer of repairs upon the road.[10]

The senior O'Driscoll's wages would seem to have enabled him to provide for his family in a more comfortable fashion than many of his contemporaries were able to provide for theirs; many of them had to live in 'Irish Shanties' near the dam. The Lawrence Street Directory for 1859 lists Timothy Driscoll's residence as being on the south side of Kingston Street in South Lawrence. In as much as the name of the street is given, the Driscoll home apparently was indeed a house and not one of the shanties, for the latter, in an earlier directory, had no such geographical designation.[11] When Charles Driscoll, who later went on to become Provincial of the Augustinian Order in America, was baptized his god parents were listed as Garrett Cotter and Johanna Foley. Garrett and Johanna were natives of Heir Island as their names appear in Aughadown Parish Records (prior to 1850). At least two of Charles' siblings survived into adulthood, an older sister, Catherine, who was born in Ireland and an older brother Daniel, who was born in Lawrence in July 1848. Parish Records show another son Denis born in Ireland in 1846. In Timothy's obituary in the Lawrence *Daily Eagle* on February 4th, 1889 it states that 'he came to Lawrence 43 years ago'. This would have been 1846, one of the worst years of the Famine.

As can be seen by the above, the Driscoll family from Heir Island certainly prospered in the United States as did many others. There are numerous second generation priests and nuns scattered across the States and many more prospered in their chosen professions.

The cities of Lewiston and Auburn in Maine have a rich history, dominated by the Androscoggin River and the power it generates. The development of water power from the Androscoggin began with the formation of the Great Androscoggin Falls Dam, Locks and Canal Company in 1839. In 1845, its reorganization as the Lewiston Water Power Company was for the purpose of generating power by waterfalls for general manufacturing, chiefly textile, cotton, and wool. Auburn's shoe industry grew steadily from the time of the Civil War. Lewiston and Auburn's common roots are inextricably entwined with the Androscoggin River and its industrial base. A group of Heir Islanders settled here and we find a number of them living on the same street, Newbury Street, Catherine Murphy from Heir Island settled here 1872/73, in 1887 her daughter married Cornelius Burke from Heir Island and they settled in No. 16 Newbury St. In 1915, we find Richard Pyburn and John Shanahan, first cousins, from Heir Island travelling out to their uncle, Jeremiah Shanahan who was living at 67 Newbury St. Among other Heir islanders who also settled in the general area of Auburn and Lewiston were Minihanes, Murphys, McCarthys, Burkes and others.

From the late 1890s and early 1900s when people from Heir emigrated, they went by liner. The ship used to hoot when passing south of Sherkin. Bonfires were lit on the Dún in Heir. Often this was their last glimpse of Ireland. Some never returned; a few came back once or twice. In later years some returned fairly frequently. Lizzie McCarthy (nee Minihane) was a baby when her eldest sister, Ellen, emigrated; they never saw each other again.

As many women as men emigrated, the majority of the women being single, unattached, who went to avail of better job opportunities and marriage prospects. Many of the emigrants had their names misspelled by officials when they landed in America. Usually the O was dropped i.e. O'Driscoll becoming

Driscoll. Each emigrant had to give their name, age, sex, whether married or single, their occupation, their nationality, their race, last permanent address, next

SAXONIA

of kin in Ireland, their destination, whether they could read and write. Their height, complexion, colour of hair and eyes were recorded and whether they were a polygamist or an anarchist. With the coming of the passenger liners, most emigrants, at least from the south of Ireland, left Queenstown (Cobh). Their last view of Ireland was the Fastnet Rock, which is often referred to as 'Ireland's Teardrop'.

The S.S. *Saxonia* left Queenstown (Cobh) on the 25th August, 1909, arriving in the port of Boston on 1 September, 1909, the voyage lasting seven days. According to the ship's manifest, aboard were four young women from Heir Island:-

Ellen Minihane (see Emigrant's Story, page 175) was 18 years of age, female, single and reported that her occupation was a servant. Her next of kin in Ireland was her father, John Minihane of Heir Island, Baltimore, County Cork. She reported that her destination was Jamaica Plain, Massachusetts, and that her sister paid her fare. She was going to live with her sister, Mrs. Mary Mahony, 2 Johnsons Ave., Jamaica Plain, Massachusetts.

Minnie McCarthy was 17 years of age, female, single and reported that her occupation was servant. Her next of kin in Ireland was her mother, Mrs. Mary McCarthy of Heir Island, Baltimore, County Cork. She reported that her destination was New Abron, Maine and that her sister paid her fare. She was going to live with her cousin, Denis O'Sullivan, 105 1st St., New Abron, Maine.

Twin Sisters, Katie and Margaret Murphy were 18 years of age, single, servants, their last permanent address Baltimore, Ireland. Their next of kin in Ireland was their mother, Mrs. Catherine Murphy of Heir Island, Baltimore, County Cork. Their destination was New Abron, Maine. Their sister paid their fare. They were going to live with their sister, Ellen Murphy, 105 1st St., New Abron, Maine.

All four girls declared that they could read and write, had never been in the U.S.A. previously, and were not polygamists or anarchists. One of the girls had twenty five dollars in her pocket, while the other three had seventy-five.

When a young man or woman was emigrating all the islanders visited the house a few nights before departure and there was a gathering or, 'American wake', as they were called. These were nights of heart-break, the parents losing a child and sometimes two, knowing that they might never see them again. For

WEST BEACH, QUEENSTOWN (COBH)

the young people emigrating it was very tough; they were leaving their parents, their friends, facing a new life and culture which was completely different to life on the islands. Most of the emigrants went out to relations who had preceded them. Margaret O'Sullivan (nee Murphy) of Heir Island middle told me her own story. Margaret left Heir Island, aged eighteen, and went to Englewood, New Jersey where she had an uncle, Michael McCarthy. Michael, in his day, had gone out to an aunt in Maine and later moved to Englewood, New Jersey. Michael McCarthy found work and after a few years paid the fare out for his younger brother, Danny. In turn Danny paid the fare for his brother Timothy, who was killed by a train shortly after emigrating. Later two other brothers, William and Eugene emigrated. Many of the emigrants settled in areas where there was a high density of Irish people already like Englewood, Worcester, Boston, Lowell. They tended to settle in clusters in close proximity to each other.

The suffering and the wrench of exile is well illustrated by the following story.

On one occasion Mike 'the Cloud' O'Neill of Heir Island had to cut short his fishing trip and return home to bid farewell to his daughter, possibly for the last time. She and another young girl from the island were emigrating. On returning home, Mike learned that the girls had been unable to arrange transport to Queenstown (Cobh) so, after hastily eating a meal, he and his crew re-baited their lobsterpots and headed for Queenstown with the two girls on board. Sailing through the night, he landed the two girls in Cobh the following morning in time to catch the tender to meet the liner out in the bay.[12]

Francis Fitzgerald, of Hollyhill and formerly Heir Island, remembers his two sisters, Maureen and Bridie, emigrating. The night before their departure was very sad. Many tears were cried. Then, in the morning, the near neighbours called again and walked with them to the slip, where there were embraces, farewells and more tears. After landing on Cunnamore Point, there was more waving before they were driven to Cobh by Seán O'Donoghue of Kilcoe. Francis said it was almost a month before their parents received a letter from their exiled daughters, a month of anxiety and worry. His sister, Maureen, was the first to make a trans-Atlantic call to the island phone, which was located in Charlie O'Neill's shop. She had indicated in a letter, the date and time of her call. The shop was full of neighbours when the call came through.

Emigration from Heir Island continued up to the 1960s. Now many second and third generation islanders visit Heir Island every year, tracing their roots and seeing for themselves the homes of their ancestors. Pat O'Neill, returning to the island for the first time, in 1947 or '48, was so delighted to see Heir Island again that he jumped out of the row boat and splashed to the shore, where he knelt and kissed the ground and rose with tears streaming down his face. Since the world is a much 'smaller' place today, with transport much easier, many emigrants return quite frequently. Karen Linden, whose grandmother was one of the four young girls who sailed out of Cobh on the Saxonia on August 25th, 1909, returned to settle in West Cork in 2000.

In the 1950s, when emigrants began to return, their arrival was often reported in the *Southern Star*. In August, 1952, the *Star* reported the return of Mrs. Katie Scanlan (nee Cahalane):

> At Parents' House.
> Mrs. Scanlan of Curtis Avenue, Staten Island, New York, is at present at home in Heir Island, where she intends to stay until October. It is twenty nine years since she left. Mrs. Scanlan was Katie Cahalane of the Reen, Heir Island, daughter of Michael Cahalane. She married Paddy Scanlan of Aughadown.

In the *Southern Star* of September 16th 1967 we read

> After an absence of forty four years, Mrs. Bridget McPartland, accompanied by her husband and two daughters, both of whom are Sisters of the Dominican Order, finally visited Ireland. They visited their relations in Dublin, Leitrim and West Cork. Mrs. McPartland is a sister of Patrick O'Neill, Ardagh, Church Cross. He was formerly of Heir Island East.

Rose Fitzgerald, who was to become the mother of the first Catholic President of the U.S.A., was a grand-daughter of Katherine Cadogan and James Fitzgerald who had 'come from Skibbereen'. It has been suggested that Katherine Cadogan was from Heir Island but there is no proof of this.

DENIS MINIHANE,
HEIR ISLAND WEST

Above Left:
ELLEN MURPHY,
HEIR ISLAND WEST

Left:
MAUREEN AND BRIDIE
FITZGERALD, HEIR ISLAND
EAST

THE HEADSTONE OF RICHARD PYBURN, HEIR ISLAND, WHO IS INTERRED IN ST. JOSEPH'S CEMETERY, WEST ROXBURY, MA.

OLD ANCHOR ADORNING A WALL ON HEIR ISLAND

— 10 —

Agrarian Trouble 1850-1900

Unrest in the Bay

The acrimony between landlords and tenants came to a head in the latter half of the nineteenth century. Some landlords were fair to their tenants, such as The O'Donovans of Lissard near Skibbereen. The record of others was less reputable and among the most reprehensible were Bence Jones of Lisselane, near Clonakilty and Lionel Fleming of Newcourt, Aughadown parish. [1]

In the autumn of 1879 the potato crop failed again and the country was threatened with another famine. But it was a different Ireland from the Ireland of 1847–1848. The Land League was formed in 1879 in Co. Mayo, with Michael Davitt as leader and Charles Stuart Parnell as President. The aim of the Land League was to procure better conditions for tenant farmers. They demanded what became known as the 3 Fs, Fair Rent, Fixity of Tenure and Free Sale. They wanted landlords to stop demanding exorbitant rents, that no tenant should be evicted for non payment of high rents and that the farmers could sell their land if they desired. At the inaugural meeting Parnell said: 'I believe that the maintenance of the class of landlords in this country is not for the greatest benefit of the greatest number. Ireland has, perhaps, suffered more than any other country in the world for the maintenance of such a class.' Parnell told the tenants: 'Hold a firm grip on your homesteads and lands.' Tenants were urged not to pay unfair rents. Landlords who evicted tenants were to be boycotted and shunned. The same treatment was to be applied to tenants who rented land from which somebody had been evicted. The word 'boycott' entered the English language when a Captain Boycott who was in charge of an estate in Mayo was shunned by all his neightbours in 1880. [2]

The Ladies Land League was established; one of its main leaders being Anna Parnell, sister of Charles Stuart Parnell. She addressed a large gathering of small farmers and labourers in Ballydehob on March 5th in 1881, one of the largest crowds ever to congregate in West Cork. Although the meeting was banned, Miss Parnell addressed the hugh crowd of at least five thousand people from a hill, since known as 'Fanny's Hill', after her sister Fanny. She urged her audience to join the 'honourable fight of farmers to put an end to hunger and misery in Ireland forever.' [3]

A riot, which took place in the town of Schull on 7 June 1881, involving an estimated 2,000 to 3,000 people, watched over by eight police and six members of the coastguard, culminated in the wrecking of the police station, the house and horse drawn car of a man who frequently conveyed the police by car. Baltimore coastguard personnel, while returning to Baltimore by boat from Schull, were physically threatened and verbally abused by three boatloads of men from Heir Island for having conveyed reinforcements totalling fifteen police by boat to Schull.[4] John Salsey, officer in charge of Baltimore Coastguard Station, revealed that the islanders had threatened that they would come over some night and wreck the station and village of Baltimore. Though the naval authorities considered sending reinforcements to Baltimore, the threat from the islanders did not materialise. When the gunboat Britomart, eventually visited Baltimore on 29th June 1881 to check the security of the newly-built station, the commander concluded that there was little fear that it would be attached.[5]

The Irish National League was formed in 1882, principally to replace the outlawed Land League. In October, 1885, the National League, mainly on the initiative of John Dillon and William O'Brien, M.P. Mallow, formulated a new strategy called the 'Plan of Campaign', which was essentially a No Rent movement, not implemented across the country, but targeted at certain despotic landlords and areas where tenants were in very poor circumstances. The strategy was to demand an abatement of rents of up to 30% and if the landlord refused, no rents would be paid at all. Tenants evicted would be helped out of National League Funds and every obstacle was put in the way of evicting landlords, such as non-purchase of stock seized and no land made vacant by an eviction to be rented by new tenants.

The main case in West Cork was the dispute between Thomas H. Marmion and his tenants on Castle Island and West and Middle Calf Islands.[6]

The *Skibbereen Eagle* of October 23rd, 1886 describes the eviction of tenants, under a heading, 'A Gunboat on an Eviction Cruise'. On Tuesday, October 19th, four tenants in different islands near Schull were evicted from their holdings by their landlord, Thomas Henry Marmion. The holdings were small and the arrears due not overmuch. The gunboat *Britomart* came from Dingle to Schull on Monday evening to land the evicting force on the islands. The tenants had argued that they had always paid the full rent when they were able, but that the terrible distressed times now left them no alternative to eviction if the landlord did not accept what the Parish Priest of Schull, Fr. Murphy, had offered him on their behalf, that the landlords should wipe out all costs, take a half year's rent, and give some time for the remainder to be paid, with the reduction that Marmion had promised. Marmion said that he would consider nothing but a year's rent in full and all legal costs. When they had made an offer of purchase under Lord Ashbourne's Act, he said he would sell, but that all the arrears and costs up to September, 1885, would first have to be paid in full. This the tenants said they could not afford to do. A few of the better-off tenants had already paid, but the rest stood united and in effect said: 'We can pay you so much and no more; the times are not as good as they were; we won't go to you to settle – you will have to approach us.'

The tenants, where they first rented the land, had the sole right to the seaweed on the shore and they were able to earn money by selling this manure to the farmers on the mainland. At that time every family was allotted certain strands and rocks where they could gather or cut seaweed. That source of revenue had dried up because everybody now began to take what he liked of the seaweed from wherever he liked. A few made some money from fishing but in that year (1886), their potatoes and other crops were wretched. Butter was selling at five pence a pound and at the fair held that week, two-year old cattle were sold for £2.10.0. to £3 each. They wondered what reduction in rent could compensate for such poor prices.

The Eagle states that when the Britomart was seen coming into Schull harbour, 'a rat was smelt' by the tenants under threat of eviction. They removed their few cattle to places of safety in case they would be seized. They also removed doors, furniture, etc, from their houses, so that when the evictions were completed, there were no doors to nail up, nothing for the emergency men or police to take possession of. The writer goes on to say that it was most likely that the tenants took back possession of their homesteads once the police had gone.

The report continued:

'Mr. John Gale, County Sub Sheriff, had command of the evicting force. He was assisted by three bailiffs from Cork and by 30 police from Schull district. At half-past eight the Britomart was steering off for Calf Island West, some four miles distant which was reached at nine o'clock. Two smaller boats of the Britomart, propelled as before by blue jackets, brought the evicting force from where the gunboat stopped to the shore of the island. But there was no necessity for policemen, as at no time were there more than fifty people assembled together, and not one expression of dissent escaped their lips. The tenant evicted on this island was Michael O' Driscoll, whose yearly rent was £14 and the writ was for £21 up to the previous March. When the sub-sheriff, headed by Mr. Marmion, got to Driscoll's house, the door was off, and all the contents of the two-storey slated house had been removed, with the exception of a few articles in the upper room, which the bailiffs at once put outside, assisted by the tenant himself, Driscoll's wife and three children being outside the house all the time. While these few articles were being taken out, Mr. Marmion asked the tenant what settlement he would offer, and Driscoll replied that he had offered a settlement before, and as it was not accepted the landlord would now have to settle with him. There was no stock to be driven off and possession was then handed to the landlord. The blue jackets then propelled the boats, containing the shrieval party, to Calf Island Middle. Here the tenant to be evicted was John Crowley, whose yearly rent was £11. 4s; £10. 6s. up to the previous March was due. A number of people were here sitting down by the strand to receive the sheriff and his force but their demeanour was most quiet and passive, In this case also, the doors, furniture, etc. were removed, except for a few articles upstairs which the tenant and his family helped remove, one tub of salted meat being among the articles removed, which Mrs. Crowley said were the carcasses of two sheep that been blown off the rock and killed during the late storm. Mr. Marmion here asked the tenant to come to him with an offer of settlement but Crowley refused to see him, thinking that no good could come of the interview. The evicting party were next brought to Carthy's islands, on none of which was a house. The tenant was Patrick Leahy, his yearly rent £8.8s and the amount sued for was £9.18s. On the main island there were only a few haycocks, and on the smaller islands there were five sheep, which had been removed, when the gunboat was observed steaming from Calf Island Middle. The islands having being duly evicted, presentation was handed over to the landlord. The evicting party again boarded the gunboat and steamed off to Castle Island, where writs were out against two tenants. The first visited was Jeremiah Regan, whose yearly rent was £17.12s. and the amount due up to the previous March was £35.4s. Regan had a schoolhouse in his dwelling, which was attended by some twenty children, (Father Murphy being patron and manager of the school) and on being questioned by the Sheriff and the landlord as to a settlement, Regan said that he could make no settlement, as there was a charge of £65 by the Government for the building of the house and that whoever would take it would be responsible for that charge. As the schoolroom was in the house, and as there were children at school of tenants who were not under the shadow of eviction, the landlord very adroitly said he would not disturb the children and he postponed the eviction. Unlike the other three tenants who were evicted, Regan had neither the doors off, nor the furniture taken out of his house. The next, and last tenant visited, was Jeremiah Nugent, on the same island. His yearly rent was £23.4s and the writ was for £34. 10s. In his case (as in the first two) the doors were off and the furniture out. The tenant, on being approached, said the only settlement he had to make was to give up possession and he was willing to do so. The tenant was evicted, the milk pans in the dairy and the contents of some outhouses being put outside by the bailiffs and the tenant's family. This concluded the day's work of the evicting party. The following day the Sheriff visited Cape Clear.'

The evictions of 1886 were followed in 1890 by the eviction of the remainder of the Castle Island tenants. The *Cork County Eagle* of March 7th, 1890 gave an account of the evictions which took place on March 1st of that year. Jerry Nugent and Jerry O'Regan and their families were thrown out on the roadside that day. The bailiff and policemen proceeded to West Calf to carry out further evictions- but were unable to land. However, about half of the evicted Castle Island tenants returned to the Island in the mid 1890s, the others settling on the mainland.

Two MPs who supported the Castle Island evicted tenants were the great nationalist figures, advocates of the Plan of Campaign, William O'Brien and the Bantry man, James Gilhooly, both of whom had spent some time in jail for their Land League activities. At the instigation of William O'Brien, timber houses were built at Dereenatra on the mainland for the unfortunate evicted. Meetings in Schull and Ballydehob, attended by Gilhooly and the Parish Priest of Schull, Fr. J.O'Connor, pledged support to the island tenants.

William O'Brien, born in Mallow in 1852, was a journalist and politician. He was elected Member of Parliament for Mallow and became editor of the Land League Journal, *United Ireland* in 1881, conducting it with such militancy that it was suppressed and O'Brien arrested. Released in 1883, he was re-elected M.P. for Mallow and renewed his campaign for the rights of farmers in the *United Ireland Journal*. With John Dillon, he started the 'Plan of Campaign' in 1886 to force landlords to reduce exorbitant rents. He took the anti-Parnell side in 1891 in the split in the Irish Party in the House of Commons. He founded the United Irish League in 1898 and played a leading part in the reunification of the Irish Party in the House of Commons in 1890. With the passing of the

Wyndham Land Act of 1903, Irish tenant farmers finally broke free of the land-lord-tenant system.[7]

The *Eagle*, in its issue of September, 20th 1890, recorded the visit of William O'Brien to the area. O'Brien was on the police 'wanted' list and the constabulary were on the look out for him all over West Cork in case he visited the Schull area. O'Brian outwitted the police by means of sea transport. Leaving Glengarriff, he went to Cape Clear where he addressed the tenants gathered at South Harbour. Leaving Cape Clear, he proceeded to the Middle Calf, where he addressed a meeting of all the Marmion tenants, who arrived 'in dozens of boats heavily laden with persons.' The report said that there were people there from Sherkin, Heir, Aughadown, Kilcoe, Schull and Goleen.

After the meeting, the whole concourse escorted Mr. O'Brien by boat to Schull and 'the flotilla, as it entered Schull was a singularly striking one.' The boat carrying O'Brien was at the front. A large crowd gathered at the pier, including three policemen who did not know what to do. The tenants then proceeded to Fr. O'Connor's house, where O'Brien was received with 'rapturous cheering.' The M.P., addressing the crowd, said he was delighted to be present and he promised his support for the local tenants. He spoke at length about the Plan of Campaign and condemned those who were trying to defraud tenants of their rights under the Land Acts. William O'Brien and the National League president, John Dillon, were arrested the following week.

Economic conditions were so bad that autumn (1890) that Fr. O'Connor P.P. Schull was so alarmed that he wrote to Balfour, Chief Secretary to the Lord Lieutenant of Ireland, telling of the total failure of the potato crop and the need for public works, such as the making of roads to give employment.

The split in the Irish Party in the House of Commons was brought about by the so-called Parnell 'scandal'. Parnell, the leader of the Irish Party in the British Parliament, advocate of Home Rule for Ireland, supporter of the Land League, was vilified by the Catholic Church for his affair with Kitty O'Shea, wife of another Irish M.P. Some of the M.P.s remained loyal to Parnell, while others, notably Tim Healy of Bantry, opposed him. Parnell seemed to be on the verge of achieving Home Rule for Ireland, but the disunity and his untimely death finished this prospect. Parnell, severely tried by the venomous attacks on his character, went on a nationwide tour in an attempt to re-establish unity, got pneumonia and died in 1891.

In all, Marmion evicted a total of 850 people over a four year period. The Heir Island landlords, the Beechers and later McCarthy Downing, did not evict any tenants although there were arrears there as well as everywhere else.

East Calf Island had been bought by the O'Regans at an earlier date (1876), from the Townsends of Whitehall, while the other two Calf Islands were still owned by landlords up to 1890.

Richard Pyburn, the Heir Island boatbuilder was nicknamed 'Pyburn the Leaguer' due to his interest in the Land League and the events of this time.[8]

Photo: Kathleen Daly

THE TEACHER'S RESIDENCE TO WHICH THE OLD NATIONAL SCHOOL WAS ATTACHED

Some of the foundation stones of the school can be seen in the foreground. The teacher's residence is where the Sisters of Mercy lived while superintending the temporary hospital which was set up in the school in August 1886.

SISTER STANISLAUS' HEADSTONE IN THE CONVENT CEMETERY, SKIBBEREEN

— 11 —

Fever

During the 18th and 19th centuries, there were many outbreaks of fever, chiefly of typhus and cholera, in Ireland and in Great Britain. West Cork and the islands in Roaringwater Bay did not go unscathed. The population of Heir Island, which had reached 358 in 1841, before the Famine, had fallen to 288 in 1851 and to 261 in 1861, began to rise again between 1860 and 1890, reaching 325 by 1891, which was almost as high as the pre-Famine population.

In the aftermath of the Famine, although there was less distress, hard times were by no means over. In 1862 for example, Fr. Leader, P.P. of Rath appealed to the English millionaire philanthropist, Angela Burdett Coutts, who came directly to the aid of the island poor in Sherkin and Cape Clear. Stores were set up in Sherkin and Cape Clear with supplies of corn, flour, meal, sugar and tea. She provided funds for nets and barrels and tried to foster trade in cured fish. Later, of course, she contributed £10,000 when Fr. Charles Davis established an interest-free loan, so that the fishermen of Baltimore and the islands could purchase larger boats for mackerel fishing and long-lining.[1]

In 1879 an epidemic of fever and measles in Cape Clear affected about one hundred persons, of whom eighteen had died by November that year. We also read of fever in several other places, such as Toe Head, Long Island and Heir Island. In March, 1880, Dr. S.W. Robinson, who had done much to help the sick on Cape Clear, reported to the guardians of the Skibbereen Union that four families on Heir were affected by fever. The houses on Heir, as on the other islands, were too small and badly ventilated. The houses were typically about 19 ft long and 18 to 19 feet wide. Built of un-mortared stone, the walls were thick, the windows small. The houses were primarily bastions against the weather and consequently were very dark. The houses consisted of a kitchen and bedroom on the ground floor, divided by a dresser. There was a loft over the kitchen and a smaller one over the ground floor bedroom.

Due to the publicity given to the fever outbreak on Heir and the other islands, Dr. Robinson received cheques for £30 from Mrs. Bayley, secretary of Ladies Bazaar Committee, Blackrock, Cork, £5 from a Mrs. Pike, Cork and £28 from the Mansion House Committee. At the next meeting of the Skibbereen Union, Dr. Robinson stated that the health of the islanders, generally speaking, was very good. He remarked that there was a complete dearth of water on the island during the summer and that the wells should be deepened.[2]

The *Skibbereen Eagle* of April 3rd carried an account of the death of Dr. Robinson.

> Many tributes were paid to the deceased doctor, whose 'abiding sense of duty rose nobly above personal considerations. Dr. Robinson had worked selflessly on Cape Clear where his constant labours contributed largely to the speedy stamping out of that most fatal epidemic. Unfortunately, soon after his labours in Cape Clear, he had to apply his energies to the outbreak on Heir. Here again

he zealously performed his duties and while doing so he himself was stricken down. The struggle he made was a short one and after nine days he died.[3]

The newspapers of July and August, 1886 give reports of another outbreak of fever on Heir Island. At a meeting of Tullagh (Baltimore) Dispensary Committee, Fr. O'Brien, stated that he had administered the last rites to eight people on Heir Island and that two people from the mainland were already in hospital. Fr. O'Brien stated that he feared a repetition of the Cape Clear epidemic which carried off so many lives.[4] Dr. Robert Hadden stated, at a meeting of the dispensary committee, that he found six families affected by fever and that one mother had died on July 27th. He blamed insufficiency of dwelling accommodation and the absence of proper sanitary services as the main causes for the reoccurrence of the fever. He stated that the majority of those affected were between eight and twenty. Fr. O'Brien C.C. Aughadown stated that the island wells needed to be improved as there was a shortage of water every summer. Dr. Jennings, consultant sanitary officer, informed the members of the Skibbereen Board of Guardians that the outbreak was due to unfavourable hygienic conditions, overcrowding of the houses and poor ventilation.

A decision was made to turn the school house into a temporary hospital and the teacher's residence, to which it was attached, would be used as accommodation for four Sisters of Mercy from Skibbereen, who volunteered to help, as they had done in Cape Clear seven years previously. The four Mercy Sisters who went to Heir Island on July 31st 1886 were Sr. M. Bernard McCartie, Sr. M. Francis Oliver, Sr. M. Margaret Mary O'Leary and Sr. Stanislaus Noonan, a lay Sister. A report in the Cork Examiner of August 6th 1886 of a visit by Dr. Jennings, tells us that he found matters much improved, since the nuns had arrived. The Mercy Nuns, the medical officer and Mr. Thomas Crowley, relieving officer 'had worked wonders' in improving matters. There were thirteen patients in the temporary hospital, only two of whom were in extreme danger, the remainder being convalescent.

The outbreak of fever was discussed at a meeting of Skibbereen Union in early August. Dr.O'Farrell, Local Government Board Inspector, stated that there were twenty four cases of typhus fever. There also had been an outbreak of whooping cough which had started in June. He recommended that 'to remedy the present state of things, what he would recommend would be frequent inspection by the medical officer and any cases detected be isolated immediately; the water to be analysed and the wells protected and last but principally, the repairing of the houses, or providing a better class of house.' At the same meeting, Fr. Charles Davis, P.P. Baltimore, said that it was to the credit of the district that there was never an eviction on the island. The tenants were allowed sub-divide and hence the overcrowding and congested population. The island contained 300 acres, a high percentage of which wasn't arable, and a population of 330. The total rental for a year was £364 per annum.

Dr. Hadden spoke to the members of the Skibbereen Board of Guardians:

> Gentleman, with regard to the outbreak of fever which occurred in Hare Island, I am glad to report that the condition of the patients continues to improve daily. The nursing sisters have been untiring in their efforts to assist the sick people and I can report that the practical lessons which they are receiving will

have a permanent effect on the inhabitants of the island. Several inmates of the temporary hospital are nearly well. I made an enquiry to the superintending Sister what clothes were required. I got the following: 60 yards of good grey calico, 60 yards coarse material for dresses (homespun), 20 yards coarse flannel, and 3 suits small boy's clothes. With regard to the wells on the island, there are a great number and the inhabitants are getting water for drinking from the best and when possible where the animals have no access. The resident carpenter was not on the Island, so one from Skibbereen had to be got and is employed putting palings around the principal wells to prevent pollution.[5]

The supplement to the *Eagle* of August 7th, carried a report of Dr. O'Farrell, who had visited the island the previous Tuesday. The report states,

> All the sick people are fairly out of danger and convalescent. The fever appears to be of a mild type and its progress has been altogether arrested for several days. One death has occurred. The presence of the Sisters of Mercy from Skibbereen is a real blessing. They have fitted up the National School as a temporary hospital and have twelve convalescents. The sisters, four in number, reside in the teachers house adjoining. The sisters also visit the other houses on the island .... Scarcely a man was to be seen on the island, they all being engaged in fishing. The utmost attention is being paid to the sick by the medical officer and nurse. It is hoped that in another fortnight all traces of the fever will have vanished.

Fr O'Brien, C.C. Aughadown, drew attention to the water supply and he proposed that a paling be placed around the three main spring wells and also to divert the course of the stream, which was bringing detritus matter into one of those wells.[6]

Sister M. Angela Bolster, in an article, on the Mercy Sisters in Ross Diocese, published in *The Fold* in June 1991, writes

> In 1879 the Skibbereen Sisters had an opportunity for what might be called navigational charity on the outbreak of a double epidemic of German measles and typhus on Oileán Cléire. Between October and December of that year they plied daily in Sir Henry Beecher's steam launch to the island, where they set up a temporary clinic and tended peoples in their homes. Funds for this project were advanced by Sir Henry and by Baroness Burdett Coutts. In 1886 came Operation Hare Island, where an epidemic of typhus occurred and Father Thomas O'Brien of Aughadown and Dr. Jennings of Skibbereen represented to Bishop William Fitzgerald of Ross the wretched state of the poor islanders and the great advantage of securing the services of the Sisters of Mercy while the epidemic lasted. Four Sisters were given charge of a temporary hospital on the island, and as on Oileán Cleire, their ministrations extended as well to home nursing. The Board of Guardians of the Skibbereen Workhouse ordered all necessaries for the sick while the epidemic lasted. Of the four Sisters appointed to Hare Island, two caught fever, one died and was replaced by a Bon Secours Sister from Cork.

In August, 1886, the *Irish Times* sent a correspondent to the island and his report was printed in both the *Cork Examiner* and *Skibbereen Eagle*. The following is taken from the *Cork Examiner* Report

As many as possible of those stricken with fever have been removed from their homes to a temporary hospital which has been established in the middle district, the National Schoolhouse being used for the purpose. This building has been fitted up with twelve beds brought from the workhouse and here the worst cases are treated. The hospital is under the personal supervision of four Sisters of Mercy from the Skibbereen Convent who, regardless of danger and hardship, have now taken up their abode on the island for the purpose of nursing the sick both in their homes and in the hospital. These ladies dwell in a cabin which was formerly occupied by the teacher, and which consists of only one room, divided into apartments by a curtain. The floor is sanded earth, the furniture is very scanty, and the beds consist of mattresses stretched on the ground. In this manner, they bravely and cheerfully perform their work of mercy and charity in the alleviation of suffering.[7]

Sr. Stanislaus Noonan was on the island for about a fortnight when she contracted the disease. She was brought home to Skibbereen Convent on August 17th, where she died on September 6th. Kate Noonan (in religion, Sister Stanislaus), was born at Rosegreen in July 1845. Kate was sent to live with her aunt, Mrs. Hurley, in Skibbereen at an early age. Here she received the rudiments of education from a teacher in the town. When the Mercy Order nuns came to Skibbereen, she attended the convent school, where she studied hard and was of 'exemplary character'. She was solemnly professed a nun in November, 1864. When the Sisters from Skibbereen Convent were appointed to take charge of the Skibbereen workhouse hospital, St. Stanislaus, with three others, entered on this new mission of mercy where she worked diligently for almost ten years. Sr. Stanislaus is buried in the Convent Cemetery in Skibbereen.[8]

The three remaining Sisters continued working on the island and were helped during this time by Sr. Theophile from the Bon Secours Hospital in Cork.

Later that year samples of water from two Heir Island wells were analysed by a Mr. Burrell, analyst, Cork, who stated that both were polluted and unfit for use and very dangerous to health. He stated that, if his suggestion to have pumps sunk at the outset had been carried out, there would be an end to the fever.[9]

It has to be said that problems with water were not confined to the island. The newspapers of the time carried many references to the polluted water in Bantry and Skibbereen towns particularly.

The last reported outbreak occurred in the summer of 1890, but it was not as severe as the previous outbreaks in 1880 and 1886, and was brought under control quickly. In 1890, Dr. Hadden reported

that fever existed in two families in Hare Island. It was of a favourable type and up to the present had not extended further. The houses had been disinfected and all sanitary precautions were being observed. He further reported that the well in the east part of the island, a little west of the school house, was in an unsanitary state, owing to the cattle obtaining access to it, and recommending that it be covered with a stone and mortar wall and a large flag at the top, leaving a small aperture at one end from which water could be obtained.

The Union ordered that the Doctor's recommendation be put into effect.[10]

— 12 —

Timothy McCarthy Downing

Timothy McCarthy Downing, son of Eugene Downing of Kenmare, was born in the month of April, 1814. In the year 1836, McCarthy Downing came to Skibbereen, where he established himself as one of the most successful solicitors in the south of Ireland. At his death he had acquired property worth over £2000 a year in rent. In 1837 he married Jane, daughter of Daniel McCarthy of Dromore near Skibbereen, a distant relative of his. They had four sons and two daughters, all of whom predeceased him, except his eldest son, Eugene.

He took a prominent part in the Repeal movement[1] and was, in 1845, the principal organiser of the great meeting held on Curragh Hill, within a mile of Skibbereen town, at which Daniel O'Connell was the chief speaker. At the general election of 1860, Timothy McCarthy Downing was elected Member of Parliament for Cork County. On being elected, he retired from his profession and soon after was made a Justice of the peace and a deputy lieutenant of the county. In the House of Commons, he was a strong supporter of the Irish National Party, then led by Isaac Butt.

McCarthy Downing, who lived in Prospect House, afterwards the residence of the Bishop of Ross and now occupied by the Administrator of Skibbereen, died in July 1879. The youngest of his daughters, Janie, married Florence Daniel McCarthy J.P. Their only child was a daughter, May Louise Bernadette.[2]

Various branches of the Beecher family were landlords in West Cork up to the middle of the 19th century. In the Griffith Evaluation of 1852, Edward and George Beecher are named as the immediate lessors of most of Heir Island. They had inherited the estate from their father, Edward, who died in 1840.

In March 1854, Edward Baldwin Beecher, before the Commissioners of Sale of Encumbered Estates in Ireland, sought that the estates in his name and in that of his brother George, deceased, be continued in his name. Beecher, heavily in debt, wanted to sell his estate.[3] Alicia Beecher, his sister, contested this and asked that the estates continue in the name of Samuel Townsend and Patrick Roynane, petitioners. The advertisement for sale continues:

The Commissioner will on Friday 5th May, 1854, at the hour of twelve o'-clock, at their Court, No. 14, Henrietta St., Dublin, sell by Public Auction, the lands of Lissaclarig West, Lissaclarig East, South Murrahin, Curravoley, East Skeam and Hare Island, with its sub-denomination, Mutton Island, (Oileán Caorach) situated respectively in the Barony of West Carbery and County of Cork, held for the residue of a term of 999 years, from May 1st 1698; and the lands of Rathruane Mor and Rathruane Beg, Bawnaknockane.[4]

The acreage of East Skeam was given as 49¾ acres with a valuation of £30 and net annual rental of £27.16s.7d. The acreage of Hare Island and Mutton Island, a sub denomination, was 393 acres with a valuation of £210.12s.6d and net annual rental of £260. It described East Skeam as an island not far from the mainland and near to the entrance to Roaringwater Bay. Heir Island, also known as Innis O'Driscoll, including Illaungunne and small rocks adjacent, was situated, 'in the entrance to Roaringwater Bay, and was about half an English mile from the mainland and four to five miles north of Cape Clear'.

The advertisement concluded, 'For Rentals and further particulars, apply at the Office of the Commissioners, 14, Henrietta St., Dublin or to McCarthy Downing, Solicitor having the carriage of the sale, Skibbereen, Co.Cork.'

Sale Advertisement

No. of Lot.	DENOMINATIONS.	Acreable Contents, Statute Measure	Valuation made Pursuant to Commissioners' Order.	Nett Annual income on Reduced Rental, after deducting Quit Rent and Tithe Rent Charge.
		A. R. P.	£ s. d.	£ s. d.
	LEASEHOLD LANDS.			
1	Lisaclarigmore (or Lisaclarig West,) and Lisaclarigbeg (or Lisaclarig East).	753 2 4	206 18 5	163 0 2
2	South Marahin	162 1 23	66 1 9	34 19 10½
3	Curravoley	341 1 38	130 7 6	140 17 2
4	East Skeams	49 3 0	30 0 0	27 16 7
5	Hare Island & Mutton Island, a subdenomination	393 3 19	210 12 6	260 0 8⅜
	FEE-SIMPLE LANDS.			
6	Banaknuckano	207 1 0	83 15 0	101 7 7
7	Rathruanemore	267 3 26	64 6 3	49 11 1
8	Rathruanebeg	302 0 18	61 16 6	53 13 4½
9	Quoleaghmore (or Coolaghmore)	243 1 29	64 1 3	62 18 9½
10	Quoleaghbeg (or Coolaghbeg)	161 2 56	62 18 0	49 15 3½
11	The Mines and Minerals on Lots Nos. 7, 8, 9, and 10	—	—	—
	Total of Leasehold and Fee-simple Lands	2974 1 33	985 17 1	957 0 7½

Dated this 9th day of March, 1854.

In 1854, Edward Baldwin Beecher sold his various estates, including Heir Island, to McCarthy Downing for the sum of £7,100; the Commissioners of the Encumbered Estate accepted the offer. The sale was contested in the Court of Chancery by Alicia Beecher who claimed that McCarthy Downing had given £600 to Edward Baldwin Beecher to entice him to sell the estates privately to him,[4] that the land was sold below its true value and that McCarthy Downing, acting as her father's solicitor, had fraudulently come into possession of the estate. Edward Baldwin Beecher had hired McCarthy Downing as his solicitor at the sale of a house and some land to Rev. Mr. Spring in 1854. McCarthy Downing pointed out that the sale was advertised in the Dublin and

Cork press, that in 1851 the estate was valued at £463 per annum rent, and that he had never bribed Mr. Beecher.

The Lord Chancellor found in favour of McCarthy Downing but this was overturned in the Court of Appeal. Finally it went before a House of Lords Committee, but before proceedings were started, the Solicitor General received a note stating that a satisfactory agreement had been arrived at between the two parties.

Heir Island was transferred to Timothy Downing on July 3rd 1854. By Will of 9/1/1879 Timothy McCarthy Downing demised an estate tail to his grand-daughter, Mary McCarthy. Mary L.P. McCarthy died a spinster on 17th May 1929 and administration to her estate was taken out on behalf of Margaret Sophia Martyn (who may have been her sister). Margaret Sophia Martyn was married and had a large family; she died on 12th March 1931 and administration in her estate was granted to Frank Martyn.

The lands were acquired by the Irish Land Commission in 1931 when they were bought from McCarthy Downing's descendants.

Title Document

When the lands of Heir Island were being acquired by Irish Land Commission the title presented was:

1. By an Indenture of 20th March 1698 John Leslie demised Hare Island otherwise Mutton Island or Gortnahorna together with other lands to James Coppinger for 999 years at a rent of £145 per annum.

2. By an Indenture of Sub Lease of 8 September 1704 James Coppinger demised Hare Island with rents amounting to £218.10.0 to Bryan Townsend.

3. By assignment of 8 September 1704 Bryan Townsend assigned certain Lands to Edward Synge and Edward Synge assigned certain lands to Bryan Townsend resulting in a profit rent of £29.11.4. payable to Edward Synge.

4. Indenture of Sub-Lease of 27th July 1716 Michael Beecher, Richard Townsend and other reps of James Coppinger to Bryan Townsend for 960 years, certain lands NOT including Hare Island but providing that this rent should be applied to the lease at 1 above, which does include Hare Island. From this time on no rent was ever paid by the owner for the Head Rent at 1 in respect of Hare Island, and none was admitted payable.

5. Incumbered Estates Court Indenture of 1st July 1854. Registered at Registry of Deeds Dublin 3rd July 1854 17/20. The Judges transferred the town and lands of Hare island or Mutton Island containing 393 Acres Statute Measure to T McCarthy Downing his Heirs Administrators and Assigns for the term of 999 years, subject, with other land, to the head rent of £145 and indemnified as therein.[5]

COPY OF RENT RECEIPT FROM LANDLORD, DATED 16TH DAY NOVEMBER 1889,
In respect of Denis Minihane showing amount of £5.10.0. paid to representatives
of McCarthy Downing

In 1926, William Barry, on behalf of the Heir Island tenants, contested the amount of rent paid to the landlord. Under the heading, 'Hare Island Tenants', the Southern Star carried a report on rents paid by Heir Island tenants. On Tuesday, 11th May, before Mr. Justice Wylie, Judicial Commissioner, William Barry of Heir Island Middle appealed against the application by the Landlord under the 1923 Land Act against a return of the rent made to the landlords, Messrs. Beecher and McCarthy. William Barry, together with all the other tenants in Heir Island, has for the previous twenty years and upwards paid one half-year's rent for every year and they sought to have this half years rent declared the proper rent. Messrs. J.J. Healy and Co. Solicitors appeared on behalf of the tenants. It was held by the Judicial Commissioner that the half year's rent of £3.18.9. paid by William Barry in each year was the proper rent to be returned as it was accepted by the landlord each year, and that the same should apply to all the other tenants in Heir Island, who accordingly are entitled to a 25% reduction on their half year's rent, and that will be the present rent until the lands are vested, when a further reduction will come into operation. The best thanks of the tenants of Heir Island are due to Rev. James O'Donovan, C.C. Aughadown, who interested himself most strongly in this matter on their behalf.'[6]

— 13 —

1890s in Heir and West Cork

The fishing industry, which had been severely affected by the Famine, began to recover in the Baltimore area from 1879, under the leadership of Fr. Leader and Fr. Davis, with financial assistance of the English Baroness, Angela Burdett-Coutts. In 1880 she gave £25,000 for the purchase of seed potatoes when the potato crop failed. When Fr. Davis became P.P. of Rath and the Islands in 1879 there were shoals of mackerel in the seas off the south-west coast of Ireland but the West Cork fishermen hadn't boats large enough to fish for them. Boats from England, (particularly the Isle of Man and Cornwall), France and Spain were reaping a rich harvest of fish.[1]

Fr. Davis led a deputation of fishermen from Cape Clear and other islands to meet Queen Victoria in 1878, who arranged for him to meet Baroness Coutts, millionaire philanthropist. The result was the setting up of an interest free purchase loan fund, to which the Baroness contributed £10,000. The Cape Clear fishermen considered that the nobbies and dandies built in the Isle of Man were the most suitable for mackerel fishing. There were fifteen of these boats fishing out of Cape Clear by 1881, forty four by 1884. By 1882, there was a total of seventy five boats fishing out of Baltimore, all owned by fishermen from Kinsale to Crookhaven. The boats were approximately 45 ft in length, many of which were built by Watson and Graves in Peel, Isle of Man.[2]

To get full benefit from the fishing, Fr. Davis was the main instigator in building Baltimore Fishery School, where local destitute boys would be taught navigation, rope making, sail making, boat building, coopering, fish curing. The school was opened on August 6th 1887 by Baroness Coutts, who had sailed into Baltimore in her luxury yacht, *Pandora*. She presented an inscribed clock to the O'Regan brothers of East Calf, who had purchased two of the Manx boats, the *Velocity* and the *Orion*, to acknowledge the fact that they were the first to have their repayments completed.

The extension of the railway line to Baltimore, which was completed in 1893, helped in exporting the fish. In the late 1890s there were four hundred boats fishing out of Baltimore. About sixty were leaving North Harbour, Cape Clear every day to fish in the surrounding water. There were curing stations in Baltimore and in North Harbour, Cape Clear. Many other types of boat, from yawls to schooners were purchased by using the loan scheme.[3]

In Heir Island, Con Burke bought several of the Isle of Man boats. Mike O'Neill of Heir, purchased *The Flying Cloud*, which resulted in him being known as 'Mike the Cloud'. The O'Regans of West Skeam purchased the *St. Keim*. See Appendix 8.

The *Skibbereen Eagle* has several articles concerning the plight of the people in West Cork in 1890, when Famine threatened again. In a newspaper report in

August 1890, the writer compares the conditions in Baltimore with Toe Head, only about 5 miles distant. Baltimore was thriving due to the success of the mackerel fishing, while in other areas the people were in great distress due to failure of potato and wheat crops.[4]

The writer continues with a description of a priest blessing the boats.

> In the beginning of the fishing season, on a sunshiny morning, the robed priest walked to the beach with the usual procession of kerchief-decked praying women coming behind him over the bare rocks, while the open-mouthed children full of curiosity and awe, lined the cliffs and looked down from their elevated stand points at the ceremonial as full of interest to them and so intimately connected with their welfare. Then the smacks being drawn into a wide and irregular semi-circle round the priest's row boat, the clergyman, standing up on the thwart supported by his acolytes, blessed the bare headed bronze faced men kneeling in the bows and blessed their craft and prayed that their fishing might prove safe and prosperous.

The writer does not specify where he saw this scene but it was the practice in every fishing village to have the boats blessed at the beginning of the fishing season.

In the issue of the following week, the journalist reports on the bad conditions in Aughadown Parish, where, he stated, the farms were generally small, averaging from eight to twelve acres of arable land. By the end of June 1890, practically all the potatoes were blighted. He gives as an example the case of a man named Timothy Mahony, in the Kilcoe area, who planted two acres about the 20th February and in early August tried to obtain a meal from the blighted field. After digging one hundred and eighty square feet he had about one stone of crahauns, a contemptuous name for small potatoes, and out of those he got a plateful of edible potatoes. He calculated, that when he planted the potatoes, that the crop would amount to twice what he would require for his family and that the surplus would make about £8 profit. Now he expected the crop to yield only enough potatoes for his family for about seven weeks. After that they would have to depend on flour and meal for the winter or for as long as the credit would last. Already the family had to eat homemade cake occasionally. Another instance of the failure of the potatoes was that of Charles Daly, Kilcoe, a farm labourer, who sowed sufficient potatoes to serve himself and his large family until about the first part of April. Wherever he found potatoes in his land, they were black, and were clinging to the stalks. He owed £2 on them for manure for which the farmer who employed him was his surety. In 1889 he sowed the same amount of land with potatoes, and after feeding his family, fattened four pigs on the remainder of the crop, and sold the surplus at 3½ d. per stone, realising £3 in Skibbereen market. The unfortunate man had a family of ten. 'A few pounds are a fortune to him, and he is almost hopeless of pulling his family through the winter with nothing to feed them.'[5]

The heavy rain of the summer of 1890 severely damaged the corn crops and made it impossible to save the turf, which was still wet in the month of August.

Tenants in Collatrum and Marsh, who had been unable to pay their rents, had received notice that the landlord had obtained power to seize their cattle, which were the only items in Aughadown Parish in that year, that they could hope to make a profit on. The older people in the district, who remembered 1846-1848, agreed that affairs were as bad as then but that the population was much reduced now so there were less mouths to feed.

With regard to Heir Island, the report continued,

> In the island portion of the parish, matters do not seem to be so bad, or rather not bad in the same way. The fisheries and their developments and success influence the condition of the people of Hare Island. Like most people in the remote districts in the famine years, they suffered greatly. At present the 'Souper' who would try the old shameful dodge on the island would instantly be told to go to Jericho

Some of the Heir Islanders had shares in craft suitable for deep sea fishing while others were employed at lobstering in the summer and spillering in the autumn. The former were in a good position to face the winter but the latter had not been very successful in their lobster fishing and other long shore fishing that year. Some of the islanders had employment on board the mackerel boats while others were employed by the fish buyers, (mainly English and American) to row long six oared yawls, out to meet the mackerel boats, fishing off the coast. So intense was the rivalry between the buyers that they went out to buy the fish rather than waiting for them to land in Baltimore. They also carried out food and drink for the fishermen. Only the best oarsmen got employment in these boats, known as 'bumming boats.' In this work a man generally made about ten pounds clear profit during the fishing season.

> This applied only to a small percentage of the Hare islanders, all of whom, with respect to crops, were not badly situated. Some would be pinched during the winter but as a general rule more inconvenience would be suffered from the necessity to frequently proceed to the mainland to obtain food. The chief danger, however, was the possibility of a fever epidemic, to which a bad supply of food on the approach of winter would act as a predisposing cause.[6]

Meeting at Kilcoe Cross

A meeting of tenants and farm labourers held at Kilcoe Cross was reported in the *Skibbereen Eagle* in December 1890 'The attendance was large and the proceedings throughout were practical and pleasant, though the occasion of the meeting was the saddest that could well be imagined'. Rev. Father O'Sullivan P.P. was chosen to preside as Chairman. In the course of his remarks, the Reverend Chairman said he was gratified to take the chair at that large gathering. They were all aware of the object of their assembling together there that day, which was the purpose of taking into consideration the great distress which prevailed and the best means that might be adopted to alleviate it. As their parish priest, he said, he could speak from experience of their condition, and he would avail of the opportunity, after long and patiently waiting, to tell the Government that at the moment the greatest distress was prevailing in the parish of Aughadown. The potato crop was a failure all through the parish, and in consequence, the poor labourers and small farmers through the length and breath of the parish found themselves without any food supply, without money to buy it, and on the very verge of being denied credit in the shops. In his opinion, unless external aid was forthcoming promptly, they would have in their midst not distress only, but 'they will have a famine as bad as they had in '47'. The Government has been promising the people that they would do all in their power to relieve the distress but their promises had come to nought and up to that time there has been nothing but red tape. If Mr. Balfour had not held out hopes and made promises to assist the people in Kilcoe as elsewhere, he would have taken the same steps that year as he had done in 1880 when he appealed to the charitable public and to his friends in America, and met with a generous response. But when the Government were promising aid, he was slow to apply for other help, but he now felt it his duty to call on the Government, not to beg of them, but to ask it as a right, to come to their assistance. Every Government worthy of the name should consider it their first duty to provide for the safety of the people – 'the safety of the people, their lives, and general happiness was the first of all laws.'

The Rev. Father Fehilly, curate, Aughadown, said that he had a few resolutions to propose. He knew several poor people who were on the verge of being refused credit; and he knew many others who had already been refused, and who had come to him, begging for help. That was a sad state of things. The resolutions he had to propose were as follows:

> That, in view of the distress now actually existing and alarmingly on the increase in consequence of the partial failure of the wheat crop and the total failure of the potato crop, we earnestly apply to the Government to take prompt measures to give employment to the people.
>
> That to avert famine some useful public works, such as roads and quays, should be commenced immediately, and what would be more useful still, the employment of the poor people in their own holdings in draining and fencing.
>
> That we beg to draw the attention of the Government to the absolute necessity of supplying good seed potatoes to the people of the parish of Aughadown in the early spring – the crop being sown here much earlier than is the custom elsewhere

Mr. R. O'Driscoll, P.L.G, of Ardnagroghery, seconded the resolutions, and in doing so said that of his own personal knowledge he knew that there were many men from Heir Island at that meeting, who had not eaten a potato that year. Heir Island had three hundred inhabitants and he assured them that if the Government did not come to their assistance there would soon be three hundred corpses on the island. In the mainland the distress was as intense as in Heir Island. As an instance of the sad want of quay accommodation, he said that he saw an old man on a frosty evening, a short time previously, down at the shore up to his arm-pits in the water emptying his boat. He knew that men were working now in the parish, whose food Balfour, Chief Secretary for Ireland, would not give to his dogs.

Fr. O'Sullivan, in putting the resolutions to the meeting said that he himself had numbers of people coming to him day after day, asking him in the saddest language for food and employment. He knew that in some instances those poor people had not the wherewithal to provide a meal for themselves, having neither money nor credit. If the state of things continued, and if nobody came to their aid, he himself would be obliged to regard it as a duty in future to aid them himself as far as his means would permit.

The resolutions were carried with acclamation.

Mr. J.O'Connor, Kilcoe, said that it was in his own recollection that in the famine of 1847, when the Government opened works, it happened too late. He thought that the farmers were worse now than in 1847 – then they had some wheat, but now they had neither wheat nor potatoes. He knew those himself who were now living on the charity of their respected parish priest. In his district (Kilcoe) there were better potatoes in 1847 than now. There were people writing in the papers who estimated that there was half a crop of potatoes – as a matter of fact they hadn't a sixteenth of a crop in the parish. In his opinion if the Government were to come forward with aid they should come in time, or it would be no use at all.

Mr. J. O'Driscoll said that the Baltimore Railway was being constructed but nobody from Aughadown got employment on it. They wanted work themselves at that side of the river, as the railway was of no use to them. If Balfour thought that people from Kilcoe/Aughadown could benefit from the employment afforded by the railway, he was greatly mistaken.

The Rev. Chairman remarked in reference to the railway, that quite a number of labourers went from Aughadown and were refused work and that only three men from the parish were employed on the line, up to the present. At the same time he thought it fair to tell them that he felt sure that if due representation was made to Father Davis, he would ensure that a fair share of the good things going at the Baltimore side would be granted them. The other day he (the Rev. Chairman) had an interview with the manager of the line, Mr. Gregory, at Skibbereen. That gentleman, said he would do all in his power to attend to the wants of the labourers of Aughadown. They should be grateful to Mr. Gregory and they might confidently hope that Father Davis would not forget them either.

Fr. Fehilly said that there was another fact regarding the railway which he thought it right to draw their attention to. He knew a poor man with eight in family, whose potatoes were so wretchedly bad, that he and his family were prostrated with sickness after the first meal of them they ate. This poor man went three times across the river to try to get work on the railway but was refused on each occasion. Mr. Balfour boasted too of the great industrial development of Baltimore and that the people there were making oceans of money at the fishing. If that was so why should he select that prosperous district for making a railway through while he neglected the impoverished districts.

The Rev. Chairman pointed out that not alone were the potatoes a failure but the little that grew were totally unfit for human food, and were sure to bring on disease. He regretted to say that there were many instances in the parish of serious sickness brought on by eating bad potatoes. Many people present could bear witness to this.

A Committee was appointed to look after the interests of the parish: Rev.

Father O'Sullivan, P.P., Chairman: Rev. Father Fehilly C.C. Hon. Sec: Messrs. R. O'Driscoll, P.L.G.: James Hickey P.L.G.: Charles Piper (The Islands), D. Gallagher, J. Sheehy, Charles Neill and John Collins.

Father O'Sullivan said that he wished to have the object of their meeting made known to all persons in the parish, no matter what creed or class, and he expressed the hope that the clergy and Guardians and others of the other denominations would kindly co-operate with them in a matter which interested everyone in the community.[7]

Aughadown

In a further report on the parish of Aughadown in the *Skibbereen Eagle* of the same date, we read,

If very little has been said up to the present about the conditions of affairs in the large parish of Aughadown, it is not because matters are less critical there than elsewhere. As a matter of fact, there is no district in West Cork in a more pitiable condition at the present moment, while, unhappily, there are many districts quite as badly off. The parish of Aughadown approaches within a mile of Skibbereen in its eastern end, and extends westwards to a point about a mile beyond the village of Ballydehob. It is an exclusively coastal district, having a sea-board of about fifteen miles, and an average width of about five miles.

The population of the parish is, in round numbers, about 3000, the vast majority of whom are small farmers and labourers. The labourers are abnormally numerous here, amounting at least to 200 for the entire parish. This unusually big number of labourers in a district, in which the large farmers are few and far between, is accounted for by the fact that when the copper mines, formerly worked in the parish, ceased working several years ago, the great body of the miners employed remained in the district. When years are good, these men get work during the busy seasons, but there never is a year in which they are not three months idle. Their potato patches enabled them to support themselves through these periods of enforced idleness but now, when the potato crop has been a miserable failure, and when the farmers who were accustomed to give employment are crippled themselves, the condition to which the wretched labourers are reduced is pitiable in the extreme. There are townlands in which as many as 20 labourers are now starving in want of employment, and scattered through the parish are very poor people who would have starved long ere this were it not for the charitable behaviour of their parish priest, Father O'Sullivan, and other philanthropic persons, who know their wants, and whose kind hearts will not let them suffer while they can afford any aid. But the outside world should have a say in this matter, and should see to it that the burthen of the distress must not be thrown on these charitable people who are themselves not too much blessed with the world's wealth, a fact not to be wondered at when we take into consideration the nature and resources of the district. As badly off as are the labourers, the numerous small farmers are in quite as sorry a plight. The land is, for the most part, rough and unreclaimed, so that the holders of small patches find it difficult at the best of times to make both ends meet. To make matters worse, the majority of them hold their farms under middlemen, who are stated to be very exacting this year. The poor cottiers have endeavoured to meet the pressing demands for rent by raising money in the bank, in order that they may stave off eviction. And now, having borrowed as much as they can get from banks and shops, they are without food, money, or credit, and while they may have succeeded in staving off eviction, they certainly have by this very means, done more to hurry on starvation than they have done to avert it. In a word, condition of things in Aughadown could not well be worse than it is. The people have neither food, money, credit, nor prospect of employment. This is the simple truth, and if anybody doubts it he can come to see for himself. Anybody who takes the least trouble to inquire into the needs of the poor people of Aughadown must come to the conclusion that this is a locality in which Mr. Balfour's schemes for road-making, pier-making, reclaiming land, and planting should be carried into effect at once.

Road-making and the reclamation of waste land are the public works most needed and should go hand in hand. Without more roads it would be comparatively useless to re-claim some of the land as in the absence of roads, neither 'sea manure' (seaweed and sand) could be brought in, nor could the produce be taken to market. But if they opened up by a few more roads, and if some better accommodation was made for landing sea-weeds and sand, the latter of which is invaluable for the peaty soil of the entire district – then the great tracts of land now lying waste could be converted into most valuable farms. These tracts could be easily drained, and as there is a noticeable absence of rocks and stones in the low lying wastes, they could undoubtedly be reclaimed at a compara-tively low cost. If the farmers get loans at a low rate of interest they would be very glad to carry on reclamation works; or, what would be better still, if the Government took over some of the waste tracts and employed men in reclaiming them, they could by this means give sufficient employment to the labourers to tide over the present period of distress while they would enrich the district enormously. There are tracts available likewise for re-af-foresting, and this is a district in which Mr. Balfour's limited plans might be put into operation with advantage. In connection with reclamation it may be mentioned that there is a plain, a mile long, lying along the banks of the river flowing into the head of Roaringwater Bay, and composed of rich alluvial soil, which is now covered with water for prolonged periods of the year, often in the harvest time when the crops are frequently destroyed. The overflowing of the river renders this plain almost valueless, and consider-ing how easy it would be to remedy this matter, it is surprising that it has never been remedied. There is a rock in the bed of the river which obstructs the water and if this was removed there would be no more flooding. A sum of £60 would do this job.

The one thing certain as regards Aughadown, is that unless public works are opened at once, the poor people must flock into the workhouse before the year is out, or their priests must resort to the last refuge of all – an appeal to the charitable public. This is the situation in Aughadown and Mr. Balfour should see to it that this and the other dis-tressed districts in West Cork shall not be neglected any longer. Delays are dangerous, they say but in this instance, delays may mean death. As I have said already, roads are very badly needed to open up the district, and very strong arguments have been ad-vanced in favour of the following:

Roads

(1) A mile and a half of a road from Collatrum to Lissaree. This would open up a district that is at present isolated and very difficult to access, and it would be of great benefit to at least a dozen farmers.

(2) A road of the same length from the main road at Skeaghanore northwards to Knockroe. This also would open a good tract of land, and would enable the farmers to cart in sea sand, and to carry their produce to the market.

(3) A road from Lissaclarig to Kilcoe. This road in particular would be very useful. Beside opening up a tract of land that is now poorly cultivated, it would lead to an important bog, and would thereby make it possible for the people in the distant parts of the parish, where fuel is scarce, to obtain a plentiful supply of firing.

(4) A road in Hare Island. At present there is no road in the island, which is about a mile long. There is neither horse nor cart in the island, which has a population between three and four hundred people. A road through the island was talked of in the famine years and there cannot be a doubt but that it would be extremely useful. The people on the island have not a potato, many of them will not be able to come to the mainland for work; while if this road were made it would afford a great deal of employment and be of incalculable service to the poor islanders at the same time.

(5) A road from Mohonagh to Gurteenroe. This is, for the most part, made already, but was left in an unfinished state forty years ago. About fifty perches want to be improved, a rock should be cut and a gully made, while all of it should be repaired after long neglect. It is estimated that an expenditure of £50 would suffice.

Quays

Along the fifteen miles of coast line in the parish of Aughadown not more than £200 was ever expended from either public or private sources for the purpose of providing suitable landing accommodation. The coast population has some eight mackerel boats, (in Collatrum, Turkhead, Cunnamore, Heir) and as many as two hundred small boats engaged in 'long-line' fishing and in drawing weeds and sand for manure. In a few of the coves the people have, from time to time, erected rude quays at their own expense; but these are now weather-beaten and all but useless, while the people are too reduced in circumstances to repair them or render them suitable for the traffic they were meant to accommodate. What is wanted now is to have the old quays repaired, and this would not be at all expensive. The following is a list of the works of this nature:

(1) The improvement of a pier at the head of Roaringwater Bay. The old one is utterly neglected, and at high tide, is two feet under water. The sand and weeds are often swept away when those who bring them in in boats cannot move them at once. It often happens that one tide sweeps away the result of a week's labour of many poor men. If raised something more than two feet the present quay would afford accommodation for large boats. At this season of the year especially, great numbers of men are engaged here in securing sand and weeds for manure.

(2) A quay at Lahertanavally, where none now exists. The consequence of this want is that men have to get into the water for seaweeds and often have to walk half a mile with their burden

(3) The quay at Kilkilleen – a small one made by the people – requires extension.

(4) A pier is sorely needed at Whitehall, which is the place from which communication is held with Hare Island. Even as it is, this place is extensively used now, as there is a good little harbour there.

(5) The old quays at Ardura, Skehanore and Fasagh need raising and extension.

(6) A small pier at Ardralla, opposite Oldcourt, on the Ilen is needed. It is here that

the coal is landed for the entire parish, and when the colliers arrive in the river, the coal has to be taken away in small boats. The place is naturally suitable.

(7) The old quay at New Court – once very extensively used, and still used by many – requires to be repaired and improved.

(8) Two small piers are wanted in Hare Island, one for the Western and one for the Eastern section. There is no boat accommodation for the island beyond a small slip on which £30 was spent in 1885 and which affords accommodation to only three or four families.

These works with reclamation of land, if carried out without delay, would relieve the distress prevailing and at the same time put the parish into 'ship shape' so that its people would be in a fair position to weather future periods of distress, without outside assistance.[8]

A report in the *Skibbereen Eagle* in February 1891 had further details of distress in West Cork and gives details of relief work on Heir Island, principally the construction of a new road the length of the island. The work started on Monday, February, 2nd 1891. Thirty men were employed on Monday, reaching 100 by Tuesday morning and no less than 203 by Wednesday, many of them from the mainland. An inspector turned up on Wednesday afternoon and speedily changed things, discharging 113. His actions were founded on the regulation which allowed only one member of a family of eight or less to be employed. He also discharged a large number of men from the mainland, many of them being knocked off because their names were not found on the official police lists of destitute persons.

It was pointed out to him that seven shillings a week was too low to support such large families, that the people from the mainland wanted work as badly as the islanders, and as no relief work had started on the mainland, they were entitled to relief work on the island. As to the police lists of destitute people, the workers stated that many people were not aware that such lists had been drawn up, and that many deserving cases were not included in those lists. The mainland labourers pointed out that some of them had to walk as much as five miles to and from work each day which showed they were in sore need of it. Many of the labourers turned away on Wednesday were already in receipt of private charity. These men were now reduced to the condition of several of the inland small farmers and labourers in the parish of Schull and Aughadown – they had nothing and they got nothing, save from private charity. A great deal of the charity, on which the people lived, came from the small diocesan fund and from American contributions. This has given the people some confidence as they learned that they were not dependent on expected and much needed works which had been proposed but most of which had not started.

The people were so destitute, that the generous priest was not always aware of it because they were very slow to resort to charity. The neighbours of the poorest respected their horror of even the smallest publicity of their misfortune until it was absolutely necessary to draw attention to it. The case of a widow, with four in family, the eldest of whom was sixteen, at last reached the ears of Fr. O'Sullivan, P.P. Aughadown and on investigation he found that the five people in the family had been living for the three preceding days on food which was not sufficient for two meals. The widow's credit was exhausted and she and her family managed to live for that time on three pounds of bread and a couple of basins of flour which a neighbouring farmer's wife had given the widow out of charity. Previous to this the family had been living in an almost similar state of semi-starvation for two months. This woman was given some of the American money and the priest sent her word that the next time she came out from her island home – one of the Skeams – he would have a sack of meal to give her. In another case a labourer came to Fr. O'Sullivan with a pig and asked for its value as he was not able to feed the animal and could not afford to fatten her for the market. It was a delicate way of asking for charity. The man received help. This man was in a rather good position, the report states because in all Heir Island, Colonel Robertson, Local Government Board Inspector, found only twelve pigs. The islanders, however, were better off than the majority of the parish, for they had employment. Many of the mainland labourers, who were turned away from the Heir Island works, got employment in the construction of the Collatrum to Poulnacallee road.

This gave employment to many men and would enable them to take seaweed and sand to their farms in the future. Up to February, 1891, they had to go to the Baltimore side of the river, about four miles distant, and work on the railway line, if work could be got. At that time only about a dozen men from the neighbourhood of Collatrum were working on the railway, and after paying for their lodgings they were able to send only three shillings a week home to support their family.[9]

The Collatrum-Lissaree Road must have started soon after the Heir Island road (later in 1891). The condition of affairs was pretty much the same in Schull, the Long Island works being of no benefit to the majority of the people as the mainland people were dismissed, like the Collatrum men who sought work on Heir Island.

As a general rule there was more distress on the mainland than on the remote islands. The non-fishing inhabitants of the coastal district earned nothing in the autumn, while a good proportion of the islanders made something either as part owners of mackerel boats or as members of the crews of these vessels. The clergy and other local gentlemen of authority in the area maintained that as well as making roads to open up the district, and constructing piers to ease unloading, that reproductive projects should be started. The relief works instigated at the time of the Great Famine were of little use as the men were too weak to work.

Congested Districts Board

The Congested Districts Board was established by the Land Act of 1891 to provide assistance to congested districts i.e. areas regarded as exceptionally poor and undeveloped, along the west coast of Ireland. The Board was set up, following a visit to the West of Ireland by Arthur Balfour, Chief Secretary for Ireland, in 1890. Following his visit he said

> The general impression left upon the casual traveller is that you are dealing
> with a population not congested in the sense of being crowded, but congested

by not being able to draw from their holdings a safe and sufficient livelihood for themselves and their children, whose condition trembles constantly on the verge of want, and when the potato crop fails, goes over that margin and becomes one of extreme and even dangerous destitution.

Heir Island was part of the Baltimore Congested District, consisting of the electoral divisions of Cape Clear, Tullagh, Aughadown South, and Castlehaven South.

The Congested Districts Board Baseline Report of 1893 for this area is very informative. Baltimore, it stated, was one of the most important fishing centres in Ireland. Two hundred and seventy boats visited it that year, including eighty six Manx, twenty eight English and Scotch, seven French and one hundred and forty nine Irish. Two hundred and eleven boats were registered with the Coastguards as owned in the district, viz:- fifty six first class boats, one hundred and fifty five second and third class boats, giving employment to about one thousand men. Facilities for the sale of fish were good, and the extension of railway from Skibbereen to Baltimore would further increase them. Fishbuyers came from England and Scotland and there were several local dealers.

There were forty lobster boats employing one hundred and twenty men in the Electoral Division of Aughadown South, engaged in summer at lobster fishing. When the fishing season ended many of the second and third class boats were used to collect seaweed and carry turf from the mainland to the islands. A boat slip was built on Hare Island and one repaired on the mainland.

The cash receipts and expenditure of a family in ordinary circumstances depended altogether on the fishing and it was very difficult to make a reliable estimate – in an average year probably £50

The estimated average value of home-grown food consumed was as follows:

	£ s. d.
Potatoes	10 0 0
Fish	5 0 0
Milk	5 0 0
Total	£20.0.0

If the potato crop was good, it lasted throughout the year; in a bad season it was consumed in three months. The report stated that the people of the district ate three meals daily: bread and tea or milk for breakfast; potatoes, fish and milk for dinner, bread and tea or milk for supper. When potatoes were plentiful they were often eaten twice a day.

The people of the district were reputed for hard work and bore 'a high character as intrepid and skilful fishermen.'

As regards the people living near the coast and in the islands, who were all fishermen, they needed better accommodation in the way of slips and shelters for boats in various places. It was stated that many of the people did not have the means to procure boats and fishing gear. Monetary assistance would be welcomed, as many of the old boats had become unserviceable.[10]

The minutes of another meeting of the Congested District Board on July 16th 1907 in the Courthouse, Skibbereen 1907 reveals much about conditions in West Cork at the time.

There were a total of eighty six large mackerel boats and eight hundred and twenty five yawls registered in the Skibbereen district, covering the area from the Galley Head to Dursey Island approximately. The numbers of mackerel boats, almost half of which were owned by Cape Clear fishermen, reflected how important the fishing industry was at the time – mackerel, herring and lobster fishing as well as long-lining for white fish (cod, ling, hake etc).

Dr. T.J. O'Meara gave an account of the dietary and physical conditions, and the housing and sanitary surroundings of the houses of the poor from Toe Head to Roaringwater Bay, including the islands. The district has an area of about 21,000 statute acres and had a population in 1907 of 5,750, of whom about 1,260 lived on the islands. The land is for the most part rocky and the soil light. The greater part came under the definition of a 'congested district', that is requiring special help. The inhabitants were for the most part poor, the diet defective, the general health of the people not good; the houses of the poor, exclusive of those who occupied 'labourers' cottages bad, and the surroundings of the houses very unsanitary. The diet consisted chiefly of potatoes, fish, bread and tea. Milk and porridge were scarcely used at all because the poor couldn't obtain milk and those who had surplus sold it to the creameries.

Dr. O'Meara declared that there was an amount of 'tea drunkenness', as people often drank tea five or six times a day as a stimulant. The most prevalent diseases were anaemia and dyspepsia, caused by poor diet and rheumatic ailments caused by the humidity and the dampness of the dwellings. Typhus fever occurred in ill-ventilated, overcrowded unsanitary houses more especially in Toe Head, Aughadown and Heir Island; although sporadic cases occurred throughout the whole district.

Pulmonary tuberculosis (T.B.) was very prevalent, especially in Aughadown and the islands of Cape Clear, Sherkin and Heir; it occurred most frequently when emigrants returned from America with the disease. The three main causes of T.B. were general weakening of health due to bad diet, defective housing and sanitation and the return of consumptive Americans.

Excepting the labourers' cottages, the houses were for the most part low, thatched, ill-ventilated, with earthen floors and had manure pits too near the dwelling. Many houses had no chimneys so that the houses were often smoke filled. The doctor advocated that grants should be made available somehow for improvement of surroundings of dwellings, putting in proper windows and cementing floors.

Aughadown South had a population of 1,400. There were up to forty uneconomic farms on the mainland, and on the islands, Heir, Skeams and Calf, all were uneconomic.

The needs of the fishing population were then described. The fishermen, especially on the islands, were greatly in need of piers. Heir Island causeway was intended as a passage from Heir Island East to Heir Island West; at high tide there was six feet of water on the strand and the tide came up very rapidly. Work had not yet begun. (The building of the causeway was started the following year and completed in 1909/10). It was originally expected that a quay or slip would be built in connection with the bridge, something that was badly needed. There were some large mackerel boats and a large number of lobster boats on the island. Lobster fishing would be very successful if there was a good permanent market but there was only one buyer and prices hardly paid for fishermen's labour. The previous year a French buyer came, whish resulted in a rise in prices due to competition.

A road was made through the island for the first time in 1892: Lord Zetland came down to the island to see it and through his influence the road was completed, also a slip at the east end of island, and a large quay at Roaringwater Bay. The slip on the east was not sufficient; there should be a quay with a slip at the end of it, allowed to run out, so that when there was a glut of fish and price was low in Baltimore, mackerel boats would come over and employ women to save fish for their own use. A quay was wanted on the mainland. All the engineers who saw the place were in favour of the proposed improvements. They also stated that two more little roads, north and south were also needed. [11]

The south road would connect with the Reen, while the road north would connect with the 'Leán Gamhan area, where Con Burke had his shop. Unfortunately the quay was not built at that time. The island people had to wait over a century for its construction. The proposed quay near the Bridge in Paris was never built.

THE BRIDGE AND CAUSEWAY BUILT IN 1909/10. THE CONCRETE SIDE WALLS WERE BUIILT AT A LATER DATE

JOHN FITZGERALD, HEIR ISLAND WEST

ELLEN MINIHANE (NEE CAHALANE), 'ÉLLICO'

MICHEÁL Ó DÁLAIGH AND HIS
WIFE, MARY (NEE PYBURN),
HIS SONS, EUGENE AND KIERAN,
WITH EDDIE PYBURN,
OUTSIDE THE FAMILY HOME
IN PARIS

— 14 —

Shipwrecks

The coastline from Mizen Head to the Kedge Rock, just east of Baltimore Harbour, has been the scene of many shipwrecks from the middle ages to modern time. We read of many ships coming to grief on the Kedge rock outside the mouth of Baltimore harbour. In Baltimore harbour is the *Loo* buoy, marking the wreck of the English Man of War, *Loo* which was wrecked in 1687.[1] As recently as 1979, fourteen yachtsmen were lost during the Fastnet Yacht race. The following is a list of some of the ships that came to grief in Roaringwater Bay prior to 1840.

The *Christopher*	wrecked on Spanish Island in 1758.
John Margaret	wrecked on west side of Sherkin July,1784.
Lady Harriet	destroyed on Long Island in 1794.
The brig *Boannius*	wrecked on Castle Island in 1802.
Rood Rech	*wrecked* on Long Island in 1807.
Hannah	of South Shields – 'a complete wreck with not one of her crew on board.' Long Island Channel, Oct. 17th 1823.
The *Albion*	wrecked on Ringaroga in 1828.
Trial of London	wrecked on Cape Clear in 1834.
The *Charles*	went on the rocks in Cape Clear in 1836.
The *Grace*	went aground in Roaringwater Bay in 1838, the exact whereabouts not mentioned; was refloated.
Lady Charlotte	went on the Barrel Rocks off Long Island in 1838.
Thomas Tucker	wrecked on Carthy's Island in 1838[2].

The *Stephen Whitney* was wrecked on Rinn na mBeann on the north side of West Calf Island in 1847 with the loss of 92, the most terrible tragedy ever in the Bay, which led to the construction of the first Fastnet Lighthouse which came into operation on January 1st 1854, replacing the lighthouse on Cape Clear which was deemed unsuitable. The *Albany* was wrecked on Carthy's Island in June 1870, the barquentine *Leonora* on south-west point of Castle Island on 4th November 1872. In February 1881 the Leyland Steamer, *Bohemian*, was wrecked on the south-eastern point of Mizen Head with the loss of 35 lives. The Leyland steamer *Ilyrian* went on the rocks at Faill Uí Chathail, Cape Clear in May 1884. All passengers were saved but the ship was completely destroyed. The newspapers report gave details of coastguards and R.I.C.[3] making extensive seizures of wool and casks of whiskey at Ballydehob, Castletownshend and other parts of the coast, part of the cargo of the ill-fated steamer, *Illyrian*.

Seven Long Island fishermen were drowned in October 1885 when their boat

capsized near Pointe an Bholláin near the entrance to South Harbour, Cape
Clear. The 14 ton schooner, *Onward,* entered the Gascannane Sound in June
1888. She went on the rocks on the eastern side of Cape but the crew escaped in
small boats.

The recovery of cargo from wrecks or the protection of cargo was done by
coastguards, established in 1822, sometimes assisted by the R.I.C. or the military. An unwritten code among island and coastal communities was that every
possible effort should be made to save life but after that it was every man for
himself. Indeed the islanders and people along the coast often put their own
lives in danger to save the sailors, as instanced, for example, in the heroic rescues
of sailors from the *Christian Wilhelm* (1894) the *Alondra* (1916) and the *Nestorian* (1917) Anything floating in the water was considered the property of the
finder. Walking the strands to search for 'wrack' was customary for coastal people, especially in winter. According to old Irish (Brehon) laws, anything washed
ashore became the property of the finder. Sometimes wrecked ships were plun-
dered. Confrontations often occurred between the local people and the
coastguards. Occasionally the military or coastguards fired at the people to prevent plunder, leading on some occasions to loss of life, as in Burgatia,
Rosscarbery, in 1834, after the wreck of the brig, *Europa* when one man was shot
dead.[4]

Grace

The barque, *Grace,* of Liverpool, bound from Virginia to Liverpool with a load of
tobacco and cotton, was driven ashore on the eastern part of Roaringwater Bay
in the dreadful gale of November 28th 1838. Hopes were entertained that she
would get off without serious damage, but she was forced deeper into the sand
by the 'Big Wind' of January 6th 1839. Her cargo of 572 hogshead of tobacco was
transhipped to Liverpool. In late January, she was floated off in remarkably good
condition. The exact location of where she went aground is not specified. [5]

Susan (of Milford)

On Christmas Eve, 1848, a ship named the *Susan (of Milford),* laden with wheat,
was wrecked on the Reen of Heir Island. One of the rocks off the south side of
the Reen is still known as Oileán Topmast (Topmast Island).[6] See story of ship-
wreck on page 38.

The Big Wind

The night of April 23rd /24th 1894 was called 'The Night of the Big Wind.' That
Monday night and Tuesday morning a ferocious storm hit the south west coast
of Ireland. No one in Baltimore could remember a gale of such ferocity. At that
time Baltimore was the headquarters of a thriving mackerel industry. The whole
harbour was full of mackerel drifters from all parts of West Cork, Baltimore,
Sherkin, Cape Clear, Turkhead, Collatrum, Heir Island, East Calf, Glandore
and Myross, Northern Ireland, the Isle of Man, Cornwall and other parts of

Britain. The storm wreaked devastation on the large fleet of boats. Nine lives were lost that night. A man named Quirke, who was a crewman of the Port St. Mary Cornwall smack '*CT.23*', was lost near the Fastnet when the crew were trying to save their nets. The unfortunate man was washed overboard and became entangled in the nets. Unable to haul their nets in the height of the storm, the crew had no option but to abandon them and leave their friend behind.[7]

The other eight men lost were the entire crew of the lugger *Florence* of Newry, Co. Down. People on Sherkin Island had a clear view of the arrival of the fleet heading for Baltimore. They saw one smack 'labouring' south of Sherkin. She was struck twice by gigantic waves and then disappeared. Later her wreckage was picked up at Trafraska, an inlet south of Baltimore Beacon.[8]

Christian Wilhelm

The Norwegian barque, *Christian Wilhelm*, which had left Port Talbot, Swansea, bound for New Brunswick, got into difficulties about ten o'clock on Tuesday morning. April 24th, 1894. The captain decided to run for shelter to the nearest harbour. In the haze she ran inside Cape Clear and went aground on rocks near Sandy Island, off the north coast of Sherkin. The men from Baltimore coastguard station put out in their rescue boat to save the crew but could not get near enough in the monstrous sea to rescue them.

John Cahalane (1838–1913) of North Reen, Heir Island, having seen the distress signals, gathered a crew of four strong oarsmen, probably including his two sons, Michael and Cornelius, who were aged 22 and 24 respectively in 1894, and who were involved in many subsequent rescues. Setting out in their lobster yawl, they reached the vicinity of the barque. Three times they failed to reach her side but at the fourth attempt, they succeeded in taking off four crewmen and landed them on Sherkin. Returning to rescue the six remaining crewmen, which included Captain Kendal and his son, they succeeded in getting them aboard the lobster boat, but just as they boarded, the barque listed over. Cahalane's yawl was swamped and sank, but fortunately the entire party was able to climb back into the *Christian Wilhelm*. The yawl, with an estimated value of £14, on which Cahalane depended for a living, was destroyed. The loss of the boat was a huge disappointment but their main worry then must have been for their lives.[9]

Many of the several English fish buyers, who bought mackerel at Baltimore, kept intercepting yawls, or as they were more commonly called 'bumming boats'. These were long, fast six-oar rowing boats. The 'intercepting boat' of Kelsall Brothers, Liverpool, manned by a crew of Heir Island men and with cox'n, William Harton in command, set out from Baltimore to go to the aid of the men trapped on the Christian Wilhelm. As they rowed out, Harton had a change of heart; he refused to risk his life beyond Green's Island (also called Spanish Island) so high was the sea running, and declared that he would go no further. Patrick O'Driscoll, one of Cahalane's regular crewmen, took command of the boat. On board with him were Michael McCarthy, Michael O'Driscoll, Michael Cotter, Peter Murphy, Dan McCarthy and John Harte, all Heir islanders. They succeeded in bringing all those on the *Christian Wilhelm* to safety.

After the *Christian Wilhelm* rescue, they gave assistance to several Manx vessels which were being hauled towards the shore by the lugger *Hawk.* They rescued the yacht *Eileen,* owned by Richard Sisk, which was in danger of being wrecked.[10]

Most of the fishing smacks suffered some damage. 'Scarcely a boat came back with gear intact and some are so damaged that they cannot resume fishing. The loss is heavy and universal', wrote the Cork Examiner reporter. By Wednesday, the *Christian Wilhelm* was a complete wreck, one of her sides being altogether stove in, while everything on board had been washed away.

The fishing boat, *Maria Jane,* of Peel, Isle of Man, didn't arrive in Baltimore until 7 p.m. on Tuesday evening, after spending the whole period at sea, riding on her nets some 21 miles off Baltimore. William Moore, her owner, told the Examiner reporter that he had 30 years experience as a fisherman on the English, Scottish and Irish coasts and during that time he never experienced a storm as bad as this one both in its violence and disastrous effects. *The Examiner* continues:

> The daring bravery and humane conduct of Pat O'Driscoll of Hare Island, and his companions deserve to be recorded in letters of gold. Not only on sea but on land has this hurricane left visible traces of its havoc. The stalks on the early potato gardens have been turned black or completely shattered by the gale, while there will be scarcely an apple in this district this season.[11]

In a report in the *Skibbereen Eagle* under the heading *The Brave Hare Island Men*: we read

> Father O'Brien, Parish Priest of Baltimore received a cheque for £35 from Mr. Edwin Hall of Cork, a subscription raised by himself and some friends. It was accompanied by a sympathetic letter asking that the money be distributed among the Heir Island lobster fishermen, in recognition of their brave conduct in rescuing four of the crew of the wrecked Norwegian barque, *Christian Wilhelm,* and who, in their endeavour to rescue the remaining six, lost their yawl, got submerged themselves, and would have been lost, together with the remainder of the barque's crew, only for the arrival of their neighbours from Heir Island. Fr. O'Brien sent the money to the parish priest of Aughadown, Fr. James O'Sullivan. Fr. O'Brien and the governor of Baltimore Fishery School, recommended £8 be given to Patrick O'Driscoll who inspired the rescue; £1 to each of the other nine men. The remainder, £18 was to be given to Cahalane, who had lost his lobster yawl.[12]

Most of the fishing boats had lost their nets, while others had structural damage. Many of the Manx fleet had to return home to replace their nets. The coast line from Baltimore to the Galley Head was strewn with lost nets and other wreckage. It should be pointed out that the coastguards hadn't any lifeboat then, only a rescue launch. Baltimore got its first lifeboat, The *Shamrock,* in 1920

Ailsawald (1900)

On Wednesday night, the 19th December, 1900, the 4,500 ton, Newcastle-on-Tyne steamer, *Ailsawald,* went aground on rocks on the north side of Sherkin near Dreolán Point, adjacent to where Mr. Matt Murphy's Sherkin Island Marine Station is located today. The vessel, belonging to Lunn and MacCoy & Company of Newcastle-on-Tyne, was en route from Penarth, near Cardiff, to Bermuda, in water ballast,with 600 tons of coal aboard. During a severe S.W. gale she was caught broadside by the wind and driven aground. Captain Muir and his crew of 24 were rescued with the greatest difficulty by the Sherkin Islanders. The Eagle, in its initial report, states, 'It is not possible to praise the Sherkin Islanders too highly for the plucky way in which they rescued the crew, in the face of the greatest peril.' The paper states that the general opinion was that she would not be got off the rocks.[13]

Skibbereen Eagle

THE SS. *AILSWALD* AS SHE APPEARED ON THE ROCKS TO THE NORTH OF SHERKIN, AND FACING HARE ISLAND

On Thursday, December 27th, there was another ferocious storm which did considerable damage on land and sea. The wind veered to the south-west and 'blew with all the violence of a hurricane'. During this severe weather the *Ailsawald* was driven further on to the rocks. The propeller was broken and the bottom damaged. Mr. Ensor, salvage operator, of Cobh negotiated with the owners, Lunn and McCoy and the insurers. As a result he sent his salvage steamer, Adelaide, to the scene. Ensor sent to Cardiff for three extra salvage pumps and these arrived in the first week of January. Each of the five pumps could clear 3000 gallons of water per hour.

On January 11th with the aid of four tug boats, she was successfully brought back to deep water. She was towed in the direction of Whitehall on to a level mud-bank, but owing to her huge draught only her bow could be properly fixed on the bank and the stern remained hanging over water. Soon her stern slipped off the mud into deep water. This was a great drawback, for instead of having dry decks to work on, there was now about 20 feet of water on the ship's aft deck at high tide. The problem now was how to lift the vessel with this tremendous mass of water was in her. To solve this problem, a coffer dam, weighing 30 tons, was built under the superintendence of the foreman carpenter, Mr John Kiely, in Baltimore Fishery School. Fr. Hill of the Baltimore School lent his staff carpenters as well as laying open his workshop.[14]

After construction, it was towed to Whitehall. It was then fastened down to the mouth of one of the largest holds making a water-tight covering. A huge pump was inserted through the top; the water inside was pumped out, while the water-tight covering prevented any more filling in, until at last, when relieved from the great weight of water, the *Ailsawald* rose again to the surface.

The *Ailsawald* was then towed to the strand on Giornán Point, the north-east point of Heir Island, where further repair work was done on her. The divers repaired all leakages and damage done to the ship's bottom. Many of the plates on the bottom of the steel-built *Ailsawald* were twisted and badly bent but not a single fracture was found in them.

The *Skibbereen Eagle* representative travelled to the site, under the guidance of Mr. S.G. Goth of Skibbereen, through whom a large staff of local labour had been employed on the vessel.

> The trip to the steamer was made in the tug boat, *Mayflower*, and was a most enjoyable one. The scenery on all sides is magnificent, especially around that spot where the *Ailsawald* herself was finally berthed, the mountains towering up on the background, with old Mount Gabriel watching and guarding as it were, the whole surroundings, whilst in front there is a distant view of Cape Clear and the surrounding islands.

He was struck by the working of the enormous steam pumps forcing out huge jets of water over the side. He describes the activity, 'In every corner of the ship there are grimy workmen straining every nerve and sinew to hasten the work.' He was most intrigued by the divers. He wrote,

> From a spectator's point of view, about the most interesting part of the work is the descent of the divers. Their ponderous helmets, heavily-weighed boots, and indeed all the cumbrous dress are objects of interest and when they suddenly appear from the depths of the sea they might well be mistaken for satellites of Father Neptune coming to visit the upper world.[15]

He goes on to state, that once a new propeller had been fitted to the vessel, she would be towed to Queenstown. He also stated that it was a great pleasure to know that a large number of local people had been employed for a few weeks and that at least a thousand pounds had been spent in Baltimore alone. He finished his report by stating that the *Ailsawald* was a steel ship, 320 ft in length with 40 foot beam and 32 foot draught. Ensor's ingenuity had saved the ship which at first seemed doomed. Bourke, in 'Shipwrecks off the Irish Coast', states that Ensor's company operated several specially equipped salvage ships at various times and was quite a large operation. As well as the *Adelaide*, he also owned the *Leonesse*.

The *Eagle* had a report on what happened in the days after the ship went aground on Sherkin.

> On Thursday morning, Head-Constable Price, Sergeant Cormac and other policemen proceeded in a boat from Baltimore to Hare Island for the purpose of searching for property taken from the steamer *Ailsawald* lying between the rocks near Sherkin. Several articles belonging to the steamer were discovered including ropes, sails, some fittings but principally provisions – tinned meat, biscuits, etc. Houses on Cape Clear were searched on December 31st.

At a special court held in the Courthouse, Skibbereen, in February, several people from Cape Clear, Sherkin and Heir Island were charged with taking coal, planks of timber, canvas, foodstuffs etc. from the *Ailsawald*. It is certain that several boats congregated from all the islands and the mainland when the vessel was on the rocks. The Eagle gives details of the charges brought against different individuals. Captain Muir, in evidence, stated that he went on board the vessel the morning after she went ashore. Seventy or eighty people were around her then. Sergeant Cormac, R.I.C., Baltimore, stated

> I was of the party of constabulary that proceeded to the *Ailsawald* on 22nd December, Head Constable Price being in charge. There were a number of boats around the ship. They were manned by people from the islands and surrounding localities. Some of the parties were engaged in lowering coal from the deck to boats alongside and others engaged in lowering planks.[16]

It is obvious that several boats from all over Roaringwater Bay and the mainland 'visited' the vessel. Why certain individuals were targeted by the authorities is difficult to say. Indeed, one of the accused, in his defence, made this point.

As for the *Ailsawald,* she was towed by tug boats to Queenstown (Cobh). However, she had a sad end. In the winter of 1901, she was lost in the English Channel. All her crew were lost.

The Savonia

On 17th January 1909 the *SS. Dominion*, bound for Liverpool, saw a ship in distress four miles south of the Fastnet in a strong south-west gale. It was the *Savonia* of St. John, New Brunswick, Canada, laden with timber. The *Savonia* was labouring heavily; her crew was taken aboard the *Dominion*, which radioed Cobh asking that tugs be sent in search of her. Tugs immediately raced towards her last position, in search of a lucrative salvage prize.

However, the *Savonia* drifted into Roaringwater Bay and struck the rocks on the S.W. side of Middle Calf Island, becoming a total wreck. The *Cork Examiner* reported that enormous quantities of wreckage were washed ashore 'off Baltimore, Sherkin, Cape Clear, Hare Island and Turkhead. The ocean is strewn with wreckage and portions of the vessel.' The *Examiner* gives the following details

The deck cargo has been already washed away and scores of boats have been engaged in securing the remainder, which is being piled up in a secure position on the island. The principal portion of the cargo is composed of deals and prepared timber, in addition to which there is mahogany, hickory and the different classes of pine.[17]

For days, quantities of timber floated on to strands all over Roaringwater Bay, subsequently used to make furniture and house fittings. Some Heir islanders used the timber as barter to settle debts with the island shop-keeper, Con Burke, who was always generous with credit. The night of the wreck there was a wedding 'ball' on Heir Island East. According to oral tradition all the men left the

wedding and headed for the wreckage. Parish records of a wedding, on January 19th, 1909 of John O'Donovan and Catherine O'Neill of Heir Island East confirm this story told to me by the late Neilly O'Donovan. At that time, all wedding parties were hold in the home of the bride.

Timber from the *Savonia* was used in making furniture and in the construction of dwellings on Heir, the other islands and on the mainland. The shelf shown here is made from timber from the *Savonia*

Alondra

The Cahalanes and Hartes of the Reen, Heir Island, were involved in many rescues. The period from the 29th December 1916 to mid January 1917 was a extra busy time for them. On the morning of Friday 29th December, 1916, the *Alondra* of Liverpool laden with wine, resin, minerals and hides went ashore in a dense fog and heavy seas, on the Kedge Rock close to Baltimore Harbour. The Cork Examiner of January 1st 1917 states: 'she now lies helplessly cradled in the rocks at the S.W. point of the Kedge.' Six of the crew, who came ashore in a lifeboat at Ballyally Coastguard Station, stated that fifteen others also left in another boat and, as they had not come ashore, they presumed they were drowned. A large crowd gathered on the high rocky ground opposite the island. Two Baltimore boats, owned by M. Cottrell and J. Logan, put off with motor boats before noon, but were unsuccessful in reaching the ship. The *Cork Examiner* correspondent reported

all rocket appliances were taken as near as possible to the scene of the wreck by the coastguards accompanied by local people … the condition of the men aboard is extremely pitiable and particularly when no assistance can be rendered to them. All are huddled together on the bridge and making efforts to keep themselves warm.

Later seventeen of the crew succeeded by means of a ladder in climbing the cliffs of the Kedge, where they spent the night.[18]

On Saturday morning, the lieutenant in charge of the coastguard patrol boat, was able to throw them some food, and he later landed on the rock, from where he was able to communicate afterwards with the fishermen who came with boats at daylight to assist at the rescue. A rope was attached to the Kedge cliffs which are over one hundred and fifty feet high. All the men, except three, were lowered in this manner, by the aid of the ropes, into small boats and transferred to a trawler. The remaining three were subsequently lowered by means of a breeches buoy.[19] On Saturday the Cork Examiner reported: 'Seventeen men who composed part of the crew of the steamer were released from their perilous position on the Kedge Rocks and were taken to Queenstown by patrol boat'. The reporter refers to. . . 'The noble and humane efforts on the part of a Hare Island crew, Messrs. Michael Cahalane and his son John, also his brother Cornelius and another man, John Hart.'

The *Skibbereen Eagle* reported the following:

> In connection with the rescue of the survivors of the Alondra wreck on Kedge Island, it should have been mentioned that Messrs. J. Anglin, junior, R. Ross, T. Browne, J. Sheehan, Wm. Nolan, Ml. Minihane, C. Cottrell and Coastguard, M. Barry of Ballyalla, accompanied by the Rev. Mr. Beecher, Rector, Baltimore, regardless to danger to themselves, did heroic work. They were instrumental, with the Cahalanes, in saving the life of the third officer, Mr. J.B. Sinclair, of Liverpool, taking him from Cahalane's boat to the patrol boat as well as hauling him off the island with the help of Mr. Beecher.[20]

Of the thirty eight sailors, seventeen were rescued by Baltimore and Heir Island boats, six came ashore in one of the ship's lifeboats. Fifteen others, attempting to come ashore in another lifeboat, were drowned.

The Nestorian

After spending all day Friday and Saturday assisting in the rescue of the sailors from the *Alondra*, the Cahalanes were at the western side of Cape Clear early on Tuesday morning to give assistance to the Daly brothers, (John and Timothy) and Cadogan brothers, (Timothy and Michael), who rescued forty six of the forty seven crew of the 6000 ton Leyland liner, S.S. *Nestorian*, which went ashore at a late hour on Monday night (January 1st 1917) at Tón an Amadáin on the S.W. of Cape Clear. Con Cadogan of Baile Iarthach (western townland) heard a gun-fired distress signal and roused his sons and their neighbours, the Dalys. They put to sea in their fishing boat which had a small yawl in tow. When they reached the scene at 7.a.m. the ship was already breaking up. There was a heavy 'draw' on the rocks. After anchoring their big boat, the Dalys and Cadogans, using the four oar yawl, rowed to the vicinity of the ship. They attached a 'travelling' rope to the *Nestorian*. The sailors were rescued, one by one, each sailor having to jump with the backwash of the sea as the tide sucked outwards. If he jumped with the swell rolling in, he would be dashed against the ship's side. Of the crew of forty seven only one man was drowned, who went foul of the wreckage.

The *Skibbereen Eagle* gives a graphic account of the rescue

> After heroic efforts made by the brothers Daly and Cadogan, of Cape Clear, and others, who went to their assistance at 7.a.m. on Tuesday morning, all the crew, save one, were saved. At an early hour on Tuesday morning all the available boats in Baltimore, Sherkin, Hare Island, Long Island and Schull hurried to the scene of the wreck, which was made in good time despite the W.S.W. gale and rather heavy sea. In this work, the brothers Daly of Cape Clear, rendered invaluable aid, assisted by the brothers Cadogan, also of Cape Clear and Cahalane of Hare Island.[21]

A presentation of testimonials of honour was made by the Lifeboat Institution to John Daly and Tim Cadogan in recognition of their outstanding bravery. A pair of binoculars presented to Con Cadogan, father of the Cadogan brothers, who raised the alarm, is on exhibition in Cape Clear Museum.

Saurnaut

Two days after helping, with others, to save lives from the *Alondra*, Mike Cahalane, his son John, and brother Cornelius, together with John and Daniel Harte, went to the aid of a Norwegian barque *Saurnaut* in distress off Toe Head. Having helped the barque to come off the rocks, they brought her safely to Queenstown. (Cobh) Their claim for salvage led to a hearing before Cork Borough Sessions in February 1917. The matter didn't end until May 1917 when, following claim and counterclaim as to the role of the Heir Islanders in the rescue, Mr. Justice Gordon delivered judgment in the Probate Court.

The sequence of events, from the claimants' point of view, were outlined before the Cork Borough Sessions Admiralty Court by Mr. W.C.A. Hungerford. The crew of the *Mary Anne*, owned by John Harte, went to Mass at Baltimore on New Year's Day 1917, after spending two days assisting in the Alondra rescue. After Mass they learned of another ship in distress. They left Baltimore in their boat and went in the direction of Toe Head. Near the Kedge Rock they met a patrol boat and, after conversation with the crew, they were taken in tow. When they arrived at Toe Head, the barque was in distress on the rocks, and at anchor. Her sails were clewed up (sic). The weather was rough, with a strong westerly breeze blowing and slack water. The crew of the Mary Ann put the captain of the patrol boat on board the barque at great risk and after great trouble. An arrangement was made to tow the barque off but the attempts made did not succeed. Eventually the cable fouled the propeller of the patrol boat and she had to drop anchors. The crew of the Mary Ann were at this time on board the *Saurnaut*, as it was too dangerous for them to remain in the fishing boat in such a sea between the barque and patrol boat. The tide was then at ebb and the patrol boat could not now help the barque. The barque's stern went on to the rocks. The crew of the fishing boat told the captain that they could save his ship if he acted on their advice. In the meantime the patrol boat collided with the barque and there was danger of her magazine exploding. The captain of the barque apparently accepted the services of the crew of the Mary Anne, and on their advice, put back the top sails. A hawser now passed to the patrol boat with the result that they swung the barque's stem over. They got wind into the sails and she moved into deep water. At that time there was considerable fog. The crew remained in the barque, and under their direction, they brought the ship to Cobh the next day. They claimed £50 each for their services. The barque was valued at £11,000. After much haggling, it appeared that they put their marks to receipts entitling them to only £5 each. The defence claimed that as an absolute defence and bar to any further claim.

At the hearing at the Admiralty Court, Cornelius Cahalane, cross-examined by Mr. A. Allen, Solicitor, representing the owners of the *Saurnaut*, said that the captain refused to give £50. Cornelius stated that they would not have accepted what they got, £5, but they were in distress and should get something. Questioned as to his sea-faring experience, he said he was all his life fishing at sea.

Allen: Tell me, are ye not known as the Hare Island pirates?
Cors. Cahalane – I never heard, sir.
Allen: Is it a fact that in Hare Island the children are taught a little prayer – 'God bless father and mother and send a fine ship ashore before morning'.
Cors. Cahalane – I never heard it.'

We see here an attempt made to undermine the character and motives of the Heir Island men. Archdeacon Beecher, Rector of Baltimore, who had co-ordinated the *Alondra* rescue effort, and who indeed had to be restrained from swimming to the Kedge, said that the plaintiffs were honest, hard-working men. The Cahalanes had saved lives before. He gave an account of the salvage of the *Alondra* and mentioned that Michael Cahalane materially helped. Cahalane's services were requisitioned frequently by the Admiralty to pilot ships into Baltimore's inner harbour.

Mr. Allen, for the owners of the *Saurnaut*, said that these 'ignorant' fishermen knew nothing about the handling of a square-rigged ship, that there was no need of them going to Queenstown and the reason they went was to stick to the ship for the purpose of remuneration. They had made a preposterous claim of £50 a man. The settlement offered was absolute and final and the men accepted it with their eyes open. He said that the amount they were given was a very substantial sum for the services rendered.

Lieutenant Saunderson, commander of the patrol boat, described the work of the crew of the Mary Ann as valuable and said there was some risk but no grave danger involved. There was a heavy sea and it was very misty. The barque was in a bad position and would have become a wreck that night if she was left there.

In giving judgment, the judge said that he and his assessor agreed that the master of the barque, Captain Tuftland, never gave up charge of the barque, but they also agreed that the crew of the Mary Anne gave valuable service. They could not accept the evidence of the captain as regards the crew of the *Mary Anne* forcing themselves on him or his telling them to go ashore before they left

Toe Head. Lieutenant Saunderson had said it would be an utter impossibility in such a situation. The Court took the view that these fishermen were co-operating with the captain of the patrol boat in rendering such service as they could and they felt they were bound to look at their services as a whole from the inception of the transaction until its end. They also felt bound to take into account the spirit in which these men entered in their work and carried it through to the end. Persons who gave service to vessels in distress were performing very meritorious work and that work ought to be properly appreciated. The Court held that £10 a man should be allowed for the services rendered, £5 a man more than given by the Captain.[22]

The matter was finally closed in the Probate Court, Dublin the following May. The plaintiffs (the crew of the *Mary Anne*) sought that the judgment of the Local Court of Admiralty be set aside and they claimed £100 as the value of their salvage services. The defendants (owners of the *Saurnaut*) sought that the £10 a man awarded should be reversed with costs against the plaintiffs. The Eagle published the Judge's findings in the following report.

The above is a photograph of Cornelius Cahalane, Michael Cahalane, and John Hart, three brave Hare Island fishermen who, on the 31ˢᵗ December last, at serious risk to themselves, rescued the Norwegian barque, Soarnut, off the dangerous rocks at Toehead.

Fishermen's Salvage Claim

In the Probate Court, Dublin, on Thursday, Mr. Justice Gordon, delivered judgment in an appeal and a cross appeal in the action by the owner and master and crew of the fishing boat *Mary Anne* against the Norwegian barque *Saurnaut*, her tackle, apparel and furniture. The plaintiffs appealed for the decree of the Recorder of Cork, sitting as Judge of the Local Court of Admiralty on February 20th last, whereby he ordered that the plaintiffs should recover the sum of £10 per man in respect of their claim for salvage remuneration, the sum of £5 per man having already been paid by defendants to each of the plaintiffs in part discharge and satisfaction of the said salvage.

His Lordship dismissed both appeals without costs and affirmed the award of the Recorder – £10 per man as payment. He paid a tribute to the bravery of the Hare Island fishermen and to the services rendered by them not only to the *Saurnaut* but to other ships the preceding December. He agreed with the Recorder that the men were not bound by their acceptance of £5 each at Queenstown and also held with him that no damage had been suffered by the *Suarnaut* because of her arrest (sic).[23]

Thomas Joseph

On Friday 10th October, 1918 the *Thomas Joseph,* owned by John Daly of Cape Clear, was wrecked on the Catalogue Rocks west of Sandy Island, between Sherkin and Turkhead point. She had been built by Tyrells of Arklow. Baltimore was a very busy fishing port at the time. Thousands of barrels of mackerel were pickled and exported. It was reported that the *Thomas Joseph* landed 67,000 mackerel in a single day in the spring of 1918. Daly decided to replace the Gardner engine with a more powerful Parsons. On that fateful evening she left Baltimore on a trial run to Schull, leaving Baltimore about five in the evening and reaching Schull at 6.20 p.m. There was a crew of three – John Daly, skipper, Mike Walsh (Cape Clear) and John O'Driscoll, (Baltimore). There were three marine engineers – Messrs. G. White, J. Inglis and Edgar Stoate and eight passengers. On the return journey they left Schull about 9 p.m. with eleven on board, three of the passengers, Constable Crowe, Messrs Shipsey (fish merchant) and Burke having decided to return to Baltimore by car. It was a foggy rough evening with a stiff breeze from the south-east. Leaving Schull, she passed through the Bealach Lao, between the Middle and East Calf, past the Reen of Heir Island and went on the Catalogue Rocks, west of Sandy Island, north of Sherkin Island.

Their cries for help were heard by the crew of a Heir Island yawl, owned by John Harte. With him were Jeremiah McCarthy and Timothy Murphy of Heir Isl. West. The desperate cries were also heard on the Reen of Heir Island. Bridie Fitzgerald (nee O'Driscoll) informed me that she often heard her parents talking about that night. They were playing cards in her father's house when the cries were heard. Her father, Patrick O'Driscoll, and his cousin, Timothy O'Driscoll and Jeremiah 'Scotty' McCarthy, went to the scene in O'Driscoll's boat, *The Non Pareil,* and assisted John Harte and his men in the rescue.[24] John Harte and his crewmen, Jeremiah McCarthy and Timothy Murphy were awarded medals for their bravery. In 'Irish Lifeboats,' 1975, we read, 'John Hart of the Reen, Heir Island was awarded a silver medal and Jeremiah McCarthy and Timothy Murphy bronze medals for their part in the rescue of five people.'

The inquest on the body of Edgar Stoate was reported in the Eagle. Mr. Albert Collins of Church Hill, Baltimore, giving evidence, stated that he was in the company of Lily and Nan Shipsey and his sister Rita Collins. When the boat struck the Catalogues, John Daly ordered everybody to keep cool and somebody shouted, 'Full steam astern'. Collins saw John O'Driscoll, crewman, jump off the boat and cling to the rock. Mike Walsh, crewman, and engineer, Mr. Inglis, also jumped out of the boat. Mr. Stoate told Collins to stay on the boat as she might settle down. Mr. Collins stated that he did not see him again. The three girls were clinging to Mr. Collins. He struggled to the rock with two of the girls. The wash took him off the rock and he went down. When he came up, the girls were gone. He saw the mast of the boat and clung on. Mr. White, engineer, and Minihane were also on the mast where they spent an hour shouting for help. A Heir Island boat came along and rescued him and afterwards Messrs. White and Minihane. They were taken to Sandy Island, where the Hegarty family lived, and where they were given a change of clothes and food.

Mr. Joseph B. Burke, Superintendent of Fisheries under the Congested District Board, stationed at Baltimore, told the inquest that on the voyage to Schull he felt the boat was not steering properly. Captain Daly and Mike Walsh lowered the mast; he thought this was not the correct thing to do as the boat would be without sail. In Schull they met Dr. Shipsey. Dr. Shipsey and Mr. Shipsey were returning to Baltimore by car. Mr. Burke joined them, but in cross examination, he stated that he was not particularly anxious about the state of the boat. Mr. Shipsey stated that if they were to return to Baltimore they would have to take the south course, south of Sherkin Island. Mr. Dan Leonard of Cape Clear was asked for his view on this and he stated that it was not necessary as John Daly was a good seaman.[25]

It seems most likely that the boat's steering was faulty. John Harte and his crew members, Jerry McCarthy and Timothy Murphy, were fishing for herring when they heard the cries for help. The part played by Patrick O'Driscoll, Tim 'Carroll' O'Driscoll and 'Scotty' McCarthy should not be forgotten. The foreman of the jury stated that Albert Collins saved three lives before he was rescued himself and that John O'Driscoll lost his life trying to save one of the girls. The cause of the accident was never satisfactorily explained. Undoubtedly, John Daly was an able seaman, not lacking in bravery, as demonstrated in his role in the rescue of the crew of the Nestorian less than two years earlier. Many theories and explanations were suggested as the cause of the tragedy. Those who were drowned were two young girls, Lily Shipsey and Rita Collins of Baltimore, John O'Driscoll, crewman, Baltimore, John Daly, skipper and two engineers, Stoate and Inglis. John Daly's body was not recovered until the following Tuesday. Those rescued were Mike Walsh of Cape Clear (crew member), G. White (Engineer), Albert Collins (Baltimore), Nan Shipsey and John Minihane, Baltimore, passengers.

JOHN HARTE – HEIR ISLAND HERO AND HIS WIFE

TIMOTHY MURPHY

JERRY McCARTHY

The Joseph Christopher

In May 1920 the London steam trawler, *Joseph Christopher*, was stranded in thick mist on the rocks between Bird Island and North Harbour, Cape Clear and 'from upwards of seven hours remained in a precarious position'. The first intimation of the matter to reach the mainland was brought by Michael Cahalane of Heir Island. The new lifeboat *Shamrock* was launched, under command of coxswain, Bill Nolan, and proceeded to the assistance of the stranded steamer. At 11 a.m. the vessel refloated herself with the rising tide and proceeded to Milford, apparently undamaged.[26]

The St. Brigid

In late April, 1922, a motor boat, the *St. Brigid* of Baltimore, went aground on a reef between the east end of Heir Island and Cunnamore Point. The St. Brigid plied as a cargo boat between Cork and the various ports in West Cork, bringing general cargo from Cork City to merchants in Glandore, Leap, Union Hall, Baltimore, Ballydehob, Schull and Crookhaven. On this particular voyage, she had a general cargo, including flour, meal, porter, tobacco, etc. She was in the charge of Thomas Taylor. When the boat struck the rock, the Captain called the islanders to remove some of the cargo and thus help to get the boat off the rocks. This the islanders did and, according to the newspaper reports, they returned in the night and took away the remainder of the cargo, believing that the boat would become a total wreck. Some barrels of porter were opened and 'the captain got into communication with the I.R.A. authorities (sic) in Skibbereen and Schull, who came into the island and made a thorough search of it.'[27] The journalist stated that much of the cargo was discovered and the islanders promised to return it the following day, Friday. In fact quite a lot of the cargo was never recovered and all of it was not removed by the Heir Islanders; they got plenty of help from people on the mainland.

Since 1922, the reef has been known as Taylor's Rock after the Captain; it is situated east of Carraig na mBó. According to the article, the boat was also carrying guano, which was used to fertilise some of the fields in Heir Island.

Map of Shipwrecks

The accompanying map indicates the site of some of the many shipwrecks in the merciless winter coast of Roaringwater Bay.

1. The *Christopher*, wrecked on Spanish Island, 1758.

2. *Lady Harriet*, wrecked on Long Island, 1794.

3. The brig, *Boannius*, wrecked on Castle Island, 1802.

4. The *Rood Reel*, wrecked on Long Island, 1807.

5. The *Albion*, wrecked on Ringaroga, 1828.

6. *The Trial*, of London, wrecked on Cape Clear, 1834.

7. The *Charles*, wrecked on rocks off Cape Clear, 1836.

8. The *Grace*, went aground on eastern side of Roaringwater Bay 1838.

9 The *Lady Charlotte*, wrecked on the Dromadda rocks at the western side of the Long Island Channel on October 23rd 1838. She had a cargo of wool, bark, hides, silver plate and dollars. The Captain and eight of the crew were lost.

10. The *Thomas Tucker*, wrecked on one of Carthy's Islands, 1838.

11. The *Stephen Whitney*, wrecked on Rinn na mBeann on north side of West Calf. Island, 1847 with the loss of 92 lives. Twelve survivors climbed the 60 ft high cliffs and were given food and shelter by the two O'Regan families who lived there. This tragedy led to the construction of the Fastnet Rock lighthouse, which threw its first beams in 1854.

12. The *Susan*, of Milford, went ashore on the Reen of Heir Island on Christmas Eve, 1848. She was laden with wheat. Four coastguards and a policeman were placed on the island to protect the cargo. On December 28th, a Heir Island man, John Murphy, was shot dead by one of the coastguards.

13. The *Albany*, 290 tons, was wrecked on Carthy's Island in June 1870. The crew of 17 were saved.

14. The barquentine, *Leonora*, was wrecked on the south-west point of Castle Island in November, 1872. The crew landed safely.

15. The *Illyrian*, a Leyland Line Steamer was wrecked on the rocks at Faill Uí Chathail, beneath the cliffs near the Cape Clear lighthouse in May 1884. The 68 crew and passengers were saved. A saloon door from the *Illyrian* is on display in the Cape Clear Museum.

16. In October, 1885, seven Long Island fishermen were drowned off Cape Clear in a fierce south-westerly gale.

17. A schooner, the *Onward*, entered the Gascanane Sound in June 1888 in dense fog. The crew escaped.

18. The night of April 23rd, is remembered as the Night of the Big Wind. A ferocious storm blew over the south-west of Ireland. The lugger, *Florence*, from Newry, Co. Down sank south of Sherkin Lighthouse; the seven crew members lost their lives. See page 87.

19 The same night, a Norwegian ship, the *Christian Wilhelm* went on the rocks north of Sherkin. The crew of 10 were saved by Heir Island fishermen. See page 87.

20 The *Ailsawald* went on the rocks near Dreolán Point in Sherkin. The crew was saved. The ship was pulled off the rocks and was repaired on Giornán Point on Heir. See page 88.

21 Three Heir Island fishermen were drowned in Roaringwater Bay on December 17th 1904. They were returning with a boatload of willow rods from Ballydehob. See Chapter 15.

22 The *Savonia* was wrecked on the Middle Calf Island in 1909. Her cargo of timber floated all over the bay. See page 91.

23. In late December 1916, the steamer *Alondra* struck the Kedge Rock. Twenty three of the crew were rescued; fifteen were drowned. The Hartes and Cahalanes of Heir assisted in the rescue. See page 92.

24 A Leyland Liner, the 6000 tons *Nestorian* went on the rocks on the South-West side of Cape Clear on New Year's Day 1917. See page 93.

25 The following day, the Cahalanes and Hartes helped to save the Norwegian barque, *Saurnaut*, which went on the rocks at Toe Head. See page 94.

26 The fishing boat, *Thomas Joseph*, went aground on the Catalogues Rocks north of Sherkin Island on October 10th, 1918. Five of the passengers were rescued by Heir Island Fishermen. See page 97.

27 On November 19th, four Cape Clear fishermen were blown into eternity when their boat, The *Roving Swan*, hit a floating mine outside North Harbour, Cape Clear. John Cadogan, Michael B. Cadogan, Patrick Molloy and Hugh Daly (brother of John, skipper of the *Thomas Joseph*), were killed. The owner, Michael Bill Cadogan made a miraculous escape.

28 In 1922, the *St. Brigid*, of Baltimore went on a reef between Heir Island and Cunnamore. The vessel was in the charge of Captain Taylor. Ever since this reef has been called Taylor's Rock. See page 99.

29. On Sunday 24th September, 1939 an English cargo ship, the *Hazelside*, was sunk by a German submarine the U.31. The Cape Clear boat, the *St. Ultan*, rescued 23 members of the crew, while eight others including Captain Davies, were lost.

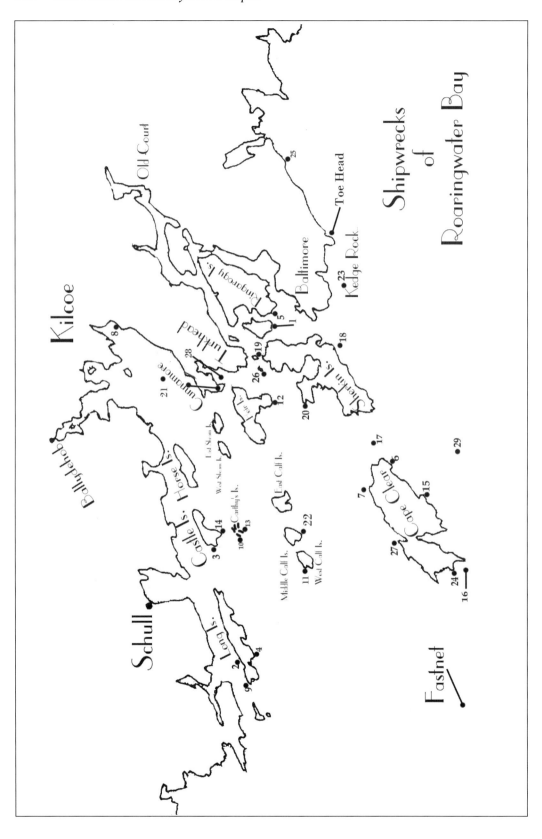

Shipwrecks
of
Roaringwater Bay

— 15 —

Tragedy and Heroism in

Roaringwater Bay

On Tuesday morning, December 13th, 1904, five Heir Islandmen left the Reen of Heir to cut willow rods in the Skeaghanore area near Ballydehob and to buy provisions in the village. The youngest of the five, Cornelius O'Driscoll, aged 23, missed the departure, but he ran to Giornán Point, the north east point of the island, opposite Cunnamore, where he was taken on board. The other four crew members were Cornelius Cahalane, John Harte and his brother Daniel, aged 23, and Denis O'Neill, aged 50 the oldest, a married man with a family.

After mooring their 25ft. yawl at Skeaghanore, they spent the day cutting rods in the area. Some of them went to Ballydehob to buy provisions. Cornelius O'Driscoll bought a grandfather clock which he had promised to buy for this mother. Eventually the boat was loaded with 'withies'[1] and they set out for Heir Island between four and five o'clock. The weather had a threatening appearance with heavy rain clouds and a rising S.E. wind. They kept to the shelter of the land for some time and made several tacks before getting out into Roaringwater Bay. When they were in the vicinity of Ilaunrahanee (Oileán Raithní, island of the ferns), north of Rincolisky (Whitehall) Castle, a sudden squall hit the sails and the boat keeled over. The upturned boat, with the five men clinging to it, was being blown away from the land.

> The wind was increasing, the darkness becoming thicker; the breakers rose and buffeted the boat, lifting the despairing men up on the crest of a wave and then dashing them down again, sometimes losing their slender hold, quickly causing them to exhaust their strength.[2]

They all clung to the upturned yawl for some time, calling for help, hoping against hope, that someone might hear their desperate calls above the roaring of the wind and the sea. As they drifted out the bay driven by the south east wind, Cahalane, the only swimmer among them, decided that their chances of being heard were very slim. He made a decision to attempt to swim ashore while he still had his strength.[3] He cut off his leather boots with a knife, threw off his coat and bade farewell to his companions, who began to say the Rosary. The boots worn by fishermen at that time were made of 'kip'[4] leather and were very heavy. The *Southern Star* describes what happened next.

> Cornelius Cahalane struck out boldly for the shore, about two miles distant from where the accident occurred, and succeeded, after a desperate struggle in the rain and sleet and in a high sea and boisterous waters, in reaching the shore. He was three hours in the water and was completely exhausted.

He crawled up the slope, until he reached the house where Mrs. Whooley of Whitehall now lives. It was then Whitehall Lodge and was occupied at the time by Mrs. Doran. Having told his terrible tale, a boat was launched from Cunnamore Point. Cliffy Minihane, of Cunnamore, remembers his father telling him that the rescue boat belonged to the Minihanes and was manned by Jerry Desmond, Tim O'Donovan, Denis Minihane and Dan Sheehan. Cornelius Cahalane recovered sufficiently to go with them in the boat. Dan Sheehan who lived in Whitehall, must have taken him to Cunnamore. After searching around for some time, they came upon the upturned boat and found only one man, John Harte, clinging to the gunnel of the upturned boat. He had a 'deadman's hold' on the gunnel (gunwhale) and the rescuers found it difficult to release his grip. The others, unable to hold on, had drowned.

While Neillus Cahalane was desperately swimming towards the shore, the men's cries were heard in Kilkilleen. That same day James Coughlan and his crew had been dredging leoithín[5] in the bay. Having landed their cargo of seaweed, they got help to pull up their yawl high as they saw the weather was worsening. After changing their clothes and eating a meal, they sat around the fire. They thought they heard distant cries for help. They ran to their boat but it took them an hour to get her afloat as their helpers had all gone home. Rowing out into the rough bay, they searched in the darkness, but heard no further calls. Hoping that the cries they had heard from their kitchen were seal cries, they returned home.

The *Southern Star* report states that,

> every effort was made to try and ascertain the whereabouts of the other unfortunate men, but without effect, and the rescue boats and their crew pulled away from the scene with sad hearts, having on board only the heroic Cornelius Cahalane and John Harte. Bitter tears crept into strong men's eyes that seldom wept when they found that some whom they loved in life and with whom they were closely associated had so suddenly gone into eternity.

Fr. O'Sullivan, P.P. Aughadown told the reporter that the boat, being a sailing yawl, would have had little ballast, which probably contributed to the boat being overturned.[6]

John Harte was brought home in such an exhausted condition that fears were entertained for his life and he was anointed the following day by Rev. Fr. O'Sullivan. The following day, Timothy Harte, walked to Skibbereen to get medical help for his brother who was 'in a dying state'. He was interviewed by a Southern Star reporter, to whom he gave particulars of the horrific night. John Harte's shins had been cut to the bone by the rocking of the boat in the storm. He spent about six months in hospital. However, he made a full recovery, and as we saw in the previous chapter, played a heroic part in several sea rescues.

All the boats of Heir, Cunnamore, Skeams and Kilkilleen went out the following day dragging the sea, under the direction of Fr. O'Sullivan, to try to recover the bodies of the drowned men. The search continued for three weeks but it wasn't until about noon on Sunday, January 8th, that the body of Denis O'Neill was washed ashore on Kilkilleen strand. The body of Daniel Harte was found the following morning about 10 o'clock and Cornelius O'Driscoll later.[7]

The funeral of Denis O'Neill took place from Heir Island on Monday 9th for Creagh, Baltimore. The Eagle describes the funeral thus:

> There were from a dozen to twenty boats in single file in the funeral procession. The boats were each about a perch[8] apart and all were connected by ropes. In the first boat was placed the coffin, accompanied by the officiating clergymen, the Rev. Fr. O'Sullivan, P.P. Aughadown, Rev. J.J. O'Hea, C.C. and the family of the deceased.[9]

The coffin was taken from Cuaisín na gCorp (the little cove of the corpses), south of the pier on Heir Island East and was landed on Inane Point in Ringaroga. It was shouldered from there to Creagh graveyard. Daniel Harte was buried on Tuesday, January 10th 1905 in Aughadown.

Richard O'Driscoll of Ardnagroghery, Church Cross, a member of Skibbereen Rural District Council, made repeated appeals to the Congested Districts Board for the erection of a pier at Kilkilleen, as there was no place of safety in Roaringwater Bay or Rincolisky harbour. In a letter to the Eagle he wrote, 'There are seven boats here (Kilkilleen) built by a loan from the Board of Fishery. In summer they are engaged in fishing and in winter in dredging manure in the bay for the land'

The *Skibbereen Eagle* gave an account of the quarterly meeting of Skibbereen Rural District Council. Under the sub-heading, 'Hare Island Hero, Cornelius Cahalane', we read that Mr. R. O'Driscoll of Ardnagrohery described the tragic drowning and appealed for some recognition to be given to Cornelius Cahalane for his bravery. O'Driscoll said,

> with regard to the disaster which occurred off this place (Kilkilleen) when that brave boy, Cornelius Cahalane, struggled for two hours and a half, amidst the roaring breakers, in the teeth of wind and rain and the inky darkness of the night, endeavouring to swim ashore to secure help and aid for those he left clinging on to the upturned boat – he was the sole means of securing aid to save the one man that was rescued and that he (Mr. O'Driscoll) did not think he was exceeding his duty as District Councillor to ask the clerk to bring the action of Cahalane under the notice of the Royal Humane Society.[10]

Despite Mr. O'Driscoll's efforts, Cahalane never got official recognition for his incredible deed of bravery.

Cornelius O'Driscoll did buy the clock for his mother, but sadly it went to the deep on that awful night. However, sometime in 1905, the family bought a replacement clock to honour his memory and it is still working to this day in the home of his niece, Mrs. Bridie Fitzgerald (nee O'Driscoll) of Riverdale, Skibbereen.

The tragedy cast a gloom on the closely-knit community where people de-pended so much on each other. The death of two young men in their prime and of the older man, who left a wife and a family, numbed the islanders and their friends on the mainland. According to parish records, there were no Heir Island marriages the following year, 1905, although there were several in the preceding and subsequent years.

The Cahalane brothers, Michael and 'Neilus were famous for their courage, strength and determination. Unusual for island people, they were good swim-mers. Neilus displayed his enormous strength and willpower on that fateful night, Tuesday, December, 13th, 1904. On other occasions, it is said, he swam out to sea to recover baulks of timber floating in the water. Born in 1870, he died in the early 1920s, in his mid fifties. His brother, Michael, who lived to be eighty one, had many nicknames including 'Stormy Mike' because he often went to sea in rough weather when other more sensible fishermen wouldn't dare leave the shore. He was also known for his massive large hands. He fell in love with Maggie Newman from Goleen. A Manxman was in competition with him for her hand in marriage. After Mass in Goleen one Sunday, Cahalane and the Manxman had a fistfight to sort out the matter. Apparently the Manxman was a good match for Cahalane, but not good enough, as Mike eventually beat him. It is said that the Newman family was against her marrying this full-blooded is-landman of little wealth, and persuaded her to emigrate. When she was being driven by her brother in a horse and trap to Skibbereen, to take the train to Cobh, they were stopped at Ballydehob by Mike. Maggie changed her mind and married Mike, with whom she had eleven children. Sadly, Maggie died, giving birth to her last child.[11]

ROARINGWATER BAY SHOWING WHITEHALL CASTLE NEAR WHERE CORNELIIUS CAHALANE
CAME ASHORE ON THAT FATEFUL NIGHT IN 1904

Photo: Kathleen. Daly

Some years later, also in the month of December, John Harte was herring-fishing in Roaringwater Bay, close to where he had nearly lost his life. The crew thought they heard cries in the distance but dismissed them, thinking they were the cries of seals. However, John Harte, who could recall vividly the awful night of December 13th 1904, when he came so close to death and lost a brother, a father-in-law and a neighbour, steered the boat in the direction from which the cries were coming. He found an upturned yawl with two exhausted men clinging on for dear life. The two men, Mike O'Neill and his son, Charlie, had been in the Ballydehob area, cutting withies, just as he and his companions had, in 1904. The carpenter, Denis O'Driscoll, had made a new donkey cart for them, so they loaded the cart on the yawl with the withies. Sailing back across the open bay, a gust of wind hit the boat; the shafts of the cart dragged in the water and overturned her. By the time they were rescued, they were completely exhausted and wouldn't have survived much longer.[12]

The Cahalanes and Hartes were involved in several sea rescues in the following years, most notably, The *Alondra,* The *Saurnaut,* The *Nestorian.* John Harte was awarded a silver medal for bravery for his part in the rescue of five people from the fishing boat, *Thomas Joseph* in 1918 He left Heir and settled in Laheratanvally in Aughadown parish, where his descendants still live.

SAFE RETURN S.198. BOUGHT BY CON MINIHANE, HEIR ISLAND IN 1948. SHE WAS SOLD TO TIMMY MCCARTHY, PARIS WHO OWNED HER UNTIL 1978.

HEIR LOBSTERMEN

In the era before radar
or radio mast,
Heir Island yawls sailed into every cuas
from the Kedge to Ardmore
seeking the blue-armoured rock denizens.
With towel-sail shelters,
breakers of drinking water,
bastable cakes and salted mackerel,
they shot their lobster pots by rock and row,
where their ancestors had fished before them.

Shallows and skerries they memorised
like psalm-verses. Seaweed forests
shone in the clear water. In warm July
the sea swarmed with jelly-fish
drifting like flowers after a sea-burial.
Gulls circled and screamed in white arcs.

Long summer nights under a net of stars,
the salt tang of the sea in their nostrils,
awakening at all hours to lift
the dripping pots, fashioned in winter
from sally rods cut in Greenmount or Skeaghanore.
They measured time by the tides,
tasted the honeysuckle of the sea,
knew its changing moods,
its power, its beauty, its timelessness.

Bronzed hardened men,
hands calloused by rope and fish-fin,
they smoked their pipes,
ate a simple diet of fish and bread.
In late August the sails yearned westwards
when the sea began to growl.
The yawls pulled high on the grass
as the days shortened.

Musical boat names:
Hanorah, Swan, Star of the Sea,
The Safe Return
dancing on the waves like a seagull.

They rest now, those vivid men – Neilus Cahalane and Peter Cotter,
Dan Harte, Mike the Cloud, Tim Carroll –
to name a few –
in Aughadown graveyard
by the sparkling Ilen river.

Eugene Daly

Photo: Kathleen Daly

PARIS FROM THE BRIDGE

Photo: Kathleen Daly

Trá na Pailíse

VIEW FROM 'PARIS'

Photo: Kathleen Daly

Photo: Kathleen Daly

PENAL MASS ROCK OVERLOOKING
THE REEN

Photo: Kathleen Daly

HEIR ISLAND WEST – CUAS A DÚNA

EAST CALF ISLAND

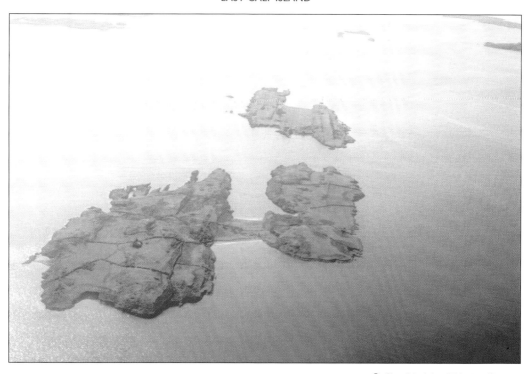

EAST AND WEST SKEAM

Photo: Kathleen Daly

OLD STEPS IN HEIR ISLAND EAST WHICH WERE CHISELLED OUT AS A LANDING PLACE
IN THE 19TH CENTURY OR EARLIER

Photo Kathleen Daly

BOLLÁN POINT ON THE SOUTH-WEST CORNER OF THE REEN WITH CAPE CLEAR IN THE DISTANCE

Photo: Kathleen Daly

TRÁ BAIRNEACH – SEA SPINACH AND
BARRAMÓTA (WORMWOOD)

Photo: Séamas Ó Máille

SOW THISTLE ON THE TRÁ BÁN

Photo: Kathleen Daly

LICHENED WALL ON THE ROAD
TO 'LEAN GAMHAN

Photo: Seamas Ó Máille

MAIDENHAIR SPLEENWORT ON HEIR ISLAND
NATIONAL SCHOOL WALL

Photo: Christine Thery

WHALES BEACHED ON HEIR ISLAND

© Mary Jordan

THE FIONN, FIRST OF THE NEW YAWLS BUILT BY HEGARTYS OF OLDCOURT FOR
COLM Ó CUILLEANÁIN AND MARY JORDAN

Photo: Kathleen Daly

A YOUNG DAN PYBURN ON THE WALL OF THE BÁN FIELD

JOHN AND FLORRIE FITZGERALD AND WILLIE HINGSTON ON THEIR WAY BACK TO HEIR ISLAND PIER, SUMMER 1958, AFTER A TRIP LOBSTERING NEAR KINSALE

THE *AILEEN*, S726, AT HEIR ISLAND SLIP. CAPTAIN, JOHN FITZGERALD, CREW FLORRIE FITZGERALD AND WILLIE HINGSTON, CUNNAMORE

PRE 1928 HOUSE OPPOSITE 'LEAN GAMHAIN
(NOW DEMOLISHED)

MCCARTHY'S HOUSE IN PARIS – ADDITION
BUILT IN 1928

PYBURN'S HOUSE IN PARIS; ONE OF THE
TWO-STOREY HOUSES REPAIRED IN 1928

MICHAEL McCARTHY'S HOUSE IN PARIS,
NOW FEWER'S

TRADITIONAL HEARTH, SHOWING TWO CUBBY
HOLES ON EITHER SIDE OF FIRE, BELLOWS AND
CLEVVY OVER THE FIRE

INTERIOR OF A TRADITIONAL HEIR ISLAND HOME, THE CENTRE PIECE BEING
THE DRESSER WITH ITS DELPH

CUPBOARD

LADDER LEADING TO UPSTAIRS BEDROOM

Photo: Peggy Townend

LIZZIE MINIHANE

Photo: Peggy Townend

DAN McCARTHY

Photo: Frank Dawe

NELL McCARTHY

Photo: Peggy Townend

NEILLY O'DONOVAN

© John Merwick

BLESSING OF CILLÍN –
AUGUST 24TH, 2003

© John Merwick

MARIA HARTE
SINGING DURING
THE MASS AT
CILLÍN – AUGUST
24TH, 2003

Photo: Kathleen Daly

AFTER MASS IN HEIR ISLAND
ON ST. PATRICK'S DAY 2000

PYBURN FAMILY ENJOYING A TEA BREAK IN THE HAYFIELD

JOHN DENIS McCARTHY IN THE HAGGARD WITH HIS SON
DENIS AND DAUGHTER TERESA

GROUP TAKEN IN MURPHY'S HOUSE, HEIR ISLAND WEST ON THE VISIT
FROM THE U.S.A. OF BEATRICE BRIGHAM (2nd from left, front)
Also included in the picture are Maggie 'Merchant' McCarthy, Kit O'Neill, Nora Murphy, John O'Neill,
Mary McCarthy, Timothy John Cadogan, Ardagh and Katie and Paddy Collins, Lissaree

Photo: Mary Kacin

PADDY JOE MURPHY,
NORA MURPHY, KIT MURPHY,
PEGGY O'DONOVAN AND
HANNAH HARTE (NEE
McCARTHY)

Photo: Mary Kacin

MARGARET O'DONOVAN,
HEIR ISLAND WEST,
RICHIE PYBURN, PEGGY, TIMMY AND
JOHN O'DONOVAN

TERESA PYBURN

Left: JACK PYBURN HOLDING HIS
GRANDFATHER'S ADZE

HARTE FAMILY, HEIR ISLAND WEST
Back, Danny, Kate, Michael;
Front, Mary, Finbarr, Rita

'BABY' BURKE, KATE HARTE,
KIT O'NEILL AND BRIDIE AND
MARY FITZGERALD

© Denis O'Driscoll

AFTER MASS, ST. PATRICK'S DAY, 2000

Photo: Kathleen Daly

HEIR ISLAND REGATTA, REEN, HEIR ISLAND, AUGUST, 2001

BRIDGE AT TWILIGHT

Photo: Kathleen Daly

HEIR ISLAND NEW PIER

Photo: Kathleen Daly

THE *LAVENEER S*. 1055, PHOTOGRAPHED NEAR THE SLIP
IN HEIR ISLAND EAST SOMETIME IN THE 1940s.

Built in the 1890s, or early 1900s, probably by Willie Skinner of Baltimore, she was a strongly built boat. She was owned by Michael (Mikeen) O'Neill of Heir Island East, who is the man with the hat standing in front of the main thauft, usually called the 'fore-sheets'. His son, Patsy, wearing a cap, is standing in the 'holt', the area between the main thauft and the aft thauft. He is holding an oar. Florence (Florrie) Fitzgerald is standing near the stern or stern sheets as they were called, the part of the boat behind the aft thauft. The boat is full of the old style withie lobster pots.

MRS KATE HARTE, EAST SKEAM, WITH HER SON
CON, PROUDLY DISPLAYING THE MODEL YAWL
MADE FOR HIM BY HIS FATHER PATTIE

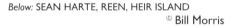

Below: SEAN HARTE, REEN, HEIR ISLAND
© Bill Morris

JOHN O'DONOVAN
AT THE BRIDGE
© Bill Morris

© Bill Morris
JOHN FITZGERALD WITH HIS SONS
FLORENCE JNR AND JOHN JOE

DANNY O'NEILL, HEIR ISLAND

DAN MINIHANE, HEIR ISLAND
AND KINSALE

CON HARTE HOLDING HIS NUMBER
GOING 'STEAMBOATING'

— 16 —
The Sea

For generations fishing was the primary source of income in the islands of Roaringwater Bay. From the Middle Ages fishermen from France, Spain and Portugal, from many parts of Britain, especially the Isle of Man and Cornwall, frequented the south-west coast in search of the rich fishing harvest. This connection is evidenced in local placenames, like Spanish Island, near Baltimore. On Heir Island on the west side of the Reen is Tráigín na Spáinneach (the little strand of the Spaniards) and Cuaisín na bhFranncach (the little cove of the Frenchmen). The little village of houses in Whitehall, which consisted of fourteen houses, now gone, was known as Scilly, presumably after the Scilly Isles off Cornwall. There was a shop here run by Maggie Sheehan, where the fishermen could buy their provisions. Many boats anchored in Whitehall during the winter in the early part of the 20th century, particularly boats from Cape Clear, as Trá Chiaráin harbour was not large enough to hold the large fleet of Cape boats.[1]

In the 1890s The *Skibbereen Eagle*, in a report describing the conditions in Carbery's Hundred Isles, stated,

> With the exception of Horse Island, which is purely agricultural, the inhabitants of the islands maintain themselves chiefly from fishing, and the majority of them are living on the hand to mouth principle. The failure of the fishing for one season means semi-starvation .... Another matter that should be attended to is the boats in which the hardy islanders earn their living. Cape Clear is fairly well equipped with mackerel boats. The other islands, however, can boast of but very few of these crafts, and a judicious system of loans could be put into force for the purpose of enabling fishermen to procure boats .... But the parties who need assistance more than any others in the matters of boats are the lobster fishermen of Hare Island, the most industrious and daring men to be found on the south coast. Every year after the conclusion of the mackerel fishing, between sixty and seventy Hare Islanders depart for a four-month expedition in search of lobsters. The men work in open boats, the yawls being about twenty feet in length. Three men go in each boat, and here they live and sleep in the open air for months at a time, cooking their meagre victuals in a small fireplace arranged on board and sleeping in their clothes. A month elapses sometimes before these men change their garments. They work along the coast from Ballycotton to Dursey Island and in all sorts of weather they are to be seen at their hazardous and not too prosperous calling. They have to run back to Baltimore with their catches, and here the cutters meet them for conveying the lobster to the markets.[2]

Heir Island Lobstermen

The eternal sea, in its many moods, bounteous, dangerous, inevitably has played a central role in the island's life. The fishermen of Roaringwater Bay's islands and the coastline of Aughadown South, but especially the Heir Islanders, will be forever associated with lobster fishing. They fished for lobster and crayfish in every cove, near every rock and skerry from Dursey to Dungarvan for at least a century. Their small open yawls were distinctive and exclusive to the coast of south west Cork.

DUNGARVAN QUAY IN 1903 WITH TOWELSAIL YAWL TIED UP FURTHEST FROM QUAY
© Dungarvan Museum

When all the crops had been sat, they set off in early May The yawls, which had been hauled up during the winter, were relaunched; they were allowed to sink and soak in the salt water, which expanded the planks, which had shrunk while out of the water. After several days soaking, they were baled out, leaks repaired, ballasted and rigged. They set off in groups of two or three, each boat manned by a crew of three. They fished until September or later, depending on the weather, returning for a few days every three to four weeks to attend to work on their small farms. Mostly they fished eastwards from Baltimore to Cobh and sometimes further. The only shelter they had was the teamhal[3] (pronounced towel) sail. The towel, made of calico or canvas, called boffity or baft,[4] was a kind of tent at the bow of the boat. It was draped across an oar or boat-hook, one end one end of which rested on the prow, with the other end tied to the mast at a height of about five feet. Here they slept on bags of hay, sheltered from the elements.

PHOTOGRAPH TAKEN IN CASTLETOWNBERE IN 1913
Spillane Collection © National Library of Ireland

At the mouth of the 'towel' they had a large cast-iron bastable 'fire pot' set in white clay, under which was a flat stone. A fire of coal and wood was lit in this. A second bastable was placed in the fire-pot; in this they baked their cakes, which was their basic diet, two cakes for each of the three meals. They also boiled potatoes, mackerel, wrasse (connor), pollock or bream, caught by hand lines. The tea was brewed in the kettle. As the twentieth century progressed, their diet improved and became more varied, with tea, sugar, 'shop' bread, rashers, sausages, bacon, baking soda, condensed milk etc becoming available.

On board the yawl, usually about 26 ft in length, six to seven feet wide and about three feet in depth, they lived for the fishing season, coming ashore during the week only to get fresh water, firewood or sour milk from friends. The lobster boats were completely open, except for a short foredeck, under which was a locker. They had two thwarts, referred to in West Cork as 'thaufts'. The area between the two thaufts was the hold, locally called the 'holt'. In the early boats, the holt was never floored. It contained the ballast, which consisted of heavy hard black stones, levelled off with smaller ones. White stones were considered unlucky and were never used as ballast. A removable plank covered the 'well', which was the deepest part of the bilge. The boats were powered by a gaff-rigged mainsail and a foresail. In later years some of the boats also carried a jib. The full regalia of mainsail, foresail, jib, and topsail was used in the yawl races at the regattas and during long voyages. The boats were coated with Stockholm tar, inside and outside, below the waterline. The topsides were usually painted.

The pots were hauled every two hours during the day. The biggest catches were usually with the morning 'change' and at nightfall with the evening 'change'.[5] When hauling the pots, two men rowed the boat along the line of the pots, while the third man hauled. He removed the lobster or crayfish, if there was one in the pot, and rebaited the pot if necessary. Crabs were considered a nuisance because they ate the bait and strangely there was no market for them then. The male crabs were killed; the females were returned to the deep because their claws resembled Our Lady's fingers. Willie Hingston, who fished in the *Aileen* with Florence and John Fitzgerald, is remembered as being so gentle that he would never crush crabs or little fish but would carefully put them all back in the sea. At night the pots were 'shot' in more sheltered waters. When the pots were hauled, they moved on, during the day, to another good fishing ground, which might be an offshore rock or reef, referred to by their Irish names of rabha or builg.[6] Hauling in deep water was very difficult work because two or three pots would be off the seabed at one time. The lobsters were kept alive in two wicker baskets, which were kept submerged while the boat was at anchor, tied to the sides of the boat. If they had a good week's fishing, the extra lobsters were kept in jute bags, hanging from the side of the yawl. At night they anchored their boats in a sheltered cove or cuas. They were known all along the coast. Miss Eileen Hayes of Reenogreena, Glandore, remembers them sheltering in Cuan Seasca (Siege Cove), east of Glandore. Pat Joe Harrington of Galley Head remembers them sheltering in Cuas a Bháid, east of the Galley. They used to land here for water. Mrs. Harrington, Pat Joe's mother, used to give them sour milk to make their cakes. They knew every well along the coast; fresh drinking water was essential.

The Congested District Board's baseline report for 1892 lists forty lobster yawls among the two hundred and eleven boats registered in Baltimore. The majority of the lobster yawls were from Heir Island, with two from the West Skeam, and the rest from Aughadown south, principally Fásagh, Collatrum, Poulnacallee, Turkhead, Ardagh, Whitehall, Cunnamore, and Kilkilleen. This unique type of yawl, with its gaff-rigged mainsail, was confined to the coastal townlands of Aughadown South but centred in Heir Island. They were known as the 'Heir Islanders' even though they might have come from Aughadown or some of the other islands, so synonymous had Heir Island become with these unique towel-sail yawls. In Glandore they were known as 'na potaeirí' – the potters. Up to the 1940s, these boats dominated the lobster fishing of the south-west coast. Jimmy Rooney of Ardmore, Co. Waterford, remembered 'the men from Heir Island in West Cork coming fishing lobsters for Fred Keane and seeing them baking bread in pot ovens over some kind of stove in the boat. The only shelter they had was the sails.'

The crews 'worked' their pots from Monday morning until the following Sunday morning. They kept their 'good' clothes in the locker under the towel, and when they landed in Kinsale or Cobh on Sunday, they went to Mass, sold the week's catch, bought some food and tobacco and relaxed in a pub for a few hours. In Cobh, they called into the 'Holyground' or English's Pub. In later years they came ashore on Saturday evening and had two nights tied up at the pier. The weekend was a time to relax after a long hard week; there was time for camaraderie, singing and story-telling. In Cobh the lobsters were bought by Clayton Love, who also had an agent in Kinsale. In later years, the boats didn't have to go to these ports; the fish buyers, like Jeremiah McSweeney of Baltimore, came to them. Clayon Love, Junior, recalls, 'As a young man in Cobh my first and abiding memory was to see these extraordinary boats and the men manning them having sailed all the way from Heir Island.'

Dan Minihane of Heir, who settled in Kinsale in 1960, in conversation with Mr. John Thulier, stated:

> The Pyburn family from the island built boats known for their running ability as the wind freshened. Not as good to windward as the Skinner boats. They were gaff-rigged and carried three sails. Often the wind running up from the west could be very pleasant during the summer. They were open boats and operated during the summer only. They had a crew of three, with a pot for a fire, lit in a pot in the bilge started with a bellows .... The boats fished 24 pots with 14 fathom of rope between them. Crew slept on hay, which was kept dry when sailing, with a towel sheet. Pots were always shot in 'foul ground' (seaweeds), often as far east as Blonde Head. At night, canvas stretched over a boom, provided some shelter. In Cobh, Loves bought for the liners. Danny Wilson in Kinsale collected for O'Driscolls of Baltimore. I remember being paid ten shillings for a dozen lobsters.[7]

Con Harte, who now lives in Melbourne, Australia and formerly of East Skeam remembers,

> They were hard times in the 1940s but people were happy. Lobsters were one pound per dozen. The living in the lobster yawls was rough, sleeping on a bed of hay or straw for six or seven weeks. When we got back home, they could smell you a mile away. No luxury in those days, only the coal fire and the smoke cutting the eyes out of you. Yet it didn't worry us.

Con remembered his father saying that one calm day they had to return home to Heir Island and he rowed non stop from the Head of Kinsale to Baltimore Pier. He finished up with his hands badly blistered. Another day when they were lobster fishing down at Cobh, he and another islander pulled up alongside a passenger liner to sell some lobsters and the young man stowed away on board to get to New York.

Each boat carried a 'train' of between 24 and 30 lobster pots, each pot tied to the next with a rope, called the badhilsgith (pronounced boil-skith), about 14 fathoms apart. Each pot was ballasted with two stones tied to the base on the inside and carried three pieces of salted mackerel as bait, which were tied to the mouth of the pot on the inside.

Every square inch of the boats was utilized. As well as the 'train' of pots, they had to carry a lot of other miscellaneous equipment – the bastables, a sack of flour, a bag of coal, the barrel for fresh water, which was called 'the keeler', two wicker baskets for holding the lobsters and crayfish, oars, anchor, a large earthenware vessel for holding milk, ropes, bailers, etc.

Inherited knowledge of the coastline, of weather signs, of the habits of the lobster, helped generations of fishermen. They had an intimate knowledge of the tides, the currents, of submerged builgs and rabhas (rows), which were located by aligning sets of landmarks. With no navigational aids, watches or lights, they coped. By careful and constant observation of their environment, they could forecast the weather. The sky, the moon, the stars, the sun, the swells, the sounds and appearance of the sea, the behaviour of sea birds and sea mammals – all were observed and 'read'. Not only was the success of their fishing dependant on this inherited wisdom, their lives at times depended on it. Most had a deep faith in the power of God; they believed in the protective power of Holy water, a bottle of which they always carried on board. Their beliefs went beyond religion to a deeper belief in signs and portents of 'good luck' or its opposite. Bad luck followed the sighting of a pig, a hare, a fox, or a red-haired woman. On board the yawl, it was considered unlucky to refer to any four-legged animal; one dared not whistle, or mention a priest; you did not stick a knife in the mast.

TWO FISHES: JEREMIAH MCCARTHY, PATSY MURPHY, DANNY HARTE, DANNY O'NEILL

With the weather becoming unpredictable after the autumn equinox, the lobstermen tended to fish locally at the end of the biaste.[8] In Cape they used to say: 'Téann an diabhal san fharraige tar éis Lá San Mhichíl, the devil goes in the sea after Michelmas (September 29th).'[9] They fished locally for 'Fall' mackerel and herring. Shoals of herring filled every part of Roaringwater Bay, even right up under Whitehall house. They 'shot' their nets just after dark, hauled at dawn and often spent the day picking periwinkles. The presence of large shoals of herrings was indicated by a type of seaweed called corraí, floating on the surface of the sea, having been agitated by the large shoals. Every type of boat was used for herring fishing, from punts to drifters. The Sands between Heir and Sherkin and the 'Éanach, west of Sherkin, were particularly good herring grounds. Sometimes the shoals of herring came right up to Whitehall House.

Around the end of November or early December, weather depending; the lobsterboats were finally pulled up above the high water mark for the rest of the winter. On Heir it took two days to haul up all the boats, the whole community 'comharing', (helping each other). The sails, rigging, masts, ballast and other gear having been removed; they hauled them up manually with the help of rollers and propped them in an upright position. The boats were hauled up in sheltered locations, near the bridge in Paris, near Burke's Shop, on Giornán Point, on the north Reen and on the south Reen. Ricky O'Regans's two West Skeam yawls were pulled up in Paris, Heir, as there are no sheltered coves on West Skeam.

There was a continuity about the lobster fishing methods and type of boat used for a least a century; it would appear the typical Heir Island towel sail yawl was used from Famine Times, (1845–49) or even prior to that, down to the Second World War. The yawls, light with beautiful lines, were ideal for sailing, suitable for narrow coves and inlets, light enough also for rowing. In the early decades of the 20th century there was a continual decline in the population of Heir and the other islands. However, there was a fleet of twenty five lobster boats still operating out of Heir in the early 1930s. Eleven lobster boats took part in the yawl race at Baltimore Regatta in 1934.[10] By the late 1930s the Calf Islands had been abandoned, West Skeam in 1940 and East Skeam in 1958. With the onset of World War Two, there was a slump in the demand for lobsters and crayfish. The fleet was reduced drastically in size. There was increased demand for more common fish, herring, mackerel and dogfish, and many of the boats, which had been drawn high and dry and neglected, were repaired and put to sea again. There had been no market for dog fish up to the war and now they got 15 shilling a stone for them. Some of the lobster boats were sold to new owners, who refashioned them, fitted them with engines and used them to fish for dogfish or to draw sand and seaweed, which were in great demand due to the absence of artificial fertilisers during the war. Some Heir islanders, who hadn't sold their yawls, continued lobstering on a reduced scale, supplementing their earnings with long-lining and fishing for mackerel and herring.

The fishing industry, like everything else, was in dire straits after the Famine. But matters improved gradually and by the 1870s English fish merchants were sending boats to the south coast of Ireland to buy lobsters and crayfish. It is almost certain that it was these English fish-buyers who introduced the wickerwork lobsterpots to Roaringwater Bay. The tradition of making this type of pot was long established in Cornwall, where they are still made today, mostly for ornamental use. It would appear that it was the Heir Islanders who, initially, learned to make this type of pot, the fishermen from the mainland and other islands learning from them.

The Lobster Pots

The hand-woven willow pots were works of art, taking great skill and patience to fashion. The pot's mouth or 'chimney' was formed first with about eleven stout rods and put on a 'stand' to hold them firmly in place. Then about 33 'bars', the ribs of

the pot, were added. The pot was bound together with a twisted spiral of willow. There was a strong thick spiral at the base, three of four other spirals (or 'wales') at equal intervals and finally the top. These thick spirals were called buinnes: the buinne cúil was the foundation layer and the buinne béil, the rim. Two buffer layers were placed around the base which helped to stop the pot from chafing on the sea floor. Finally the base was woven and a spiked rod pushed horizontally through the 'navel' in the centre of the base to hold the pot together. Two weighty stones were lashed in with thickish twine; these were to keep the pot from rolling or turning over on the sea bed. Most pots lasted only a year, so new ones had to be made each winter with 'withies' cut

mainly around Ballydehob, but also in Ringaroga.

In the late 1940s the fishermen were getting only sixteen shillings per dozen for lobsters and about a pound for crayfish. In the early 1950s prices began to rise again due to increased demand and competition between buyers. The price

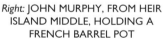

Left: JIM 'CON' MCCARTHY HOLDING A WITHIE LOBSTER POT OUTSIDE HIS HOUSE IN PARIS

Right: JOHN MURPHY, FROM HEIR ISLAND MIDDLE, HOLDING A FRENCH BARREL POT

shot up to £2 per dozen for lobsters. The era of the towel-sail yawls was over, however. Some had rotted, some had been sold as pleasure craft, others were converted with raised gunnels and fo'c'sle, and motor driven, usually by a Kelvin 13/15. Among the yawls converted and fitted with engines were *The Pride of Toe Head,* owned by Neilly O'Donovan, *The Safe Return,* owned by Con Minihane, and John O'Donovan's V*aletta.*

As the old yawls disappeared, they were no longer replaced with the traditional towelsail yawls. Most of the new boats had cabins where the men slept. Instead of a bastable pot, they used a primus for cooking.

New French barrel-pots replaced the old withy pots. The Hegarty, boatbuilders, of Oldcourt were the first to make the barrel pots locally. The towel-sail yawls disappeared, rotted on strands; some ended their lives as roofs on hen houses or other chambers. From the early 1950s, as lobster fishing became more lucrative, it was no longer dominated by Heir Island boats. The whole coast was dotted with lobster pots, fished from a variety of boats, from punts to 40 foot boats.

The Lobster Pond

Large English and French 'cutters' had for years fished for lobster and crayfish off the south-west coast. Up to sixty feet in length, they could carry up to five ton of fish in their wells so they did not have to rush to market every week. One of these Frenchmen, Pierre Trehiou, opened a lobster pond in Crookhaven. He collected lobsters along the coast from Crookhaven to Carrigaholt, near Loop Head in Co. Clare, stored them in his pond and shipped them out to France. He also bought lobsters from the Blasket Islanders. For export to England, the lobsters were packed in boxes with sawdust and ice, transported by lorry to the railway station at Schull or Skibbereen. The Skibbereen to Schull train, or 'tram' as it was called, was in operation from 1886 to 1947. It was Trehiou who introduced the French barrel pots, which were much more efficient than the old withie pots, for catching crayfish. The laths were imported from France and the buyers sold them to the fishermen. The construction was quick and simple and the art of making traditional pots was gradually forgotten. No longer did they have to go cutting the 'rods' on winter days. Probably the last man making the 'old' pots was the late Den Murphy of Heir and later of Schull.

With the demise of the towel-sail yawls, larger boats, fitted with engines, were bought by the Heir Islanders. Neilly Harte of the Reen bought the 31 ft. *Sally Brown,* an English built boat, in 1951. Jack Pyburn bought the 28 ft. *Mary Joseph* in 1953; Timmy Cahalane bought the 30 ft. *Wild Wave*; Seán Harte bought the *Ebinezer*, a 36 ft mackerel drifter. John Harte bought the *Colleen,* another mackerel drifter.[11]

The fine art of sailing and rowing gradually disappeared as the new boats were all engine-driven. Mechanised pot-haulers were introduced in the 1950s. The era of the old gaff-rigged yawl came to an end. By 1957 lobsters had reached the incredible price of £3 per dozen. From 1960 on, the lobsters were bought by weight rather than number. Lobster pots were 'shot' everywhere by all types of boats; over fishing reduced the stocks drastically. In the mid 1960s, salmon fishing with drift nets, was started and it proved so lucrative that it replaced lobstering as the main occupation of the small boats. Lobstering was now only done when the salmon season ended. In the late 1960s shrimp pots were introduced and Roaringwater Bay turned out to be the richest shrimp fishing grounds on the south coast.

In the 1960s, Bord Iascaigh Mhara which had taken over the boatyard of the Fishery School, in Baltimore, started making a series of 32 foot Béal boats, so called because the first part of each boat's name was Béal (mouth, as in mouth of a harbour). The Yard also started building some twenty six foot clinker built boats. Skinner's Boat Yard in Baltimore and Paddy Hegarty of Oldcourt were building new boats as well. The Béal boats were half-decked, with comfortable accommodation and a wheel house. They were fitted with pot-haulers and echo sounders so they were able to find new lobster 'grounds' of which their ancestors were unaware. Jack Pyburn bought the *Béal Bán* in 1962, Sean Harte the *Béal Boirne* in 1963 and John Harte the *Béal Ceare* in 1966.

Spillering

In autumn some of the Heir Islanders spent weeks spillering (or long-lining) on the Sands, a fishing ground between the Fuarán Rocks south of Heir and the Gais-ceanán Sound, between Sherkin and Cape Clear. The lines were made of hemp or manila, three or four strands interwoven. The lines and ropes were 'barked' first. Burma cutch (catechu) was boiled in large cast-iron tubs and the lines and ropes immersed in it. Shorter lines, called losnaí ('nostles' as they were known locally), made of lighter material, were attached to the main line, a fathom and a half apart. The lines had 300 to 400 hooks contained in a tub with projecting skiff, to which the hooks were attached. Great agility of hand was required for handling the lines which stretched to the bottom of the sea, being sunk by a weight at each end, called a pole stone. The buoy line was attached to each end and attached to a buoy on the surface. The usual bait was salted mackerel. They caught ling, cod, whiting, bream, pollock, hake and the different varieties of flat fish.[12]

The bay was 'full' of gurnard, locally called gurnet, which are now very scarce. They were caught with tangle (puzzle) nets as well as by lines. They are a bony fish, but very tasty fresh or salted, and were a valued addition to the islanders' diet. There are two types of gurnet, the grey (cnúdán) and the red (an píobaire dearg, the red piper). Of the two, the grey is superior to eat. Gurnet, pollock and wrasse (connor) were salted as well as the 'oily' fish, mackerel and herring. Cod, ling and hake were salted first, then dried on the stone walls and the sloping roofs of outhouses and then hung from the rafters in the kitchen.

Nets and Ropes

Nets and sails also were 'barked' with Burma cutch or catechu, as were lines and

EXAMPLE OF A BARKING POT IN UNION HALL

ropes. The cutch was boiled in a large cast-iron pot until it was hot liquid. The nets were then pulled through the cutch. One man 'fed' the net slowly into the pot, another continued stirring the liquid, while a third pulled out the nets with a hook or pike. It was then placed on a draining board. A splash of the boiling cutch would cause severe burning, so the work had to be done slowly and carefully. 'Barking tar' was applied to the ropes after the cutch.[13]

Sails

Sails were made of boffity (calico), to which a mixture of cutch and linseed oil was applied. The bigger sails were strong and stiff and made of hemp. For sewing the sails, the men used a thimble with an encircling 'rail'. Pulling the needle through the heavy material required great strength of hand. The sail makers used hempen thread to make or mend the sails, using different needles to suit the thickness of the material. Beeswax, egg yolk, and later, alum, was also applied to the sails. If a sail was holed or ripped, it was mended with yarn and oakum.[14] This was termed 'to fother'[15] the sails. Oakum was old tarred ropes untwisted and teased out with a fid[16] for caulking the seams of boats or patching sails. The canvas sails were sometimes made by the fishermen themselves. Tom O'Regan of West Skeam made his own sails. Other noted sail-makers were Ricky O'Regan, also of West Skeam, and Patrick O'Driscoll of Heir Island East. The most renowned sail maker in the area was Willie Logan of Baltimore, who had come from Co. Antrim to the Fishery School in Baltimore, to teach sail-making.

Mackerel and Herring

By 1880, a change in the migratory habits of the mackerel changed with large shoals heading for the south west of Ireland in the spring. Baltimore replaced Kinsale as the centre of this industry. Fleets of boats followed the mackerel – English, Manx, Welsh, French, Spanish, and boats from other parts of Ireland, Arklow, Co. Down, Waterford, etc. Foreign fishermen were reaping a rich harvest; the small local boats could not compete. In 1879, Fr. Charles Davis became Parish Priest of Rath and the islands – Baltimore, Sherkin and Cape Clear. He brought a deputation of fishermen from Cape Clear to meet Queen Victoria, who arranged for them to meet the English philanthropist, Baroness Burdett-Coutts, who agreed to help. An interest-free purchase loan fund was established, towards which the Baroness contributed £10,000, an enormous amount at that time. Within a year, fifteen boats had been bought by Cape Clear fishermen. In 1887, Baroness Coutts came to Baltimore to assess the progress of the scheme. She presented an inscribed clock to the O'Regan brothers of East Calf Island in acknowledgement of their hard work in replaying their boat loans. The O'Regans had purchased two boats, the *Orion* and the *Velocity*.[17] under the scheme. Con Burke of Heir Island had several mackerel boats at different times. The *Marion*, The *Mary Ann*, *Réalt na maidne* (*Morning Star*), the *Siubhan*, The *St. Margaret*, the *St. Finbarr*. Timothy O'Regan of Skeam West had the *St. Keams*, Mike 'The Cloud' O'Neill of Heir had the *Primrose* and the *Flying Cloud* and Mike 'The Heber' O'Driscoll owned the *Heber*.

'Fall' fishing for mackerel and herring was very important. All types of boats were used, from punts to large mackerel boats. The nets had depths of ten to sixteen fathoms, i.e. up to ninety feet. On Heir, as on all the islands, every household had a barrel of pickled mackerel.

Pilchards

Pilchards, mature sardines, belong to the herring family. They are so like herrings that even fishermen may sometimes mistake them. Generally they are smaller and rounder. One method of distinguishing them is to hold the fish by the dorsal fin between two fingers. If the fish remains level then it is a pilchard, but if it droops, it is a herring. In past centuries, they were found in great abundance off the South-West coast of Ireland. Pilchards are a very oily fish and were harvested for both eating and oil extraction. They were caught in great numbers, but because they decompose quickly, quick preservation was essential. They were either smoked or pressed into barrels after salting and oil extraction. The pilchard fishing industry drew a large number of vessels from England, Spain and France from the early 17th century on. 'Fish pallices' for extracting oil were constructed all along the coast.[18]

The most common process for curing pilchards was that described by Smith in 1750

> The fish are brought out of the boats in large baskets and laid in the fish house (which they call a Palace) in the following manner. They first cover the pavement with salt, which is made so as to have a fall to let the pickle run off; then they lay the fish with the heads all outwards on the ground and strewing salt between 2 or 3 feet or higher. Thus they remain for 21 days if in the summer and 15 or 16 in the winter; then they take them and shake off the salt and wash them at least twice until they are perfectly clean. After this they are brought to the yard where the presses are and having filled them in casks (in which they are closely packed) having holes in the bottom to let out the water, blood and oil, they are then pressed. The casks are all placed in a row against the press walls, being supported on wooden stands which prevent the bottoms from being pressed out. On the top of each cask is placed a round piece of timber or plank, an inch thick, somewhat less than the head of the cask which they call bucklers. These bucklers are squeezed in by placing one end of a pole or leaves a hole made in the wall for the purpose and by applying weights at the outward end, the bucklers are forced into the cask; and the pilchards are squeezed down. The barrels are again filled up until they can hold no more. Under the casks are convenient receptacles to hold the oil, blood and water; the oil is got by skimming off the top. The fish being thus pressed, the barrels are headed and sent to market.[19]

'Train Oil' was the oil pressed out of the pilchards as described in the previous paragraph. Quantities of oil, mixed with blood and water, drained into a specially constructed tank or container. The oil was separated from the mixture in the following way. When a quantity of the mixture had collected in the sump, it was transferred to a barrel which had a spiel (plug) in the bottom. When the spiel was removed, the water and blood was allowed to flow out. The fish oil, being the lightest, was on top. As soon as oil appeared, the spiel was replaced; the barrel was filled with water, the mixture stirred vigorously and the process repeated until the oil was clean. The oil was then bottled and sold.

This train oil was used in one of the earliest form of lighting. The oil was placed in a slige, a receptacle like a scallop shell. The wick most commonly used was the white pith of rushes (geataire).

Train oil[20] was also obtained by removing the livers of the large fish like ling, cod, halibut, placing them in an open barrel and allowing them to melt in the sun.

In 1758, the Anglican Bishop of Ossory, Doctor Pococke, saw Spaniards extracting train oil from pilchards in Cape Clear and Sherkin Island. The Spaniards were summertime visitors, who sometimes lived in huts, clustered on Spanish Island. When the pilchards migrated to Cornish waters in the 1760s, Baltimore pilchard processors migrated with them. The shoals returned in 1870, but by then mackerel was becoming the main source of income.[21]

The remains of 'fish palaces' are visible all along the South West coast, in Kinsale, Courtmacsherry, Castlehaven, at the Cove in Baltimore, near the Abbey in Sherkin, Ringaroga, near South Harbour in Cape Clear, in Rossbrin, several near Schull, in Crookhaven. Pilchard fishing was so rewarding in Bantry Bay that it could be claimed that the town grew because of the industry.

In Heir, the strand north of the pier is Trá na Pailíse, (Palace strand), so there must have been one there. Paris (Heir Island West) is probably a corruption of the word 'palace'.[22] Opposite the pier on Heir, a strand in Ardagh is known as 'Palace'.[23] This is ample evidence of the importance of the pilchard in coastal life over a long period.

Bumming Boats

During the boom years of the mackerel industry in Baltimore, roughly from 1880 to 1925, there were many English and American fish buyers in Baltimore and Cape Clear. Some of the fish buyers had local agents, who did the purchasing for them. The demand for mackerel was so great that the merchants used large six-oared yawls to go out to sea to meet the mackerel drifters. They employed only the best oarsmen for this back-breaking work. The buyer, after reaching the drifters, wrote the price of the fish on a piece of paper, rolled it around a stone and threw it aboard the fishing boat. Great rivalry in rowing grew out of this and the rowing races at Baltimore and Schull regattas were eagerly awaited, as were the lobster yawl races. Willie O'Regan of Whitehall tells of a race between two bumming boats, one manned by a Baltimore crew, the other by Heir Islanders. They were stroke for stroke as far as Cape Clear, a distance of eight miles from Baltimore. As they headed towards the Fastnet, the Heir crew gradually pulled ahead. Local folklore has it that Mike Cahalane, of the Reen, Heir Island. after a night rowing in a 'bumming' boat, sailed to Schull Regatta to take part in the lobster yawl race, having had no time to eat his breakfast.

Connor

Wrasse (or connor as they are called in West Cork) were an important part of island diet. They could be caught without going to sea. They are a fish of 'foul' ground or 'connor holes' as they were called. They were fished by rod and line off the Dún, the Reen, 'Lean Caorach, the north side of 'Lean Gamhan and off West Skeam. The rods used were home-made, usually of bamboo, washed ashore as wrack, ten to twelve feet in length. The usual bait was lugworm, dug in muddy strands at ebb tide. There is also a more colourful wrasse called the 'cuach' (cuckoo) wrasse which is not as tasty as the brown wrasse. On West Skeam they used crab meat or limpets as bait, as there are no muddy strands there to find lugworms. From years of experience the islanders knew all the 'connor holes', the best places to get them. People also knew where there were 'crab-holes'. Crabmeat made a welcome change from salt fish.

Bream

Heir Island boats used to catch bream in the Sands and south east of Cape Clear. They were dried on walls or slanting roofs. They turned a lovely yellow colour when dried and were sold in Skibbereen in the pre-Christmas market. South of Heir are situated the Deargán rocks, derived from deargán, the Irish for bream.

Scallop

Some of the Heir Islanders use to dredge for scallop north of the Skeams, in the Caol between Sandy Island and Turkhead, in the Gaisceanán Sound and else-where. The dredges were usually made by the Ballydehob blacksmiths, especially Jer. O'Sullivan.

Leoithín

The boats of Roaringwater Bay islands and the adjacent mainland dredged the bay for a seaweed called leoithín or 'wool.' In the *Skibbereen Eagle* of December 1904, in a report on the drowning tragedy, when three Heir Island men lost their lives (page 104) they state that the Coughlan fishermen of Kilkilleen had spent the day dredging for 'wool', so called because of its soft wool-like texture.

Periwinkles

Periwinkles were collected from October to April on the island strands. Since there were so many 'picking winkles' on the island, they often sailed or rowed to strands along the coastline from Schull to Baltimore. On short winter days they often rose in the dark, rowed to places like Rossbrin, or Turkhead, spent the day picking, before returning again in the darkness, with very little to eat during the day. As well as periwinkles, there was a plentiful supply of mussels, limpets (bairneachs), cockles and clams to be eaten, full of vitamins and goodness. Sometimes the water in which the limpets were boiled was bottled and drunk. To a lesser extent, periwinkles are still gathered on the island today They fetch a great price now, but it is slow, cold, back-breaking work.[24]

Carrageen Moss

Many of the islanders plucked carrageen moss (ceann donn, chondrus crispus) from the rocks at spring tides. It grows low on the rocks. Spread out on the grass, it was bleached and turned brown in colour. Some of it was used to make a healthy pudding, while the rest was sold to merchants, like the O'Driscolls of

Baltimore, when there was demand for it. The O'Driscolls came to the island to urge the people to pick carrageen. They supplied large bags into which the carrageen was packed. It was also fed to calves.

Wrack

Gathering flotsam and jetsam on the strands was always an important activity for the islanders, especially in winter, when they were at home and when there was a better likelihood of finding something worthwhile after winter gales. The old Celtic (or Brehon) laws gave coastal inhabitants the right to collect wreckage or wreck, usually called 'wrack' in West Cork, cast ashore from ships lost at sea in bad weather. After the Battle of Kinsale in 1601, when Irish customs and laws had to yield to English law, this right was withdrawn; nevertheless wrack was still collected by coastal dwellers. Pieces of wood were prized in the islands as they are virtually treeless. Pieces of good timber, washed ashore, were used in the construction of boats, buildings, furniture and tools. The less valuable pieces were burnt as fuel. Pitch pine from shipwrecks is incorporated into the structure of many houses on Heir and the coastal townlands of Aughadown.

Local custom governed the right of ownership of 'wrack', based on the principle of 'finders keepers'. Anything found on the shore belonged to whoever brought it up above the high water line. At sea the first person to tie a rope around a floating object became the owner. As well as spars and baulks of timber, the sea often threw up objects like barrels of rum, whiskey, bales of tobacco, flour and other foodstuffs. Tobacco Point in Whitehall is named after bales of tobacco coming ashore here from a wreck.

THE *SAFE RETURN* WAS BUILT FOR JIM BARRY OF EAST SKEAM. SHE HAD THE REPUTATION OF BEING A GOOD SAILER. SHE WAS SOLD TO DICK SALTER OF BALTIMORE, WHO ALTERED HER AND INSTALLED AN ENGINE AND FOREDECK. SALTER SOLD HER TO JOHN HOSFORD, WHO HAD A HOUSE IN HEIR ISLAND FOR A NUMBER OF YEARS, AND WHO NOW LIVES IN GLANDORE.

THE BÉAL BÁN, BOUGHT BY JACK PYBURN IN 1962, NEAR 'LEÁN GAMHAN PIER.

THE *MARY HANNAH S896* BUILT BY RICHARD PYBURN 0F HEIR ISLAND, FOR JEREMIAH McCARTHY.

Seen here are his mother Mary McCarthy on shore and *left to right*, Michael McCarthy, Cornelius Harte, Timothy Harte, Jeremiah McCarthy. This picture is taken on the northeast side of the goleen in Paris. East Skeam is in the distant background.

— 17 —

Heir Island Boatbuilders

The Pyburns of Heir Island were boat builders, as were other branches of the family in Crookhaven and Toormore, Schull. Pyburn is a rare name in Ireland, confined exclusively to the West Cork area. It is rare also in Britain, where the name originated. The largest concentration of Pyburns in England is in County Durham in the north east in the Sunderland area. That fishing boats from that part of Britain visited the south west coast is verified by the 1901 census of boats for Baltimore, where we find a fishing smack from North Shields and another from South Shields, Co. Durham.

Tradition has it that the first Pyburn came from Cornwall, that he settled on the banks of the Ilen and that he had four sons. It is conjectured that the Pyburns moved from Durham to Cornwall, the two counties having mining in common, tin in Cornwall, coal in Durham. Alternatively, the first Pyburn may have come directly from County Durham. What is certain is that a Richard Pyburn lived in Mohonagh, Aughadown, near Newcourt, according to the Tithe Applotment List of 1828. Aughadown parish records reveal that he had three marriages and four sons, one bearing the father's name, Richard. It is believed that one settled on Heir, one in Toormore, one in Crookhaven and one in the Durrus area. We do not know exactly when the first Pyburn moved into Heir Island but Griffiths Evaluation of 1852 records a Richard Pyburn, almost certainly the son (or grandson) of Richard of Mohonagh. It is also certain that they were boat builders or shipwrights

RUIN OF THE ORIGINAL PYBURN HOMESTEAD IN MOHONAGH,
SITUATED ON THE BANK OF THE ILEN

VIEW FROM THE ORIGINAL PYBURN HOMESTEAD IN MOHONAGH
WITH THE RIVER ILEN AT EBB TIDE

In 2003, Albert Pyburn, originally from Co. Durham who had settled in Australia, returned to Sunderland, Co. Durham and crossed over to Ireland to visit Heir Island, having heard from a friend that there were Pyburns here. Amazingly he had a very striking resemblance to Jack Pyburn of Heir Island and interestingly all this man's ancestors were shipwrights, who lived and worked in County Durham.

The Pyburns, whether in Mohonagh, Heir, Toormore or Crookhaven, lived near the sea, which facilitated launching the boats when completed. We can safely assume that the first Richard on Heir was a boat-builder, because his son, Christopher, and grandson, Richard, fashioned many of the yawls, in which the Heir Islanders and other fishermen of South Aughadown fished for lobsters from the time of the Famine to the middle of the twentieth century, most of a century of boat-building.

Christopher and Richard Pyburn built their boats in the Bán field, south west of the Bridge in Paris, Heir Island West. Here the boats were constructed in the open. These boats were usually about 26 ft in length, 6 to 7 ft wide and about 3½ ft deep. They were large enough to carry a 'train' of lobsterpots and all the other equipment required. The frames were made of oak or elm, usually cut in Newcourt and the boats were planked with pitch pine or red or white deal. The timber was cut in a 'saw pit', a deep hole in the ground. Two men, one in the pit and the other on the timber, cut the timber with a pit saw. To be able to use an adze skilfully was essential for the boat builder. The adze, a curved blade attached to a handle, was used to 'dub' the timber. The adze[1] with which his grandfather 'dubbed'[2] the wood is in the proud possession of Jack Pyburn.

Richard Pyburn, and the other old boatbuilders, the Pyburns of Toormore and Crookhaven, Willie Skinner of Rathmore, Henry Skinner of Baltimore, Flor

O'Neill of Sherkin, used no plans or drawings. The boats were built by rule of thumb, guided by the buyers' very precise instructions. Every boat had the stamp of its maker and could be identified by its shape and curve.

The *Hanorah* was one of the last boats built by Richard Pyburn, registered in 1893 for Con Harte of the Reen, Heir Island. She was sold to Seán Barnett of Schull in 1958 when the Hartes bought new boats. In 1959, she was bought by Den Murphy of Schull, who fished her right up to the 1970s. She was eventually bought by a man from County Clare but she never left the area. She was abandoned at Mill Cove, Schull, where she deteriorated over the following fifteen years. Luckily this unique boat type was rescued from oblivion. Nigel Towse of Sherkin Island and boat-builder, Liam Hegarty of Oldcourt, realising that the remains of the *Hanorah* were probably the last example of this type of boat, rescued her from the mud and transported her to Hegarty's boatyard in Oldcourt in 1999. Here she has been used as a prototype for the construction of new yawls. Colm O'Cuileanáin and Mary Jordan's *Fionn,* Micheál Crowley and John Colleran's *Mary Colette,* Cormac Levis' *Saoirse Muireann* and John Punch's *Rose* have already been launched. Once more these beautiful boats sail the waters of Roaringwater Bay.

As well as building boats, Richard Pyburn also repaired them. Con Burke, merchant and fishbuyer, had several large mackerel boats and Pyburn was often employed doing repair work to them.

Richard Pyburn's son, also Richard, was trained to carry on the boat-building tradition but he emigrated to America in 1909. His younger brother, Jim, did some boat-building, but the era of the Heir Island lobster boatmen was coming to an end. Jim Pyburn's grandson, John, also trained as a boat builder in Baltimore. He is now fishing out of Whitehall. As well as boat-building, the Pyburns also made furniture, tables, chairs, children's cots etc. Jack Pyburn, grandson of Richard, seeing the carpenter's chairs for the first time in the Pyburn household in Toormore, recognised them as being of the same design as those made by the Pyburns of Heir Island.

Proud of his skill as a boat builder, Richard Pyburn, like any craftsman, did not like his work being criticized. In the island folklore, it is said that one day when he was at work on one of the many boats he built, 'Big Johnny' Minihane came alone and passed some disparaging remark about his work. Pyburn, angered by having his work criticised, cast the adze at Minihane. Luckily, all the damage done

JIM PYBURN, SON OF RICHARD, WITH HIS SONS, CHRISTOPHER AND EDDIE AND HIS WIFE LOU (ELLEN, NEE CAHALANE).

was the removal of the tip of Big Johnny's hat.[3]

Richard (Dick) Pyburn was involved in William O'Brien's National League. A saying by Richard Pyburn is still remembered. 'If I put on a clean suit to go out to say a word for my country, there's a gang down there on the Rock talking amongst themselves, "There goes Pyburn the Leaguer".'[4]

THE AUTHOR, ADMIRING THE FRAME OF THE *HANORAH*, BUILT BY
HIS GREAT-GRANDFATHER, RICHARD PYBURN

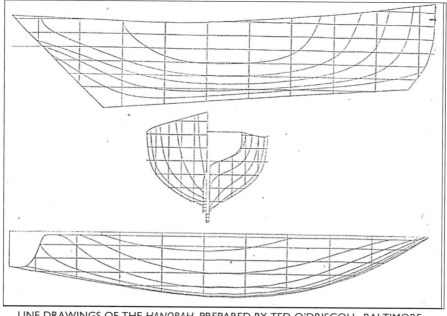

LINE DRAWINGS OF THE *HANORAH*, PREPARED BY TED O'DRISCOLL, BALTIMORE

List of Boats built by Pyburns, Heir Island

(not necessarily complete)

OWNER

Eleanor	Denis Minihane, Paris, Heir Island.
Fear Not.	Mike Cahalane, Heir Island.
Flower of May S.350	Rickie O'Regan, West Skeam.
Hanorah S.463	Con Harte, The Reen, Heir Island.
Lily S.125	Rickie O'Regan, West Skeam.
Mary Hannah S.896	Michael McCarthy, Heir Island.
Safe Return S.12 & S.141	John Dwyer, Collatrum.
St. Anna S.136	Patrick O'Neill, Heir Island.
Two Fishes S.722 (originally *Mary Ellen*)	Michael O'Neill, Heir Island.
Swan S.121	Richard Cotter, Heir Island. By tradition she was the last boat built by Richard Pyburn.
Village Maid S889	John Harte, Heir Island.
Valetta S852	Dan Murphy, later John O'Donovan both Heir Island
Dove S. 692	Denis Nolan, Sherkin.
Ocean Star S903	Denis Nolan, Sherkin

As well as the towel-sail yawls listed, Pyburn constructed other boats, punts and smaller yawls which used a lugsail.

In John Hawke's article on Ardintenant (White Castle)[5] there is a reference to the name Pyburn. The Down Survey, which was commissioned by Cromwell to facilitate the confiscation and redistribution of lands, shows Ardintenant (east of Schull) extending over a large area, covering a number of townlands. Sir Geoffrey Gallway was owner of this area in 1641 according to the Book of Survey and Distribution. Two lots, one of 937 acres and the second of 150 acres were confiscated because Gallway was a Royalist who opposed Cromwell. Criste Pyborne was granted 149 acres. This indicates that Pyburns were in the Schull area as early as the 1640s. Whether the boat-building Pyburns of Mohonagh, Heir, Toormore and Crookhaven are connected with this Criste Pyborne (Pyburn) or are descended from another Pyburn, we are not sure.

TIMMY CAHALANE, HEIR ISLAND AND SHERKIN, WITH HIS GRANDSON TURLOUGH O'CONNOR

RICHIE AND DAN PYBURN COLLECTING COCKLES ON THE SLOB NEAR 'LEÁN GAMHAN

Above, NEIL AND MARY McCARTHY

Left, RICHARD PYBURN

MAISIE AND PETER
MURPHY

JEREMIAH McCARTHY, LOU AND TERESA
PYBURN WITH DANNY CAHALANE

BRIDIE AND LIAM BARRY, KATIE O'DRISCOLL, TERESA
PYBURN WITH FRANCIE AND NELLIE HEALY

FINBARR AND MARY ELLEN HARTE IN NEW YORK WITH MARGARET MARY SCULLY (NEE O'DRISCOLL)

JOHN AND MAGGIE MCCARTHY, HEIR ISLAND

MAGGIE AND GERRY MCCARTHY, HEIR ISLAND WEST

ANNIE FITZGERALD

MINIHANE FAMILY, HEIR ISLAND AND GARRETTSTOWN

— 18 —

Heir Island Memories 1901-1923:
Nonie Nance Cahalane

This is an edited transcript of a taped interview of Nonie Nance Cahalane Cesareo by her son Steve Cesareo

Nonie Nance Cahalane was born on the 24th August 1901 in Heir Island. She was the youngest child of Cornelius Cahalane and Ellen McCarthy. Ellen, a

widow, came from a farming family on the mainland and married into the island. Cornelius was her second husband. Nonie remembered living on a small farm, where they grew enough food to live on, and stored some for winter use. From May to September her father went fishing for lobster and crayfish. He owned his own boat and made his own lobster pots. There were three men on the boat and they stayed away for three weeks at a time. She remembered him going as far as Cobh and Youghal, where he sold his lobsters and from where he mailed money home to her mother. They also fished for herring and mackerel and for white fish with lines and hooks. After September the boats were pulled up and painted and put into dock until May. Cornelius's boat was called *Annie,* after Nonie's grandmother.

She also remembered him making his own sails during the winter.

They grew wheat, which was cut in August, bound in sheaves and brought in for flailing. She remembered the sheaves being slashed and pounded until all the grain came out. The grain was bagged and any surplus taken to market. They had two gardens of early vegetables. She remembered 'blue-eyed' potatoes, cabbage, turnips – white for the animals and yellow for the house – carrots and parsnips. There was not much work to be done outdoors from November to March, when the ground was ploughed by two donkeys.

Nonie remembered about sixty families on Heir Island in the early 1900s[1]; many families had ten or eleven children. Around age seventeen, most of the children left home for America. Nonie was the youngest of eleven and she had only seen two of them growing up, as all the others had emigrated. They only left the island on Sunday when they went to Mass by boat.

She remembered going to school, where there was only one large room, where all the classes were taught. The male teacher taught from third to sixth classes and the female teacher up to second. The male teacher had the reputation of being strict. They went to school five days a week and also had 'Sunday School'. They had one month off in August. The teachers never left the island during school term. She never heard of Protestants – all were Catholic and they always had a prayer at the start of class. She learned reading, writing, arithmetic, geography. All she remembered of World War I was sitting in school looking at a calendar on the wall and being told, 'we are in the war'.

After school ended at three o clock, she went home, changed her clothes, and went out into the fields. Nonie simply hated farming – she longed to stay in the house and make bread with her mother. She remembered setting the potatoes in ridges which were dug with a spade – she remembered picking the potatoes, saving the bigger ones for the family and for seed and the little ones which were boiled for the animals. Nonie remembered going to Skibbereen twice as a child. She recalled that it was like going to the circus. She recalled the fish market in Market St.

They lived in a thatched house and also had a cow chamber. They had two cows, also a pigsty and chicken coop and a barn for the wheat. The hay was put in the loft. In their house, there were two bedrooms upstairs, one downstairs and the kitchen. They had an open fireplace in the kitchen, in which they burned coal which was very expensive. They had a keresone[2] lamp for light and there was a well close by for water.[3] They had no bathroom, only an outhouse. The house was right on the bay (where O'Connors live today). She remembered visiting the little island in the bay[4] on Sundays with other children gathering gulls' eggs.

At the time, there was one shop where they could buy most things, flour, sugar, kerosene etc. They also bought tea in the shop. It was sold loose by the pound weight and sugar and flour by the stone. She recalled the £note, 10shilling note, 5 shillings, half-crown, shilling, pennies, three-penny bit.

The priest came to the island twice a year to say Mass at the Stations and if you were very sick he came in to give the last rites. The houses were decorated with flowers and they had an altar for the Stations. Every family had them in turn.

Around age fifteen Nonie remembered having to work harder. Women took over the farm work when the men were away fishing. Each family helped each other planting wheat, flailing corn, etc.

When she was seventeen or eighteen Nonie knew that she would not spend her whole life on the island. She could have married on the island – the marriage was all settled [5] – but she refused. She had made up her mind that she was going to America as she felt there was no future for her on the island. Her half brothers and sisters in America sent cheques home regularly to her mother – all the family were in Boston – and she was determined to go also. She recalled that in most families the eldest son would be left the land but would have to wait until all his younger siblings had left home before bringing in a wife of his own. In some case he might have to wait until he was aged forty or more.

Nonie Nance remembered the Black and Tans coming over to Ireland and shooting the people. She also remembered 'our boys' hiding in hay stacks and barns on Heir Island. The islanders kept them for four or five days, fed and looked after them. They were quite safe as nobody would ferry in the Black & Tans; they would rather drown them. She remembered it being a sad time.

She remembered the sinking of the *Lusitania*. The previous week, her half-sister, Elizabeth, had left for America and her mother prayed the Rosary every night for a safe passage for her. She also remembered the lobster fishermen being afraid of being blown up by German mines. Her mother was very worried at this time, as two of her sons, who had emigrated to America, Michael and Thomas, were involved in the war.

Nonie remembered visiting other islands in Roaringwater Bay, going to dances in Sherkin and going to Cape Clear, from where they could see the liners passing on their way to America. She recalled the 'gentry'[6] coming into Heir Island on Sundays with food baskets and having picnics in the fields and strands. Sometimes they gave cookies to the children.

When Nonie was twenty her mother became ill. She thought at first that she had swallowed a fish bone. It was October and during the winter months they ate a lot of salted herrings. Her condition deteriorated and she died after five days from a heart condition. She was aged sixty-one.

Nonie stayed on Heir Island for another two years but the call of America was getting stronger all the time. She left in 1923. Her father Cornelius went to live with his sister on the island and the land was divided up between the neighbours.

Nonie Nance's father, Cornelius, who survived the 1904 tragedy, page 103 died a few years later.

NONIE LIVED IN NEW JERSEY. SHE LIVED A LONG HAPPY LIFE, VISITING HEIR ISLAND TWICE.
She is pictured above with her family, *left to right*, Steve, Betty, Vincent and Penny.
See 'Ballad of Nonie Nance' – appendix 11, page 320

JOHN O'NEILL

FLORRIE FITZGERALD

JOHN HART

JOHN MURPHY

© Bill Morris

— 19 —

Family Names of Heir Island, Skeams and East Calf Island

Although Heir Island is named O'Driscoll's Island, O'Driscoll wasn't the dominant surname, at least after 1822, when Aughadown Parish Records (Births and Marriages) began. Catholic Parish Records, The Tithe Applotment list of 1828, Griffiths Survey of 1852, the Census of 1901 and 1911 give us a picture of the distribution of surnames on Heir, the two Skeam Islands and East Calf, all part of Aughadown Parish. West and Middle Calf are in Schull Parish.

McCarthy was the dominant surname in Heir Island West. Five branches of the McCarthy clan were represented: McCarthy Mountain, McCarthy Mór, McCarthy Ceonach, McCarthy Rábach and McCarthy Samhnaigh (Sowney). In fact the names Mountain and Sowney are sometimes given as surnames in Parish Records. The Parish Records, an invaluable source of information, are nevertheless incomplete because some of the priests didn't record the townland in registering births and marriages.

O'Neill was the dominant surname in Heir Island East, Harte in the Reen, while Heir Island Middle had a varied list: Shanahan, Burke, McCarthy, Murphy, Casey, Foley, Minihane, Barry, O'Donovan.

In East Calf and West Skeam, O'Regans were dominant, indeed the sole surname in the early part of the twentieth century. East Skeam, on which the Townsends of Whitehall, built a summer house, was inhabited by families, descended from men who worked for the landlord, Townsend. Barry, Desmond, and Cadogan. The Horgans, who were in East Skeam in 1852, had moved to Kilsarlaght, Aughadown by 1901.

The Tithe Applotment List of 1828 gives us a list of all landowners on the islands; it is not a complete list of families because those who had no land didn't have to pay tithes.

Surnames on the Tithe List:

Heir Island: McCarthy, McCarthy Mountain, McCarthy Rábach, O'Donovan, Casey, Minihane, Shanahan, Murphy, Burke, Kearney, Harte, Collins, O'Driscoll, Harrington

East Skeam: Desmond, Horgan, Cadogan,
West Skeam: O'Regan
East Calf: Townsend

The names listed in Griffith Evaluation of 1852 is a complete list because all householders are included, with immediate lessors and value of property. The occupiers are listed in groups because the people built their houses close to each other to form little villages or clacháns. The surnames, Kearney, Collins, and

Harrington, who were on the island in 1828 were gone by 1852 as they are not included in the Griffith List.

A. Heir Island West: McCarthy, McCarthy Mountain, O'Donovan, Murphy Minihane, Hurley, Pyburn,

B. Heir Island Middle: Burke, Foley, Murphy, McCarthy, Shanahan, Minihane, Harte, O'Regan

C. Heir Island East: O'Neill (spelled Neale), O'Driscoll, Casey, McCarthy, Fitzgerald, O'Regan

D. Reen North: O'Driscoll, Cotter, McCarthy, O'Neill, Cahalane (various spellings)

E. Reen South: Harte.

The surnames, Hurley, Foley and Casey, listed in Griffiths were gone by 1901.

The following is a list of families and documented first year of reference. Since Church records only start in 1822, there is no way of ascertaining when most families first settled on the island.

Barry   The first Barry came from Bawnahow near Skibbereen to work for Townsend of Whitehall. They settled on East Skeam. The first reference to a birth there was in 1870 when James was born to John Barry and Margaret Cadogan. This James Barry had moved to Heir by 1901.

Burke   (variously spelled Bourke, Bourk, Burke). Traditionally, they came from the Baltimore area. The earliest reference to Burke is for May 1824, when Florence was born to Thomas Burke and Catherine Horrigan (Horgan) on East Calf. The earliest reference to Burke on Heir is in 1824, when Michael was born to Cornelius Burke and Ellen O'Driscoll. There were Burkes on the Skeams also, in 1826, where we find Ellen, born to Patrick Burke and Mary O'Regan.

Cadogan   (variously spelled Cadagan, Cadigan, Kadigan, Cadagane) It is believed that the Cadogans came from Cape Clear. The name Cadogan, derived from céad gamhan, (one hundred calves) is a branch of the O'Driscoll clan. The Heir Island Cadogans were called the 'Harrys' after Harry Cadogan. They were in Heir in 1825, when Cornelius was born to Michael Cadogan and Margaret Daly. The first reference to Cadogan in East Skeam is in 1868, when Catherine was born to Cornelius Cadogan and Ellen Murphy.

Cahalane   (variously spelled Cohalane, Cahalane, Coughalane, Couhlane). The first reference is in 1824, when Catherine was born to Cornelius Cahalane and Mary McCarthy. They are believed to have come from the Baltimore area.

Casey   Caseys had the first shop on Heir, near the boreen leading to Nelly O'Donovan's house in Heir Island Middle. A son, Humphrey, was born to Thomas Casey and Mary O'Mahony in 1824.

Collins   The first recorded Collins was John, born to Jeremiah Collins and

Elizabeth O'Regan, on 31st March, 1826. on the Skeams. A daughter, Catherine, was born to Timothy Collins and Mary McCarthy on Heir on the same date 31/3/1826. They are listed in the Tithe but not in Griffiths, so they must have left before 1852.

Cotter   The Cotters, it is believed, came from the mainland of Aughadown. The first documented Cotter is Ellen, born to Garrett Cotter and Ellen O'Brien in January 1824. The Cotters, like the Hartes and Cahalanes, lived in the Reen.

Daly   The earliest reference is to Patrick, born in 1824, to John Daly and Hanora O'Regan. The name is not listed in Tithe List, Griffiths or 1901 census. The last recorded birth is Elizabeth, born to Denis Daly and Catherine Hurley in 1869.

Desmond   There were Desmonds on the East Skeam as far back as records go. There are two recorded births for 1825. A daughter, Mary, was born to Denis Desmond and Mary Cadogan in January and in May a daughter, Ellen, was born to Timothy Desmond and Ellen Horgan.

Fitzgerald   Usually called the Gearrlachs from the Irish, MacGearailt. The earliest mention of the name is for 1836 when a daughter, Joanna, was born to John Fitzgerald and Mary McCarthy on Heir.

Foley   One of the few surnames which gives its name to a place on Heir – the strand called Foghlú (Irish for Foley) opposite Oileán Gamhan. They were on the island as far back as 1824 at least; in that year Ann was born to Michael Foley and Margaret Burke.

Harrington   Listed in Tithe but not in Griffith, so they were gone by 1852. They were on Heir and on the Skeams during the Famine. A daughter, Mary, was born to Dan Harrington and Hanora O'Neill in December 1844 on Heir. A son, Michael, was born to Dan Harrington and Johanna McCarthy in July 1846 on the Skeams.

Harte   Usually spelled Hart in early references – the first documented birth is of Ellen, born to Cornelius Harte and Ellen Cotter in 1824, so Harte is a long established island name.

Horgan   Often spelled Horrigan. Jeremiah Horgan and Ellen Minihane lived on Heir in 1856 when a daughter, Margaret, was born to them. They had moved to East Skeam by 1858 when another daughter, Catherine, was born. Later in the century the family moved to Kilsarlaght in Aughadown parish.

Hurley   There were Hurleys on Heir in the early and mid 19th century. The earliest reference is to Jeremiah, born to Andrew Hurley and Mary McCarthy, in March 1827. They were gone by 1901.

Kearney   The Kearneys lived on the Reen of Heir, where there is a place-name – Caladh Kearney, Kearney's landing place. The earliest reference to the name is to Thomas, son of Daniel Kearney and

Ellen Bourke, born in May, 1841. There were no Kearneys left on Heir by 1852.

McCarthy   (Carty) The most populous surname on Heir Island, with five different septs. The earliest recorded birth is of Catherine, born to Michael McCarthy and Hanorah, in August 1823. Mother's surname is not clear in records.

Minihane   (Minihan Mór, Minaghan, Minihan, Minahan). There were two branches of the surname on the island, in Heir Island West and Middle. The Paris Minihanes came, either from Cape Clear or East Calf. There were Minihanes on Heir in 1824, when a daughter, Ellen, was born to Daniel Minihane and Anne Cadogan.

Murphy   A long established island name, the first reference is to John, born in February 1824, to Daniel Murphy and Anne O'Driscoll.

O'Donovan   Usually spelled without the O. The first documented record is to Mary, born to Daniel O'Donovan and Mary Cadogan, in July 1824.

O'Mahony   A son, Daniel, was born to Timothy O'Mahony and Mary O'Driscoll in 1824 in Heir. An inlet on the northwest side of the island is called Cuas Mahoun – Cuas Mathúna (O'Mahony's inlet). In island lore, the O'Mahonys did live in Heir Island West.

In July 1846, a son, John was born to Timothy Mahony and Ellen Desmond on the Skeams. Probably Timothy O'Mahony married Ellen Desmond of East Skeam and later left the island.

O'Driscoll   (Also spelled Driscoll, Driskol, Driskil). Margaret, the first recorded in parish records, was born to John O'Driscoll and Mary Harrington in October 1823, so they were there from the beginning of parish records and for centuries before that.

O'Neill   (Also spelled Neill, Neil, Neale, Nale) The most populous name after McCarthy, their stronghold was at the eastern end of the island. The first recorded birth was in October, 1823 when a son, Daniel, was born to Florence O'Neill and Hanorah Sheehan.

O'Regan   The O'Regans were employed by the Townsends to take charge of the seaweed 'stations'. Every family has an allotted strand and/or rock from which they could get seaweed to fertilise the land. The Townsends sold the East Calf to them in 1865. Some of them settled in West Skeam. According to parochial records the first O'Regan named was Eliza, born to Timothy O'Regan and Mary Horgan in May 1825 on West Skeam. The first reference to the name on East Calf was Mary Ann, born to Thomas O'Regan and Hanorah Cogan, in 1865. The first recorded O'Regan birth on Heir Island is Patrick, born May 1846, to Timothy O'Regan and Hanorah O'Brien.

Pyburn   (Phibairn, Piborn, Phyburn). They were on the island in 1852 (Griffith Evaluation). The most unusual of the 'old' names on the island. The first Pyburn birth recorded for Heir was Mary, born in

March, 1864, to Christopher Pyburn and Ellen McCarthy (Rábach).

Shanahan A long established island name, they were there when records began, the first recorded being Johanna, born to Daniel Shanahan and Mary Cadogan in August 1824. The last Shanahan, John, who had been the island postman for a long period, left the island with his wife in the 1950s, having had no issue. There are six Shanahan households listed in Griffiths Evaluation (1852). A hundred years later they had disappeared.

It seems certain that there was migration into Heir Island from the mainland during the Great Famine period. For example, a son, William, was born to Dan Daly and Catherine Fitzgerald, in Cunnamore in November 1846. A daughter, Margaret, was born to the same couple in May 1849, but now they are located on Heir Island. The following families are recorded only once in Parish records for the island. It would appear they moved into the island, possibly because they were related to some of the islanders, stayed for a while and then returned to the mainland, died or emigrated.

Crowley A son, John, born to Patrick Crowley and Ellen (surname illegible) in June 1846 on the Skeams.

Griffin A son, Patrick, born to Jeremiah Griffin and Mary Burke in March 1845. The godparents were Denis and Mary Horgan, who lived on East Skeam.

Hegarty There is only one reference to the name in Heir; a son, George, was born in June 1848 to George Hegarty and Mary Minihane.

Duggan In October 1844, a son, Thade, was born to Jerry Duggan and Mary O'Regan on Heir.

Spillane There is only one reference to this name. A son, Timothy, was born to John Spillane and Ellen Mountain (sic) McCarthy in 1839 on Heir.

Two other surnames to which there is only one reference are Keating and Kelly:

Keating Catherine Keating was born in April 1824 to Michael Keating and Ellen McCarthy on East Calf Island.

Kelly In January 1838 a son Thomas, was born to Thomas Kelly and Joan Linahan on the Skeams. This is the only reference to this surname in the 19th century. In the 1911 census we a find a Richard Kelly occupying a house in Heir Island, owned by Michael O'Neill. This Richard Kelly, who came from Skeaghanore, near Ballydehob, was the island school teacher for three years.

In Parish Records, we find Burkes and Keatings on East Calf in 1824, but they are gone by 1852. The landlords, Townsends, cleared eleven families off the island to build a summer house, which presumably is the reason there are no further references to other surnames. Townsend, soon tiring of the summer house in East Calf, sold the island to the O'Regan family and built a summer house on East Skeam, later to become the home of the Barry family.

The following families lived in the Skeams for short periods, some of them possibly moving there during the Famine, to stay with relations. Burke (1841), Collins, (1826), Harrington (1846), O'Mahony (1846) Crowley (1846), Griffin (1845) and Kelly (1838).

DENNY AND MARY ANN
McCARTHY

© Michael Minihane

TIMMY McCARTHY, HEIR ISLAND WEST

— 20 —

The Land

PLOUGHING WITH THREE DONKEYS IN HEIR ISLAND IN 1961
Photo: Michael Minihane © Cork Examiner

A report was published in June 1893 in the *Skibbereen Eagle* describing the conditions in 'Carbery's Hundred Isles'

> The bulk of the islanders cultivate little plots of land, mainly for the growth of potatoes, but only the very few have sufficient ground to produce potatoes enough to adequately support an average family the entire season. Besides the rent of land is so high that unless the fishing proves successful, the payments to the landlords, which are made with extraordinary punctuality, reduce the people to an utterly helpless condition in times of distress. It is hard to credit it but is nevertheless a fact that as much as £2 per arable acre are paid in these islands. When I enquired as to the reason why rents are so high in places where people should almost be paid to live, I was informed that in the old days the landlords charged for the seaweed cast up on the shore. As the seaweed could be disposed of for manure, the landlord put on an impost accordingly.

The reporter goes on to advocate the cultivation of early potatoes and vegetables as a source of income.

> The islands with a few insignificant exceptions possess a climate which rivals that of the Scilly Isles or the Cornish coast for the production of early potatoes and vegetables. Rugged as they are, the sheltered nooks between the rocks are of great fertility, thanks to the careful cultivation of the cottiers .... What the islanders suffer from is the want of changes in the seed and some instructions

as to improvement in their methods of cultivation. How very profitable it would be if they sent early potatoes on to Cork now that the railway comes down to Baltimore.[1]

Smith, in his *History of Cork*, in 1750,[2] noted that there were potatoes grown in Cape in 1750, the first reference to the potato in West Cork. Brought to Ireland by Sir Walter Raleigh in the early 17th century, the potato provided an easily grown crop that thrived in Ireland's moist Atlantic climate. It supported a huge increase in the population of Ireland in the late 18th century and early part of the 19th century, but led to an over dependence on one food source. The Potato Famine changed that forever.

The potato was the most essential part of the islander's diet, together with fish and bread. Many of the islanders grew early varieties like Red Elephant or Epicure. The beautiful yellow fleshed Champion was the main crop, later replaced by Kerr's Pinks and Golden Wonder. The potatoes were set in a bán or lea field, which had been well fertilized with seaweed during the winter and spring. The potatoes were grown in ridges, (or lazy beds as they are called in other parts of the country) about three to four feet wide. These were raised seed-drills separated from each other by narrow trenches. The ground was broken up by a plough pulled by a team of three donkeys or two ponies. Some of the ridges were made by breaking the soil with a spade and grafán[3] which was like a grubber or heavy hoe. Grass, weeds, furze and briars were removed with the grafán and were burned when they dried and wilted – this was termed 'grafadh dóite.'[4] The seed potatoes, which would be some of the previous year's crop which were left to sprout, or new bought seed, were cut into two or three parts, which were called sciolláns.[5] Every sciollán had to have an 'eye' or sprout. The biggest piece left had a súil tóin.[6] and was not sat. When the ridges were made, the planting was done by making a hole with a spade, dropping a seed into it, the seed being carried in a púca[7] by the planter. Once the seed were sat, the holes were closed with a pucadóir,[8] a flat piece of timber with a handle.

Earthing the potatoes was done about three weeks after planting and again a month later, when the stalks were well above ground. To 'earth' the potatoes, a shovel was used to scoop up loose soil from the trench and distribute it over the ridge. The potatoes got a 'second dressing' of seaweed when the shoots began to show. Spraying against blight was done before the blossoms appeared. A solution of bluestone and washing soda was mixed in a barrel of water at the top of the garden. In earlier times the solution was sprinkled on leaves and stalks with a besom.[9] In more recent times a spraying machine fastened to a man's back was used. This had a pumping handle and a spraying nozzle which broadcast the solution over the leaves. Spraying was done three or four times a season at least. Sultry humid weather is the worst for the spread of potato blight. Aran Banners, which were larger and less appetizing, were grown to feed the pigs. Turnips and cabbage were grown in the same garden as the potatoes, the young cabbage plants often bought from Timothy John Cadogan of Ardagh. On West Skeam, the ridges of early potatoes were covered with mussels, often collected at Mussel Point near Ballydehob. The fish would rot, enriching the soil, while the shells drew heat from the sun, encouraging growth.

Hay

JERRY McCARTHY SAVING
THE HAY
© B. Morris

Once the grass was tall enough, the hay in the meadows was cut, usually in June. Since this was the height of the lobster season, the women, children, and older men did most of the work. Sometimes, men like Batt Cadogan of Ardagh, were hired to cut the hay with a scythe. Sometimes the fishermen had to return for a few days to 'save' the hay. It was cut in swathes (swarths is the usual West Cork pronunciation), left lying on the field for a few days; it was then turned and shaken up with two-pronged hay pikes and made into cocks in the field. The haycocks were then drawn into the haggard and built into a rick (pronounced reek). The sides of the rick were manicured with a hay rake. The base of the rick was pulled, leaving an inward slope called the cos[10], which prevented wetting. The blacksmith fashioned the scythes to the farmer's specifications so no two scythes were exactly the same. The blade was sharpened with a special honing stone, called a 'scythe-stone.' After World War II a mowing machine, pulled by a single horse, replaced the scythe. The first mowing machine on Heir Island was bought by Patsy O'Neill, Heir Island East. The scythe was still used, however, to cut small patches of hay where it would be difficult to manoeuvre the mowing machine. The scythe continued to be used to cut rushes, briars, ragw,ort etc.

Grain Crops

Smith, in his *History of Cork*, in 1750, describes Heir Island thus:

> To the N.W. of Inishircan (Sherkin) lies Hare Island, a large fruitful spot; and near it are four (sic) small islands called the Schemes, not expressed in any former chart. All these islands, together with the adjacent coast, produce large crops of fine English barley by means of sea sand, which is the manure mostly used.

In the nineteenth and in the first half of the twentieth century every household grew a 'patch' of wheat and often some oats or barley. In olden times the corn was cut with a sickle and later by a scythe. The cut corn was bound into sheaves. Six to eight sheaves were stood, leaning against each other, to form a stook. After a few days the corn was drawn into the haggard[11] by donkey and cart, (or pony and cart) and built into a rick. The threshing, which was postponed until the lobster season finished, was done by slashing the wheat ears on a stone or baulk of timber placed on a bench. The thresher would take a dornán (handful) of wheat from an opened sheaf and holding the bottom of it, bend it by rubbing it up and down against the side of the bench. The dornán of wheat was then threshed by repeated slashing against the square-edged stone. Slashing was superior to threshing with a flail because it did not break the straws which were required for thatching. The corn grains fell onto a piece of canvas, often a piece of sail cloth, placed on the ground and the threshed straws were bound into sheaves again.

When the threshing was done with a flail, the sheaves were taken from the rick, opened and placed on a sheet on the floor. As the walloping got under way, a steady rhythm developed. Usually two men worked in unison, sometimes three, (buaileadh dó or buaileadh trír) – two beating or three beating in unison. The flail consisted of two parts, the handle (colpa) and the beater (buailteán), which were tied together by a leather thong or animal sinew which was called a gad. This had to be tough and strong to withstand the powerful belting : from it we get the expression, 'as tough as a gad', to describe a hardy, tough person.

The straw was used as bedding for the cattle. The grain was still mixed with chaff, so the next step was the winnowing. For this one needed a day with a 'sweet' breeze, not too calm, not too windy. The heads of corn were placed on a bodhrán or criathar.[12] The man winnowing stood on a height and shook the

THRESHING IN HEIR ISLAND – AT LEAST TWELVE MEN AT WORK

PATSY O'NEILL, HEIR ISLAND EAST, WINNOWING ON THE TOP OF THE GIORNÁN STRAND

container vigorously in the wind, so that the chaff dislodged from the corn kernels and blew away in the wind.

Jerry McCarthy, Heir Island West, had the first threshing machine on the island, bought from Dalys of Dereenatrá. It consisted of a drum and engine and could be moved by pony from haggard to haggard. The engine was operated using paraffin oil. Later, Patsy O'Neill of Heir Island East bought a larger one from Denis Cadogan of Turkhead, who had used it for milling grain for a few years at Church Cross. On West Skeam, their first threshing machine was a drum turned by manual effort. Another man fed the sheaves into the thresher while working pedals with his feet.

In West Skeam the wheat seed was 'pickled' before sowing. The seeds were placed in a barrel of salty water. All small grains, chaff and weeds would float to the surface. The pickling continued for up to three weeks, fresh salt being added at intervals. The pickle was considered strong enough when a raw potato would float on it. The grains were enlarged in the salty water. Sometimes the wheat was sat as early as January if the weather was suitable. At harvest time the grain was washed in salt water before being taken to the mill. It was strained and 'dead' grains discarded. This gave the wheat a lovely flavour. On Heir they usually tarred the wheat seeds before planting to keep the crows from eating them. The wheat was brought to Ballydehob for milling and to Cotters of Lissaree, Aughadown, in later years.

Threshing

When the threshing was done by machine, the neighbours had to comhar[13] (help one another). A 'meitheal'[14] of men followed the machine from haggard to haggard. The Irish work 'meitheal' means a group of men working in co-opera-tion. The threshing required a minimum of eight or nine men. A couple of men piked the sheaves onto the machine, where another man opened the sheaves and fed the corn into the drum. The grain came out and was filled into jute bags. It took a couple of men at least to take charge of the filling and to draw it into the barn loft. It took four or five men to pike the straw and construct the rick of straw. When the threshing was completed for one householder, the meitheal moved on to the next house. Mutual help was absolutely essential. At the end of the day's work, the men ate a hearty meal. It was usual to have a few bottles of stout for the men, which they drank during a break or when they were finished in the evening.

The haggard was the storing place for hayrick and cornstack. A berth of stones, briars or fuchsia was placed underneath the ricks to prevent wetting in winter. The ricks were usually covered with luachair (rushes), under a piece of old netting, torn sail or jute bags, weighed down with stones.

Ploughing

The ploughing was done with donkeys and later by ponies. It required three donkeys to pull the plough; two ponies sufficed. The early ploughs were made of timber. They had a v-shaped iron into which the sock or ploughshare was fitted. The sock of the plough was taken to the blacksmith. The farmer required the correct depth and the proper lay to fold the furrow back.

The following is a list of some of the families who 'comhared' for ploughing in the 1950s, as recalled by John Fitzgerald, Riverdale, Skibbereen and formerly of Heir Island.

1. Patrick Murphy, Jeremiah McCarthy and John Fitzgerald (all Heir Island West).
2. Florence Fitzgerald, Danny O'Neill and John O'Neill (All Heir Island East)
3. Charlie O'Neill, Johnny Harte and Richard Cotter.
4. John Denis McCarthy, Danny Harte and Mike 'Stephen' O'Neill.
5. Timmy Cahalane, Timmy Harte and Jim Pyburn.

Those who 'comhared' with ponies were.

> John Barry and Jerry McCarthy,
> Pat Burke and John McCarthy.

The Quern

Most houses had a quern (bró), a small hand mill, comprised of two round stones. The upper stone had a hole into which the grain was fed at a regular rate. When grinding corn with the quern, it was placed on a sheet on the table. The

© Bill Morris

CHARLIE O'NEILL WHO HAD THE FIRST TRACTOR ON HEIR ISLAND

© Michael Minihane

TRANSPORTING BALES INTO HEIR ISLAND

BASE STONE ON THE LEFT; UPPER STONE WITH
LARGER OPENING ON RIGHT

upper stone has a timber stick or spindle, called the míolaire, attached to it by which the upper stone was turned. Any overflow came out around the edge and was gathered into a container. With the milled grain some delicacies were made. Riabún[15] was made out of pure hulled wheat which was first roasted in a bastable to harden the grains. It was then ground in the quern. The finely milled grain was

mixed with milk and sugar to make a delicious meal. The island people used other methods of treating the wheat to produce two other popular dishes. Gráinseachán was made by boiling unground grain in water. Milk and sugar were then added to make a tasty treat. Próinsimín, frumenty in English, toasted grain, eaten with sugar but without milk, was especially attractive to children.

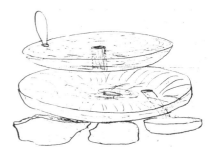

Sand

The Griffith evaluation carried out in West Cork from 1847 to 1853, aimed at establishing a uniform taxation on property. Local circumstances, climate, manure, and markets had an effect on the valuation of a holding. Manure consisted of coal, turf, limestone, seaweed, and sea sand. Griffiths stated that where seaweed of good quality was plentiful and easy of access, the land within one mile of the strand from which it was drawn was increased in value by 4 shillings in the pound at least (20%), and where the soil consists of a strong clay or clayey loam, the value of shelly sea sand when abundant increased the value by 2 shillings and 6 pence in the pound, for a distance of one mile from the shore (12½%).

Farmers in coastal West Cork had a history of applying sea sand to the soil for at least three hundred years prior to Griffith's Evaluation. The influence of 'sea manure' (sea weed and sea sand) had the biggest bearing on land valuation in the islands and townlands adjacent to the sea. Added valuations from Aughadown parish include: Turkhead, Cunnamore, Heir Island, the Skeams 10 shillings per £ (50%); Ardagh, Calf Island East, Fásagh, Poulnacallee, 5 shillings per £ (25%). This raised the valuation of the land and consequently the rents. Undoubtedly the application of sand and seaweed improved soil quality but it inflated rent paid to the landlord, making it very difficult for tenants to keep up with payments.[16]

In the 1950s, the farmers got government grants to buy sand. Sand was taken from the strands or was dredged in sandy places. On Heir, there are many fine sandy strands – the two Trá Báns, an Tráigh Mhór, 'Leán Caorach, etc. Boats from Ballydehob, Sherkin, Turkhead, Collatrum, Ardralla and other places were involved. Dominic Casey of Collatrum often collected sand from the strands on the Reen in his boat, the *St Anthony*. Three men shovelled a load of sand into the boat at low tide. When the boat rose with the flood tide, the load was transported up the Ilen to be deposited on one of the quays. The two Pyburn brothers, Jack and Eddie, drew sand in the early 50s. They often filled the *Mary Joseph* and landed the sand at the Quay, near Jack Minihane's pub, in North Street. Mr. Minihane bought the sand. Eddie remembers taking sand from 'Lean Caorach, from the Trá Bán strands on the Reen, from Silver Strand in Sherkin. They were paid £5 a boatful in 1953. It had to be shovelled into the boat by hand and shovelled out onto the quay again by hand. Boats from Ballydehob, and Ardralla dredged for sand.

Seaweed

Much of the soil of Heir Island is rocky, the western end being dominated by heathland. There are some very fertile fields and fertile patches between the rocks. The fields were constantly being enriched with seaweed during the winter and spring months. This was gathered on the strands or cut from the rocks at low tide with an implement called the corrán cam or scamhdóir, a sickle with a long handle. With it they cut different types of seaweed – lóch (loke), dúlamán, (doolamaun) ráimh and clabhtaí (clouts).

The seaweed was transported from the strands to the fields by a donkey bearing a top-load, which consisted of two wickerwork baskets, one on either side of the animal, attached to a piece of timber across the donkey's back, underneath which was a soft súgán band, called a saoistín.[17] The top-load comes from the Irish word, lód. The straddle-mats (saoistín) woven in three-strand plait, provided protection for the donkey's back, placed under the timber yoke, from which the creels or top-

loads hung. The bottoms of the creels were hinged and when the field was reached, the owner pulled the ropes so that the two baskets unloaded together. The seaweed rotted into the soil, enriching it with minerals. The long strand on the western side of the inlet in Paris is called 'Trá a Bhliana' (strand of the year) because seaweed is washed ashore here throughout the year. Every family had their own seaweed 'station', marked by stones. For example, the Pyburn family had a station in Trá a Bhliana and another in the south Lochán.

Rocks off the shore were also allotted to families. In later years people began to draw seaweed from anywhere they could get it, but in earlier times a householder dare not collect or cut seaweed in an neighbour's allotment.

Livestock

Most families in the early part of the century had only one or two cows. The cows who grazed in the fields from spring to autumn were wintered in the cow-byre or 'chamber' and were fed hay, mangolds, turnips and (later) fodder beet.

MRS KATHY 'CON' MURPHY FEEDING HER TURKEYS.

The people suffered greatly during the economic war of the 1930s; bailiffs would come and round up the cattle. Farmers were paid 12/6 for a hide which was more than you would get for a bullock.

Most households fattened a pig or two, usually bought at Ballydehob fair with the first money of the lobster season. The women used to row or sail to Ballydehob in May in one of the smaller lug sail boats. They bought two bonhams, one to kill before Christmas, the other to sell. Every housewife kept a flock of hens, which supplied them with eggs. They sold the extra eggs and the homemade butter at the end of the week to the island shopkeepers. It paid in part for the weekly groceries. Michael John Whooley of Lisheen also bought eggs and butter from the islanders, collecting them at Fásagh. Some of the islanders kept geese and ducks. In latter years some of the householders raised turkeys which they sold at the Christmas market, which was usually held on December 8th.

The resilient nimble donkey served the islanders well for a long time. Ideal for work in the confined small fields, and ideal on the strand from where toploads of seaweed were drawn. Harnessed to a cart, they were used to carry loads from the shop, coal, flour, meal, etc.

Milk

Before the coming of the separator, fresh milk, which was left after home use, was kept in a cool pantry in big dishes. At the end of the week the cream was scooped off with a saucer or scallop shell. Later a separator was used to separate the milk after enough of the leamhnacht (fresh milk) was kept for the house. It was then made into butter in a churn, of which there were several types. In the dash churn, a staff was used to swirl the cream around until it 'broke' and you had butter. In the dash churn a special twist of the staff was called a 'cor'. The dash churn continued to be used by many of the families, but others bought the end-over-end

churn, also known as a barrel churn, because essentially the cream holder part of it was a stave-built barrel. The barrel churn was turned by hand. If someone called during the churning, he or she was expected to say 'God bless the work' and take a turn. In sultry warm weather it often took a long time for the cream to 'break'. Once the butter was 'clean', butter pats were used to mould it into shape. Some of the butter was shaped into wedges after salting. The butter was salted for home use and the rest was sold. The milk left after the churning was called butter-milk (bláthach) and was great to 'kill' the thirst on hot summer days. Sometimes small amounts of butter were made in a sweet tin. The old boiled sweets like Bull's Eyes, Clove Rocks etc. came in ½ gallon tins. The cream was placed in the tin and shaken vigorously until the butter was made. The above picture is of an Alfa Laval Separator used in Heir Island.

Fairs

When the people of Heir wanted to sell an animal they had to go to Skibbereen fair. The animals had to swim to Cunnamore the previous evening. Their friends on the mainland – the Desmonds, the Hingstons, the Minihanes, Pattie Whooley – would look after the cattle until the morning. The islanders had to wake in the middle of the night and walk the cattle to Skibbereen in the early morning. Sometimes the cattle buyers came out towards Newcourt to meet

© Michael Minihane

SWIMMING CATTLE FROM HEIR ISLAND

them. The fairs were hold in different streets – Ilen St., Market St., Townsend St., and later in the Fair Field. The islanders were at a great disadvantage; because of the difficulty in getting the animals back to the island they often had to accept prices below the animals' value. Sometimes cattle buyers went into the islands to buy cattle.

Sometimes they drove the cattle to Skibbereen the evening before the fair and stayed overnight with friends in Skibbereen. Minihane's and Hall's of North St., and Tom Teape, formerly of Sherkin, who had a pub in Bridge St., were favourite lodging houses for the Heir Islanders. In later years, when bigger boats were bought, they carried the animals by boat as far as Oldcourt and walked them to Skibbereen.

Blacksmiths

Paddy Daly and his son, Tom, of Ardnagrohery (Ard na gCrocairí) townland were blacksmiths ; their forge was in Lisheen near Jack Daly's Hill, east of Minihan's Pub. They went into Heir and the Skeams to shoe the donkeys and ponies. The men congregated near William Barry's house west of the school with their animals. The people of Heir Island West used to bring their animals to Jerry McCarthy's yard in Paris.

Hardship

The hardship that the island people had to endure is well illustrated by the fact that some of them had to haul bags of gravel up steep slopes from the strands when the houses were being built in 1928. Jeremiah McCarthy had to haul gravel up the incline from Cuas a Bhrághaid. John Fitzgerald did likewise, pulling gravel from the strand near Cuas Mahoun. Everything was done by the sweat of the brow.

In the School Folklore Collection 1937/38,[18] John McCarthy, Heir Island West told of the hardship of living on East Calf.

> Michael O'Driscoll, now residing on Heir Island, but born on Calf Island, told me that his family, when living on Calf Island, were often forced to live for weeks during stormy weather, when they could not venture to the mainland for food provisions, on flour ground from wheat.

Furze

Irish furze (aiteann Gaelach), cut with a sickle and gabhlóg, (a Y-shaped piece of stick), was chopped up and fed to the donkeys and horses. The stronger French furze (aiteann Gallda) was used for stopping gaps in a field. Small bits of furze clinging together was called an ortóg. So many ortógs made a bundle, or beart, as it was called in Irish and still widely used, 'I cut a beart of furze' or 'give a beart of hay to the cows'. Some houses had a furze-machine to chop the furze into little pieces. Before the coming of the furze machine, a special mallet was used to crush the furze thorns to make it edible for the cattle and donkeys.

With the mechanization of farming from 1950 on – use of tractor, mowing machines, threshing machines etc., the coming of electricity, the islanders fell further behind their neighbours on the mainland with regard to income from agriculture. At a meeting of the Cork Committee of Agriculture, held at County Hall, Cork on 22nd March, 1973, the Chairman outlined to the meeting the desire of the Central Development Committee to improve the lot of islanders in any way possible. For this purpose, it had set up a sub-committee to carry out a survey to ascertain what could be done. The Chairman of the sub-committee outlined the scope of the proposed survey and stated that as far as West Cork was concerned, he proposed to start with an investigation of Heir Island. The Chairman outlined the position with regard to island agriculture. He felt that almost all farms would be termed 'non viable' by mainland standards for reasons of size, minimal, if any, use of fertilizers, attitudes – slowness to change to new methods, etc. Milch cows were the main enterprise, with butter sales per cow realising about £30 per annum. The average farm income would be about £300 from sale of cattle, butter, eggs, turkeys, geese, etc. Sheep or pigs were not kept on the island. There was only one tractor on the island – farmwork was done by horse or manually. Mr. J. Cadogan, of the Department of Agriculture and Fisheries, suggested that improvements could be achieved by increased use of fertiliser and lime mechanically spread, and the use of special calf suckling scheme instead of butter scheme.

The meeting was informed that there was very little fertiliser or lime used on the island. The islanders felt aggrieved that lime, at half price, was not supplied to them, as was the case with Cape Clear farmers. The meeting felt that there should be a special island scheme for supply of fertilisers and lime to all islanders at half-price, delivered in bags at mainland pier of Cunnamore. It was pointed out that the only agricultural machinery available on the island was one tractor. There were no attachments for fertilizer spreading, etc. In was the unanimous view of the meeting that there was little hope for island agriculture if modern equipment was not introduced.

At the time of this meeting in 1973, there were forty one island houses, twenty occupied, eleven used as holiday homes and ten unoccupied.

DOMINIC CASEY OF COLLATRUM
AND HIS SON DRAWING LIME
TO THE ISLANDS FROM
COOSHEEN PIER, TURKHEAD

Photo: Peggy Townend, Turkhead

PATSY O'NEILL'S MOWING MACHINE

CUTTING
CORN
WITH A
SCYTHE

— 21 —
Growing up in Heir Island 1920s-30s:
Catherine O'Connor

The following are the memories of Catherine O'Connor
(nee McCarthy, Heir Island Middle) who was born in
Heir Island in 1914 and who now lives in London.

My father, Michael McCarthy, and my mother Mary (nee O'Donovan) both came from the Western part of Heir Island. Whey they married they settled in Heir Island Middle facing 'Leán Gamhan. My mother told me that her father gave her a dowry and they bought ten acres in Heir Island Middle. There were ten children in our family and I was the second youngest. My older brother, Jeremiah, went to the States when he was about nineteen. My father died in 1921, aged about 45. I was seven and the oldest was sixteen or seventeen. We were poor and my mother struggled to bring us up. My sister, Mary Hannah, went to America in 1922, followed by my brother Charlie two years later. He lived in New York. I am the only one left now. My dear husband Vincent died last September. Vincent was a wonderful man and I loved him dearly. He loved Heir Island and we were last there about 13 years ago. We visited Jack Pyburn and Teresa – she was my first cousin and Jim Pyburn was my mother's first cousin. I went to school with Charlie O'Neill and Patsy O'Neill – we were all about the same age. Denis O'Donovan, our teacher, had a little house in Whitehall and used to come in to Heir Island when the weather permitted. If the weather was bad, he stayed over in William Barry's, the house next to the school. We were taught the Irish language and I spoke it fluently but now I only know a few phrases – time dulls the memory I am afraid.

I left Ireland in 1937, aged 23, to come to the Isle of Wight to my sister Betty, who was already working there. I met Vincent in St. Mary's Church – he came from Youghal. I stayed in the Isle of Wight for two and a half years. Vincent was working in London and he wanted me to join him, which I did, after a lot of persuasion. We were married in Richmond in 1941. Getting back to Heir Island, all the families had nicknames to distinguish them as there were so many of the same name : Donovans, McCarthys, Murphys, Hartes. I knew most of the boats, also Taylor's Rock; it was the year my father died. I can remember the guards coming to collect the loot but they didn't get it all! Bales of material, shoes and whiskey were hidden – I remember my Uncle Denny, my mother's brother, falling about drunk. I don't know if it was the whiskey or porter he had drunk.

Con Burke lived very near us and my mother did a lot of her shopping there and exchanged butter and eggs for goods. She had large bills but she paid them all eventually. When the boys grew up, they lobster-fished as they were able to buy a boat.

My mother was a great nurse and she delivered babies. When people were sick she nursed them, much to our resentment, as my brother Owen had to look after us, younger ones. He baked cakes etc. He was very good. I remember my mother going to Creagh, when her sister Bridgie had her first child and staying there for two weeks. My Aunt Hannah, my mother's sister, was in Boston and she was very good to us. She used to send clothes and materials to make dresses. My mother made all our clothes by hand – she was a wonderful needlewoman. She also made patchwork quilts on a wooden frame. In the summer we went to school barefoot and in the winter wore second-hand shoes sent by Aunt Hannah from America. We were very grateful as my mother couldn't afford to buy them. When we first started school, we had slates to write on. As we progressed, we had copybooks, pencils and pens which we had to buy. We also had to buy our reading books – nothing was free. Our books were passed down to the younger children.

Our staple diet was potatoes, gruel, fish and cured pig. The pig was killed and cured in a barrel of coarse salt. Mackerel were cured in the same way. We had three cows and we made our own butter in a barrel with a handle – anyone who came in, gave the handle a turn, as it was supposed to bring good luck! The island people were very superstitious. One winter when no one had any milk, the government sent milk each week and we collected a sweet-tin full at the Slip. My mother or Owen made 'bastable' cakes with the sour milk, kept after the cream was skimmed off the pans to make butter. Bastable cake was made from a dough and then cooked in the pot with a lid covered with hot turf or scalps. It took about an hour to bake and was really delicious. We used to drink cups of buttermilk. I also picked winkles to sell to Con Burke.

My Uncle Denny made lobster pots and also did thatching. Harry Cadogan was also a thatcher. They were the only two men on the island with that skill. Our house now belongs to an Englishman. My brother sold the house to Pat Burke, who sold it to the Englishman, who uses it as a holiday home. When we last visited Heir Island, Neilly O'Donovan was the caretaker and he took us to see my old home. I got very emotional when I saw it.

There has been a lot of improvements and it really looked lovely. Vincent took a photo of myself and Neilly Donovan sitting on the wall outside the back door. (*left*)

It is such a pity that so many had to leave, but there was no alternative. We had to leave school at fourteen and go into housework as we couldn't afford further education. It was very hard but we managed. Thank God both my girls got a wonderful education and married well. Vincent and I made a lot of sacrifices but it was worth it. I was determined that they wouldn't have to work like I did.

CATHERINE'S BROTHER, OWEN.

CATHERINE'S MOTHER, MARY (JACKY) McCARTHY (NEE O DONOVAN) AND HER SISTER MARGARET ANNE McCARTHY

MARY HANNAH, CATHERINE'S SISTER, ON THE DAY SHE ARRIVED IN AMERICA IN 1922

CHARLES McCARTHY, MARY HANNAH McDONOUGH (NEE McCARTHY) JEREMIAH McCARTHY

LIZZIE MCCARTHY,
HEIR ISLAND WEST

MARY FALVEY (NEE MCCARTHY)
HEIR ISLAND WEST

MARGARET AND KATHLEEN
MURPHY

MRS. CECELIA O'NEILL, HEIR ISLAND

PAT LORDAN (NEE O'DONOVAN) AND NELLIE
HEALY (NEE FITZGERALD)

JOHN HARTE WITH PADDY AND HUGHIE O'NEILL

LIZZIE FITZGERALD AND HANNIE HARTE

— 22 —

Population

Excluding summer visitors and part-time islanders, the population of Heir Island today is twenty five.

The population of Ireland rose rapidly in the early decades of the 19th century, reaching a total of over eight million by 1841. This was due to landholders sub-dividing their farms between their sons, large families, and the fact that potatoes, which give a large yield, could feed a big population. Despite the fact that we have no census figures for earlier dates, we can assume pretty confidently that the highest number of people ever living on Heir was three hundred and fifty-eight in 1841. Prior to the Great Famine (1845-49), landowners subdivided their tiny farms among their children, which was the norm all over the country at that time. There is no way that the island of 380 acres, a large portion barren and rocky, could maintain a population of three hundred and fifty eight, given that they were depending almost entirely on fishing and what food they could grow in their little farms.

The decade 1841-1851 marked a fall from 358 to 288, a fall of 20% reflecting the pattern nationwide. Death, from starvation, but mostly from 'famine fever', and emigration caused the decline in population. Despite fever and other diseases, emigration and years of partial famine, when the potato crop partly failed again e.g. 1881 and 1890, the population had increased from 288 in 1851 to 325 in 1891, an increase of almost 13%, almost as high as it was before the Famine.

In the century 1891–1991, the population fell from 325 to 22. During the decades following 1891 there was increased emigration, the people now leaving on board liners from Cobh, instead of in small ships from Baltimore, Schull, or Crookhaven.

The first big rift in the population, apart from emigration, came in the early 1950s, when three island families were allotted farms on the mainland by the Irish Land Commission. The Barrys and Minihanes got farms in the Old Head of Kinsale area and left the island on the same day, April 10th, 1954. Two years previously on March 26th, 1952, the McCarthys of Heir Island East got a farm in Velvetstown, near Kanturk, in North Cork.

A new factor in the fall of population occurred from 1970 onwards. With delays in providing electricity and piped water, the younger generation compared the hardship of life on the island with the advantages of living on the mainland and persuaded the older generation, who were more reluctant to leave, that they too should move. Some sold their houses and land to people from England, Germany, and other parts of Ireland, mainly Cork City. Some of the islanders kept their homes and sold their land, while others sold their houses and kept their farms. All of these homes were sold at a time when prices were deflated. Today the reverse is true; sites for houses being sold at a very high price.

The decline of the resident population of Heir reflected the general trend toward the demise of the island way of life around the Irish coast.

I describe the two Skeams and East Calf as 'satellites' of Heir, because they are all part of Aughadown parish and there were close social and family connections between the inhabitants. The decline on the 'three satellite islands' of Heir, showed the same trend in decline in population. Eventually all three, being smaller and lonelier, and in the case of East Calf, more remote, were abandoned by the inhabitants. The East Calf was deserted sometime between 1911 and 1926, West Skeam in 1940 and East Skeam in1958, when the last inhabitant, Mrs. Hannah Cadogan, moved to Heir Island, the Harte family having moved to Collatrum earlier in the same year.

1901 Census

The 1901 census was carried out on the 11th and 12th April of that year. A total population of 317 in 44 inhabited houses gives the average number per house to be 7.2 persons. The number of inhabitants per house varied from two to twelve. The average in 1911 was 6.5.

Population

YEAR	POPULATION	PERCENTAGE	
1841	358		
1851	288	20%	Decrease
1861	261	9%	Decrease
1871	279	7%	Increase
1881	302	8%	Increase
1891	325	8%	Increase
1901	317	2%	Decrease
1911	294	7%	Decrease
1926	216	27%	Decrease
1936	169	22%	Decrease
1946	143	15%	Decrease
1951	139	3%	Decrease
1961	94	32%	Decrease
1971	79	16%	Decrease
1979	54	32%	Decrease
1981	35	35%	Decrease
1986	19	48%	Decrease
1991	22	16%	Increase
1996	16	27%	Decrease
2003	25	56%	Increase

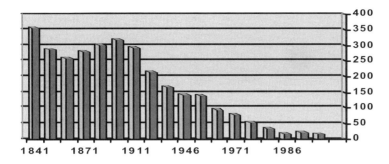

Graph 1 – Heir Island Population.

Population

	EAST SKEAM	WEST SKEAM	EAST CALF
1891	20	16	16
1901	22	11	7
1911	27	15	9
1926	11	13	0
1936	8	8	
1946	8	0	
1951	7		
1961	0		

The population chart shows that apart from the decade of the Great Famine when the population fell by 20%, the other significant decreases occurred (a) between 1926-1946. when the population fell by almost 34%, one third of the population, which was caused mainly by emigration and (b) the rapid recline from 1961 to 1996 when practically all the families left the island to settle on the mainland, mainly in the parishes of Aughadown, Schull and Skibbereen.

The island population reached an all-time low (16) in 1996. In recent times, six families have settled permanently on the island, while others have built houses, to which they come frequently, especially during long weekends, at Easter and at Christmas. In summer all the houses are occupied for periods and in some cases for most of the summer. It is also encouraging that two native families have returned to settle on the island.

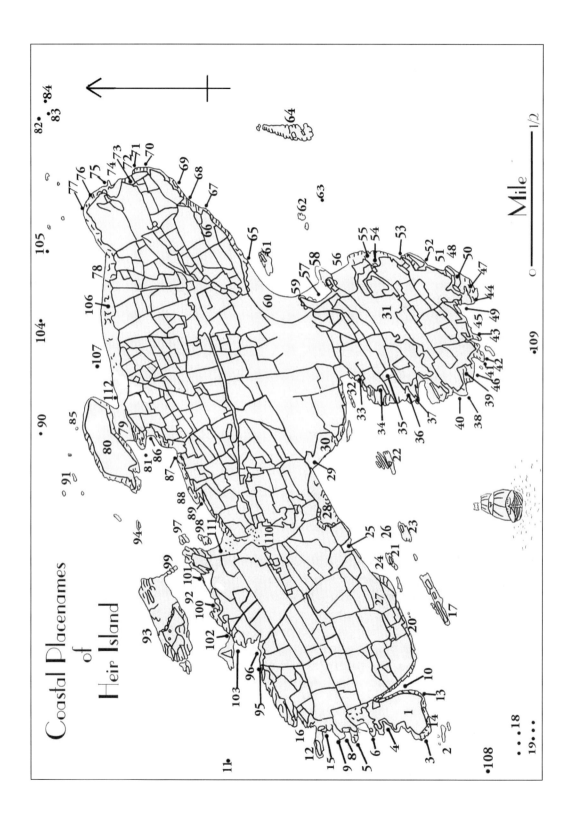

Coastal Placenames of Heir Island

— 23 —
Heir Island Placenames

In total, over two hundred placenames have been identified, the vast majority in Irish. Every strand, cliff, rock and skerry in the vicinity of the island was known by the islanders. They knew, from centuries of experience, where there were builgs (submerged rocks) visible only at low tide, or rabhas (pronounced rows), a line of rock or skerry, which had to be avoided. Around the offshore rocks and builgs was plenty of seaweed or 'foul ground' which is the habitat of lobsters, crayfish and crabs and also some fish like ling, pollock and cod.

Inland there was a name for every field, rock, well, hill and hollow. If these placenames had been collected and recorded fifty years ago, I'm sure the number would be doubled at least. When somebody dies they bring with them a part of the history of the island.

The landscape, the history of a place can be 'read' to a large extent by studying the old Irish placenames, which refer to the topography, to people, to events, to folklore. A few words recur regularly in the placenames. On the coast you find cuas, a cove or inlet, faill, a cliff, trá or tráigh, a strand, carraig, a rock, oileán, an island, inis, an island.

A higher percentage of coastal names than inland names are still remembered. On the farms, each householder knew the names of the fields in his own farm but might not know some at the other end of the island.

Coastal

1. The Dún: Comes from the Irish dún, a fort or a fortress. It is a rocky heath covered peninsula, almost cut off from the island by deep inlets. It commands a panoramic view of Roaringwater Bay. The O'Driscolls, possibly, had a promontory fort here as the name suggests. However, there are no traces left.
2. Carraig a Dúna: The rock of the Dún.
3. Sciollán Point, the S.W. corner of the island. Sciollán, a thin slice, slaty-type rock.
4. Trá a Dúna: The Dún strand.
5. Carraig na Seagaí: rock of the shags or cormorants.
6. Faill a Dúna: The Dún cliff.
7. Cuas a Dúna: The Dún inlet or cove
8. Léithoileán: a lump of rock with some vegetation, otherwise it would be called carraig.(rock) It is pronounced lah-oileán, meaning literally half-an-island, almost an island. It could also be liath-oileán meaning grey, windswept, almost devoid of vegetation.
9. Dún Beag: the little dún, compared to the larger outcrop further south.
10. Cuas a Bhrághaid: The inlet of the gorge. Brághaid means a long narrow opening, a neck, throat.

11. An Rabha Mór – the big row (skerry). In O.S. maps it is termed Builg an Anama the reef of the soul, spirit.
12. Oileán na Mná Boichte: The island of the poor woman.
13. Faill a Bhrághaid: the cliff of the gorge.
14. Dún Sound. A narrow passage between the Dún and the rock.
15. Faill a Scéim. Possibly from scéimh, an overhanging verge of cliff. Pronounced like Skeam islands. More likely, it comes from céim, a step, a rise.
16. Faill a chréisc. Probably, Faill a chorréisc – the cliff of the heron.
17. Oileán an Ghiolla: from giolla, a page, servant, or guide; probably from pilot as many of the O'Driscolls were employed as pilots in Baltimore Harbour up to the 1590s.
18. Fuarán Rocks: Fuarán – a spring or well – cannot apply here. In O.S. maps they are listed as Toorane Rocks.
19. Deargán Rocks: from deargán, bream, which were once very plentiful in the bay.
20. Cuas Phartaláin: from Partalán, Bartholomew – Bartholomew's inlet.
21. Carraig a Róinte: from rón (seal) Rock of the seals; when seals come inside these rocks to shelter it is a sign of bad weather approaching.
22. Carraig a Róinte (2):
23. Carraig na Seagaí: Rock of the shags or cormorants.
24. Faill Leac: the cliff of the flat stones.
25. Trá Faill a Sleach: it may mean 'the strand of the cliff of the drisleacha (briars)' or possibly from saileach, a willow or osier.
26. Cuaisín a Rais – Probably from frais, spray, the little cove of the spray.
27. Leagacs: sloping land.
28. Lochán: a little pool or lake. This is directly opposite the narrow inlet which almost makes Heir Island West separate from the rest of the island.
29. Trá Bán North: the white sandy strand.
30. Trá Bán South: On the headland south of this strand is a large stone marking the grave of a sailor who was washed ashore here.
31. An Rinn: The Reen – a headland, divided into North and South Reen. A line from Cnocán Reamhar to Tráigín na Spáinneach is the dividing line.
32. Na Feoirí Beaga: or Na Fothaireacha Beaga; probably from fothair, wasteland sloping to a cliff.
33. Cuas na hÉanlaith: cove of the birds.
34. Carthy's strand.(from McCarthy)
35. Cuaisín Brandy: little cove of the brandy – sometimes barrels of brandy, wine or whiskey were washed ashore.
36. An Cuas Dubh: the black inlet. There are black rocks here.
37. Tráigín na Spáinneach: The little strand of the Spaniards – Spanish fishermen have been coming to the S.W. of Ireland since medieval times.
38. Bollán Point: from bollán, a rounded rock – S.W. Point of Reen
39. Cuaisín na bhFranncach: The little cove of the Frenchmen.(or of the rats)
40. Trá na Muice Mara: strand of the sea pig (porpoise)
41. Oileán an Mhuintearais: The island of friendship, possibly.
42. Pointe na Rinne: Reen Point.

43. Rinn a chorra: Rinn a chorréisc – the headland of the heron.
44. Rinn na Screadaíola: Headland of screeching or crying – probably refers to the seal's wailing.
45. Sailor's Strand.
46. Léithoileán: as the rock off the Dún – see no. 8
47. Oilean Topmast: Here the *Susan* (of Milford) was wrecked in 1848.
48. Oileán Geidhreach: Island of the willows or osiers, possibly.
49. Shelly Strand.
50. Trá Berry: probably Trá Biorraigh (bulrushes, reeds), strand of the reeds.
51. Colú Kearney: Caladh Kearney, Kearney's landing place. A Kearney family lived in this area in the 1800s.
52. Kearney's Point.
53. Tráigín na Bearna: Little strand of the gap, chasm.
54. Cúl Trá: the back strand.
55. Stephen's Point:
56. Trá an Uisce: strand of the water. A little stream flows onto the strand here.
57. Trá Báirneach: Strand of the limpets.
58. Peter's Point: Traditional landing place for the Cotters of the Reen. Peter Cotter lived near here.
59. Cnocán Reamhar: a fat rounded hillock. Traditional landing place for the Cahalanes.
60. An Tráigh Mhór: The big strand. The northern side of this strand is referred to as the *Dog of the Stray,* as it was believed that a ghostly apparition, in the form of a dog, was often seen there.
61. Cos: a small island with a little vegetation still. From cos, a sandbar – a sandbar connects strand to rock. This is called Deadman's Rock in O.S. maps.
62. Carraig a Duilisc: The rock of duileasch (palmaria palmate) dulse, an edible seaweed.
63. Carraig an Phiopaire: The rock of the piper. Also called 'half tide rock.'
64. Oileán Dá Bhán: Generally called Two Women's Rock, to which there is a tale about two women from Cape Clear fighting on a boat, resulting in the captain leaving them on the rocks to cool off. However, this would be Oileán na Beirte Mná in Irish, so it more likely refers to island of the two plots of land.
65. Spring's Landing Steps: Here steps were chiselled out of the rock to facilitate unloading of goods from a boat. Refers to Rev. Edward Spring –See Chapter 9, page 41.
66. Leacain: sloping hillside.
67. Faill na Leacaí: cliff of the slope.
68. Cuas Cam: the crooked inlet.
69. Trá na Geitirí: strand of the rushes. Geataire, common rush, the pith of which was used as wicks in old oil lamps.
70. Trá na Fideoige: strand of the plover, possibly, or of the soft rush. Also pronounced Trá na Fuinneoige, which would make it the strand of the window.
71. The Steps: This was the old landing place for boats, before the slip was built

in 1892. Chiselled out of the rock, it is a suitable landing place; because of the depth of water boats can land at low tide. However, it is unsheltered so a slip would be useless here.

72. Cuaisín na gCorp: Little cove of the corpses. Traditionally the coffin was placed here before being put into the boat. Liostrums (flag iris) were said to grow here in the form of a cross.

73. The Carraig Liath: name of the rock on which the coffin was placed. (grey rock).

74. The Pier, constructed in 2000-2001.

75. Trá na Pailíse: Pallice or Palace strand. There was a 'fish pallice' here – see page 122.

76. Traigh an Ghiornáin: Strand of the Giornán.

77: An Giornan or An Guairneán: North-east point of island, opposite Cunnamore. Comes from guairneán, swirling water, vortex, or gearr -fhionnáin (wild grass) possibly.

78. The Lic: Lic or leac – slab, flat rock surface.

79. The Strule: An srúill –a stream, channel.

80. Oileán Gamhan: Island of the calves or possibly Oileán Gann – bare or unproductive island.

81. Oileán Gamhan Beag: Little Oileán Gamhan

82. North Carraig na mBó: The rock of the cow, possibly of the cow seal.

83. South Carraig na mBó

84. Taylor's Rock: Here the St. Brigid was shipwrecked in April, 1922. The captain's name was Taylor.

85. Carrigeens of Oileán Gamhan: Little rocks of Oileán Gamhan.

86. Foghlú: This is a strand which gets its name from a Foley family that lived nearby. Foley is English form of O'Foghlú (pronounced fow-loo).

87. Cúilín na hátha; little backstrand of the ford. A stream flows into the strand here.

88. Cuas na gCat: The inlet of the cats.

89. Trá Gannaí or Tráigín na Gainimhe: the little strand of the sand.

90. Carraignagal: Three different meanings have been suggested as the basis of this name.
     (A) Carraig na gCapall: of the horses.
     (B) Carraig na Gal – of the foam.
     (C) Carraig na nGealt –of the mentally imbalanced person.

91. Na Carraigíní Buí: the yellow little rocks.

92. Sunnta: a sound or channel, between Heir and Oileán Caorach.

93. Oileán Caorach: Island of the sheep.

94: Carraig a Stacáin: from stacán, a pointed peak of rock, rock of the peak.

95. Cuas Dubh: Black inlet.

96. Cuaisín na Faille: Little cove of the cliff.

97. Carraig a tSunnta: rock of the sound – channel.

98. Carraig an tSasanaigh: Rock of the Englishman or Rock of the Protestant. Rev. Spring did lease 'Lean Caorach from the Beechers for a while in the mid 1800s.

99.   An Chos: Sandbar, passable at ebb tide.
100.   Trá na Cabhlaí – from cabhlach, a ruined house. The strand of the ru-
       ined house.
101.   Lochán (North): a little pool or lake.
102.   Manna Trá
103   Cuas Mahoun: Cuas Mathúna: O'Mahony's cove.
       O'Mahonys did live on the island in the 19th century.
104.   Oileán na gCroch: Island of the hillocks.
105.   Oileán Gé: Island of the Geese.
106.   Cuas na gCapall: inlet of the horses.
107.   Carraig na Searrai: Rock of the foal, possibly.
108.   An Láir: Greymare Rocks. An lair bhán, the greymare is the local name
       for dabberlocks (alaria esculenta), an edible seaweed.
109.   Muileann Dá Ros: The mill of the two headlands – a rock between the
       Reen of Heir Island and Dreolán Point, Sherkin. in o.s. maps, Mullen
       Rock
110.   An Góilín: Goleen – the long inlet over which the causeway is built.
111.   Tráig a Bhliana: The strand of the year. Derived from the fact that sea-
       weed was washed ashore here all through the year.

Inland

The inland placenames (fields, wells, rocks etc.) which are still remembered are generally not as interesting as the coastal placenames. The words for different types of
field are repeated. They include: (a) páirc, a pasture or grass field, (b) gort, a cultivated field, (c) garraí, a kitchen garden near the house, where potatoes and
vegetables were grown, (d) bán, a lea or uncultivated field, (e) clais, a low narrow
field. When the prefix –ín or –án is used, it signifies small, so you get páircín, a
little pasture field, claisín, a little low field, goirtín, a little cultivated field.

   Other words relating to the island topography consist of: fán, a slope, leacain,
sloping land, cnoc, a hill, sliabh, literally a mountain, but in this context, high
ground and bóthar, a road. There are at least three Fáns: Lizzie's Fán, Danny
Murphy's Fán and Fitz's Fán (Fitzgeralds). Here again the prefix –ín or án is
sometimes used as in Cnocán Ramhar (the fat rounded little hill) south of the
Tráig Mhór on the Reen, and boithrín, the little road, as in Bóithrín Spring
(Spring's little road). The word currach (usually prounounced crock) meaning a
damp, marshy place, is used in the name of at least two areas. West of Dan Mc-
Carthy's house there is a 'crock', a little lake, out of which flows a stream which
flows into the góilín, the long inlet which is spanned by the Bridge. There are numerous instances of Tobar (a well) and conair (a path). Because the islanders
always had difficulty in getting water in dry summers, the names of the wells are
all remembered.

   Inland Place Name Map on page 172 shows a sample of the more interesting
inland placenames. There is a more comprehensive list of inland place names in
Appendix 5

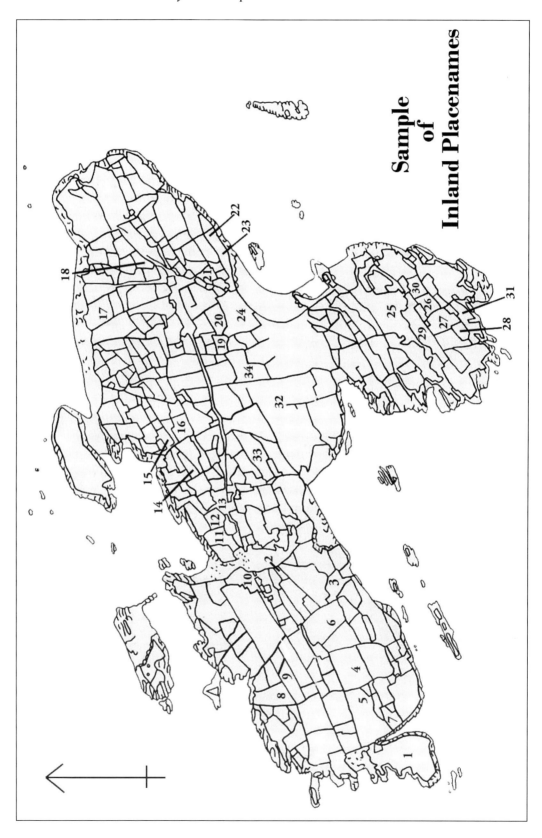

Sample
of
Inland Placenames

Index to Map

1. The Dún; fort, fortress. Possibly the O'Driscolls had a promontory fort here although no traces remain. Off East Calf and in Whitehall harbour are Dúinín (Dooneen), little fort, rocks.
2. Clais a Phoirt, low field of the landing place.
3. Cabhlach well : well of the ruined house.
4. Gort Fiannach: cultivated field or field of coarse mountain grass
5. Gort Brághaid: cultivated field adjacent to Cuas a Bhraghaid.
6. Gort na Luínseachán: Cultivated field of the lepreachaun.
7. Cac na bhFaoilean: seagulls' droppings.
8. Clais an Óir : low field of the gold, probably from golden furze flowers or from a story about buried gold.
9. Clais an Chapaill: low field of the horse.
10. Tobar na mBan: well of the women. The women used to congregate here to collect water. This well is at the edge of the strand, now closed in with gravel.
11. Latrach, rough marshy ground.
12. Béilic, a large overhanging stone, under which one could shelter.
13. Father's Hill; named after a Cadogan man, whose nickname was Father.
14. Gort na gClann: cultivated field of the families.
15. Gort na nGallán; cultivated field of the standing stones.
16. Gort na nGiollaí: cultivated field of the servants.
17. The Lic: lic or leac, flat ground or flat rock.
18. Carraig na Stácaí: Rock of the stacks, small hill west of the pier.
19. Tobair Charnáin: Wells of the cairns or mounds of stones.
20. Carriag an Aifrinn: Mass Rock.
21. Garraí Thaidhg: Tadhg's potato garden.
22. Leacain: sloping hillside.
23. Boithrín Spring: Spring's little path. Apparently the Rev. Spring used to walk along here
24. Dog of the Stray: on the northern side of An Tráigh Mhor. In folklore it is claimed that an evil spirit, in the form of a dog, was seen here on several occasions.
25. Mullach: peak. There is high rocky ground here.
26. Clais a Bhaicín: low field of the little twist or bend.
27. Brisí Fraoigh (Brishee Free): from fraoch, heather, a break of heather.
28. Póna: a pound where stray cattle were impounded until the owners paid for their release.
29. Tobar Síofra: The fairy well.
30. Liúire Báine: there is a little lake here – shining bright.
31. Claisín Airgid: little low field of silver, possibly from the plant, meadowsweet, airgead luachra.
32. The Doucks: from dabhacha, sand dunes.
33. Tobar a Lúibín: Well of the little bend. This was once considered a 'holy well'.
34. Breacain Mhór: the big speckled field.

BABY BURKE ON DONKEY

Back, l. to r., MARY JANE SHEEHAN, MRS. HEALY,
CON MINIHANE,
Front, JOHN PAUL HEALY, MARTIN MINIHANE, MARY HEALY
AND MARY MINIHANE

MRS. NORA MCCARTHY,
HEIR ISLAND WEST

PATTIE O'DONOVAN

NEILLY AND KITTY HARTE

Captain Con Burke

CAPTAIN CON BURKE AND HIS WIFE KATE

Kate Murphy, sister of Timothy Murphy, worked for Mrs Casey, who had the first shop in Heir Island. When Mrs Casey was getting old, having no family left to continue the business, she gave all the shop equipment – weights etc. to her assistant when the shop closed. When Kate Murphy married Cornelius (Con) Burke she brought these to her new home on the north side of the island near 'Leán Gamhan, where John Moore has his shop today. Con Burke set up his business early in the 20th century, selling groceries, coal etc.

Con Burke, a large impressive looking man, was the greatest entrepreneur the island produced. He was never afraid to invest his money in fishing and other enterprises. He often travelled, in one of his many boats, to the continent – France and Belgium mainly, as well as to Britain with loads of lobsters and crayfish, often accompanied by his wife.

The lobsters and crayfish were kept alive in two large submerged tanks, which were anchored off the eastern side of the island. The 'tanks' were wooden cages, semi-submerged, in which the lobsters were stored until they were shipped out. For export to Britain the lobsters were packed in crates, insulated between layers of butter-paper and wood shavings, to a total of 65 pounds in weight per box, carried by rail to Cork and by ship to England. Sometimes they were collected by French cutters, who also supplied ice. Occasionally he transported them in his own boats. He sold periwinkles to Barkers of London.

The *Savonia*, loaded with timber, was

wrecked on Calf Island Middle in January 1909. Roaringwater Bay was full of fine timber, pitch pine, teak, deal etc. It was collected by the people of Heir, Skeams Islands, Calf Island and Aughadown south who used the timber to build furniture, doors, rafters and lofts for their houses. It is said that Con Burke accepted the timber from the islanders in payment for goods purchased.[1] Everyone I have spoken to researching this book maintained that Con Burke was a good friend to the islanders in the bad times, during the Economic war of the 1930s and during World War II. He was generous with credit, giving the islanders plenty of time to settle accounts. The main source of income for the islanders was lobster fishing in the summer. The people did their best to pay their debts with money earned from selling the lobsters or when they sold their pigs or cattle. He also bought eggs and butter from the islanders. Some islanders remember during World War II paying for a stamp with an egg. The Post Office was located there at the time.

He set up a small creamery, the base of which was to be seen until recently at the eastern end of the house. The creamery was a large separator which separated the cream from the milk. In the early decades of the 20th century, people did not possess their own separators. The cream was scooped off the milk with a saucer, placed in large dishes in a cool room, before being churned into butter. It was much more efficient to have the separating done mechanically. As well as separating milk for the islanders, some of the Cunnamore people used to bring their milk in to the creamery every morning – the Desmonds, Minihanes and Hingstons.

He had the first pony on the island.

The islanders augmented their small incomes by picking periwinkles. Islanders remember that when picking periwinkles or cutting seaweed, Con Burke would often bring them bread, which was much appreciated. Willie O'Regan, of Whitehall, and formerly of West Skeam, remembers a quote made by Con Burke when somebody asked him if he was rich. 'How could I be rich with Clarks and Warners coming to me every day?' He was referring to Clarke's tobacco and Warner's bread, baked in Bantry, which was delicious, according to the older people. During World War II, people were issued with 'ration books', which indicated how much of each product a family could purchase. Since importing was impossible, supplies of oil, tobacco and fruit stopped.

The island school teachers usually boarded in Burkes. Freke Hingston, who lived in Cunnamore, used to ferry the teacher or teachers from Cunnamore to the island on Monday morning, collecting them again on Friday evening. The school books were also bought in Burkes. Con Burke, and later his son, Pat, ran a ferry to Skibbereen every Saturday in the *Surf* or the *Barker* when he went to buy provisions from wholesalers, J.J. Daly of Ilen St. Earlier they used go to Ballydehob to collect provisions.

Con Burke owned several large boats at different times. They were engaged in mackerel fishing, which was thriving in the Baltimore area from the 1880s to the 1920s. Many islanders were employed on his boats. He had boats of varying sizes which were involved in a variety of duties, transporting goods to ports along the south west coast, transporting loads of turf to ports in Britain, returning with loads of coal; exporting lobsters, collecting lobsters at Baltimore, Kinsale and Cobh. A report in the *Skibbereen Eagle* of April 3rd 1920 covers the burning of one of his boats, the *St. Finbarr.*

> Yesterday morning about 3.30, 12 miles west by north of the Mizen Head, Mr. Con Burke's splendid fishing boat, the *St. Finbarr* was destroyed by fire, caused by an explosion in the engine room, and sank with all her belongings in a few minutes. Interviewed by the Eagle reporter, Mr. Burke said the crew, consisting of his son, John, John Harte (mate), John McCarthy (third hand) and six others, all able seamen, immediately took to a punt and spent three hours in the small boat before they were picked up by an Arklow boat which landed them at Brow Head at 9.a.m. They had a very narrow escape from being lost. The *St. Finbarr* had a registered tonnage of 15.7 tons and was insured. Nobody but the engineer could account for the explosion which caused the fire. The vessel is a serious loss to Mr. Burke but he, nevertheless, is full of thankfulness to Providence that his men and himself escaped with their lives.

After Con Burke's death the following obituary was published:

> The death at Hare Island, Baltimore, of Mr. Con Burke removes from our midst one of the most outstanding personalities. A man of sterling worth and humorous disposition, with a heart almost as large as himself, he was a friend to everybody, and particularly to fisher-folk and sailormen. He was well known at almost every port in Eire, Great Britain and on the West European Coast. For a great number of years he engaged in the export trade of lobsters, crayfish and shell-fish, and personally sailed with them to ports in Belgium, Holland and France. The funeral to Creagh on Wednesday was of large dimensions and was a fitting tribute to a worthy man. Local fishermen came in from sea to attend the graveside.

A list of the various boats owned by Con Burke is included in Appendix 7.

HEIR ISLAND 1936
l. to r.: PAT BURKE, KATE BURKE, CON BURKE, SR. MAUREEN O'NEILL

DANNY CAHALANE, REEN, HEIR ISLAND

JOHN AND BRIDGET HOLLAND (NEE O'DONOVAN),
CREAGH, WITH MARY HANNAH McDONOUGH
(NEE McCARTHY)

CHARLES 'SHAW' MINIHANE,
KATHLEEN BURKE, 'BABY'
BURKE AND KIT O'NEILL

— 25 —

Emigrant's Story

This is the story of Ellen Helena Minihane from Heir Island West,
told by her grand daughter Karen Linden

ELLEN WHEN SHE FIRST ARRIVED IN AMERICA

My grandmother's life was typical of many of the emigrants to the States. She left her home in Heir Island, arrived in Boston, worked, married, raised her children and mourned many of her family and dear friends before she left this world at the age of ninety-two. She never made millions but her life was rich and full, a profound influence on those important to her and especially on me, grandchild number seven of twelve.

My grandmother was Ellen Helena Minihane, the eldest daughter of John Minihane of Heir Island West and Ellen Cahalane, originally from the Reen, Heir Island. Mom was born on 12th December. Coincidentally, my mother was also born on 12th December (same day, different year). We believe that Mom was born in 1890, but were never positive, as there are no civil or baptismal records marking her birth. This was John Minihane's second marriage, the first being to Margaret Harte also from Heir Island. There were three children from John's marriage to Margaret Harte and six children from his marriage to Ellen Cahalane, five of whom survived. Like most families, John and Ellen lost a daughter, Catherine, when she was quite small. Catherine is probably buried in the Cillín in Heir Island Middle.

Mom left Heir in August 1909, aged eighteen. Her older sister Mary (from the first marriage) had already come to the States in 1900 and married John Mahoney. Aunt Mary paid Mom's fare and according to the passenger manifest of the *SS Saxonia* I, Mom arrived in Boston with $25.00 in her pocket; a small fortune for those days. She lived with Aunt Mary and her family for a time, and then worked as a domestic/cook for the Taylors, a wealthy Boston newspaper family and the Wellingtons, another wealthy Boston family. She particularly liked

179

Louise, one of the Wellington daughters, enough to name my mother, Mary Louise. Mrs. Wellington also took a liking to my grandmother, as she would visit Mom after her marriage.

Nine years after her arrival in Boston, my grandmother married on 11 June 1918. My grandfather was William Eugene Leehan, (Americanised spelling) the youngest son of two Irish immigrants, John Lehane originally from Carrigtwohill, County Cork and Mary McCarthy from somewhere in County Cork.

Grandpa was a boiler maker/iron worker. Because of the economic depression, times were hard. Typical of so many people, his work was sporadic and Mom made do with his pay cheque, when there was one. I remember my mother saying that, regardless of how difficult things were, there was always a piece of meat for my grandfather, making sure that he had the best that she could provide him. I remember Mom sitting down to her favourite lunch, a boiled potato, boiled onion, cream and butter, all smooshed together and of course, a cup of tea.

There were four children, all girls. Helen Dorothy was the eldest, then Elizabeth Veronica (Betty), Mary Louise (my mother) and Rose Patricia. Little Betty died when she was about 8 months old. I believe that Mom was very proud of her daughters and the good men they married. I believe that she was also proud of all of her grandchildren. I do know that she was proud of where she came from, Heir Island. She made Boston her home. Looking back, I don't think that my grandmother regretted coming to Boston. So many of her family were in the States, I suppose that in some ways she could feel a bit like she was home when they were around her.

As Mom got older, there were some times when she would feel blue and lonesome for her own, the people that grew up with her. She missed her eldest sister, Mary. She missed her brother Jerh, who died young in Ireland, sometime before 1911, as a result of an accident. She missed her brother Din, who never fully recovered from being gassed while serving in the Canadian Expeditionary Force in World War I and who lived in Boston with Aunt Mary. She missed her sister Nonie, who married Mike Shea from Cape Clear and raised her family not far from Boston. She missed her sister Margaret, independent and full of fun, who lived and made her way in New York. She missed her brother John, whose wife Caddie O'Neill and daughter Maureen came to the States after his death in Ireland in the late 1920s. And she missed her sister Lizzie, who remained in Ireland, married and raised her family in Heir.

Mom buried Betty, her infant daughter and survived the deaths of four of her grandchildren. She buried Grandpa, her husband of forty-nine years on Friday and had the strength to attend her eldest granddaughter's wedding on Saturday. She saw the passing of her parents, all her brothers and sisters, favourite cousins and dear friends, yet still retained her deep religious beliefs. I remember as a kid that she made sure that all of us would go for a dip in the ocean on the Feast of the Assumption because there was a cure in the water. Mom never swam, but always made sure that she at least dipped her toes on that feast day.

We grew up listening to the tales and stories of Heir Island and her family. I remember hearing the name Shanahan, Cadogan, Murphy, O'Neill, Harte, Cotter, Pyburn and of course, Cahalane. I remember asking Mom who these people were and she would always answer 'Oh, they're cousins.' It was amazing to me that she came from such a huge family. Mom always called her father 'Black Jacket,' a name that impressed me. I could just picture this big strong man walking along the road in his black jacket and hat, a force to be reckoned with. I remember hearing of her cousin, Father Jeremiah Minihane. Like everyone else in the family, she was very fond and so proud of Father Jerry. There was her cousin, Curley Minihane, and how much fun he was. I remember hearing that, when Curley was around, there was so much laughter and story telling (even more stories than she would tell). I remember that she was always very explicit in making sure that we knew how to spell Heir, ' It's 'H-E-I-R, not H-A-R-E.'

I remember hearing stories of how poor they were growing up, obviously a lesson to us, so that we would appreciate all that we had and still have for that matter. The house in Heir had a dirt floor, no electricity and the kids all slept head-to-toe together in bed. And, allegedly, at times the chickens slept with them too. She told us how strict her mother was with all of the children. Of course, with eight children in a two-room house, my great-grandmother, Ellen Cahalane, just had to be strict with her brood. Mom told us of the dances that she went to and one time being in the worst kind of trouble with her mother because the crowd of kids were so late coming home. She told us that when someone was lost at sea, people would go to Baltimore to wait for the dolphins to bring the body home. I remember hearing stories of the regattas, such an important day in those times, all of the fishing boats in the harbour; it must have been a beautiful sight. I remember hearing about going to Cape Clear and Baltimore for some of those regattas.

I remember hearing about Sherkin Island, the long walk to Mass in Lisheen Church, a walk made often, in happy times and sad times. She told us of the goleen, which divided Heir Island. At low tide you could walk across in the mud. She told us of walking to school with a piece of coal and in bare feet, with shoes tied over the shoulder. They were so poor, carrying the shoes saved wear and tear and the coal was used to keep the school's fire going. It must have been quite a sight in those days to see the crowds of children walking along the road to school in their bare feet. I remember hearing about how rough and dangerous the water around the island would get in bad weather, the high spring tides and how the brave men would still go out fishing in those rough waters.

My grandmother passed from this world in 1983. The last years of her life were filled with the birth of great grandchildren, something that pleased her. Her health was failing as the years passed, until finally her heart gave out. She held on until one more great grandchild was born. She had a peaceful death, dying in her sleep a week after Erin was born. She was the last of her family to leave this world. I am sure that they were waiting for her when she finally caught up with them.

I was the first person in the family to return to Heir, sixty-nine years after she left. There were a lot of changes, but Lizzie, Mom's 'baby' sister was still living in the 'West.' When I came home from that visit and showed Mom the pictures of Lizzie, Jerh and John, of Heir Island and of Lizzie's home, she was quite happy. She was glad that they had such a nice home, with electricity and water no less!

I came home with stories that she wanted to hear, saw some of the people that she wanted to see and some of the places that she wanted to visit. From a selfish point, I have something that no one else in my family has of Mom. Mom and I shared Heir Island.

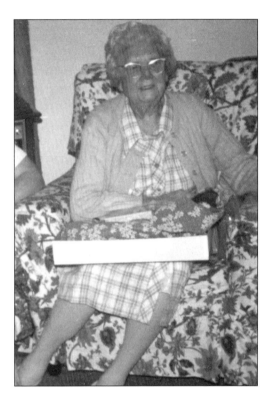

'MOM', ELLEN LEEHAN (MINIHANE)

MARGARET MINIHANE, ELLEN'S SISTER

© Michael Minihane

JOHN MURPHY CASTING HIS VOTE IN HEIR ISLAND SCHOOL

© Michael Minihane

GENERAL ELECTION 14TH JUNE 1969
Left, Jer McCarthy, John McCarthy, John O'Neill, Freke Hingston, Cunnamore, Garda Ned Cleary
and presiding officer, Dan O'Leary, Skibbereen

Photo: Kathleen Daly

1900 SCHOOL

Photo: Kathleen Daly

OLD SCHOOL (1845)

— 26 —

Education

The Penal Laws of the 18th Century discriminated against Catholics being educated, in that no Catholic was allowed teach or run a school. This was the era of the so called 'hedge-schools', where teachers taught pupils in secret in some secluded house, or sometimes in fine weather, out of doors, hence the name. The establishment of the National School system in 1831 incorporated many existing hedge-schools, Bible schools and parish schools.

In a Catholic School Census of 1807 there were 8 schools in the Parish of Aughadown (including the islands) which were attended by a total of 530 pupils. The main subjects taught were the 3 Rs – reading, writing and arithmetic. The charge were 2s/2d for reading, 3s/3d for writing and 4s/4d for arithmetic.[1]

The earliest school on Heir Island was situated in the 'Doucks'[2] in North Reen. A thatched cottage, thirty six feet long by thirteen feet wide, it was a pay school, operating on a term basis. The children were charged per subject. Children attended mainly to learn the 3 Rs and were taught religious instruction (catechism) and some Latin.

The old school, or 'schooleen' as it is called, was built during the early 1840s and classes began in April 1845. The children paid one shilling per quarter for each child of the poorer islanders and one shilling and six pence for the less poor. Fr. Troy, P.P. Aughadown applied to have this school incorporated with the Board of Education, stating that it had been built at his own expense. Religious instruction was given in the school house on Saturdays. When the application was submitted, there were three Church applicants; the Established Church, Presbyterian and Roman Catholic (Robert Troy). Some of the school books used were spelling books, Murray's Grammar and Chamber's Geography. The landlord visited the school and was so delighted with the appearance of the children that he forgave the rent. The School was incorporated into the National School System on the 28th November, 1845. The school consisting of one room, 25 ft long by 12 ft wide, was built of stone with a thatched roof. The teacher in 1845 was Myles Mc-Sweeney and there were 32 males and 25 females on roll.[3]

The Island and Coast Society, spearheaded by the Rev. Edward Spring established a 'church' and a school in Heir Island East in 1847 (see Chapter 9) and for the following six years, at least, there were two schools in Heir Island, with the following numbers on roll.

	1847	1848	1849	1850	1851	1852
National School	50	73	50	42	49	72
Island Society School	69	73	39	26	55	16

As can be seen, both schools claimed an attendance of 73 in 1848. If both numbers are correct, there were 146 pupils in total on the island in that year, which is very unlikely. One or both schools obviously exaggerated the total on rolls or some of the pupils moved between the two schools, remembering that this was when the Famine was at its height and food was given to the children in the Island Society School. Daniel Foley, Island Society Inspector, visited West Cork in 1849, and in his report wrote ....

> I was greatly delighted with the School on Hare. The children answered remarkably well; and the sight of a large pot of stirabout boiling in the Teacher's house for their breakfast, was a truly gratifying one, many of the poor little creatures looked so famishing.[4]

During this period there was tension between the Catholic Clergy and the Church of Ireland regarding the control of education. The importance of education as a means of promoting proselytism was recognised by the clergy of both sides. As can be seen from the number on roll in the Island Society School, the high of 1848, had fallen to 16 in 1852 and the school was closed before Spring left Kilcoe in 1867.

Myles McSweeney was appointed principal of the National School in 1845 but was dismissed by Fr. Troy in 1847. However, he was appointed Schoolmaster of the Island Society School in 1848. James Sweeney succeeded Myles McSweeney as Principal of the National School on 1st October, 1847. There seems to have been a succession of appointments and dismissals right through the 1850s and 1860s. James Sweeney was succeeded by James Buckley, Thomas Young, Daniel Sullivan, Denis O'Leary. In 1856, Cornelius Keane was granted £15 and books were supplied for 75 pupils. In 1860, Patrick O'Leary was Principal, in 1865 a Mr. Duggan and in 1867 John McCarthy. In the 1890s, Julia O'Leary and Katherine Sheehy taught on the island. Miss Sheehy married John O'Regan from West Skeam in 1898 and transferred to Lisheen School in 1906.[5]

The last school on the island was built in the late 1890s. The quarter acre site was bought by Rev. James O'Sullivan, P.P. of Aughadown. The stone for building the school was quarried on Oileán Caorach by Michael Cahalane and others.[6] The school opened on August 16th 1900. Funding for the new school was by local subscription and a grant from the Commissioners of Education. It was vested with the Commissioners of Education, the Parish Priest of Aughadown being Chairman. It measures thirty-one feet six inches long, eighteen feet wide and thirteen feet high, comprising one single classroom with no partition. The Principal taught the higher classes – from 4th to 8th at one end of the room, while the assistant taught the lower classes, from infants to 3rd, at the other end. Some children did not leave school until they were fifteen or sixteen or even seventeen. Since there was no opportunity to get secondary education, bright pupils remained in school up to 8th class. Most left when they had completed 6th class, aged about 14 This school had no connection with 'religious houses' except Rev. James O'Sullivan, P.P. of Aughadown, who was patron of the school. The grantor in lease was Mary Louise Bernadette McCarthy, 9, The Crescent, Queenstown (Cobh). Miss McCarthy was the Island landlord after the death of her grandfather, Timothy

McCarthy Downing. A grant of £180 was given in February 1899 to build the school and £41.16s.8d. on expenditure. In October 1899 the Commissioners gave a special grant of £20 for carrying materials to the island by boat. The school was built to accommodate eighty pupils in maximum attendance. On September 21st, 1900, the Commissioners ordered that all grants be transferred from Heir Island National School (Roll No. 7335) to the new vested school (Roll No. 15274).[7]

On the 18th September, 1900, Hannah O'Donovan was appointed assistant at a salary of £39 per annum. On 21st December, 1905, Richard Kelly, an untrained teacher, was appointed Principal of the School, sanctioned 'in view of the exceptional circumstances'. The exceptional circumstance was the inability to find a trained teacher to accept the position. In the 1911 Census, Mr. Kelly was resident on the island.[8]

In my research on education in Heir Island, it is clear that a school was incorporated into the National School System in 1845, that its Roll Number was 4611 and that there were three clerical applicants:, Established Church (Protestant), Presbyterian and Roman Catholic (Fr. Troy). We also know that there were two schools operating on the island from 1848 to sometime in the 1850s, one a National School and the other an Island Society School, under the guidance of Rev. Edward Spring.[9]

The Griffith Evaluation and accompanying map indicated that in 1852, the National School was in the Doucks, where the earlier 'Pay School' was and that the principal was Thomas Young. From Griffiths Map, it is clear that the area around the 'schooleen' was the centre of Island Society activity with a 'church', a school and a teacher's residence leased from the landlords, Beechers.

The last school which opened in August, 1900 had no connection with 'religious houses'. The roll number was 15274. The roll number of the school closed in that year was 7335, not 4611, which was the roll number of the school incorporated into School System in 1845.

According to Griffiths Evaluation, the National School was in the Doucks in 1852 and the Island Society School was the 'Schooleen', east of the Island Restaurant, or was in that area, hence the three roll numbers. It would appear that when the Island Society left the island that this became the National School until 1900.

Teachers

	PRINCIPALS	ASSISTANTS
1909	Richard Kelly	Miss O'Driscoll
1912	John O'Donovan	Miss Hannah Desmond (1917)
1923	James McCarthy	Miss Margaret O'Regan (1923)
1926	Denis O'Donovan	Miss Ann Murphy (1925)
		Miss Ann McCarthy (1926)
		Miss Siobhán O'Regan (1928)
		Miss Kathryn O'Mahony (1936)

When numbers fell below thirty, it became a one-teacher school in 1945, with Miss Catherine Hegarty as principal.

Principals of School when it became a one-teacher school.

1945	Miss Catherine Hegarty
1953	Miss Margaret Hayes
1955	Miss Mary Hickey
1957	Miss Mary Shanahan
1961	Miss Kitty O'Donovan
1962	Mrs. Catherine Whooley (nee Hegarty), who had previously served as Principal, from 1945–1953.

After 1970, when Mrs. Whooley moved to Lisheen National School, no trained teacher took the position until Miss Cáit O'Driscoll from Cape Clear was appointed Principal in 1975. The following served as substitute teachers between 1970 and 1975: Charles O'Neill, Pauline O'Shea, Ann O'Connell and Jane Ann O'Donovan. Cáit O'Driscoll was the last appointed Principal of the school. There were only four on roll when the school was closed on 8th July, 1976. Three, Danny Pyburn, Peter Murphy and John O'Donovan had completed 6th class. The last pupil, Maria Harte, transferred to Kilcoe National School.

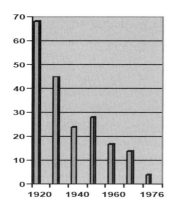

GRAPH SHOWING SCHOOL ATTENDANCE NUMBERS FROM 1920 UNTIL CLOSURE.

For some years after its closure, the school was used as a meeting place for the islanders and for nights of celebration, such as the night that the electricity was switched on, and for voting. The priests of Aughadown said Mass there on a regular basis. A branch of Cork County Library was based in the school for a period in the middle of the twentieth century

Left is a copy of Mrs. Hannah Cadogan's library ticket. Mrs Cadogan, who had lived in East Skeam, moved to Heir in 1958. She was a voracious reader.

CORK COUNTY LIBRARY
READER'S TICKET

Mr.
Mrs. Hanna Cadogan,
Miss,
Heir Island N.S.,
Church Cross, Skibbereen.
Borrower's No. 23.5.2.3.

This Ticket is valid for one year from 3.-3.'66'

The local Librarian should be notified of any change of address.

MS MARGARET HAYES, PRINCIPAL 1953–55

MRS. CATHERINE WHOOLEY (NEE HEGARTY)

MARIA HARTE, PICTURED WITH HER PARENTS AND HER TEACHER, CÁIT NÍ DHRISCEOIL, AFTER SHE HAD BEEN CONFIRMED AT KILCOE

The above picture appeared in the *Cork Examiner* of 28th May, 1976, under the heading 'Last child from the island' .... by Jim Cluskey. He went on to say, 'now that they have all been confirmed, the future of the school must be as much a matter of doubt as is the future of the lovely island, which is no more than ten minutes by boat from the mainland.' The school closed on the 8th July, 1976.

LAST DAY AT HEIR ISLAND SCHOOL – 8TH JULY 1976
MARIA HARTE, JOHN O'DONOVAN, DAN PYBURN AND PETER MURPHY
© Michael Minihane

MARIA HARTE
AND HER
FATHER JOHN
AT CUNNAMORE
SLIP 6TH JUNE,
1977 ON HER
WAY TO
SCHOOL
ON THE
MAINLAND

© Michael Minihane

Back: HANNAH CONNOLLY (NEE DESMOND), MISS MCSWEENEY
Front: JOHN O'REGAN, KATE O'REGAN (NEE SHEEHY)

HANNAH DESMOND
HEIR ISLAND SCHOOL 1917–1923

Below: GROUP OUTSIDE HEIR ISLAND
SCHOOL 1970s

© Michael Minihane

CHRISTMAS NIGHT MASS IN HEIR ISLAND SCHOOL 1979

Religion

Religion, as manifested by attendance at Mass, saying morning and evening prayers, devotion to the Holy Rosary, the use of holy water to bless homes and boats was an integral part of island life, where all the natives were Roman Catholic. Most people, excepting the very young, the old or the sick, tried to attend Mass in Lisheen every Sunday and Holy Day.

It was customary to say the Rosary in the home at night. In the lobster boats most captains led the crew in saying the Rosary each evening. Holy water, usually brought from the church on Christmas morning, was used to bless the house and cattle 'chambers'. A bottle of holy water was always taken on board the boats.

The Stations, when Mass was prayed in the house, is a custom going back to Penal Times, when Mass was not celebrated in public but in some private house and very often under the open air. Mass Rocks commemorate these open-air places of worship today and on Heir there is a Mass Rock on high ground overlooking An Tráigh Mhór. Each householder 'had' the Stations in turn. The house was painted, the yard tidied up and the house made to look as impressive as possible. The Stations were held twice a year, in spring and in autumn. After Mass, which was said early in the day, the people remained on for a meal. The night of the Stations was an important social event, with people gathering in the 'station-house', for the station party or ball.

There is a Mass Rock on the island on the side of a hillside overlooking the Reen and Mass would have been said here in Penal Times, in the 1700s, when priests were on the run and forced to say Mass in houses or sometimes in the open air,

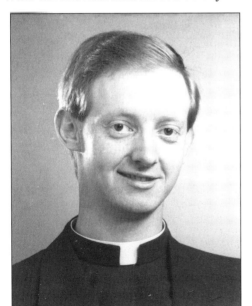

hence the 'Mass Rocks', of which there are hundreds all over the country.

Heir Island has one native priest, Fr. Dan Pyburn, who studied in Maynooth and who was ordained a priest on the 6th June, 1987. In a report in the *Cork Examiner*, of June 2nd, reporter Eddie Cassidy wrote,

A Hare islander is one of three young men from West Cork that will take the final step into the priesthood this coming weekend. Deacon, Dan Pyburn, is the youngest person on the tiny island at present and he will be the first permanent resident to be ordained .... Dan Pyburn, born and bred on Hare Island is a son of salmon fisherman and farmer, Jack Pyburn and his wife Teresa. He will celebrate his first Mass in the Parish Church at Lisheen on Sunday next.

Fr. Dan ministered in Glandore, Co. Cork, Ballyphehane, Cork and now ministers in Knocknaheeney in Cork.

The parish of Aughadown, to which Heir Island belongs. has given the Church more priests and nuns than many a parish twice its size and population and Heir Island has played its part. Fr. Peter Queally, grandson of Peter Cotter of the Reen, who migrated with his fishing boat to Courtmacsherry in the middle of the 19th century, is a frequent visitor to Heir Island. A native of Broadstrand, facing Courtmacsherry's outer harbour, Fr. Queally spent 25 years on the mission fields of Sierra Leone. He is attached to Rockwell College and commutes to Cape Clear at the weekends, where he serves as curate.

Heir Island had many second and third generation religious, working as priests and nuns around the world, especially in the United States. Among them are the following:

Charles Mary Driscoll, O.S.A. 1859–1934, a son of Timothy Driscoll and Bridget (Foley) Driscoll, both from Heir Island was born on the 18th June 1859. The baptism of the future Augustinian took place on 19th June 1859, with Garrett Cotter and Johanna Foley, ex Heir Islanders, serving as godparents. Charles was ordained to the priesthood at the age of 24 and rose to the rank of Provincial of the Augustinian Order in the United States. He enjoyed the personal acquaintance of Popes Leo XIII, Pius X, Benedict XIV and Pius XI, the latter giving him a recognised standing in the Vatican. Fr.O'Driscoll visited Heir Island in 1902 on one of his many trips to Rome. In his obituary we read that he had no immediate relatives when he died, but left several cousins, among whom where Rev. Charles P. Hart, O.S.A. of St. Mary's Church, Lawrence, Rev. Leo A. Hart, O.S.A. of St. Augustine's church, Andover, Rev. Daniel W. McCarthy O.S.A. of Washington D.C. and Rev. Edward Carney, O.S.A., of Chicago, Ill. All the above are Heir Island stock, Harte, McCarthy, Kearney.[1]

William Edward Shanahan, son of Jeremiah Shanahan, Heir Island and Catherine Salter, was born on August 5, 1908 and baptised in St. Patrick's Church Lewiston, Maine. His godparents were Cornelius Burke and Mary Burke. He was ordained a Jesuit on June 17th, 1939 and served on the missions in Jamaica before returning to lecture in Latin and Religion in Boston College. Fr. Shanahan made several visits to his relatives in Heir Island before his death in 1979.[2]

Rev. Jeremiah J. Minihane was born in Skibbereen on November, 16th 1888. He arrived in the Port of Boston aboard the *S.S. Saxonia* on 6th October, 1910 He studied at St. Bonaventure's Seminary, New York and at St. John's Seminary in Brighton. He was ordained by William Cardinal O'Connell on May 23, 1924. Fr. Jerry served in St. Patrick's, Brockton, for 24 years, before becoming pastor of St. John the Baptist Church, Essex and in Our Lady of Good Counsel in Quincy, MA. until his death in 1954.[3] He was a brother of Cornelius and Denis Minihane, Cunnamore and son of Denis Minihane, Heir Island. While stationed at St. Patrick's, he was in charge of the parish's sports programmes. This was an afternoon sports programme to help keep the local children occupied and away from mischief. Father Jerry encouraged a young football player by the name of Rocky Marciano, who started his boxing career while in the Army. He followed Rocky Marciano's career when he turned professional and won the World Heavyweight Boxing title, retiring undefeated champion of the world.[4]

Other second generation Heir Island priests include Fr. Lynch, of Buffalo, Fr. Burke of Auburn, Fr. Leo O'Neill, of Gulf Shores, Alabama, Fr. Dan O'Neill and many others.

Religious Sisters

Many first and second generation women became nuns. The list includes the Burke and Pyburn Sisters from Heir Island, who emigrated to the U.S.A., Sr. Mary Magdalene Cronin, daughter of Catherine Harte (Heir Island) and Michael Cronin, Sr. Mary and Sr. Peggy McPartland, O.P. daughters of Bridget O'Neill, Heir Island and Myles McPartland, Leitrim, Sr. Catherine Sienna O'Neill, O.P. daughter of Daniel O'Neill and Nora O'Donovan, both emigrants from Heir Island, St. Mary Denis O'Neill, O.P. sister of Sr. Catherine, Sr. Maureen O'Neill, daughter of Michael O'Neill and Bridget Burke, Heir Island, Sr. Brenda O'Neill, daughter of Patrick O'Neill, Heir Island and Hester O'Regan, West Skeam Island and Sr. Teresa O'Donovan, daughter of Daniel O'Donovan, Heir Island and May McCarthy, Kilcoe, born in Watford, England in 1949, and Sr. Mildred Burke, daughter of Patrick Burke and Ann Barry, Heir Island.[5]

Heir Island's contribution to the Church has been enormous in terms of second generation vocations and is a clear indication of the great faith held by their parents, who emigrated from the little island, off the south west corner of Ireland.

ELLEN BURKE (MURPHY) WITH HER CHILDREN CATHERINE,
SISTER MARY LEONA AND FR. NEIL BURKE

SISTER MAUREEN O'NEILL ON A VISIT HOME TO HER FAMILY IN 1936

ARRIVING FOR THE STATION MASS – HEIR ISLAND

L. to R., PATTY WHOOLEY, LISHEEN; PATSY O'NEILL, HEIR ISLAND; FLORRIE FITZGERALD
WITH HIS SON JOHN; SR. MAUREEN O'NEILL; *in front,* KATHLEEN O'NEILL

© Michael Minihane

HEIR ISLAND WEDDING AUGUST 1964 – FINBARR HARTE HELPING HIS BRIDE MARY ELLEN O'DRISCOLL
INTO THE BOAT FOR THE RETURN JOURNEY TO HEIR ISLAND TO CELEBRATE THEIR WEDDING BALL

GROUP OF HEIR
ISLANDERS OUTSIDE
MICHEÁL MINIHAN'S
PUB IN LISHEEN
including
Pat and Baby Burke,
Mary Ann O'Neill,
Florrie Fitzgerald,
Jerry McCarthy,
Betty Cadogan,
Cape Clear,
Noreen Desmond,
Bridie Fitzgerald,
Sean O'Donoghue,
Eileen Cadogan,
Cape Clear,
Mary Ellen
O'Driscoll,
Finbarr Harte,
Peggy O'Driscoll,
Jimmy Fitzgerald,
Michael John O'Neill,
and
Sonny Desmond

— 28 —

Birth, Marriage and Death

In earlier times, women usually gave birth to their children at home, with the aid of a 'midwife'. The midwives, untrained, were women who were skilled and were trusted by the pregnant women. In the early half of the 20th century, the two Heir Island midwives were Ellen Minihane (nee Cahalane), nicknamed Ellico, and Mary McCarthy (nee O'Donovan, mother of Catherine O'Connor, whose story is told in Chapter 22). If there were complications, there were no doctors or medical aid readily available. In latter years most women gave birth in Skibbereen or Bantry hospital. Babies were slways baptised a day or two after birth.

Marriage

In the nineteenth and early twentieth century, many marriages were arranged. It was very much an arrangement to protect property and property rights. Matchmakers were used as go-betweens, to bargain between the two families. Quite often the bride had no choice in the matter. The matchmakers extolled the young man's virtue and how good a farmer or fisherman he was, while he praised the young woman's virtues, how hard working she was, her neatness. Usually the father of the bride had to give a dowry to his son-in-law. This custom faded out in the middle of the twentieth century. Most of the island men married women from the island or neighbouring islands.

The month of May and Fridays were considered unlucky to marry. The marriage was usually held in Lisheen or Kilcoe Church and the wedding party (bainis) held in the bride's home on the island. This was usually a long night of celebration, song and dance.

If a farmer had no son, the land would be given to a daughter. When she married, her husband came to live in the home. A 'cliamhain isteach' is the Irish for a man who marries into his wife's home.

Death

After death, the body was 'waked' at home; this was a momentous occasion which involved the whole community. News of a death spread quickly around the island and no work was done by the neighbours that day. It affected the whole community. The waking of the dead is a very ancient custom throughout the world, and we have accounts of wakes in Europe going back almost a thousand years. When a person died, the clocks in the house were stopped. First there was the laying out which was usually done by certain women in the community. After being laid out, the corpse was never left alone until it was put in a coffin the day of the burial. Candles were lit by the bedside. All the neighbours came to the 'wake' and prayed by the bed. Keeners[1] (from the Irish word caoineadh, crying), usually women (mná caointe[2]) would

© Michael Minihane

FUNERAL PROCESSION OF CHARLES 'SHAW' MINIHANE HEADING INTO
RINCOLISKY HARBOUR ON 22ND APRIL, 1979

start up a wail of crying over the body, filling the house with lamentations to keep the atmosphere solemn. Up to the middle of the 20th century women used to keen, set up an olagón (lamentation). Jack Pyburn remembers women keening at Mike Cahalane's wake in 1950. The Rosary was recited at midnight and again towards morning. If the dead person was young, the occasion would be very sad but if the dead person had lived a long full life, the atmosphere would not be quite so solemn. People who called to the wake would be given something to eat, tea, and cake. A glass of whiskey was given to the men, and in olden times tobacco and clay pipes (dúidíns) were also provided, as well as snuff for the women. On the third day the body was put into the coffin, which was placed on two chairs outside the door, before being brought straight to the graveyard, unlike today, when the corpse is usually brought to the church the evening before the funeral. These chairs were then left unused, and often kicked over, until the corpse was buried. The coffins in the first half of the twentieth century were made by Denis O'Driscoll of Ballydehob.

The corpse was shouldered a part of the way to Cuaisín na gCorp south of the pier in Heir Island East. A pony and cart carried it the rest of the way. The coffin was always placed on the rocks in Cuaisín na gCorp, where it was believed the flag iris (liostrums) grew in the form of a cross. The coffin was then placed in the boat belonging to the family or a near relative. The boats were rowed in cortege, each boat tied by a rope to the boat ahead of it, about ten to twenty yards apart. The coffin was landed on Grove Point, in Whitehall on Gerald McCarthy's land and then shouldered by men across the strand as far as the road. If the tide was in, the coffin bearers would be up to their knees in water. At the road it was also shouldered to the bottom of Pound Hill in Whitehall. Before the advent of the hearse, it

was carried from here by horse and cart to Cross of the Corpses in Marsh. From there it was shouldered in relays to Aughadown graveyard (pictured left) near the Ilen. In recent years Lisheen graveyard is the usual burial place for the islanders.

Families who had come to Heir from the Baltimore area used to be buried in Creagh graveyard. The Burkes, the O'Donovans and the O'Neill families were buried there. The coffin left Cuaisin na gCorp and was landed on Inane Point, Ringaroga, always on a special place where a flag iris was said to flower. The coffin was shouldered from there to Creagh graveyard. People from the funeral used to drop in to the home of Margaret O'Driscoll from Heir Island, (who was married to John Holland) for a cup of tea or some of the men walked to the nearby Sibín Pub, then owned by Mrs. Davis.

After the funeral, close relatives were 'in mourning' for twelve months. Many wore black clothes; the men wore black ties and diamond shaped pieces of black cloth sewn to the upper ends of their sleeves.

The Cillín

There is no consecrated graveyard on the island but there is a cillín[3] in 'Barry's land' in Heir Island Middle. This was a grave for still-births and for children who died before they were baptised. Most families connected with the island have a child buried there. The field is called Gort na Cille (the field of the graveyard). The custom of burying children in a separately designated place appears to have been practised in Ireland from at least late Medieval times. Although this practice reflects in part the refusal by Church authorities to allow the burial of unbaptised infants in consecrated graveyards, it also reflects the underlying view of traditional societies that unnamed children had not attained full membership of the community into which they were born. Occasionally, adults who were considered to be outsiders or beyond salvation in some way, such as suicides and unrepentant murderers, were also buried in such places.

One young baby was found by Jim Cotter of the Reen. He was searching the strand for wrack when he found a timber box. When he opened it, he was astonished to find a baby dressed in beautiful clothes. Two stones were placed on either side of the child. Apparently the baby died and was buried at sea but the stones were not heavy enough to sink the box. The box was new and had not long in the water. The baby was then buried in the Cillín.

Dan Murphy found two bodies on the Reen; they are buried in the Cill although it was more usual to bury dead sailors near where the body was found. Another body was found in Cuas Mahoun on the N.W. side of the island.

In medieval times, it is almost certain that the dead islanders were buried in the graveyard in West Skeam.

A Special Mass for the consecration of the Cillín and dedication of the cross was celebrated in Heir Island on Sunday, 24th August, 2003. The Mass was concelebrated by Fr. Danny Pyburn, who was born on Heir Island, Fr. Peter Queally whose grandfather was born on Heir Island, and Fr. Donal Cahill, Administrator,. Aughadown. Many former islanders and their relations returned to Heir Island for the consecration of the cillín.

THE CILLÍN – AUGUST 2003 AFTER THE ERECTION AND BLESSING OF THE CROSS

Pictured below is a large stone above the South Trá Bán, marking the burial place of a sailor, who was washed ashore nearby.

— 29 —

Houses

OLD HOUSE IN PARIS, PRE 1928

The old houses on Heir were described by Michael O'Neill, aged 73, (Heir Island Middle) in the School Folklore Collection of 1938, collected by Denis O'Donovan who was Principal teacher at the time. [1]

When I was a young boy, all the houses on this Island were thatched with wheaten straw. The cupboard and dresser were usually placed as a partition between kitchen and little room. The fire place was always at the gable-end, and at that time turf was used in every house. There was no chimney or flue in these houses, and the only escape for the smoke was through a hole in the thatch by the gable end. On a calm day the house used to be filled with smoke, and often the smoke was so thick that we failed to see one another in the house.

I remember some time after this to see flues built in the old houses. A strong beam was fixed across the house from one side-wall to the other. This beam was about four to five feet from the floor and from three to four feet from the gable. Strong sticks were driven into the gable. The lower sticks were driven at level of cross-beam, and as they reached the top of the gable they became shorter, so that the top sticks were only about a foot long. Then through these sticks – on sides of front – briars and twigs were woven and this closed up the flue. I saw twigs and briars plastered with 'cow-dung' in my father's house. Bottom cross beam was called 'mada clúir.' [2] Afterwards this type of flue was replaced by a stone and mortar one.

The space on each side of the flue was called the 'cutóir.' This was planked from the cross-beam to gable, and cured dried fish was stored in the cútóir. Every house used to have the two 'cútóir' (recess, cubby hole) filled with fish for the winter.

The loft over the kitchen was called the main loft. In this loft the beds were on the ground. The loft over the room was about a foot or so lower than the main loft, and here a 'standing bed' was kept.

About sixty years ago there were no 'standing' tables on the Island. The tables then in use consisted of two nine inch planks about three feet long nailed together with 'treasnáns.' [3] They had ledges about an inch and a half high to prevent potatoes from rolling off. When in use they were placed on top of boxes or keelers.[4] After every meal they were scrubbed and placed against the side wall of the house. Afterward, the tables were hinged to the back of the 'settle', and when not in use were held upright against the wall by a clamp.'

There were usually only two tiny windows. The floor was made of white clay (blue till) put in very wet and packed as hard as possible. There was only one door in the front. The coop for the hens was usually at the side wall inside the door. There was usually a perch for the cock, whose morning call brought the household out of bed.

The roof was of thatch. Wheaten straw, after slashing, was the most common thatch. Spars made from strong old briar stems – pointed at both ends – and

OLD ISLAND HOUSE   © Pierce Hickey

about 2½ ft long were cut to bind the thatch. The straw was first laid down evenly. It was then sewn through with a needle[5] (like a poker). The thatching needle, shown at left, was found by James Cadogan of Ardagh in the ruins of an old house in Ardagh, where Thady McCarthy of Heir Island came to live. White cord was used for the sewing. A second person inside fastened the cord around the taobhán (the purlin). The spars were then driven in at even intervals around each sheaf. The thatching always began at the eaves and finished at the ridge of the roof. Súgán[6] mats, made of plaited straw, were hung on the inside of the door on cold winter nights to keep out the draught.

Ruins of some of the single-storey dwellings still remain and can be distinguished from animal houses by the presence of a chimney. Examination of the Ordnance Survey maps of the island, drawn in the 19th century, show the houses grouped together in little villages, referred to, in some areas, as clacháns.

Mike Cahalane, who was a good stone mason, put chimneys on many of the old houses. Dick Cotter, Denny O' Donovan and 'Harry' Cadogan were acknowledged to be skilful thatchers.

In the 1901 census, carried out on the 11th and 12th April of that year, there were forty-four inhabited dwellings classified under four categories, depending on material used in the construction of walls and roofs, the number of rooms and the number of windows in front. There was no class one house, the highest class, or class four, the poorest type. Eight were classified as class two and the remaining thirty six come under class three. All the houses were built of stone and the vast majority, thirty seven, had thatched roofs. Seven had slate roofs.

The number of windows at the front varied from one to five, the majority, thirty four, having two. Seven houses had only one window at the front, while the other three houses had five windows at the front. Twenty eight houses had two bedrooms occupied, fourteen had three bed-rooms and two houses had four.

The total number of out-offices and farm-buildings totalled eighty seven: thirty nine cow houses, thirty two piggeries, four potato houses, one dairy, one barn and six other buildings.'Out' houses for cattle, pigs, etc. were usually called 'chambers' on Heir and in the locality of Aughadown South.

Looking at the picture, page xix, taken by Mrs. Foy of Baltimore, sometime between 1909 and 1927, probably around 1920, we see the houses in Paris have chimneys.

The kitchen was the heart of the home and its hearth-fire the focal point. The fire was never allowed to go out, even at night, and was a strong symbol of family continuity. The housewife tended it last thing before going to bed. She poured ashes on to the gríosach (embers) to keep it quietly alive until morning when a raking with the poker brought it to life in a few minutes. All the old houses, pre 1928, had an open hearth with a bellows to the right. A pipe went from this under the fire. By turning the bellows wheel, air was pumped under the fire making it glow. Turf was bought at times from the bogs in Ballybane and other bogs in the Ballydehob area. The turf was brought to the island in the yawls and carted from the pier in a cart with high rails, called a 'crib', pulled by donkey or pony. Turf was rarely cut by the islanders themselves as the men were away lobstering at the time of turf cutting. Timber found in 'wrack' was often used as fuel. The women and children collected cipeens for starting the fire or bringing it to life in the morning. These cipeens were also known as brosna. Spéanach – burnt furze stumps – were burnt as were dried cow-pats which were called boorawns (buaithreáin). The open hearth was truly the heart of the home and with the advent of the range none of those things were ever quite the same, the dreams or the stories, the fire or the flames. As well as bringing warmth and comfort to the family, all meals were cooked on the open hearth fire, clothes dried in front of it and sick and ailing animals revived by its healing warmth. It also kept the thatch dry and preserved the roof timbers.

Every house had a three-legged cast iron pot, in which the potatoes were boiled, and a bastable pot in which brown cakes and soda bread were baked. Currant cakes were baked for special occasions. Howard's One-Way flour was popular for making brown cakes. Sour milk was usually mixed with the flour. The dough which incorporated breadsoda as a raising agent, was placed in the bastable, the lid drawn over it and then glowing coals were heaped on the lid. During the war years or when coal was scarce, boorawns were heaped on the lid. Kettles were generally heavy and black, made from cast iron. They were suspended from one of the pot hooks on the crane. People who kept pigs had a big pot for boiling a mixture of potato skins, small potatoes, turnips, cabbage and various types of meal for the pigs.

The furniture in the houses was always basic and functional. Every house had a kitchen dresser, where the lady of the house displayed her crockery, her willow-pattern delph and collections of ornaments and souveniers. The lower part of the dresser was closed and held large jars, buckets, pans etc. Furniture was made by Denis O'Driscoll of Ballydehob, Jim Pyburn of Heir Island, John O'Sullivan of North St., Skibbereen, and Paddy 'Timsey' O'Driscoll of Cape among others. When John O'Sullivan of North St., Skibbereen was asked about the type of furniture that he made when he was young and working for his father, he described an average day's work in the workshop while his father was out overseeing other jobs – 'a kitchen table now, my father would send me into the workshop and he'd say – make a kitchen table there for a man from Heir Island and put a drawer in one end of it. The table with the drawer was twenty five shillings.'[7]

O'Sullivans built the old 'chicken-coop dressers' which were commonplace in lots of homes. This is how he describes them. 'The great dresser, gay with willow-pattern plates, with dishes of various shapes and colours and, here and there, a jug. In the lower part of the dresser instead of cupboards was a long coop in which were sitting hens, it seems to me that they sat there perpetually except when two geese took their place in early spring.' The later dressers did not have a 'chicken-coop'.

As a small boy, John O'Sulivan used to go around the houses with his father where they were working. He said in nearly every one there was what he called a coom. It would be about six feet long at the lower end of the kitchen, made like a press in the bottom and there were two shelves for two rows of hens, and little sliding doors in it where the hens went in. It was stained like any other bit of furniture, but was often the first thing to be thrown out when the furniture was updated.

Most houses had iron bedsteads. These had hair mattresses, but the older beds had either a plank floor which supported a thick straw mattress and then a feather 'tick' quilt. Bed clothes were often home-made. Sheets were often made from flour bags which had been washed and bleached, four bags joined together making a fine sheet for a double bed.

Every family had their little stone-built outhouse or 'chamber' as it is called on Heir, where they kept the cows and pigs. They also had a hen house. Most of the old dwelling houses had a stone projecting from under the thatch, where the cock rested and from where he announced the new day with loud crowing.

The houses were whitewashed inside and outside. Whitewash is a solution of lime in water, made by blending quicklime with water to the coinsistency of thick cream. Good quicklime was pure white in colour. Whitewash, which in effect is diluted lime plaster, formed a protective skin on the surface to which it was applied. Whitewash also acted as a disinfectant and a preventative against the spread of diseases. The houses were always 'done up'before the Stations. This included whitewashing the walls and painting every timber surface in the house.

The 'New Houses'

The *Southern Star,* of October 9th 1926, gives an account of President Cosgrave's[8] visit to Skibbereen on Friday 1st October. W.T. Cosgrave was President of the Executive Council of the Irish Free State. In today's parlance, Prime Minister or Taoiseach (leader), which became the title when Ireland became a Republic. He was accompanied by the Minister for Justice, Kevin O'Higgins, on his journey to West Cork, where they had business in Bandon and Clonakilty, before reaching Skibbereen. Kevin O'Higgins was assassinated two years later in Dublin.

The President met a number of deputations from various parts of the area in The West Cork Hotel, Skibbereen. Rev. Fr. F. McCarthy, P.P. Aughadown, introduced a deputation of inhabitants of Heir Island with regard to housing on the island. 'The cabins, on this island,' Fr. McCarthy said,

> are of the most miserable type and they wanted to erect more and better houses for the people. He was glad to see by that morning's paper that the Free State Government, as explained by the President in Bandon, were endeavouring to solve the housing problem by building 12,000 houses in a few years. He hoped the Government would consider a scheme for housing on the island, where the accommodation was of the worst description. Landing facilities were also necessary on Heir Island.

President Cosgrave asked were the people prepared to contribute something toward the cost of erecting houses. Fr. McCarthy said they were prepared to meet all their liabilities in regard to annuities, but they were miserably poor.

Mr. C. Connolly, T.D. explained that the valuation of the holdings was not a fair one, and said the conditions under which the people lived were deplorable. The people of Heir Island had the smallest houses and the largest families in the world, he believed.

President Cosgrave speaking to a member of the deputation, asked – 'Have you any family? The man replied – Yes, sir, I have nine, four boys and five girls and my house is 19 feet long by 19 feet wide.' The President said he would bring the matter to the notice of the Local Government Minister when he returned to Dublin. It would not be easy to settle the question as there were people elsewhere with the same valuations as the islanders, who were badly in need of housing accommodation, and all they were doing for them was what they had undertaken in the Government Housing Scheme.

Fr. McCarthy said the amount of the valuation of the houses was misleading. The holdings on the island would in most cases feed only one cow. The President asked several members of the deputation how many cows they had and in most cases they replied that they had only one.

Mr. Connolly said that a couple of years previously the Minister for Agriculture sent down an Inspector to report on conditions on the island and he said they were the worst he had ever experienced. The President again said that he would bring the matter before the proper department on his return to the capital.

In the Dáil on February 16th 1927, Mr. T. Murphy, Labour T.D. for West Cork asked the Minister for Lands and Agriculture whether the Land Commission had yet approved the suggested housing scheme for the people of Heir Island, and if so, would he state when the scheme would be undertaken. Mr. McGilligan, Minister for Lands and Agriculture, stated that proposals for the improvement of the housing accommodation of the tenants were at present under the consideration of the Land Commission.[9]

The deputation to President Cosgrave must have had influence because the new housing scheme began in 1927 and was completed within a couple of years. Denis O'Driscoll of Ballydehob, always a good friend of the island people, got the contract to build the houses. Paddy 'Timsy' O'Driscoll, of Cape Clear, who was an accomplished carpenter, also worked on the scheme. The owners had to supply the sand and gravel for the building of the houses, which were made of mass concrete. There are many sandy strands on Heir Island. People like John McCarthy (Nell's house) at the far end of the island had to draw bags of sand up the slope from Cuas a Bhrághaid. A few of the houses are almost the same today as they were the day they were built. Others have been adapted slightly. New private houses built on the island in recent years have been restricted to keep the basic shape of the 1928 houses and blend well into the landscape.

Each of the 1928 houses consists of a porch in front, leading into a kitchen with two bedrooms on the ground floor and one bedroom upstairs. All the houses had an open hearth with two cubby holes,[10] one on either side of the fire. One was used for keeping firewood, coal and turf. The bellows was situated to the right of the fire in the other cubby hole. Over the fireplace was the clevvy, on which was displayed photographs and miscellaneous items which needed to be kept dry, sugar, salt etc. Twenty eight new houses in all were built.

Of the original stone built houses on the island, six were two-storey: Burkes, Barrys, Charles (Shaw) Minihane's, John O'Donovan (Paris), Pyburns, O'Neills, where artist Percy Hall lives today. These houses were repaired and enlarged at the time of the construction of the new houses and concrete floors put in. The houses on the Skeams had concrete floors installed at the same time. Two houses in Paris, those owned by Dan McCarthy and the late Jim 'Con' McCarthy, were also converted, enlarged and cement floors put down in 1928.

In most of the houses, solid fuel burning stoves were installed at a later stage.

Light

In bygone times often the only light in the houses was the dim light from the fire in the hearth. Sometimes there were jobs to be done at night, although the work corresponded more closely to the day light hours, dawn to dusk. They repaired

NEW RANGE INSTALLED IN FLORENCE
FITZGERALD'S HOUSE,
HEIR ISLAND EAST

nets, made lobster pots, slashed or flailed the corn. The first form of light was light-ed bog-deal splinters or vir as they were called. These could be bought in Skibbereen, Ballydehob and Baltimore. The vir splinters gave way to the slige, a creusset of iron, about ten inches wide, on three legs. It had two pointed ends and a handle on the side. It was placed in a hole in the wall. The holders were called slighte because seashells were used as containers prior to the iron creussets.

The fuel used was 'train' oil, from the Irish word treighin (pronounced train) which was obtained from the livers of big fish, cod, ling, halibut, etc. which were placed in a barrel and melted in the summer sun. 'Train-oil' was also obtained from pressed pilchards. The soft pith of peeled rushes was used as a wick, extending over the narrow pointed end. The common soft rush (luachair) was collected in late sum-mer, when mature but still green.

The Islanders often found candles in wrack. Also big lumps of tallow were often washed ashore. They melted the tallow in a pot and poured it into a mould made of copper piping. Threads from cotton bags were used as wicks. Others crocheted their own wicks. The first commercial candles that came on the market were thin and short and were known as 'penny dips'.

'Train' oil was replaced by paraffin oil, which could be bought in the shops. Oil lamps with one wick were replaced with lamps with two wicks, called Alladin lamps, and these were followed by the Tilley lamp which also burned paraffin oil. Each house had a storm lantern, so that they could go about their work in the dark and the men also had a storm lantern on board their fishing yawls.

When bottled gas became available in 1961, many of the islanders installed gas lights. Nearly everybody purchased a small gas cooker and finally electricity was brought to the island in 1976, almost twenty years after rural electrification reached the mainland.

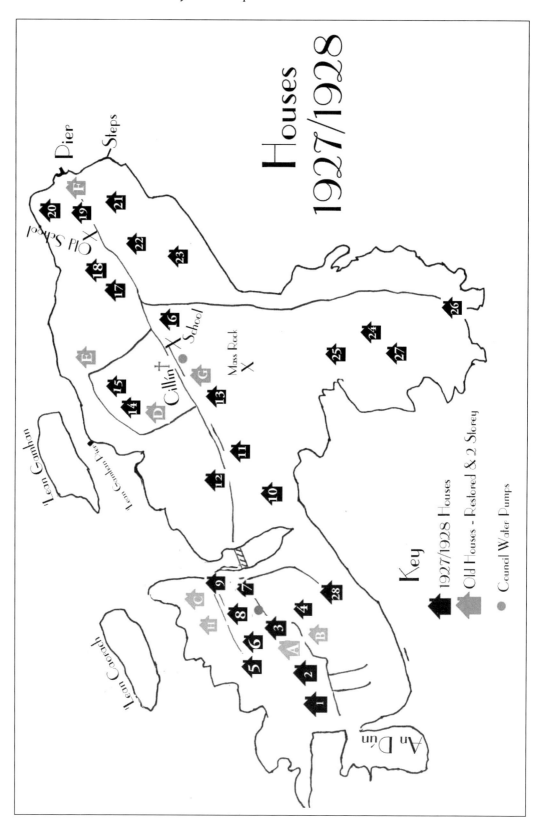

Houses 1927/1928

Key

1927/1928 Houses

Old Houses – Restored & 2 Storey

• Council Water Pumps

1928 Houses

1. John McCarthy, inherited by his family, Jeremiah and Nell.
2. Charles McCarthy, inherited by his son, Jerry.
3. Cadogans.
4. McCarthy, later, his son-in-law, John Fitzgerald.
5. John Minihane, inherited by his son-in-law, Jeremiah McCarthy.
6. Denis Minihane, inherited by his daughter, Lizzie.
7. Catherine Murphy, inherited by her son, Patrick.
8. Michael McCarthy.
9. Timmy O'Donovan, inherited by his son, Neilly.
10. Dan Murphy, inherited by his son, Patsy.
11. Denis Murphy, later, John Murphy.
12. Michael Minihane, inherited by his son, Con.
13. John Shanahan.
14. Michael McCarthy.
15. Michael O'Neill, inherited by his son, Danny.
16. John O'Neill.
17. John McCarthy.
18. Michael O'Neill (Stephens)
19. Michael O'Neill, later John Harte.
20. Michael O'Neill, (Mike the Cloud) inherited by his son Charlie.
21. Florence Fitzgerald.
22. Michael O'Neill (Mikeen), inherited by his son, Patsy.
23. Patrick O'Driscoll.
24. Michael Cahalane.
25. John Harte.
26. Dan Harte, inherited by his son, John.
27. Timothy Harte.
28. Michael Harte, inherited by his son, Danny.

Houses roofed and renovated.

A. Denis McCarthy, inherited by his son, John Denis.
B. Jim Pyburn.
C. Michael McCarthy (Con) inherited by his son, Jim Con.
D. John O'Donovan.
E. Paddy Minihane, inherited by Charles (Shaw) Minihane.
F. Con Burke.
G. Michael O'Neill. (Donaleen).
H. William Barry, inherited by his son, John.
I. Jerry McCarthy (Scotty), later his brother Seán (Hanny).

INSCRIPTION ON THE GABLE WALL OF CADOGAN'S 'NEW HOUSE' IN PARIS
SHOWING DATE THE HOUSE WAS COMPLETED
JEREMIAH CADOGAN, DECEMBER, 1928

ONE OF THE 'NEW HOUSES' IN HEIR ISLAND
MIDDLE. (BUILT 1928)

— 30 —

The Women's Role

The day started early on Heir, especially in summer. The fire which was banked up before going to bed, would be rekindled. Then water was fetched from the well. In dry summers getting water for domestic use and for the animals was difficult. There were many wells on the island but most of them were unsatisfactory in very dry summers when the water level lowered. People who hadn't a well on their own land had to rely on the generosity of neighbours until Cork Co. Council erected a public pump in Heir Island Middle in the 1930s and later another one in Heir Island West in the 1950s. In summers of drought the women had to rise early to be first at the well, the water level having risen during the night.

At harvest time, when a meitheal of men gathered together to save the hay and the corn, the housewife always provided a good meal, as well as bringing bottles of hot sugared tea and cake etc to the field where the work was in progress. The women had many of their own tasks as well as helping the men. Along with rearing a large family, the woman of the house milked the cows, took care of the calves and the poultry, earning some money by selling the eggs and butter, which was made at home. After the milk for the house was taken, the remainder was placed in earthenware milk pans and kept cool in the dairy. At the end of the week, the cream was scooped off the milk with a saucer or scallop shell. The cream was placed in the churn, operated by hand. Everybody who called to the house was expected to spend a while at the butter-making. Butter was kept fresh in the summer by storing in cold water. In warm weather, they placed cabbage leaves around the home-made butter, wrapped in muslin, to prevent it from melting when it was being taken to the shop.

Normal housework, such as making meals and washing clothes, was done without the aid of modern appliances. Wonderful wholesome brown bread was made each morning with wholemeal flour, buttermilk or sour milk and bread soda. The dough was baked in a bastable, a round cast-iron pot with a lid, which was set in the ashes of the fire and heaped with burning coal or turf which created a miniature oven. White cake, using refined flour, was also made. There were other pots for boiling potatoes or meat, all hanging from a crane which hung over the fire. Big families were the norm, some having twelve or more children.

On winter mornings, if there was a period of settled weather, many islanders, both men and women, rose early and went picking periwinkles. They picked them on strands near Schull, Rossbrin, Sherkin, Ringaroga, Baltimore, Turkhead, Inis Laoich, as well as on the island strands. Long cold days were spent searching under the cold seaweed to find the small shellfish. They were sold by the firkin[1] (which was four stone) and paid eighteen shillings per bag from the fish merchants in the early fifties. Michael Minihane of Cunnamore, who depicted island life so well in his photographs, said that he often saw the Heir islanders picking periwinkles on raw winter mornings..

On Heir much of the summer work in the fields was done by the women, when the men were lobstering and were reluctant to spend too many days away from the fishing. The women often had to save the hay, the teenagers and older men helping.

The saying 'A woman's work is never done' is nowhere more appropriate than on an island farm. The women of the house were very adept at sewing, knitting, crocheting, darning and lace making. The making of patchwork quilts and knitting of pullovers (geanseys) and socks often occupied them during the long winter nights. When the socks became frayed, they were darned faithfully. Nothing was wasted. The skeins of wool were usually bought in Skibbereen in one of the many drapery shops, Trinders or Levis & Sweetnams. Children usually helped by holding the skeins of wool over their outstretched hands, while their mothers wound it into a ball. Practically all the women were talented at needlework; Maggie 'Merchant' McCarthy and Teresa Pyburn were good at crochet. Kate Harte (nee McCarthy) used to make lace. Many of the women made First Communion and Confirmation dresses for their children. Bed clothes were often home-made. Quilts and bedspreads were often showpieces, knitted or patchwork.

The women were experts in many things that mattered in their lives and many of them were specialists. The women were highly skilled in many vital activities. They were skilful in setting the new milk in large earthenware pans in the era before the separator. They were good at making home produced butter, which had real colour and taste. They were experienced in the care of the 'clocking hen'

'MINDING THE GEESE'

during the three weeks of sitting, in the care of the chickens when they emerged from their shells. They were even adept at detecting the glugger in the nest almost before it was a glugger.[2] They were expert in picking out the proper seed potatoes, which had to be neither too big nor too small, with the correct type of eye out of which the season's stalks would grow. They were expert in cutting the sciolláns (seed potatoes), for which they possessed specially prepared sciollán knives, making sure that no seed potato had more than two 'eyes'.

In the 19th century and into the 20th clothes and household linen were still made of tough natural materials, wool, linen, cotton and calico. These stood up to vigorous washing – they could be boiled, beaten, scrubbed and wrung out without damage. The washing of clothes was done in a galvanised bath. Clothes were hung out to dry and bleach on the hills and bushes. In the South Reen one of the field is known as the Hill of the Clothes. Starching of cloth was very popular. Starch was made by grating raw potatoes and squeezing out all the liquid. This was left to stand until all the solid matter – the starch – sank to the bottom. Blouses, dresses and shirts were starched for special occasions, as when relations returned from America, weddings, etc.

Gradually as the 20th century progressed, new products arrived in the island shop or were available in Ballydehob, Baltimore and Skibbereen. 'Sunlight' and 'Lifebuoy' soaps, Rinso washing powder, Robin starch, Reckitts Blue became household names and made the laundering of clothes a little easier. Brushes of all sorts became available, from the heavy yard brush to the scrubbing brush and the hair brush. Mangles for wringing the clothes and the Singer sewing machines became familiar household items.

Many of the women could handle a boat as well as any man. Most of them could row; some were able to use a lug sail. Often in the summer they rowed or sailed across the bay to Ballydehob to buy provisions and to buy a couple of bonhams with the first of the lobster money.

OVER-ALTAR CLOTH WHICH
WAS PINNED TO THE RAFTERS
FOR THE STATION MASS

Made by Mary Ryan (nee Harte)
South Reen, Heir Island

CROCHET TEA COSY

Made by Mary Ryan's daughter, Hannah O'Driscoll (nee Ryan), Coolanuller, Skibbereen

PIECE OF CARRICKMACROSS LACE

Designed and made by Mary Ryan's grand-daughter, Eleanor Calnan (nee Ryan), Leap, Co. Cork

The above is an example of some of the beautiful needlework created in many island homes, the skill passing down from generation to generation.

— 31 —

The Cycle of the Year

In the past an extensive framework of beliefs, customs and superstitions (piseogs) underpinned everyday existence on land and sea, profoundly influencing people's perspectives, outlook and conduct. Some of these traditions were linked with religious holidays and saints' feast days, but many had ancient pre-Christian roots and continued to be respected for many centuries. In Heir and the islands, as elsewhere, the strength of these customs began to die in the latter half of the nineteenth century as the Irish language declined and during the course of the twentieth most of them faded away. However, even among the most sophisticated or learned, if you probe, you will find an undercurrent of pre-Christian paganism.

Shrove Tuesday

This was a night of plenty before the 'black fast' of Lent. Even the poorest people tried to have a little meat for their supper. For many centuries Catholics were bound by Church law to abstain, not only from meat, but from eggs, milk, butter and cheese during the Lenten season. These restrictions eased as time went by, but Ash Wednesday and Good Friday were still observed as days of strict fast. Pancakes were always made on Shrove Tuesday. The idea was that surplus butter, eggs, milk and cream should be eaten before the fast began on Ash Wednesday.

Shrovetide, (from Epiphany, January 6th to Ash Wednesday) was the traditional time for marrying in rural Ireland in the 19th and into the 20th century. In parish records one can see that most of the weddings took place in February or March, which resulted in a high percentage of births in November and December. Being a bachelor or spinster was frowned upon up to recently. A man that married at twenty five was considered a man while his neighbour at fifty would be looked on as 'a boy' if he had not married. From the Famine to the middle of the 20th century, many men didn't marry until they were middle-aged because of a reluctance to bring a 'new' woman into the family home. When they did marry, it sometimes led to friction between the mother and daughter-in-law. Often the man's parents did not welcome a new woman into the house and wanted to hold on to the land, leaving the men as slaves to the land, lonely and frustrated. From the Famine to the 1960s, Ireland has controlled its population growth by three measures: celibacy, late marriage and emigration. (Irish Times, May 8th 1971)

From Little Christmas (Epiphany) onwards, the matchmakers were busy and many unions were planned and eagerly awaited, not only by the couple to be married, but by the whole district, who would share in the merrymaking, feasting and drinking. After the marriage ceremony the wedding party, which would consist of all the islanders, except the very young and very old, returned to the house of the bride's parents, where feasting, music, singing and dancing continued until morning. The Council of Trent in 1563, decreed that marriage could not be solemnised during Lent. Legend has it that the monks on the Sceilg Rocks off the Kerry coast continued to marry people during Lent, as they hadn't heard of the Papal decree.

If a man or woman or marriageable age had not married by Shrove Tuesday, it was clear that they did not intend to marry that year. The local 'boyos' poked fun at these unfortunate people. 'Sceilg Lists' were composed by local scribes to embarrass those who hadn't married, often put to rhyme and learned in the locality, some of which are still remembered.

A Sceilg verse, written by some one in the Whitehall area, went like this –

> Katie Sheehan of Whitehall
> She can't be pleased at all,
> Since Captain Tim did her enthral
> And leave her in the lurch.

According to custom a local bard would compose rhymes linking the unmarried men and women in the locality and these rhymes which would be circulated on Shrove Tuesday and for some time after, caused much discomfort to all those singled out for still being unwed.

Shrove Tuesday was the favourite day to get married. For example, there were twenty eight marriages in Aughadown on Shrove Tuesday, 1844.

Ash Wednesday

This was a day of black fast when only one full meal was allowed. Some people went further and ate nothing except a cup of tea and a slice of unbuttered bread. Some member of the family tried to go to Mass and returned with an amount of ash, which was put on everybody's forehead.

St. Patrick's Day

March 17th was a welcome break from the Lenten austerities. Everybody, if they could, would have meat for dinner that day. It was a holiday of obligation, so everybody went to Mass. Springs of shamrock were worn. Men who had taken the 'pledge' – to abstain from alcoholic drink during Lent – could drink that day. Most of the men 'drowned the shamrock' on St. Patrick's Day

Palm was blessed on Palm Sunday and distributed at Mass. Since there is no 'palm' on Heir, Mrs. Trinder of Whitehall used to leave sprigs of greenery out for the islanders, which they collected en route to Mass.

For centuries people abstained from meat for the forty days of Lent. Most existed on fish and potatoes. Good Friday was a day of black fast, tea without milk and dry bread. In later years when the fast was relaxed, it was a day for fish and or cnósach trá:[1] limpets, periwinkles, cockles and edible seaweed like dulse.

April 1st

Lá na n-Amadán (Fool's Day). People played practical jokes on each other.

Laethanta na Bo Riabhaithe, (The days of the brindled cow) usually a period of broken weather, comes at the end of March and early April. According to folklore the brindled cow boasted that she had survived the cold weather of March. However, April 'borrowed'a couple of hard cold days from March, which killed the cow.

Scairbhín na gCuach are days at the end of April and early May which coincide with the coming of the cuckoo. The weather is usually cold and blustery, hence the name scairbhín or more correctly garbh-shíon (rough weather) of the cuckoo.

Easter Sunday

Easter was welcomed as it meant the end of fasting. Everybody tried to have meat for dinner on Easter Sunday, lamb, chicken or corned beef. Eggs were in plentiful supply at Easter and were consumed in large quantities.

May Day – Lá Bealtaine

In the pre-Christian era, the druids led the celebration of Bealtaine, May Day, the start of summer and at Samhain (November), the start of winter. Imbolg, February 1st, Christianised as St. Brigid's Day, heralded the beginning of spring and Lughnasa (August) the beginning of autumn.

May Day, when the Fastnet sailed north to meet the Bull and Cow Rocks off Beara.[2] when sleeping out of doors was dangerous, when the fairies had a particularly detrimental effect on butter, on cream, on cows, you dared not give a loan of anything to a neighbour, because you were giving away your luck. On May morning young maidens washed their faces with the dew on the grass. On that morning people always 'brought in the summer' – leaves of trees, or flag iris (liostrums) in the case of Heir Island and other parts of West Cork, and hung them in a bunch on the front door or stood them in a vase on the windowsill. Bealtaine is derived from Bile Tine, the fire of the sacred tree or Baal Tine, the fire of the Celtic God Baal. Lighting bonfires was associated once with May but this was transferred to the Eve of St. John, June 23rd coinciding with the summer solstice.

Baal was the sun god, giver of life, fount and donor of fertility. In pre-Christian times, all household fires were extinguished on the eve of May Day and nobody ventured out of doors before dawn. Druids lit the fires of May; people brought rowan branches of new growth to dance deiseal (clockwise) in the direction of the sun around the fire. Turning deiseal is still preserved in Irish customs – turning boats at sea, the route of a coffin around a house etc. There were many superstitions associated with May Day. If a person had a grudge against a neighbour, he might dump an animal carcass or a hen in the other person's land to take away their luck. It was considered lucky to have the first water out of a well on May morning. People would rise very early to try to be the first to draw water from a particular well. If the neighbour was unfriendly they would try and borrow something from you. Nothing was given away, not even the time of day.

On May Day, children used to nettle each other by slapping each others hands and legs. Harmless fun, but sometimes it ended in tears.

St. John's Eve

The twenty third of June, St. John's Eve, was traditionally midsummer's day. Lighting a bonfire near the potato garden was customary all over West Cork. It was done to bring blessings on the crop.

The feast of Lughnasa, at the beginning of August, had no local festivities or practices associated with it, at least in recent times. Baltimore Regatta, which has always been held on August Monday, was a big day for the islanders of Roaringwater Bay, Aughadown and Baltimore. The lobstermen came home to participate in the lobster-yawl races and the sailing and the rowing events were keenly contested.

Halloween (Samhain) was the beginning of the Celtic year. At this time, it was believed, only a thin veil separated the physical world from the world of spirits. Halloween was celebrated indoors with games like Snap Apple, using water, apples or coins, Blind Man's Buff etc. Barm brack, containing a ring, a stick, a rag, a bean and pen, was part of the evening meal.

Christmas

The ancient pagan Irish adored the sun, a fact recorded by early Christian writers. According to these writers, the Irish swore oaths by the heavenly bodies, giving rise to thos expression in the Irish language – dar bhrí na gréine is na gealaí (by the strength of the sun and of the moon). Early Christianity, aware of the importance attributed by the Romans and others to midwinter, when the sun was 'reborn', decided to celebrate the birth of the Saviour at that time, and thus December 25th was settled upon as Christmas.

Christmas was of paramount importance in traditional Irish life. It was believed that the gates of Heaven were open at this time and that anybody who died during the twelve days of Christmas had an easy passage there. On Christmas Eve, a special big candle, coinneal mór na Nollag, was lit in the kitchen window as a symbolic guide to the Holy Family, wandering the lonely roads outside, as they had the first Christmas. It was said that, in memory of the holy birth, all creation rejoiced at midnight on Christmas Eve and that the cows in their byres went on their knees briefly at that hallowed time.

Preparation for Christmas began many days in advance. There was a general and thorough cleaning of house and farmyard. The men cleaned and tidied all the outbuildings and the yard; sometimes the dwelling house was whitewashed. Meanwhile the women were busy inside the house, sweeping, washing and cleaning. The welcome task of providing the decorations usually fell to the children.

On Heir Island most families 'fattened' a pig which was killed before Christmas, pieces of fresh pork being shared with less fortunate neighbours. Most housewives kept a flock of geese and/or turkeys which were sold before Christmas and provided welcome cash for the Christmas purchases. Many families had sons 'steamboating' (working in the Irish, or more usually, the British merchant navy), who frequently returned to be with their families at Christmas. Every family had relations in America and the 'American letter', which was sure to contain not only good wishes but also a present of money, often a substantial sum, was eagerly awaited.

Some members of the family always went to 'town' (Skibbereen) a few days before Christmas 'to bring home the Christmas'. They made their Christmas purchases of meat, fruit, sweet cake, barm brack, candles, tobacco, whiskey and porter, toys and sweets for the children, new clothes and household goods. Shopkeepers gave presents to their customers, a 'Christmas box' of seasonal dainties. Shopping in the local island shop before Christmas was called 'bringing home the loan'. People had a book on which items bought were recorded. Payment was made when an animal was sold or money earned from fishing.

On Heir Island, Christmas Eve was a day of great excitement, especially for the children who helped decorate the house with colourful baubles and long trails of ivy, but without holly, as it does not grow on the island. The traditional Christmas Eve dinner on Heir, and indeed in many parts of West Cork, consisted of 'stockfish' (usually dried ling) with onion sauce and potatoes. As darkness fell, the candles were lit, the big one in the kitchen being lit by the youngest child, with help from an older person if necessary. The lighting of the candle was accompanied by the wish, 'Go mbeirimid beo ar an am seo arís' – may we all be alive this time next year. The rich Christmas cake was cut for the evening tea. Punch was made and bottles of porter opened if a neighbour called.

The children hung their stockings by the fire or at the foot of the bed and were hastened to bed with warnings that Santa Claus wouldn't call with his presents if they were up late. There was something magical about Christmas night. The island was dotted with lights flickering in every window. Looking across Roaringwater Bay one could see the little dots of light in the homes on Sherkin and Cape Clear; to the north lights brightened the windows on the Skeams and on the mainland.

© Christine Thery

HEIR ISLAND CHRISTMAS

Christmas Day

The first of three successive Masses started in Lisheen Church on the mainland at half-past seven. This necessitated rising as early as four, often in the black darkness, rowing to Cunnamore or Whitehall, depending on the tide, walking the two to three miles to the Church, hearing three Masses, returning on foot to their boats and rowing back to the island, landing at the pier, at Paris, at 'Leán Gamhan pier or at the Reen, depending on what part of the island one lived. If the early morning was calm and moonlit, it helped a lot. If the night was dark the people carried lanterns as they walked towards the strand. Islanders speak of watching the lights of the lanterns moving towards the shore along the winding boreens.

Everybody, except the very young and the very old or disabled, went to Mass in Lisheen on Christmas morning, unless the weather was very bad.

On the mainland, Christmas Day was a quiet family day but on Heir, it was a day for fun, dancing and sports. All the young men and women gathered at the Trá Bán, where they danced and sang. The men competed in races, long jump and weight-throwing. A football tournament was played, with four teams competing, a team representing the four 'townlands' of the island, Heir Island West (Paris), the Midlands, Heir Island East and the Reen. Tired and happy, they returned to their homes about four o clock when Christmas dinner was eaten, the biggest and most elaborate meal of the year. The housewife, who hadn't joined in the frolics at the Trá Bán, took pride in setting a generous table before appetites, sharpened by dancing, football and athletics.

On St. Stephen's Day the children went from house to house, dressed in gaudy clothes and masks, singing the wren song.[3] They always called to the houses where sailors would be home from sea, Shaw Minihane's, Neilly O'Donovan's, John O'Donovan's, Pyburn's and others. Money was scarce on the island but there would be money in the house when the merchant seaman returned. They would be rewarded at each house with money which might range from a réal (sixpence) to a leath-chóroin (half-crown). Charlie O'Neill used to open the shop for half an hour in the evening so that they could buy sweets.

St. Stephen's night brought the Christmas festivities to a climax on Heir. This was the night of the big party or 'Ball', as it was called by the islanders, organised on Christmas Day and held on St. Stephen's Night. A committee was selected to make all the arrangements. The first task was to find a householder who would be willing to make his house available for the night's fun. They tried to rotate it as much as possible and very few houses refused to have the 'Ball' in their houses. John Fitzgerald told me that one year, when he was a committee member, they decided to ask Timmy Cahalane of Reen South to make his home available. Timmy had no hesitation, saying, 'Row it along'. Very often the islanders used nautical terms and expressions in many unrelated aspects of everyday life. Money was collected to buy drink and food, the men contributing ten shillings and the women a half-crown. Those home from sea usually contributed more as they had more cash.

On St. Stephen's Day, they went to Baltimore to get supplies for the night; four or five quarter-tierces of porter, a few bottles of whiskey and wine, and minerals for the ladies. Food was also supplied; sweet cake, sandwiches, barm brack etc. The alcoholic drinks were always bought in Salter's Pub. They returned about eight o clock at night, a donkey and cart bringing the porter from the pier to the house. A long night of song and dance followed.

From talking to the Heir Islanders on the island and elsewhere, it is very obvious that the people were very musical. Nearly everyone could sing and many could play an instrument. The Heir Island Set was danced many times during the night. The party continued until dawn and sometimes was resumed the following night if all the drink had not been consumed.

By December 28th life was coming back to normal and the daily routine of work was resumed. There were no special celebrations connected with New Year's Eve or New Year's Day except that January 1st was a holy day of obligation.

The Epiphany was, and still is, known as Nollaig na mBan – the women's Christmas. However, only a little of the delicacies would have survived until then, giving rise to the saying:

> *'Nollaig na bhFear – Nollaig mhór mhaith,*
> *Nollaig na nBan- Nollaig gan mhaith.*
>
> *Men's Christmas – a good big Christmas,*
> *Women's Christmas – a useless Christmas.*

MAGGIE McCARTHY, LOU PYBURN, DANNY CAHALANE, BABY BURKE AND DAN O'DRISCOLL

HEIR ISLAND WEDDING, APRIL, 1958.
GROUP TAKEN OUTSIDE LISHEEN CHURCH AFTER THE WEDDING OF JOHN FITZGERALD
AND BRIDIE O'DRISCOLL

From left to right in front, Maura Shanahan, Ardura, Mary Ann O'Neill. Noreen Desmond, Eileen Cadogan, Cape Clear, Francis Fitzgerald, Betty Cadogan, Cape Clear, Gerry McCarthy

From left to right back, Maggie McCarthy, Jimmy Fitzgerald, Mary Ellen O'Driscoll, Hannah McCarthy, Kilsarlaght, Bridie Fitzgerald, (nee O'Driscoll) Michael John O'Neill, John Fitzgerald, Peggy O'Driscoll, Sonny Desmond and Bridie Fitzgerald.

— 32 —

Social Life

Despite continued emigration the island was still crowded with people up to the middle of the twentieth century, the population in 1951 being 139. The pace of life was slow, dictated by the seasons and the weather, in tune with the natural cycle of the year. There was always time to chat, exchange stories. The men would congregate for a chat at The Rock in Paris, by Coorey's Chamber or at John Murphy's Hill. Parties or 'Balls' as they were called, were frequent: when an emigrant returned, the night of the Station, the night of a wedding.

When an exile returning from the U.S.A. or Australia it was a good 'excuse' for a party. 'Balls' were held in Pyburns, when Katie Scanlan (nee Cahalane) returned from Staten Island, New York, with her husband Paddy Scanlan. Charles (Shaw) Minihane had several emigrant sisters and brothers and their return was usually marked with nights of singing, dancing, drinking, and jollity. There was always a 'get together' when an islander was emigrating, more a gathering of neighbours in a sense of unity, for they were sad occasions. Happier were the parties when an emigrant returned for a visit. Margaret O'Sullivan of Clonakilty, and formerly of Heir Island Middle, remembers listening to the music in Harte's house on East Skeam when Con returned from Australia. The music wafted across the waves. She was too young to go. Later she emigrated herself, but returned and settled near Clonakilty. Margaret remembers the first radio on the island which was in the late Neilly O'Donovan's house and was bought by one of his brothers who worked as a merchant seaman. Crowds used to gather to listen to music programmes like 'Take the Floor'. People often rowed over from the Skeams to listen to the programmes. The islanders loved music – Margaret remembers her father dancing twenty one sets in Sherkin one St. Stephen's night, dancing so much that he wore the soles off his shoes.

The first television set on Heir Island was bought by her father, John Murphy. It was battery operated, as electricity had not yet reached the island. Before John Murphy bought his T.V., some of the islanders used to row out to Turkhead to watch special programmes in John Cadogan's house or to Hingstons in

Cunnamore. John Cadogan of Turkhead was the island postman in the 1960s and had a special relationship with all the islanders. A good crowd went out to watch the Mohammed Ali fights, which were televised at that time.

Words of songs were learned from *Ireland's Own*, songs like *Danny Boy*, *The Wild Colonial Boy*, *The Rose of Tralee*, *The Rose of Mooncoin*, *Dear Old Skibbereen*, *The Butcher Boy* and many more. Songs became associated with certain singers. Jeremiah (Corney) Murphy is remembered for reciting *The Sailors Alphabet*, Tom 'Jack' O'Donovan for *The Memphis*.

There was a dancing platform of mass concrete near Coorey's shed in Heir Island East. Here on summer Sunday evenings the young men and women gathered to dance the island set, waltzes etc. Music was provided by those who could play the accordion or mouth organ. There was another platform in the Midlands, across the road from the entrance to the boreen which leads to Neilly O'Donovan's house.

At night the neighbours gathered to discuss the events of the day, the fishing, farming, the weather. Ghost stories were told; returned emigrants described their adventures, 'steamboat' sailors told of places seen, stories heard. This was called scoruíochting. Some houses were 'good' scoruíochting houses; Seán McCarthy's (Seán Hanny) house in Paris was a favourite gathering place at night, although it is a very small house.

Playing cards was a popular pastime during the long winter nights. If a few neighbours dropped in scoruíochting, an impromptu card game might begin. In the 1940s and 50s, there were organised card 'championships', played on winter Sunday nights. The card-playing was held in a different house each Sunday night in rotation. Paying one shilling to enter, they played for prizes, a turkey, a goose or a 'surprise'. When a card player had won three games, he went forward to the final. While the card playing was in progress, the others danced seventeen sets every Sunday night. Other dances which were popular were the *Two-Step*, the *Stack of Barley*, the *Highland Fling* and *Step a Chipín*. When a person was dancing, they could nominate another to play the cards for them. The usual game was Twenty-Five, Thirty-Five and Forty-Five. Ten people used to play at a time.

The Heir Island Set has been revived. A group of Heir Islanders and their friends danced *Set na n-Oileán* at Fleadh Cheoil na Mumhan in 1995. The team consisted of Bridie Fitzgerald, James Collins, Anne Collins, Danny Murphy, James Whooley and Bridget Hourihane. Now a group of céilí dancers meet every Tuesday night in Casey's in Baltimore where the tradition of set dancing is kept very much alive.

During the summer the islanders often travelled across to the larger islands on Sunday evenings, to Paddy Burke's pub in Cape Clear or to Jim O'Connor's Pub in Sherkin. Paddy Walsh of Cape Clear, who was married to Maggie Cahalane from Heir Island, was a good melodeon player. A great night of dancing and singing was often held on Cape and sometimes the islanders did not return until morning. Melodeon players on Heir Island included Pattie O'Donovan, Florence O'Donovan, Seán Harte, and Pat Burke among others.

Men and women walked to Mass from Cunnamore or Whitehall on Sunday mornings. The men would have a few pints in Minihane's on their return. The women were not allowed in at that time; they would be served four-penny packets of biscuits at back of pub.

When the men were away 'lobstering' in the summer, the island women would congregate at Coorey's platform to dance and sing. Music was provided by mouth organ or accordion; sometimes the tunes were hummed. The Heir Islanders were considered the best dancers in the Fisherman's Hall in Baltimore.

Wedding parties, or 'the hauling home' as they were called, were always held in the bride's house. Everybody in the island was invited to the wedding party. The night was spent dancing, singing and eating. 'Tide' washing powder was scattered on the concrete floor to make it livelier. A couple of half tierces of stout were always drunk. Couples were married in Kilcoe or Lisheen, the two churches in Aughadown Parish. A sibín or pub, run by the Minihane family in the midlands in the late 19th century, is remembered for its 'Wrestler' stout which was brewed by Deasys in Clonakilty. The Sibín closed when Deasys stopped brewing stout and there hasn't been a public house on Heir since.[1]

FLORRIE FITZGERALD PLAYING THE MOUTH ORGAN AND HIS WIFE ANNIE

Regattas

Baltimore Regatta, on the first Monday in August, was the great 'day out' for the islanders. The lobster men usually came home for the regatta. Baltimore used to be thronged with people, whether the day was wet or dry and it often rained. The pubs were packed; ferry boats brought crowds of people to Sherkin.

There were many hawkers' stalls on the pier. People walked around, meeting friends whom they might have not seen for a year. Most interest centred on the rowing races, the two-oar boat race, the four-oar and the six-oar gig races. Gigs from Myross, Ardralla, Ringaroga and Glandore were the usual contestants. The lobster yawl race aroused great interest, especially for the Heir Island people. Two of the fastest yawls were The *Leader,* owned by Con Minihane, and *The Pride of Toe Head,* owned by Neilly O'Donovan, which is borne out by the results which were published in the *Southern Star.*

A man from Skibbereen, named Paddy McCarthy, was often the centre of attraction; he entertained the crowd with feats of strength and agility. He performed all sorts of tricks with a whip, balanced a ladder on his chin, laid down on a bed of nails, pulled a motor-car by a rope held between his teeth.

Schull Regatta was another outing for the islanders. Schull Regatta used to be a two day event. Sailing, rowing, and other aquatic events were held on the first day, while athletic events, like weight throwing, racing and tug-o-war took place on the second day. At Schull Regatta, the T.B.C., owned by the Scullys of the Middle Calf, often won the lobster yawl race.

© Michael Minihane
COMING FROM THE PIER
including MRS. KATHLEEN HARTE, MRS. KIT MURPHY, PETER MURPHY AND MARIA HARTE

LEFT TO RIGHT: KATHY MURPHY, TIMOTHY O'DONOVAN, MS. NEWMAN, DANNY CAHALANE,
LOU AND EDDIE PYBURN.

— 33 —

Shops

Mrs. Ann Casey had the first shop on Heir Island. It was situated in Heir Island Middle, near the boreen leading to the late Neilly O'Donovan's house. She sold a wide range of groceries and bought butter and eggs from the islanders. Mrs. Casey had two sons who were renowned for their strength. It is claimed that they could turn the stream millwheel in Skibbereen by hand. They both emigrated to the U.S.A. and the shop had closed by 1901, as there are no Caseys on Heir in the census of that year.[1] The next shop on the island was Burkes (See Chapter 24)

O'Driscoll's Shop

Patrick O'Driscoll had a shop in Heir Island East where Don O'Connor lives today. This was a general grocery store, selling a wide range of household goods, flour, meal, sugar, paraffin oil. Mr. O'Driscoll used to sail in his yawl, The *Non Pareil,* to Baltimore or Skibbereen to collect goods for his store. The *Non Pareil,* built by O'Neills of Sherkin, was also part of the lobster fleet. He also bought eggs and butter from the islanders which he brought to Baltimore to the Railway Station. Patrick O'Driscoll used to go up the Ilen to Skibbereen to purchase provisions from the wholesalers, John J. Daly and Sons of Ilen St., Skibbereen. Mrs. O'Driscoll closed the shop soon after her husband's sudden death in 1942. The family were known as the Merchants because of their business.

O'Neill's Shop

Mr. Tagney of Millstreet was married to Katie O'Neill of Heir Island. In the 1940s he set up a shop in Fásagh, directly opposite the eastern end of Heir Island. When he closed this shop, his brother-in-law, Charles O'Neill, bought the shop, weights, measures, scoops etc and set up business in Heir Island. The licence to sell stamps was transferred from Tagneys to Charlie O'Neill. O'Neills was the only store on the island from the forties until the early 90s when Charlie died. For a while his son, John, continued the business. When he closed, the present shop, owned by John Moore, was opened for business. This

THE SHOP © Christine Thery

229

business is carried on in the house where Con Burke had his shop.

The telephone 'came' to the island on September 5th 1941. It was situated in Charlie O'Neill's shop/post office. Battery operated, it was worked by a windmill situated on the hill south of O'Neill's shop. A paragraph in the *Southern Star* of September, 20th 1941 reads

> The establishment of a wireless telephone system between Baltimore and Sherkin, Heir and Cape Clear islands, at which Post Office engineers have been working for some months, has been completed and tests carried out during the past fortnight have given excellent results. The system which is now officially in operation will be of immeasurable value to the islanders, particularly during the winter, for months of which communications have heretofore been extremely hazardous and at times impossible.

Post Office

The first Post Office on the island, was in Con Burke's. When Burkes closed their shop, Charlie O'Neill, of Heir Island East, took over the Post Office.

For many years John Shanahan of Heir Island Middle was the postman.[2] Famous for his punctuality, he called his watch 'Big Ben'. People who kept turkeys or geese often sent one to relations in England for Christmas. Richard (Dick) Herlihy of Church Cross brought the mail to Cunnamore Pier, where it was collected by the Heir Island postman. Dick, who collected the Heir Island mail, had to carry the heavy loads of parcels around on his bicycle while he was delivering letters on the mainland. The heavy weight of parcels was too much for the bicycle. Seán O'Donoghue of Kilcoe, who had a hackney car, was then given the job of collecting the mail from Heir Island and delivering it to Church Cross Post Office.

In time Dick got a van, which made life easier for him. John Cadogan of Turkhead was the postman on Heir Island in the 1960s. He motored from Turkhead to Cunnamore every morning in his punt, which had a Seagull outboard engine, to collect the post and distribute it to the island homes. He also ferried Mrs. Whooley of Whitehall, who was the island teacher from 1962 to 1970, to the island and in the evening brought her back to Cunnamore. Finbarr Harte of Heir Island West, now living in Skeagh, was the island postman for four years.

The Post Office closed on the 30th April, 1988. John O'Neill continued to collect the post at Cunnamore and delivered it to the houses. The post is now delivered by John Moore. As shown by the postmarks below the official name for Heir Island was Inis Uí Eidirsceoil. Today the shortened version, Inis Uí Drisceoil, is used.

— 34 —
Water and Electricity

Water, or the lack of it, was often a serious problem in Heir, especially in dry summers. If a landowner had cattle and no well on his land, he had to depend on a neighbour's generosity to get water. During summers of drought, people used to rise very early in the morning to get the water that would have risen during the night. Some boundaries between farms were disputed, so getting water became a cause of friction between families on occasions. Although there are numerous springs, all of the wells were shallow and couldn't be deepened without electric power. The people of the island had to wait until 1983 to get a proper supply, piped in under water, from Cunnamore.

The main wells in the island were:

Tobar Garraí Thaidhg (The well in Timothy's garden) This is in the North Reen, near where O'Driscolls had their shop. It is said that it never went dry. People from the South Reen came to this well, carrying the water home in buckets. Nell McCarthy, who lived in the most western house on the island, often walked the island to the different wells for water for her cattle and for domestic use in dry summers.

Tobair Charnáin (The wells of the heap or hillock) are three wells in close proximity on 'Barry's' land in Heir Island Middle, adjacent to the Mass Rock.

Tobar na mBan (The women's well) is situated at the western end of the bridge, very close to the high water mark and in 'spring tides' the sea water got into it. In dry weather the women of Paris used to congregate here and wait for the trickle of water to rise. They passed the time chatting. A Mr. Manley who supervised the building of the bridge said, 'The Devil must be planted in that rock as there is so much gossip and back-biting going on' [1]

Tobar a Lúibín (The well of the little nook) is in Heir Island Middle on the hillside North East. of the Trá Bán. In older times it was considered to be a holy well. People went there to pray and rub water on sores, etc. 'This well is situated on the south side of the hill which is called 'Cnoc a trágh bháin', overlooking the strand known as the 'Tráig Bán' I remember when I was a young man, people suffering from sore eyes used to visit this well. There was no fixed day for those visits. They used to go there three mornings – early – in succession, and on each visit they used to recite a decade of the rosary, and then bathe the eyes with the water from well. People suffering from a pain and other sickness used also visit the well. The custom no longer prevails on the Island.' (I.F.S.C) [2]

Tobar na mBannaí (well of the women or the headland) is in Heir Island West, north of Faill a Dúna, on Fitzgerald's land.

In the Dún area there is a well very near **Faill a Bhrághaid**.

The Cabhlach well (well of the ruins) is in Heir Island west, near Faill Leac (cliff of the flagstones). A boreen leads down to the well from the road but is now blocked by furze and blackthorns. This boreen was made by one of the Pyburn family so it is known as Pyburn's Boreen.[3]

A well on the north side of the island was known as '**Michel's Well**', after Michael McCarthy, who lived nearby. There was also a good well further west near Cúilín na hÁtha, where a little stream of water runs into the sea. There was a well in a field, called the Garraí Glas in Heir Island Middle, near where Gubby Williams lives today.

A well on the South Reen was known as Tobar Síofra (the fairy well) in a field called Clais an Airgid.

Cork County Council erected two public pumps, one near the school in Heir Island Middle in the 1930s and one in Paris (Heir Island West) in the 1950s.

This is a report by Mr. D.J. McCormack. L.G. Inspector, in 1928, published in the *Southern Star*.

> The well at Hare Island is situated beside the road at a much lower level than the road surface. It has been covered over in concrete, and an attempt has been made to protect it from pollution, but without success, as during rainy weather surface washings from the road will pass into the well at the entrance. In view of the very excellent housing which has been carried out on the Island, it seems a pity not to provide a water supply free from contamination. It might be possible to protect the present well by enclosing it entirely in concrete and erecting a pump for drawing the water, instead of the present method of dipping buckets, which are not always too clean. If this is possible, it should be done without delay. The only alternative would be to erect a pump over some new source.

This refers to the pump near the school, which was erected soon afterwards.[4]

The *Southern Star* in 1929 published a report about the difficulty of getting water on the island, especially in dry summers. Dr. T.J. O'Meara stated that the Board of Guardians had erected a pump over the well in Heir Island Middle, but because of frequent breakages, they had to give up the attempt of keeping it in repair. The well gave a fair, but unsatisfactory, supply of water. In his view, wells should be considered an obsolete method of supplying water, especially for young children. Since there were many people drawing from the same wells, there was bound to be contamination if every vessel used was not completely clean.

Water was an ongoing problem. In an article in the *Cork Examiner* in 1975, under the heading, *A Paradise Lost for Want of Water*, Jim Cluskey reported as follows:-

'To the people of Heir Island, just a quarter of a mile out in the Atlantic off the West Cork coast, the lack of water for themselves and their livestock is a constant nightmare and one which they are no longer prepared to tolerate. The same lack is, as I have seen, a very real source of physical danger, a barrier to the island's progress and, very possibly, a health hazard. Now a committee has been formed on the island and one of its members, Mr. Danny Murphy, told me, "For the first time in our lives we are organised and we are going to fight this thing to the bitter end". Danny, whose job is in Bantry, has been forced to go and live on the mainland, because he was not prepared to leave his wife to face the drudgery of walking three miles each day just to get sufficient water to meet the needs of their home. Danny, who led a deputation to the May meeting of the Western Committee of Cork Co. Council, and made a strong demand for action, wants to go back to his island home. But unless a sufficient supply of water is found it may well be that others will follow his footsteps to the mainland.

An effort has been made by the Western Committee to provide a water scheme for the island. Five bore-holes were sunk but three of them were useless and two did not provide sufficient water for a scheme. The islanders, however, are not satisfied that everything possible was done to find an adequate source and I was present when they pointed out to Mr. Cornelius Murphy, M.C.C. two wells which they say had never gone dry and which they maintain, show that the water is, in fact, there.

Mr. Murphy, a consistent campaigner to bring both water and electricity to the island, came away with a new sense of the urgency of the situation, because even apart from the fact that water is a vital every-day need, it was, he told me, quite obvious that the lack of it was impeding the development of a profitable tourist business on this beautiful unspoiled island.

Arising out of the deputation to the Western Committee, the Assistant Co. Engineer, Mr. Jerry O'Regan, is soon to visit the island where local people will point out to him where water will, they believe, be found.

Committee member John Harte said, "we know that the water is there and at this stage we are prepared to settle for nothing less than a piped scheme to every house. We have been putting up with this drudgery for years and it is time that it came to an end".

Quite obviously there is a mood of militancy on the island. A "no rates" campaign is under way and there are those who say that this is but a first step, with others to follow until their demands are met. The militancy is easy to understand. Because people, women as well as men, awake every day to the misery of those long treks to the two island pumps. And frequently, too, they awake to the same misery as early as 4 a.m. The reason, Danny Murphy explains, is that the demands on the meagre supply are such that sources for the pumps must be "rested." Very often it is before the crack of dawn that they recover and then, goaded by sheer necessity, the people, buckets in their fists, plod wearily from their homes.

In all of this I found one aspect which, to me, was particularly dangerous and frightening. When the level of the water drops in dry weather, the people lift the heavy manhole covers beside the pumps and clamber down iron rungs to the dark pits underneath. There, standing on narrow platforms, they lower their buckets on ropes and haul up the water before clambering out again. The fact that they stoically accept the need for this makes it no less appalling.

Whilst the need for water dominates the mind of the islanders, there is anger, too, at the fact that electric power – apparently promised five years ago – has still not been provided. Islanders point to the fact that rock formations between the island and the mainland provide natural platforms for the erection of pylons, and wonder why, after all this time, they stand still barren in the sea.

As our boat curved out over the sunlit waters towards Cunnamore Point, we looked back on an island paradise. But it is a paradise lost – for want of light and water.'[5]

When the County Council was boring holes in 1976 to find a good 'spring', they stated that their work would be much easier if they had electricity. The campaign for a good water supply resulted in the E.S.B. finally connecting the island to the main supply in 1976, underwater cables connecting Cunnamore with the islands. Piped water soon followed in 1983.

© Michael Minihane

JOHN O'DONOVAN, OF HEIR ISLAND WEST, FILLING A BARREL OF WATER AT THE PUMP
IN HEIR ISLAND MIDDLE, WEST OF THE SCHOOL

ISLAND PUMP ERECTED 1930s

DANNY MURPHY, HEIR ISLAND

© Michael Minihane

KIT O'NEILL BEING INTERVIEWED
BY TOM MCSWEENEY ABOUT THE
WATER SITUATION IN HEIR ISLAND.

FRANCIS FITZGERALD COLLECTING WATER
WITH HIS NIECE, MARY

© Michael Minihane

22ND NOVEMBER, 1976, HEIR ISLAND SCHOOL ON THE OCCASION OF THE E.S.B. SWITCH-ON.
MICHAEL PAT MURPHY, JUNIOR MINISTER, *(below)* PERFORMED THE SWITCH-ON.

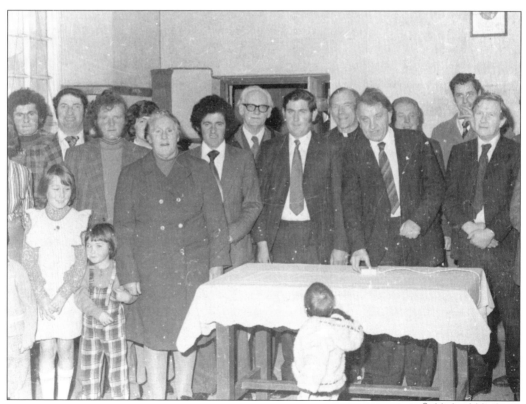

© Michael Minihane

MAGGIE DESMOND (NEE MEHIGAN) WITH HER
DAUGHTER, BREDA DESMOND

HANNAH AND TIMMY HARTE,
HEIR ISLAND AND EAST SKEAM

PATTIE AND KATE HARTE (NEE BARRY),
EAST SKEAM

TIM DESMOND, EAST SKEAM

CON HARTE, EAST SKEAM

EAST SIDE OF WEST SKEAM WITH CHURCH RUIN AND GRAVEYARD IN THE CENTRE

— 35 —

The Skeams

The two Skeam Islands, East and West, are very close to Heir Island. In the past they were interconnected socially, economically, geographically. All the residents of the Skeams had relations on Heir. They moved from the Skeams to Heir to marry and vice versa. The children went to school on Heir Island, coming across every morning and were collected again at three of clock. Sometimes the children from the Skeams stayed on Heir with relations during the school week, going home for the weekend.

They fished together; Ricky O'Regan of West Skeam always had his yawls pulled up high in Heir Island West because his own island has little shelter from winter gales. The Heir Island postmen delivered post to the Skeams twice a week.

Traditionally the belief was that the Skeam Islands got their name from a Saint Céim (Kame), supposedly a brother of Ciarán of Cape Clear. Daniel O'Donovan (in 'Sketches in Carbery') corroborates the local tradition about St. Céim.[1] However, no such person appears in the 'Calendar of Irish saints'. The Coppinger Inquisition of 1694 gives the name as 'Iniskeame' and Bishop Dive Downes, writing in 1699, calls them East and West Iniskeam. Canon O'Mahony, however, states that the islands belonged to the O'Mahonys and got their name from Cian, a popular O'Mahony name, and that the islands passed to the O'Driscolls under a marriage settlement between the two tribes. He wrote: 'The islands, now called the Skeams, were anciently named East and West Inniskean. They belonged to Ivagha.' (O'Mahonys of Mizen Peninsula)

The islands names, are West Inishcame and East Inishcame recorded in 1614, when the island was assessed as ¾ of a ploughland in area and granted to Sir Walter Coppinger. They are called East and West Eniscame in the Book of Survey and Distribution, about 1641.[2] Historical written names for the island suggest that the name ends with an m (scame) or n as Canon O'Mahony refers to it, Iniscian, the island of Cian, Cian being a common O'Mahony name. It is impossible to be certain of the exact derivation. Certainly on Cape Clear and in Heir and Skeams, the tradition was very strong that there was a St. Céim (Kame), a brother of Ciarán, which would suggest that there was a church here in pre-Patrician times. On Cape Clear, the local belief that Ciarán preceded St. Patrick has been nearly certainly established by historical research, mainly done by Dr. Éamon Langford. *St. Kéim*[3] was the name of an O'Regan mackerel boat, built in Peel in the Isle of Man, in the 1890s.

West Skeam, although blessed with fertile soil, is much more inaccessible than East Skeam, in that there is no good mooring place for boats. Like Heir, finding good drinking water was a problem, especially in dry summers when the inhabitants had to resort to getting water on East Skeam, where there was a well which did not go dry even in summers of drought, transporting the water in wooden barrels in a rowing boat. In bad weather the south-western end of West Skeam is frightening with waves rising up to 40 feet, going right into the fields.

A natural sea-arch on the south-west side of East Skeam is known as 'The Bridge'[4] or 'Timothy's Whistle'.

Situated on West Skeam are the ruins of an ancient chapel, erected in honour and to the memory of St. Keam, who is said to have lived in the 5th century. O'Donovan refers to the ruins of the ancient chapel and burial ground,

> Here, in former times, numerous interments used to be made, persons on the mainland bringing the remains of their deceased relatives to the island that they might be buried in the sacred precincts of the old chapel, over which, the memory of St. Keam had thrown so great a halo. A few years ago, by the undermining action of the sea, a portion of the cliff, near the site of the old chapel, was detached from the mainland, and the soil being broken up to a considerable depth at the same time, exposed to view numerous skulls and other bones of persons, the period of whose interment is unknown.[5]

The remains of the church with antae and a burial ground stand on a low cliff at the north eastern end of the island. The eastern end of the church has been partially destroyed by coastal erosion. In 1990 the Office of Public Works proposed a scheme to underpin the north and south wall of the church at the cliff edge.

Archaeological excavations were carried out within the burial ground and revealed three phases of burial. The remains of sixty two individuals were exposed and many more were visible in the eroded cliff face. There were twenty four burials associated with phase one, the bodies placed in simple body-shaped graves. The only artefact found was part of a bronze loop-headed pin of a type used between the 5th and 8th centuries.

One individual was buried in a stone-lined cist grave, probably indicating that he was a person of importance. Radiocarbon dating indicated that this burial took place some time between 430 to 770 A.D.

Fifteen people interred at the north side can be assigned to phase two. Two stone weights were found which were probably line sinkers or net weights. Radiocarbon dating places these burials at 550-855 A.D. Phase three burials were assessed to be of a later age, 1165-1365 approximately. It is likely that the graveyard went out of use shortly after 1400 A.D.

A kitchen midden was found over the last phase of burials, containing periwinkle, whelk and oyster shells, also scallop and crab. Seven species of fish were identified. Domestic animal bones, cattle, sheep and pig, horse and cat were also present.

The church was 6.85 meters long and 3.84 meters wide and originally had a stone roof. Archaeologists suggest that the church was built in the 9th or 10th century. Probably it was built on the site of an earlier wooden structure. If Céim did really exist, then this church dates back to pre-Patrician times.

The burial ground appears to have been used over a long period, perhaps as long as nine hundred years. Unlike Sherkin and Cape Clear, none of the smaller islands, Heir Skeams or Calf Islands had a consecrated burial ground so it is quite feasible that the burial ground on West Skeam was used by a wide community from the neighbouring islands and coastal district.[6]

Father Charles Davis (in *Cape Clear: A Retrospect*) writes about the church in West Skeams. He stated that he had landed on an island near Cape Clear called St. Keames .... He continued

> This island consists of about fifty acres and is occupied by two families. On the brow of a cliff are the ruins of a monastery or convent founded by this saint. So holy was this island considered, that until a later period the inhabitants of the mainland adjacent were wont to bring their dead miles across the sea for internment there. The waves of time and ocean have made sad havoc of the foundations of the monastery, and as they crumble away, the bones of the long-buried dead are frequently carried away by the receding waters.[7]

Writing from Melbourne, Australia, Con Harte, formerly of East Skeam recalled:

> There have been so many changes since I left the Skeams in 1948. I didn't get back until 1969. It was nice to see so many improvements, motor cars and outboard motors etc. Of course there were changes in Heir Island too. I remember my mother telling me that there were about one hundred and forty four children going to Heir Island School when she was there, sixteen going from the Skeams alone. They used to come and go in Desmond's flat-bottomed cot. There is greater luxury in Heir Island now, water on tap, electric power, good landing piers. It should have been there years ago for the poor battlers of the island.

Flax was grown in West Skeam by Tom O'Regan's family; it was not grown in the other three islands. It is one of the oldest cultivated plants; the mummies of ancient Égypt were wrapped in cloth woven from the fibres of its stems. This cloth is called linen, a word that comes from linum, the Latin name for flax. Linseed oil is obtained from the flax seeds.

The flax grown on West Skeam was for the production of its fibre. It was harvested directly after the blue flowers wilted. The tall stalks were pulled by the roots, a particularly hard job because the tough fibrous plants were extremely hard on the hand, causing blisters and welts. The continual stooping was backbreaking. The sheaf of stalks were put steeping in water, weighed down with stones. This was called 'ponding'. The stalks were allowed to ret[8] for about ten days. The beets (stalks) were slimy, ugly and difficult to handle; a foul odour permeated the surroundings.

After the ponding, the stalks were left to bleach on grass. Once dried, the stalks were bound into sheaves (like corn), or beets as they were called. When the bleaching was completed, they were built into stooks. It was soon ready for scutching, the beating which tenderised the tough stalks. The fibres were hit repeatedly against a hackle,[9] which separated the coarse brittle fibres, called 'tow', from the finer strands. The cleaned fibres were made into sheaves again and were ready for spinning. Finally the spun fibre was ready for weaving.[10]

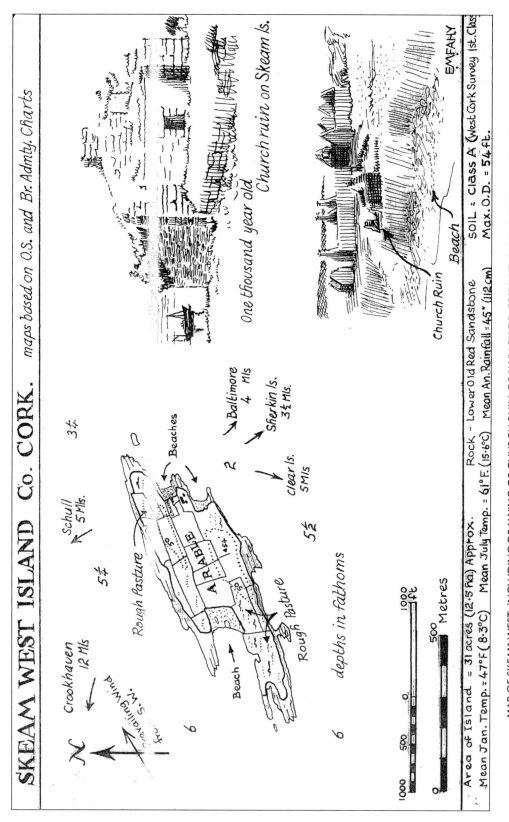

MAP OF SKEAM WEST, INCLUDING DRAWING OF CHURCH RUIN, DRAWN BY DR. EDWARD FAHY, OF U.C.C. IN THE 1960S.

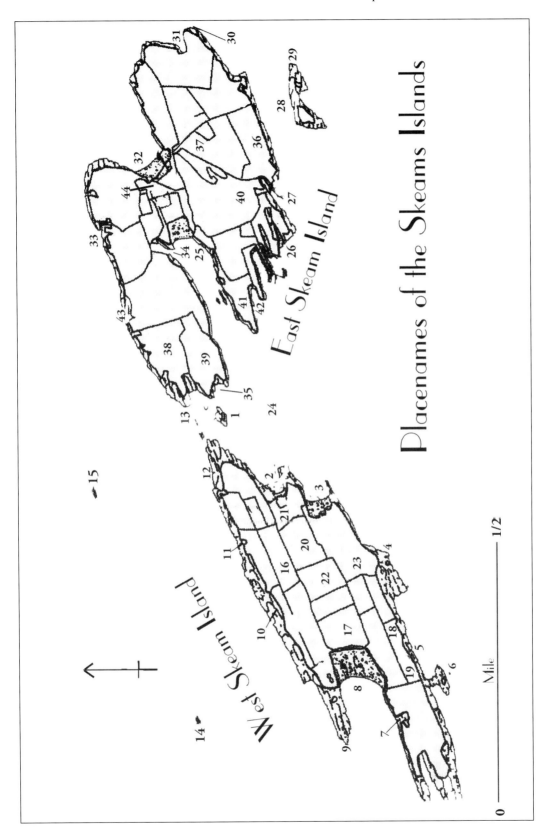

Placenames of the Skeams Islands

East Skeam Island

West Skeam Island

Mile

0   1/2

Placenames of West Skeam

1. Carraig an tSiúnta: the rock of the sound (passage between the two islands)
2. Skeam Church (Cill Inis Cáim)
3. Cé an Tobac, Quay of the Tobacco
4. Léith-oileán: half-an-island, meaning a rock accessible from the shore at low water with some vegetation, or Liath-oileán, the grey island, meaning bare, grey, almost devoid of vegetation.
5. Cuas an chapaill: the cove of the horse.
6. Oileán an Triopáin: island of purple laver, edible sea laver, porphyra umbilicalis, which was eaten raw or boiled in milk or water. It grows on beds of small mussels.
7. Cuaisín Naomhóg: small inlet of the little boats
8. An Trá Mhór: the big strand.
9. Pointe an Rabha Biora: headland of the pointed reef or row (rabha in Irish)
10. West Cuas an Bháid (inlet of the boat)
11 East Cuas an Bháid
12 Gob Rinncín: point of land of the dancing waves. Here the waves off the N.E. point of the island twist and turn as currents of water collide.
13. The Bones: three ridges of rock (rabha) which show at low water.
14. An Rabha Mór (The big rabha, row)
15. Tom's Rabha from rabha (a sunken rock or reef), discovered by Tom O'Regan. It was important to know every builg and rabha for safe navigation and also for fishing as some fish and shellfish, like lobsters, crabs etc are found only on 'broken' ground.
16 The Three Long Ridges : Ridge, a raised potato bed.
17. An Pháirc Dhearg, the red field, indicating good quality soil.
18 The Crock: from corrach, a marshy boggy field; very common in placenames of West Cork.
19 The South Leaca, from leaca, a slope.
20 Páirc an Teampaill, the field of the church (medieval)
21 An Séanta-Fhód: the holy ground – the burial ground adjoining the Church.
22 Ceann Árd, literally, 'high head', a hill.
23 Páirc an Tobair, field of the well.
24 Skeam Sound, passage between the two islands.

East Skeam

25 An Trá Bhán : the white strand, sandy.
26 The Bridge (An Droichead) : a natural sea-arch. The whistling sound of sea and wind in a nearby cave was used to forecast a south-easterly gale, and giving it an alternative name, Timsy's Whistle.
27 Cuas an Uisce, inlet of fresh water; there is a spring well nearby
28 The Sound, passage between East Skeam and Oileán na gCruach.
29 Oileán na gCruach: Island of the hillocks, a small island with a little vegetation
30 Pier erected by Board of Works.

31 Trá na gCruach: the strand of the hillocks or Trá na gCearc, strand of the hens. Hens used to go down to the strand to peck food.

32 An Trá Bhán East

33 Cuaisín na n-úll: little cove of the apple trees; nearby are the rough branches of a crab apple tree.

34 An Cúl Trá, the back strand, difficult to get into.

35 Trá na mBó, strand of the cows.

36 Leaca na gCruach, the sloping ground of the hillocks.

37 The Crock, from corrach, a marsh.

38 Páirc na Gaoithe, field of the wind.

39 Páirc na gCaorach, field of the sheep..

40 The Vein, marshy tract of land.

41 Ceann Chapaill, headland of the horse.

42 Cuas an Chapaill, inlet of the horse.

43 Cuas an tSeaca, inlet of frost. On north side of the island, which gets little sun in winter.

44 Tobar na Wella, The Wells. The best well in any of the four islands. When there was a long drought, people came from West Skeam, and even from Heir Island, to get water here. The water was bucketed into a barrel and brought back by boat.

Place-names and their meanings in English are from the *Natural Environment and Place-Names of Skeam Islands* by Anthony Beese, published in *Mizen Journal No. 8* (pp. 74–82) with some from *Logainmneacha Inis Cáim* (Skeam Islands) Coiste Logainmneacha Chorcaí, 1997.

BARRY'S HOUSE ON EAST SKEAM

THE PLACE I CALL HOME

There is a little plot out in the ocean
Surrounded by sea and by foam
Where the seal and the otter are venting
And now they have made it their home.

That's the place I was born and reared in
Where I grew up from childhood to man
Where we grew all our wheat
Our potatoes and beet
And even the clothes we put on.

That's where I learned to walk and to swim
To row and to sail and the sails for to trim
't was never sign-posted or never will be
The place I call home is surrounded by sea.

There are no Traffic lights, no cops to be seen
That awkward old warden never has been
They can keep writing dockets from morning 'till night,
But they could never sort out the green waves from the white.

I long to go back there
But alas 'tis too late
Because the one that keeps time
Has been marking the slate.

The old folks are gone now and I linger on
To join them at some later date.

Willie O'Regan, West Skeam and Whitehall

BRIDGIE O'REGAN, WEST SKEAM
WITH HER MOTHER MRS. RICKY
O'REGAN AND MRS. KATE
HARTE, EAST SKEAM

— 36 —

Life on East Skeam:
Mary Dwyer

***The following are the memories of living on the Island of East Skeam
of Mary Dwyer (nee Harte, Collatrum, Aughadown)***

I was born on the island of East Skeam in the early nineteen forties. I have lots of memories of what it was like as a child. I was the oldest girl in the family; my brother, Con, was thirteen years older and my sister, Bridie, five years younger. My father, Pattie Harte, was born in Heir Island in the year 1889, the youngest of eighteen children. My mother, Kate Barry, was born in 1897 on East Skeam, one of five girls. I think she was the second youngest. There were four other sisters, Molly, Hannah, Maggie and Helena. Helena died when she was only eleven. I have the most wonderful memories of my mother, who was both mother and friend. Growing up with no other children of my own age, she was a big influence in my life. My Dad was also a fantastic person; he was the main breadwinner and was away at sea, steam-boating or fishing most of his time. He went fishing either in his own four oar yawl or in one of the boats from Heir Island. That time they would go away for about six weeks at a time either to Kinsale, around the Seven Heads, or Crosshaven, fishing for lobsters and crayfish. Previous to that, my dad was away at sea. I remember Mam telling us children that Dad went back to sea a week after they were married. She did not see him again for three and a half years. By then she had a son of two years and nine months. There was also another boy in the family, Michael, who died when he was only seven years old. He died before I was born. It was a tough life for mother, looking after a family on the island, but in those days she had no choice. She worked very hard. There were no luxuries, no electricity, no radio or television. Candles and paraffin oil lamps provided light. There were no outboard engines, just the pair of paddles to row the punt to Heir Island to school and get the shopping.

My mother always had lots of hens and chickens. She would often take forty dozen eggs to either Burkes or Charlie O'Neill's shop and buy the shopping for the week. In the winter time the hens would not lay many eggs because of the cold weather. We had two cows. My mother used to milk the cows and put the milk in the big earthenware pans and let it sit for a few days, then skim off the cream to make the butter. The butter was made in a round wooden barrel with beaters on the inside. It sat on a stand and the barrel was turned with a handle at the end, to turn the cream into butter. There was not much milk or butter in the winter times as the cows usually go dry about October or November and calve in the spring. In those days we used *Killarney* condensed milk which was great to have. We loved it and if we got a chance we would spoon it out of the tin and eat it. Mam told me I was reared on it as there was no milk when I was born so she diluted the condensed milk with boiled water to feed me.

We always had plenty of fish and meat cured for the winter. I remember getting the pigs killed and salted down. They used coarse salt and made a couple of buckets of pickle. To test it they either floated an egg, or a large potato with a six inch nail, in the pickle to test its strength. I remember John Barry from Heir Island coming over to kill the pig. As children we thought it great to see someone come to the island.

Fish was pickled in much the same way as the pig but first the fish had to be caught. That was done in those days with what they called spillers or long lines with hooks fastened on about a fathom apart. They usually baited them with lugworms that were dug out of the strand and attached to each hook. They would go away very early in the morning and sometimes stay away for two days and come home with a boat full of hake, cod, ling, pollock and other white fish. Then the work of salting and curing the fish began. It was put into big timber barrels and pickled the same way as the meat, but removed from the pickle after a week and hung out in the sun to dry. When it was dry enough, it was taken indoors and was hung up on the beam over the fire to dry out properly. I remember seeing rows of fish hanging from the beams. It was wonderful to eat with white onion sauce and potatoes. Another favourite was carrageen moss. We used to pick and bleach it and that was a treat we always looked forward to. It was boiled in milk and strained through a muslin cloth and left set for a few hours. It was delicious with nice fresh cream skimmed off the pans of milk.

Living on the island was very tough at times, especially going to school. We had a wonderful teacher in those days, Miss Hegarty. She used to put our bottles of milk around the fire to heat it up on those cold frosty mornings and gave each child a turn standing by the fire to heat us all up. For us, going to school was great, as we had other children to play with at lunch time in school. Lunch was homemade brown cake and homemade butter. We only ever got a loaf of white bread when Mam took the butter and eggs to sell once a week. With a bit of luck there would be a penny halfpenny to buy a few 'bulls' eyes' or 'brown cushions' sweets after the shopping was done. That would be a real treat or perhaps even a penny worth of Marietta biscuits.

Our nearest neighbour, Mrs Cadogan, also came from Heir Island. She was a Hannah Harte from the Reen. She was such a handsome lady. She married Denny Cadogan but the poor man died within three years of getting married. Her brother, Timmie, went to live with her on the island to help her out after her husband's death. They remained there until 1958, when they left the island for good.

I have wonderful memories of the island at that time. There was nothing to do at night but listen to stories or play cards. I remember my mother telling the story of how they launched her father's four oared boat, herself and her sister, with the help of Joe Desmond and some of his sisters, and went off to Long Island to a dance, arriving home in the early hours of the next morning to discover her father had come home. Then all hell broke loose. He nearly lost the head to think that they took the boat. Her two sisters, Maggie and Hannah, got such a beating they left the island a short time later and never saw their father again. They went to America. One of them died about 1960. The other sister came back home after fifty-four years, but of course that was a long time after her father was dead. She is now dead as well, God rest them all.

Joe Desmond was the last of the Desmond family to leave East Skeam. He married a Whooley woman from Lisheen and they lived in Ballydehob for years. I met him on one of my trips to Ballydehob with my father and mother. There was a large family of the Desmonds, either sixteen or eighteen, I'm not rightly sure. Most of them went to America and one of the family went to England, I think Jim was his name. All the rest of the family went to America and never came back except one grandson, Tim, who comes to visit each year with his wife, Cynthia.

Winter time on the island was very tough as the weather was so severe and getting across to the mainland or Heir Island could be very rough at times. I remember a few times going to Heir Island and being unable to return that evening owing to a storm that came up very quickly. The waves would sometimes be as high as thirty feet in the channel between the islands. Quite a few times when going to school, we could not get back home and had to stay with my uncle Timmie in the Reen. As children that did not worry us as we enjoyed the company of our older cousins. I remember a few times, in south east wind, my Dad would turn the punt in the strand to face the tide and wind, before he took off with his pair of paddles to row us to school. If the tide was out we landed on the north side of Oileán Gamhan and walked across the Strule (srúill) in our bare feet to keep the shoes and socks dry.

We used to go to Mass in Lisheen. It was a long walk but we always seemed to make it most Sundays. At Christmas time for the dawn of day Mass, we left home at 6 a.m. to make it to the church in time for the Mass which was celebrated at 7.30. In those days, there were three Masses and we all waited for all the masses as was the custom then. Bringing home the Holy Water on Christmas Day was a big thing. It was brought home and our mother or father would shake it over us children and also sprinkle it on the cattle and outhouses to bless them for the year. I also remember when they cut the seed potatoes, before they were stuck in the ground, the Holy Water was again sprinkled on the seed and they prayed for a good crop. It was the custom in those days and was the same with the wheat and oats.

The cutting of the corn was done with a hook or sickle and the sheaves of corn were bound and stacked to dry off and ripen better before being taken into the house my father called the slashing chamber. He had a big heavy baulk of wood on which he used to beat all the heads of corn, separating them from the straw, then he took out the grain and winnowed it on a big sail to get the chaff out of it. He used to lift it up in bucketfuls and let it fall gently in the breeze. That was the corn we had for making the brown flour for baking. Another thing they used to do was to heat the wheat in the big bastable pot until it was really hard and crunchy and grind it between the quern stones to make riabún. It was a lovely crusty flavoured cereal eaten with milk and sugar. From the yellow maize, the fine ground corn, they would make yellow meal gruel and that was often eaten for supper before going to bed. I remember mother making yellow meal cakes with just a little of the white flour put in to keep the dough together. These made a pleasant change from the home made brown cake all the time.

It was often very lonely for two little girls growing up on the island on their own, as my brother was gone to sea. He left home in his early twenties. I could scarcely remember him. I was only seven and a half and my sister only three when he left. The next time I met my brother, Con, was when I went to Australia in 1958. That was the year we left East Skeam Island. It was a big change to head off to a strange land, twelve and a half thousand miles away.

SEA ARCH ON EAST SKEAM

— 37 —

East Calf Island

East Calf Island, from the middle of the 18th century, was the property of the Townsend family, then owners of Whitehall House and lands in lower Aughadown. The last Townsend owner was Samuel Nugent Townsend. Earlier, the Townsends had cleared thirteen families off the island and built a summer house there for themselves where they also kept a yacht.

The Townsends were not long getting tired of their summer house and in 1876 sold East Calf and the West Skeam islands to the O'Regan families for a total sum of £625, subject to a yearly ground rent of £32.17.0 and an annuity of £19.13.0. The purchasers were Patrick O'Regan and Daniel O'Regan who, with their families, had already been living on the West Skeam and where they remained. These two O'Regan brothers sold East Calf to another brother, John and his cousin, Big Tom O'Regan, who with their families, occupied the island from 1876, having moved there from Derreenard, parish of Aughadown. The O'Regans had been tax-gatherers for the Townsends from earlier times in Reenascreena, Rosscarbery Parish, where there is a townland called Maulyregan.

The O'Regans of East Calf were fishermen/farmers. John O'Regan married Hanora Duggan and they had a large family of ten children. Around 1880, they bought two boats, the *Orion* and the *Velocity* under the scheme devised by Fr. Davis, who had persuaded the millionaire philanthropist, Baroness Burdett Coutts, to make £10,000 available for boat purchase. These boats, constructed in the Isle of Man, were purchased for about £400 each. The O'Regans of East Calf were the first to have their loan repaid in full and as a memento of this, she presented the family with a magnificent clock, still to be seen in Seaview House, Aughadown, bearing an inscription which says:

> A gift from Baroness Burdett Coutts to Mrs. Hannah O'Regan, mother of the brothers O'Regan, fishing out of East Calf Island, Co. Cork. to record her appreciation of their integrity and regular payments in foul weather and fair, of advancements made to them from 1880 to 1890 and of their skill, industry and perseverance in their calling. Long may this clock strike its remembrance of pleasant memories.

The Baroness visited Baltimore in 1887 to open the Baltimore Fishery School, where she was hailed 'Queen of Baltimore'. She sailed in on her yacht, 'Pandora'. Newspaper reports of the time tell of 'a hundred small fires twinkling on the hillsides signalled a welcome that was repeated in the booming of a salute from the shore.' During this visit, she made a special journey to East Calf to visit the O'Regan family.

Some time after selling the East Calf, Townsend built a three storey house on East Skeam, later reduced to two by the Barrys who bought it. Townsend emigrated to Australia, where he was committed to a mental home where he died, leaving his estate frozen for many years.

John O'Regan died relatively young as a result of an accident with a plough, on part of which he was impaled. Many of the children of John and Hanora contracted tuberculosis, as a result of the unhealthy low-lying nature of the island and four died there before the family moved to Schull. One of the sons, William, founder of Aughadown Creameries, was the father of the late Bernard, famous historian and ornithologist, and Joseph, for many years editor of the Southern Star, and eventually the owner.

William O'Regan's grandmother, Mary O'Mahony of Three Castle Head, moved to Whitehall to earn a living when her husband died. She married Tadhg O'Regan of Reenascreena Castle. They had been estate managers for the McCarthy Riagh family but this collapsed. The Townsends brought Tadhg O'Regan to Whitehall, where he was given the job of letting the 'seaweed stations' on the Townsend estate.

An unusual story concerning the Calf Island has been told like this – a Crowley man from the Middle Calf came to the aid of his neighbours the O'Regans in East Calf, when of the their sons, Freke Allen, was dying of T.B. The Crowley man risked the bad weather to go to the mainland to a priest to anoint him. With him went William O'Regan. They were able to bring in the priest to anoint Freke Allen, who died in January 1894.

Around this time, a ship laden with copper, was stranded on the Mizen Head, in the process of sinking and breaking up. Many fishermen took copper bars off the ship, including the Crowley man from the Middle Calf. Some time later, Crowley was weeding mangolds when he saw what appeared to be Freke Allen standing in the field with his back to him. Crowley's working partner did not see the 'apparition.' Some time later the incident was repeated. Crowley went to the see the parish priest of Schull, Fr. O'Connor, for his advice. The priest told him that the next time he would see the vision he should ask him what he wanted. The vision appeared a third time and Crowley, on asking who appeared to be Freke Allen what he wanted, got the reply, 'give back the copper'. This Crowley did, handing it back to the authorities. Freke Allen did not appear again.

Michael O'Driscoll, owner of the mackerel yawl, *The Heber* was born in West Calf. He lived for a while on East Calf then moved to Whitehall, before settling in Heir Island. He was always known as 'Mike the Heber'.

The Calf Islands

The Calf islands lie in a N.E-S.W. line, about midway between Cape Clear and Schull harbour. West and Middle Calf are part of Schull Parish, while East Calf is in Aughadown Parish.

Samuel Lewis' Topographical Dictionary of County Cork, published in 1837, states that the total population of the three islands was eighty six. The acreage of the three islands is Middle Calf, 78 acres, East Calf 75 acres; and West Calf (also called Leacrer) 65 acres. There were two families in West Calf, six in Middle Calf and five in Eact Calf. A school was established in 1835 on the Middle Island 'in which all the children and adults may receive gratuitous education;

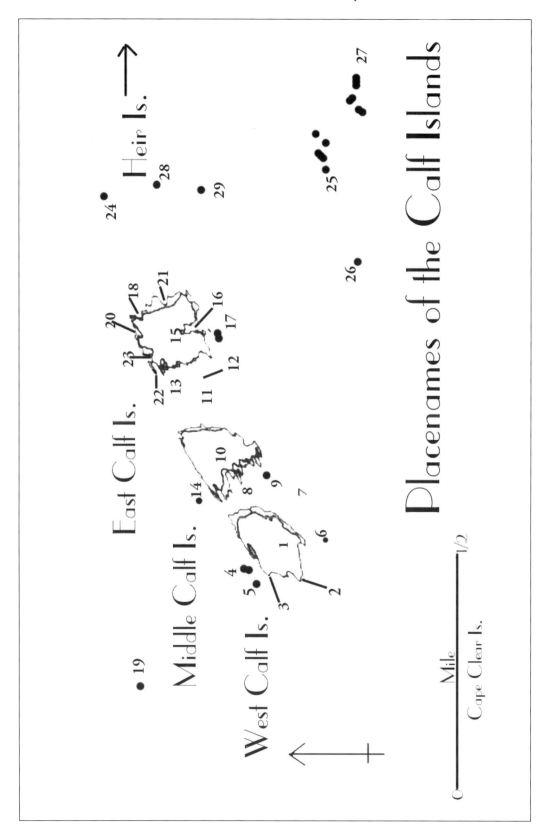

Placenames of the Calf Islands

eighteen children and fourteen adults were in this school at the start of 1836'.

In Irish they are called Na Laonna (the calves): Lao Iarthach (west), Lao Mheán (middle) and Lao Oirtheach (east). The alternative name Leacrer for West Calf is probable derived from the Irish word, Leac (a flat stone).

Placenames

1. West Calf (Lao Iarthach)
2. Ceann Lao: Calf head (headland)
3. Rinn na mBeann: the headland of the peaks or cliffs. The Stephen Whitney was wrecked here in 1847, with a loss of 92 sailors.
4. Carraig an Áhda, possibly rock of luck.
5. Boilg Rinn na mBeann: sunken rock of Rinn na mBeann
6. Boilg Chathal Uí Riagáin, Charlie O'Regan's boilg.
7. Boilg Bill Mór: submerged rock of Bill Mór Cadogan, who lived on Cape Clear in early 19th century.
8. An Doirseoir (doorkeeper). The channel between West and Middle Caf, narrow, rocky and dangerous. Sometimes called the Doirseoir Dhobrónach (the sorrowful doirseoir)
9. Boilg an Doirseoir: the submerged rock of the Doirseoir.
10. Lao Mheán : Middle Calf
11. Bealach Lao: The Calf passage, between Middle and East Calf, much safer than An Doirseoir.
12. Boilg an Bhealaigh; the submerged rock of the passage.
13. An Luascach, part of the passage (from luascach, swinging, rocking)
14. Carraig Duibhir, Carrigdwyer, dark rock, possibly.
15. Lao Oirtheach: East Calf.
16. Trá na Loinge: strand of the ship.
17. Illaunapisha (1839/40 Ordnance Survey). Oileán na Píse.
18. Trá Bhán: white sandy strand.
19. An Bhá Thuaidh, the North Bay, between Cape Clear and Schull.
20. Cuas an Doimhin, possibly cuas doimhin, the deep inlet.
21. Cuas an Bháid: inlet of the boat.
22. Oileán Dúinín, Dooneen island, the island of the little ford.
23. Cuas an Ghainimh: inlet of the gravel.
24. Boilg an Anama, submerged rock, possibly from anam, a spirit.
25. Na Fuaráin, O.S. Toorane Rocks, possibly from tuarán, a little fort.
26. Boilg na bhFuarán Mór, the submerged rock of the Fuaráns.
27. Carraig na nDeargán: rock of the bream.
28. Carraig an tSáile, rock of the seawater
29. Rabha Charraig an tSaile; the reef of Carraig an tSáile.

Other placenames on East Calf:

Trá Bréan: foul-smelling strand, probably from rotting seaweed. It is also the name of the strand west of Whitehall House, where there is a strong smell of rotting seaweed.

Páirc an Chapaill: Field of the horse.

WILLIAM O'REGAN, FOUNDER OF AUGHADOWN
CREAMERY, AND HIS WIFE NORA

CORNELIUS O'REGAN
DIED 1893

HANNAH O'SULLIVAN (O'REGAN)

BROTHER TIM O'REGAN

WILLIAM O'REGAN

RICKY O'REGAN AND FAMILY,
WEST SKEAM

TOM AND KATE O'REGAN,
WEST SKEAM

— 38 —

Connections with the Mainland

Because Heir Island is so close to the mainland of Aughadown south, there weren't many times when the passage couldn't be navigated, except in the height of a strong gale. Despite its nearness to the mainland, life on the island had many difficulties not experienced 'outside'. Going to Mass, for example, necessitated rowing to Cunnamore Point and then walking the two to three miles to Lisheen Church. This had to be done without breakfast in olden times if one was to receive Holy Communion, as Church Law at the time required one to fast from midnight on Saturday until after Mass. After Mass, usually at 11.30, the people had to walk back to Cunnamore again. If the tides were favourable, they could row up to Rincolisky (Whitehall) which halved the walking distance.

The Hingstons

The Hingstons of Cunnamore were good friends to the islanders of Heir and the two Skeam islands. If the weather was not suitable for crossing to the islands, Matthew Hingston gave lodgings for the night to stranded islanders. His son, Freke, was for years the unofficial ferryman to Heir Island. He was known to go 'missing' on occasions, if the dog warden or some other unwelcome visitor, came to Cunnamore looking for a ferry to the island. Jim Kingston of Dunmanway, a brother-in-law of Freke Hingston, sold clothes on the island, bringing them from house to house with a donkey and cart.

FREKE HINGSTON IN CUNNAMORE
© B. Morris

Ballydehob

There was a long association between Ballydehob and Heir Island. Most of the 'withies' (willow-rods) for lobster-pot making were cut in the Ballydehob area, in Greenmount, Foillnamuck and Skeaghanore townlands principally. Ballydehob, in the first half of the twentieth century, was a busy town, a town of tradesmen and business. Jer O'Sullivan, the blacksmith, 'laid' the scythe, made bastable pots, 'barking' pots, anchors, scallop dredges, etc. for the islanders. Denis O'Driscoll, builder and carpenter, got the contract to build the 28 'new' houses on Heir in 1927-28. He had a special grá (respect) for the Heir people. He built furniture for them, dressers, settles, tables, many of which are still in houses on the island. He made their coffins and regularly came to the 'wake' of a dead islander.

They brought their grain to be milled by the Coughlans or Kellys. In later years, Cotters of Lissaree, Aughadown did most of the milling. They could buy hardware goods in Young's, clothes in O'Farrell's or Levis'. The people of Heir and the Skeams, used to row or sail to Ballydehob on Thursdays which was market day. They brought eggs or butter to sell; some would have a plough sock to sharpen, 'wrack' timber to be cut. During the summer months the Heir Island boats were navigated by the women, all the men folk having migrated for the lobster season. If the weather was unsuitable for sailing, they rowed the four miles to Ballydehob. During the war years, when coal was scarce, many of the island boats went to Skeaghanore in the autumn to collect boatloads of turf.

Skibbereen

After the war going to 'town' meant going to Skibbereen rather than Ballydehob. Hardware and seeds could be bought in Kennellys or Cian O'Mahonys, clothes from Levis & Sweetnam, Trinders, Levis', radios from Walleys, bicycles from Robbie Gill. Pat Burke now motored up the Ilen in the *Barker* every Saturday to Skibbereen to Steam Mill Quay to buy provisions from J.J. Daly, wholesalers, of Ilen St. and also provided a ferry for any islander going to town. The O'Sullivan of North St. Skibbereen made furniture for the islanders.

Baltimore

Baltimore, of course, was often visited by the Heir Islanders. Jeremiah McSweeney bought their lobsters. There was Skinner's boatyard, Denis O'Driscoll repaired their engines; coal and hardware could be bought in Fullers. When the lobstermen set out for the season's fishing, they always called to Baltimore to buy mackerel bait and other provisions. On their return journey, when they reached Baltimore, they were almost home and there was time for a few pints of stout in Salters. The Fisherman's Hall in Baltimore was a well-known rendezvous for dancers and many romances started there. The Cork-Skibbereen railway was extended to Baltimore in 1893. Often the islanders went to Baltimore by boat and travelled from there to Skibbereen or Cork on the train until the line was closed. The dispensary serving the islands was in Baltimore up to the mid twentieth century.

Lisheen

Michael John Whooley of Lisheen had a grocery shop. He bought eggs and butter from Heir islanders, collecting them at Fásagh. He collected the same products at Coosheen pier, Turkhead, from the people of Sherkin. People came from Heir, Sherkin and even from Cape Clear to shop in Whooley's Shop, which was a thriving business up to the 1960s or later.

A regular visitor to the island was the late Mrs. Molly Cadogan of Ardagh, who sold religious magazines and sometimes stayed overnight with friends on the island. She brought news of all the happenings on the mainland.

Many young girls, who didn't emigrate, got employment in shops or other businesses in Skibbereen, Baltimore, Schull and farther afield. Often they worked locally for a while before emigrating.

Whitehall

The old name for Whitehall was Rincolisky, Rinn Cúil Uisce, headland of the back water. The name Whitehall is supposed to have been given to the townland by one of the Audley family, some of whom were Earls of Castlehaven in 17th century. Lord Audley, who had a command in the English army at the Battle of Kinsale (1601), was created first Earl of Castlehaven in 1616 by James I. Near the coast, north east of the house are the ruins of Rincolisky castle of the O'Driscolls which was built circa 1495. It was the O'Driscolls only castle in Colleybeg, probably.

There was a little fishing village near Whitehall house in the 19th century. It was called Scilly, which reflects the Cornish connection with the South West of Ireland. The 1901 census records that there was a shop here owned by Katie Sheehan. Some of the servants in Whitehall House lived in the village of fourteen houses.

The fishing boats used to buy food in Ms. Sheehan's shop. There was a lime-kiln here also. Flat-bottomed boats (sloops) used to transport the lime. Because of the mild climate, the Whitehall/Cunnamore headland is a good area for growing early potatoes. The late Jerry Minihane grew potatoes here up to 2002.

According to local tradition, a Heir Island man was hanged by the Townsends.[1] He landed in Palace Point in front of Whitehall House and took a short cut across the lawn of the 'Palace' as the Townsends called it. The lodge house of Whitehall was situated where Mrs. Whooley, former Heir Island teacher, now resides. An avenue led from here to the 'Palace'. Near here was a 'pound' where straying cattle used to be impounded, until the owner paid a fine. There was a gallows here as well, as evidenced by the name of the townland – Ard na gCrochairí – Height of the Hangman. The hill is still known as Pound Hill.

According to local folklore, after the hanging of the man who dared to walk across the lawn, the priest put a curse on the house and it became infested with beetles. It is said that Townsend went to the priest, who removed the curse, Townsend was so grateful that he donated a plot of land for a church to Fr. James Mulcahy in 1832. This was the old Lisheen Church, situated near Minihan's Pub.[2]

In winter time, the inlet used to be full of boats as it is quite sheltered. Many of the Cape boats wintered here because Trá Chiaráin (North Harbour) was not big enough to shelter all the island boats. Some Heir boats anchored here also. 'There's hookers in the Scilly' was a saying of the time, referring to the large number of boats there.[3] One of the Townsend yachts was wrecked on Dooneen (Dúinín) island in Whitehall. Part of her frame can still be seen at low water.

Denis Minihane of Heir, a brother of Big Johnny of Heir Island, lived in Cunnamore and was in charge of Townsend's boats and was his right hand man. Jim Barry was Townsend's coachman. Townsend built a summer house in Skeam East and this later became Barry's home.

When the Townsends left Whitehall, the next owner was Mike Trinder, whose wife was a Daunt from Newcourt. Much of the estate was overgrown with furze. He gave permission to the neighbours to cut the furze so that it could be fed to horses and donkeys. The Trinders were very generous to the island people, and even though they were members of the Church of Ireland, used to put 'palm' out on the lawn on Palm Sunday for the islanders to collect as they walked past to Mass. Practically no trees grow on Heir, the Skeams or Calf Islands because they are so bare and windswept. The Trinders were also very generous with the apples from their large orchard and often left bags of them at the gate for the island people to collect when returning from Mass.

The next owners were the Allayne family. It passed then to the Schmidt family from Germany, who farmed it, keeping a big herd of Jersey cows. Now it is owned by Richard and Rebecca Posgate.

The Minihanes and Desmonds, with relatives on Heir and East Skeam, had close ties with the islanders. Denis 'Mór' Minihane had a towel-sail yawl, the *Mary Ellen* (S1013). Connie Desmond and his late brother, Timmy, started school in Heir Island as it was quicker and easier to row the children from Cunnamore to Heir and have them walk the short distance to Heir Island School than to walk from Cunnamore to Lisheen School. As the boys got older they were transferred to Lisheen.

Mary Cotter of Fásagh, who later married John Cadogan of Poulnacallee, attended school in Heir Island. She spent the school-week with relations on Heir Island and returned to Fásagh at the weekends. Their daughter Maureen, who married the late Seamús Davis, musician, footballer, poet, balladeer, now resides in their home in Poulnacalee.[4] Her sister, Nancy, is married to Michael Minihane of Cunnamore and Skibbereen, who with his camera, captured on film the changing life of West Cork.

Health Services

The doctor was called only in emergencies. The islanders' favourite doctor seems to have been Dr. Paddy Burke of Skibbereen. When an islander had a sprained or broken leg or arm, he often went to Mike O'Brien of Rossbrin, a bonesetter, who had the gift of being able to fix sprains.

— 39 —

Language

'To lose your native tongue, and learn that of an alien, is the worst badge of conquest, it is a chain on the soul'.   **Thomas Davis**

The defeat of the Irish chieftains at Kinsale in 1601 sounded the death-knell of Irish culture. The bards or poets, who recorded the history of the race, no longer had patrons and their influence waned. The Bardic Schools, like the Daly bardic school at Dromnea near Kilcrohane, lost their importance. At these schools the students studied history, law, language and literature. The history was that of Ireland, the law was that of Ireland, namely the Brehon law system, the language was Irish and the literature was Irish.

The 19th century saw a rapid decline in the use of Irish among the ordinary people. Many factors contributed to this. The people equated Irish with poverty and hardship. Since they realised that many of them would have to emigrate, they encouraged their children to learn English, which would be of benefit to them in the U.S.A., England or Australia. Children, who heard only Irish spoken at home, were forced to speak English in the new primary schools, which were established by an Act of Parliament in 1831, and disallowed the teaching of Irish. English was also the language of commerce. Fish-buyers, cattle-buyers, government officials, all spoke English As the late poet, Michael Hartnett, put it in his *Farewell to English*, 'finding English a necessary sin, the perfect language to sell pigs in'. To be on equal terms with these people, they had to use English and encouraged their children to speak English because they saw no future in the Irish language. Daniel O'Connell, 'the uncrowned king of Ireland,' in the first half of the 19th century, who fought ferociously for Catholic Emancipation, made his speeches in English, although he could speak Irish fluently. This was a major influence also on the people. The Famine and resulting emigration also hastened the decline of the native tongue because the worst hit area was the western seaboard, where the Irish language was still very strong.

In the 1901 Census and again in 1911, the head of each household on Heir, the Skeam Islands and the Calf Islands are attributed with the ability to speak both Irish and English. As the century progressed, English gradually became the first language but enriched with words and turns of phrase from Irish. The older native inhabitants, like Lizzie Minihane and Jack Pyburn, Willie O'Regan of Whitehall and formerly of West-Skeam, Mary O'Flynn (nee Cotter) of Bantry and formerly of Heir Island, among others, still use Irish words and phrases in their speech, as indeed do the younger islanders. The last fluent Irish speaker was John McCarthy of Heir Island West, who gave much information to the School Principal, material contained in the School Folklore Collection of 1937/38. Dan Murphy used to say the Rosary in fluent Irish up to his death in the 1950s. There are still hundreds of Irish words used in conversation.

Most of the placenames are still referred to in their Irish format. The words in the following list illustrate a way of life, dominated by the sea and the land, a way of life almost forgotten. This is not a complete list of words still used, just a sample. The majority were given to me by Willie O'Regan.

The Land – Farming

Aiteann Gaelach	Irish furze.
Aiteann Gallda	French furze (ulex europaeus)
Bacán	foot rest on old type spade.
Bacla	an armful.
Bán	lea, untilled ground. e.g. The Bán field in Pyburn's land.
Banbh	a bonham, piglet; also, Ace of Hearts in playing cards.
Bearrachán	a potato cut by the spade while digging.
Beart	a bundle, usually carried on back or shoulder, i.e. a beart of hay
Bothán	hut, cabin, small house.
Brus	tiny fragments of bread etc
Buaithreán	dried cow pat, used as fuel in open fires.
Buinne	a thick border in basketry, also in the old lobster pots. The buinne cúil was the foundation layer of basket or lobster pot. (bottom ray) The buinne béil (mouth ray) was the ridge at the top.
Bodhrán	a winnowing sieve, also a musical instrument.
Bró	quern or stone hand-mill, consisting of two round stones.
Buarach	a spancel for tying a cow's hind legs when milking.
Barrfhód	literally the top sod of turf, also sods of heath, used as fuel. Barrfhód was cut on the Dún during the war when coal was not available.
Bláthach	buttermilk, the milk left after churning, good for thirst. Literally 'flowering' from bláth, a flower.
Cipín	a little stick, used to start the fire.
Ciseán	a basket, woven from twigs.
Criothán	a small useless potato, fed to pigs.
Coinleach	a stubble field, after corn is cut.
Corrán	a sickle.
Cúb	a wooden plug in the under millstone of a quern to recline the pivot. A cúb was also a hen-coop. Many of the old houses had hen-coop dressers with shelves for delph above, with the lower part divided into sections for hens.
Cos	a. the base of the hay rick, shaped inwards to prevent wetting. b. also a sandbar. The little rock off Reen North, marked in O.S. maps as Deadman's Rock is known as Cos. A sandbar connects it with the strand making it accessible at low water. There is also a cos running from Heir to Oileán Caorach.

Cornóg	six score sheaves of straw made a cornóg for thatching.
Cloch Speile	a scythe stone for honing the cutting edge of a scythe.
Cloch Bhuailte	threshing stone.
Cuilithe	the middle sheaves of a stack of corn.
Cromarasc	a spancel or rope tied from neck to forefront of cow to stop her from breaking loose.
Cnósach	a little bunch of fruit, grass, shell-fish etc.
Cúnsóg	a bees'nest.
Drúichtín	a light dew; also a species of small whitish snail. If cattle swallowed them, they got sick.
Dornán	a fistful, from dorn, a fist. A dornán was four times the amount of a teadhall (towel), a handful. Three dornáns made a sheaf of corn (punann)
Gabhlóg	a small two-pronged fork made from limbs of a tree or furze, held in the left hand when cutting cereal crops or furze with a sickle. Also used in divining for water; for this purpose a hazel gabhlóg was best.
Gad	a tie or cord, tying the two parts of a flail, made of strong material.
Gallán	a standing stone.
Garraí béal dorais	garden at mouth of door, literally. Small field of potatoes and cabbage near the house.
Gliogar	an infertile egg.
Grafán	a strong hoe or grubber for breaking the soil.
Gráinseachán	boiled wheat, frumenty or frumentry in English.
Gruaiscín,	a grunt, a cow complaining when sick.
Grua	side of the potato ridge.
Ladhar	space between toes or fingers, also a handful. e.g. ladhar mine, a handful of meal.
Lár	ground on floor where the threshing was done by slashing corn heads on a large stone or block of timber.
Leac,	a flat stone, also lic, common in placenames in Heir i.e. Faill Leac (The cliff of the flat stones).
Lochán	a little pool, puddle.
Luachair	rushes. Used for covering potato pits, for bedding cattle etc.
Mogall	a defective grain of wheat seed.
Múnlach	puddle, dirty water.
Próinsimín	also called prampsa, wheat roasted in a bastable pot over fire.
Púca	(a) pouch-like bag used for holding the seeds when the farmer was planting them in the ridges. (b) a ghost.
Pucadóir	a short block of timber with a handle used for closing the holes in which the potatoes were being placed. Also called a fairrichín
Raithneach	ferns. North of Whitehall castle is Oileán Raithní (Island of the ferns).
Sciathóg	a smaller wicker hand basket.
Sciollán	a seed potato. Each potato was cut into two or three pieces, each

	with an eye or sprout.
Smoirt	dirt, refuse or 'rust' in wheat.
Speáthanach	refuse of burnt furze, used as firing in open hearth.
Speal	a scythe.
Súiste	a flail. The flail consisted of the handle (colpa) and the beater (buailteán). These were tied together by a strong leather thong called a gad, giving rise to the term 'as tough as a gad.'
Tortóg	a tussock or bunch of grass, rushes etc.
Uachtar,	cream , literally 'the top'. When making butter in a dash churn, a special twist of the plunger was called a cor.

The Sea

Edible Seaweeds

Ceann Donn	Carrageen Moss, chondus crispus (literally brown head) collected at low water, dried ,and eaten later as a pudding which is made by soaking the carrageen first in water and then boiling in milk. It is then strained, sugar added to sweeten and is left to set. It is often taken as a hot drink and is a cure for sore throats and colds. It was also fed to calves.
Duileasc or Duilisc	(dulse, pulmaria palmate) red, grows on rocks on lower shore and on or among kelps. Carraig a Duilisc is east of Reen headland, the rock of dulse.
Glasláth	Green laver
Glasán	Sea lettuce
Gruagach	Grows in little bushes on a single stem, streamers coming out of its centre, dark brown in colour.
Rábh	long stringy seaweed
Scamhdóir	a sickle with a long handle used for cutting 'clouts' of seaweed in deep water.
Sleabhchán	sloke , purphyra spp, red or purple edible seaweed.
Triopán	brownish green, found on hard clean rock. Oileán a Triopán. (the island of triopán), is situated on the south side of West Skeam.
Boilg	underwater rock, visible at low water.
Clabhsúr	closure, the end, like the end of the fishing season or to finish the harvest.
Cuas	a cove, inlet
Faill	a cliff
Madra uisce,	water dog, an otter.
Prais	anything broken into smithereens, especially broken shellfish, thrown into water to attract connor (wrasse) or bream, before starting to fish with rod and line.
Rabha	a skerry. (row) All the builgs and 'rows' were known by the islanders. They used landmarks to locate them. Lobsters, crayfish as well as 'rock' fish, like pollock and wrasse, are found near these underwater rocks in 'foul' ground, where there is a rocky

bottom with plenty seaweed.

Rón	a seal. South of Heir there are two Carraig a Róinte, seal rocks.
Seaga	a shag or cormorant. South of Heir is Carraig na Seagaí, (Rock of the cormorants).
Tine ghealáin,	phosphoresce in the water.

Shellfish

Báirneach,	limpet. On the Reen is Trá Báirneach, (strand of the limpets).
Dúilicín	mussel.
Gliomach	a lobster
Miongán	periwinkle (also faochain).
Portán	a crab
Ruacan	cockle.

Trí chineál bia: Bia rí ruacain, Bia tuata báirnigh, Bia caillí faochain (Is í dá bpio-cadh lena snáthaid)
Three types of food: Cockles, a king's food, Limpets, a peasant's food, Periwinkles, an old woman's food (and she picking them with a needle)

People, House, etc

Ablach	an awkward, useless person.
Ainniseoir	a miserable person. I'm feeling ainnis (angish) – feeling miserable.
Amadán	a foolish man.
Aerach	merry, light-hearted.
Aguisín	an addition, something added.
Balcais	a rag
Bastún	ignorant stupid person
Botún	a blunder, a mistake.
Braon	a drop, i.e. braon bainne, a drop of milk.
Braonín	a little drop
Bréan	putrid, evil-smelling. Trá Bréan in Whitehall, bad smell coming from rotting seaweed. Breán Trá is the Irish for Union Hall.
Bean si (Banshee),	fairy woman. Said to 'keen' when a member of certain families was about to die.
Bastún	a lazy fellow.
Bronnach (or barr catha)	Drink made from fine husks of oats to quench thirst.
Brosna	broken wood, twigs for fuel.
Bligeárd,	a blackguard
Buaileam sciath	a boaster, literally 'a striker of shields', one who makes empty useless clatter.
Cabhlach	ruins of an old building.
Caoin (keen)	to lament, to cry. In olden times women used to 'keen' at the wake for a dead person.
Ceardaí	a tradesman, a person good with their hands. Could also mean a prankster.

Chomh n-aos	people of the same age.
Ciotóg,	a left handed person.
Cliamhain isteach.	a man who married into a household. Usually this happened only where there was no son in the family.
Codhladh grifín	'pins and needles' in hands or feet.
Crúíbín	pig's trotter.
Comhar	neighbours co-operating in farm work, etc. e.g. A has B, C, D, E. at his threshing. Then B in his turn will have A, C, D, E and so on. Co-operation was essential in an age before machinery.
Cabaire	a chatterbox, usually a noisy child
Cáipéis	a written document
Cladhaire	villian, rogue.
Corraghiob	rump, haunches – 'down on your corraghiob'
Cráite	bad humoured or annoyed.
Críochnúil	neat, tidy, tasty
Croí	heart – To put croí in something was to finish a job carefully, literally to put 'heart' in it
Ag cnáimhseáil,	complaining.
Deoch an dorais	'one for the road'
Diabhal	the devil
Diúrnín	handle on scythe
Dríodar	dregs, waste
Dúchas	heredity, inherited traits.
Dúidín	a pipe for smoking, especially a clay pipe.
Eirí in airde	vanity, big-feeling.
Fáilte	welcome
Faire	Alas! Said after hearing bad news or to show disapproval of some word or action.
Flaithiúil	generous, big-hearted.
Flúirseach	plentiful. Flúirse bia, plenty food.
Fústar	fuss
Fuadar	hurry, to be in a fuadar.
Fuarthé	a pathetic, negligent person.
Gábháil	as much as can be taken between the two hands outstretched i.e. a gabháil of hay.
Gaisce	great achievement. A feat of heroism.
Gamal	a simpleton (male)
Gamalóg	a simpleton (female)
Geab	talk, chatter
Gligín	a foolish person.
Geansaí	a pullover or jumper. (gansey)
Go brónach	sad, downcast.
Gob	a bird's beak, a point of land, a headland.
Ag giuirneail,	giurnawling, 'tinkering' around, doing odd jobs.
Gríosach	red fire embers.
Giobal	rag, tattered clothing.

Grá-mo-chroí	love of my heart; usually, sweet but insincere, talk.
Leadhb	untidy, slovenly person.
Leath-scéal	an excuse, usually a lame one. Literally, 'half a story'.
Leadaránach	slow-moving, tedious, dragging.
Lód	pannier, basket.
Lúbaire	twister, devious person, trickster.
Lúidín	the little finger.
Liobar,	an untidy person.
Lochta	the loft of a house.
Leamhnacht,	new milk
Lúb ar lár	a 'dropped stitch', a discrepancy, something missing.
Mallacht	a curse
Masmas	feeling of nausea from overeating
Méagram	dizziness in head.
Meas	respect. 'I've no meas on him'(I don't think much of him).
Meascán mearaí	mixed up, mentally disorientated.
Meidrisc	discord, confusion.
Meidhreac	merry, tipsy.
Meitheal	a group of neighbours who mutually co-operate at threshings etc. when there was a necessity for many hands.
Méirscre	a windgall scar on hand or foot, a scar hardened by cold weather.
Mí-ádh	bad-luck, misfortune.
Mocainsear	long dress worn by girls in early 1900s
Múnlach	mixture of cow dung, urine etc.
Óinseach	a foolish woman.
Olagón	loud wailing cry, a lament.
Piseog	superstitious belief, or practice
Plamás	flattery
Racait,	a wide dress worn by young girls and boys in early part of 20th century.
Ráib	a stroll. To go for a ráib.
Ráiméis	nonsense, blather.
Raidhse	plenty, raidhse bia = plenty food.
Ré	a rope tied to the buinne (wale) of a wicker basket. (b) the moon.
Sceilimis	frightful commotion.
Sceóin	fear.
Seachrán	wandering, straying.
Scoruíocht	visiting neighbours at night for a chat or story telling.
Seanchaí	a storyteller.
Sceabha,	aslant, sideways, askew
Slacht	tidiness.
Slachtmhar	tidy, a slachtmhar person.
Smacht	control.
Smidíríní	broken into little bits, smidereens.
Smeachán	a small drink.

Strácáil	striving, struggling
Súgach	merry, slightly inebriated.
Táthaire	cheeky person.
Tadhg a Dá Thaobh	Literally 'Timothy of the two sides'. One who agrees with everybody, takes all sides, therefore not to be trusted.
Taoscán,	a quantity of any liquid poured into a vessel. He drank a good taoscán of porter.
Taobhán,	purlin, rib or cross rafter on which rest the creataí (laths)
Teaspach	exuberance, 'taspy'.
Trí na chéile	confused.
Tromluí,	a nightmare.
Tuaiplis	a blunder
Ubh gliogair	an addled or empty egg.

Animals, birds

Sile Portaí: (Sheila Portee)	Sheila of the bogs, the heron.
Pilibín Míog	the lapwing.
Gabhairín reo	the male snipe – literally 'the little goat of the frost.'
Beach ghabhair	horse fly.
Dreoilín	a wren.
Spideog	a robin.
Gearrcach	a nestling.
Geimhsleach	an earwig.

Weather

Sí gaoithe	a fairy wind. A sudden whirlwind or mini tornado which could blow haycocks out of a field.
Gaidhsce,	a blister, a speck of rainbow, seen in morning or evening on both sides of the sun, and a portent of very bad weather.
Saotrún,	Often pronounced say-turn. The sun's course, the wind following the course of the sun all day (returning to an easterly direction after sunset), This is sign of very good settled weather.

Plants

Barramóta,	Wormwood.
Buachallán buí	ragwort.
Caisearbhán	dandelion.
Copóg	dock plant. Leaves were used to assuage nettle stings.
Feocadán,	a thistle.
Liostram, feilestram,	flag iris.
Meacain an tathabha	root of hellebore or great common burdock. Its roots were

pounded, boiled and applied as a poultice for ringworm.

Neantóg	a nettle; used to be chopped and fed to hens.
Praiseach Bhuí	yellow charlock.
Saiste Cnoic,	wild sage.
Táithfléithlean	honeysuckle, woodbine. Gives rise to the expression 'as tough as táithfhéithlean' as the stems are very hard to break.

Unusual English words used in everyday speech

adze (tál)	an adze was a tool for smoothing wood . It had an arched blade set at right angles to the handle. To 'dub' the wood with an adze was to smoothe it.
Chamber	An outhouse for cattle or pigs.
Fid	a fid was a pointed piece of timber used to unravel the strands of a rope.
Galluses, gallowses	Trouser braces.
Linney.	An outhouse.
Painter.	Rope for mooring boat.
Scun	a scun was a template used in making nets e.g. for 4 inch mesh a four square inch piece of wood was used.
Scudding	to sweep along easily before the wind – used to describe a sailing boat.

Short phrases, interjections, prayers and curses in Irish are still used. What they took to be curses were often prayers in disguise.

Mhuire, Mhuire	Blessed Mary.
T'anam ón Diabhal	Your soul from the devil.
Mo léir!	Alas
Arú!	Really! Indeed!
A Bhíorsa (ar ma bhiathar-sa)	On my word!
Míocram ort:	Bad cess to you – ill luck to you.

FAMILY GROUP OUTSIDE THE FITZGERALD HOME IN HEIR ISLAND EAST

— 40 —
Flora and Fauna

The North Atlantic Drift, carrying warm water from the Caribbean, flows past the southwest coast, helping to keep the climate mild and giving us warmer, if wetter winters. Very cold winters or very hot summers are a rarity, so much so that old people will still talk of the 'hard' winter of 1946/47, the very warm summer of 1995 etc. There is evidence that the seasons are changing due to global warming, that the winters have become milder. Rain and the mild climate create a lush and varied flora in the Roaringwater Bay area. Some rare plants, known as the Lusitanian Flora, found in southern Europe, particularly Spain and Portugal, are to be found in Ireland, further north than one would expect. It is likely that these plants survived the last Ice Age there and then moved northwards in the milder, damp climate from Europe to Ireland, while a lot of water was still locked in the ice and the level of the seas around Britain and Ireland was low. This happened about 10,000 years ago. So there are plants in the South West of Ireland and particularly in the islands of Roaringwater Bay which have been there for 10,000 years. They are called the Lusitania Flora, as Lusitania was the Roman name for the Iberian peninsula.

In my description of the flora of Heir, I depend to a great extent on 'The Wild Plants of Sherkin, Cape Clear and the adjacent islands of West Cork', [1] edited by John Akeroyd, and published in 1996 by Sherkin Island Marine Station, in addition to folklore and my own personal observation. I am also grateful to the observation of my friend, keen botanist Seamus Ó Máille, who, on our walks through the island, alerted me to plants I would not recognize myself. The Sherkin Island botanists found a total of 592 different flowering plants, conifers and ferns on the islands in Roaringwater Bay. In the introduction, the editor states that the flora of the area is of immense importance, both nationally and internationally, and that the area is as rich as anywhere in North-Western Europe. Of the total found in Roaringwater Bay, 381 are found on Heir, 241 on East Calf, 227 on East Skeam and 167 on West Skeam .

Heir Island, often windswept, is almost devoid of trees, with the exception of elder, which is grown near most houses. There are no woodlands on the island; young trees are prevented from establishing by the strong, salt-laden winds. A shelter belt of the wind and spray resistant Monterey Pine has been established in recent years in Heir Island East. With the abandonment of grazing on large tracts of the island in the last forty years, scrub, consisting of bramble (briar), blackthorn, furze and hawthorn has spread. The western end of Heir around the Dún, is an extensive heathland, as are parts of the Reen peninsula. It consists of low dense growth of dwarf gorse, ling and bell heather, producing a beautiful purple and yellow mosaic in autumn.

There are a total of over 30 rare plants on the islands, vulnerable and precious. They should not be uprooted or even picked.

Sandy strands carry a flora of salt-tolerant, often fleshy plants, like sea purslane, fleshy-leaved orachs, sea holly and sea radish. South of the school is an extensive marsh, dominated by a reed bed. The main inlet or goleen, which separates Paris from the eastern side of the island, has some salt marsh on its margins. The choicest plant on Heir is the very rare Spotted Rockrose found in at least two heathy places. It is also found on the East Calf. It has survived since the glaciers retreated 10,000 years ago and hopefully will survive another 10,000 years.

The following is a list of some of the more familiar plants found on the islands.

Bramble (Briar)	(Dris) Blackberries, the fruit of the bramble, are picked in late August and September and make delicious jams and pies. In olden times, potato pits were covered with rushes, straw and some briars.
Blackthorn	(Draighean): common in scrubs and ditches, making an impenetrable hedge.
Dock	(Copóg) Leaves were used to ease the pain of a nettle sting. Leaves of pennyworth were used for the same purpose.
Elder	Practically every house on the island had an elder tree growing near it. They can still be seen near the ruins of the old houses, indicating that people believed in its magic powers. On one hand, it was feared and associated with witches, but was also valued for its protective qualities, to ward off evil. It was used in many herbal remedies and as a fly repellent. People believed that it gave protection from lightening. The Irish for elder, trom, was used commonly in placenames, such as the townland of Collatrum in Aughadown south. Caladh, a landing place and trom, an elder, the landing place of the elder trees. Willie O'Regan remembers elderberry wine being made on the West Skeam.
Fern	Ferns (ráithneach) was burnt to provide a 'blast' of heat in the open fire when cakes were being baked in the bastable. North of Rincolisky Castle is Oileán Raithní (the island of ferns).
Hawthorn	(Sceach geal): common in hedges and scrubs. Commonly known as the fairy tree, where the fairies meet or live. There is a wealth of folklore associated with this tree/bush. It was considered unlucky to bring any part of it into the house. The flowers look white, pure and wonderful over the early summer landscape.
Heath:	Fraoch. Scalps of heath were grubbed on the Dún and used as fuel, especially during World War II when coal was unavailable.
Irish furze	(Aiteann Gaelach), smaller than aiteann Gallda (French or foreign furze), its bright yellow flowers are an integral part of the landscape. It used to be chopped and fed to donkeys and ponies. Some islanders had a furze machine for this purpose. The bigger bushes of aiteann Gallda were used to block gaps in ditches. Bushes of furze and blackthorn, pulled by a donkey, were used for 'brushing' cereal seed into the ground after setting. Since gorse or furze

can be very invasive, the half-burnt stumps, called speáthanach, were used as a fuel. After washing, the clothes were spread on the furze bushes to dry.

Nettle
: (Neantóg) were chopped and fed to hens. Young nettle leaves were boiled and eaten in May as a good blood-cleanser. It was eaten during Famine times.

Ragworth
: (Buachallán Buí), abundant in pastures, heaths and waysides, poisonous for cattle. An obnoxious weed, despite its bright yellow flowers. Grows profusely on land that is not being grazed or tilled.

Rushes
: (Luachair) were used as bedding for cattle, for covering potato pits and hay ricks. The white pith of the soft rush, geataire, was used as a wick in the old sligthe (oil lamps).

Willow
: (Saileach or sally) was grown on the island for basket making. The stronger 'withie', with which they made the old lobster pots, didn't grown there and had to be cut on the mainland, mainly in the townlands near Ballydehob.

Wild garlic
: (Gairleog) a relic of cultivation, used to be eaten for stomach complaints.

Wild Sage
: (Saiste Cnoic) was a popular medicinal herb used principally to heal internal injuries. Sage is a wonderful plant. The Greeks said: 'how can a man die who has sage in his garden'. Wild sage, boiled and bottled, was drunk as a tonic.

Wormwood
: Is still known on Heir by its Irish name, barramóta, a sure indication of its former importance. It was widespread on Heir 40 years ago but is much less common now. It is found near houses and ruins. It was a traditional remedy for a bad stomach. It has a strong pungent odour and was placed under mattresses to kill fleas.

The mild moist climate helps create a lush and varied flora. Walking through the island, from February on, one may notice the pale yellow flowers and crinkled leaves of the primrose along the banks which will be massed into clumps by April. After the long dark winter days it is a delight to see the furze begin to bloom. The lesser celandine with its glossy yellow flowers twinkle on banks, roadsides and damp shady nooks. The violet peeps from dry banks and grassy walls from late March.

Thrift or sea pink appears along the seashore in late April, often growing in cracks and crannies a few feet above the high water mark. Profusions of pink tussocks are at their best in late May and flower until late summer. An old Irish name for sea pink is 'tonn a chladaigh', beach wave. Irish spurge is another May flowering plant, found in sheltered places along lanes, in heathland and on sea-cliffs, prominent with leaf-like flowers of surreal yellow green. The white sap that exudes from the stems of spurge was a traditional cure for warts. Irish Spurge has a beautiful Irish name, bainne caoin na nÉan (gentle milk of the birds) because of the white sap or bainne cích na n-Éan (breast milk of the birds). Also found is Common Milkwort with its lovely blue flowers.

Early June brings profusions of ox-eye daisies in meadows, waysides and grassy walls. About the same time the poppy flourishes. The daisies and poppies of Heir have become well known in the beautiful paintings of island artist, Percy Hall.

On Heir, we find four different orchids; Early Marsh-orchid, Western Marsh-orchid known locally as the West Cork orchid, Heath Spotted-orchid and Autumn's Lady's Tresses.

In June we find the pea-like yellow blossoms of kidney vetch, abundant in coastal grassland. Tall spikes of foxglove regale the roadsides, bees delving into the speckled thimbles growing on the tall velvety stalks. In damp and marshy fields we find ragged robin with its clusters of pink flowers. The exquisite scent of the rambling honeysuckle fills the evening air. In Irish, táithfhéithlean, its stems are very tough, giving rise to the saying 'as tough as táithfhéibhlean'. The yellow flag iris (liostram or feileastram) is profuse in damp or marshy fields.

In July the white daisy like flowers of camomile bloom in heathlands near the sea, often forming extensive mats, emitting a sweet soothing scent. A delicious fragrance also wafts from the creamy clusters of meadowsweet found in damp fields. The delicate shy pink flowers of dog-rose are found in the hedges of July. In Irish one of its names is uisceoidin – *uiscesheoidín* – (little water jewel), a beautiful name for an exquisite flower.

The yellow-orange flowers of bird's foot trefoil, the purple heads of self-heal flourish in mid summer. A taller plant of the roadside is yarrow, well known as a medicinal herb, with a profusion of aromatic feathery leaves and clusters of white, cream or pink flowers.

As well as the 381 plants and ferns noted on Heir, mosses and lichens flourish. Lichens are tolerant of the prevailing conditions; they thrive on clean air, colonizing the rocks near the shore as well as the stony fences.

In the boggy parts of the island is found pale butterwort, which traps tiny insects to satisfy its carnivorous appetite. Thirteen different types of sedges and many types of grass are found such as fionnán – purple moor grass. Raithneach – bracken, provides a habitat for a host of other smaller plants and associated insect life, such as the sciortán (or tick) that can become embedded in your skin causing much annoyance. Fuchsia is found on the island as well as another import, montbretia (cock's comb), with its bright orange flowers in late summer. Elecampane (meacain aillín) is found near derelict houses and can be found growing on the north side of the island near the strand called Foghlú. It was formerly used as a medicine for coughs and chest complaints and also for skin ailments. Its roots were pounded, boiled and applied as a poultice for ringworm.

Two white flowers of summer are brookweed, found in wet places and rocks near the sea and heath bedstraw, common on dry heathland.

In late summer we find yellow centaury, found on damp peaty and gravelly ground near the sea. Common Centaury, a little plant with a beautiful Irish name, Our Lady's Ladder, grows on heathland and short, dry or damp grassland by the sea. Up to the end of September, too, one can see the blue-violet clusters of tufted vetch, common in tall grasslands, tendrilled leaves sprawling over the rocks.

Growing through the carpet of heathers and furze throughout the summer one can find the little yellow tormentil, the deep blue purple flowers of heath and milkwort. Tormentil has tannin in its roots and in the past was used in the treatment of burns. The tall pink spike of Purple Looseshife and Willowherb enchant the eye in late summer.

During late summer, right through September into October, the mosaic palette of colours is enhanced by dominant tones of yellow, magenta and cobalt-blue in the flowers growing abundantly on roadsides and in the fields. Flowers like devil's-bit scabious, field scabious and goldenrod are found on hedge banks and cliffs and knapweed or hardheads found on coastal heathlands. On September days when it is warm, bright and calm, these colours are heightened by the special quality of radiant autumnal light under blue skies when calm translucent waters near the shore reveal languidly swirling seaweed tresses.

The different types of hypericum or St. John's wort, which get their name from the fact that they flower around St. John's Day (June 24th), is well known as a cure for depression. Many flower on Heir, slender St. John's wort, marsh St. John's wort, trailing St. John's wort, and square-stalked St. John's wort.

The old school house on Heir is a notable place to find ferns. Several occur in abundance in the playground walls. Of special interest is Rusty-back Fern, where this is its main station in Roaringwater Bay and Wall spleenwort, which is found nowhere else in the islands of Roaringwater Bay. Both benefit from the lime in the mortar. The almond willow, salix viminalis, is found on Heir, especially in the more sheltered eastern side. This is the willow of the basket-maker; it was used to fashion different types of baskets, including the top-load or pannier, used for drawing seaweed.

Many plants have interesting, unusual and often quite beautiful names in Irish. The usual name for an orchid is magairlín (the scrotum or testicles). For example, the early purple orchid is magairlín meadhrach (the joyful testicles). Kidney vetch is méara Muire (Mary's fingers), ragged robin, an lus síoda, (the silken plant), Poppy, an chailleach dhearg, (the red hag), meadowsweet, airgead luachra (silver rushes).

Yarrow, athair thalún in Irish figures prominently in folklore. It was one of the sacred plants of the ancient Druids. Girls danced around it and sang:

Yarrow, yarrow, yarrow,
I bid thee good-morrow,
tell me before tomorrow,
who my true love will be.

See Appendix 10 for a list of Heir Island Flora.

Sea Mammals

Seals were killed on Heir and Skeams, but not in large numbers, as in the Blasket Islands. Seal oil was used as a cure for burns. When the seals were killed, the blubber was cut away; the melted blubber was rubbed to the old leather boots to make them soft and flexible. Seal oil was used in the old lamps. It was rubbed to sails and to the planking of boats to keep them waterproof. Seals figure prominently in Irish Folklore. Sometimes on fine nights seals lie on their favoured rocks, uttering long mournful cries – the 'song of the seals' which sounds very like the laments raised for the dead in olden days. The common seal and the grey seal are common in Roaringwater Bay. There are two rocks south of Heir called Carraig a Róinte (Seal Rock). The Reen headland is sometimes called Rinn a Screadaíola (the headland of the wailing) from the seals' cries.

Otters (madra uisce) were killed occasionally. Merchants in Ballydehob used to pay a few shillings for their skins. Coolim Island, west of Cunnamore, was a favourite haunt of otters. In the West Skeam they often got fish from the otters. When they saw an otter with a fish, they threw a stone to frighten off the otter who would drop the fish. Sometimes an otter would return for the fish so they might have to throw a second stone to scare him off again. The O'Regan children used to steal down to the holt; the otters would run, dropping the fish. The fish the otter usually had was a connor (wrasse). Sometimes part of the fish would be eaten by the otter.

The south west coast is one of the most important breeding and feeding grounds for whales and dolphins. Up to twenty three species have been recorded off the coast, including the common dolphin, bottle-nosed dolphin, Risso's dolphin, porpoise and minke whale. Dolphins sometimes come into the bay in fine weather and are welcomed as a harbinger of good settled weather. There was a very friendly dolphin in Baltimore harbour during the 1940s. He used to swim near the fishing boats, escorting them into the inner harbour. He allowed the fishermen to rub him and used to take bread or other food from them. Albert, as he was named, met a tragic end when somebody, for whatever cruel reason, shot him. He was missed by the fishermen who had grown to love him. Porpoises were quite common in the bay but seem to be less plentiful.

The sea has excluded hedgehogs, badgers, stoats, hares, and rabbits from Heir Island but not rats and mice. However, there are no mice on the Skeam Islands.

An unwelcome new resident is the American mink, descended from escaped or deliberately released captives. Their numbers have swelled all over West Cork and they have found their way to Heir. Sometimes a fox is seen on the island, most likely one that swims the short passage.

Birds

Because of the amount of uncultivated ground and the preservation of most of the hedgerows, the island is an ideal home for many birds and butterflies. In summer and in autumn, when fine weather brings good numbers of migratory butterflies, the many species delight the eye. The peacock, painted lady, clouded yellow, red admiral, common blue and wall brown are some of the species that can be seen.

The buildings on the island, both derelict and occupied, provide nest sites for many birds including swallow, house-marten, jackdaw, starling, house sparrow, wren and blue tit. The sea cliffs in the Dún area in Heir Island West provide nest sites for shag, kestrel, raven, rock pipit and chough.

The choughs, small crows with red legs and red beaks, are found only by the seaside. It is a delight to see them swirling over the Dún rocks. On the rocky shore we can see waders like the oystercatcher, curlew, common sandpiper and others. The beaches are an important feeding habitat for the waders and also for wagtails and pipits. The off-shore islets and rocks are habitats for cormorant, shag, herring gull, lesser black-backed and great black-backed gulls. The grey heron can be seen on many of the strands. In the inlet near the bridge, mute swans float majestically, followed by their brood of cygnets. The pheasant's loud call can be heard in the long grass throughout the island.

On the mainland, changes in farming methods, intensive cultivation with increased use of artificial fertilizers and destruction of habitat, has led to a steep decline in the numbers of birds once plentiful, like the lark and the yellowhammer and to the disappearance of the corncrake over most of the country. The lack of intensive cultivation and grazing on Heir and the other islands results in species like the skylark still surviving there.

Much of the island is dominated by a mosaic of gorse, bramble, heathers and bracken interspersed by grassland. In this habitat of heath and rough pasture many birds breed, including cuckoo, meadow pipit, wren, dunnock, robin, stonechat, blackbird, thrush and linnet.

The island is an ideal habitat for the stonechat, who likes open farmland, particularly near the sea, especially where there is gorse (or furze). Walking along the roads of Heir, quite often you will hear the distinctive 'whit-chick, whit-chick' call of the stonechat, like a stone banging on stone, hence its name in Irish, caislín cloch. About the size of a robin, with a bright orange breast, he likes to perch on top of a bush, or post, so he is easily seen. Stonechats figure in Irish folklore, the male's pet name being 'Donncha an Chaipín, (Denis of the Cap), from its black head and the female Máirín a Triúis, Mary of the Trousers.

EILEEN O'DONOGHUE (NEE O'NEILL)

CHARLES *KING* McCARTHY

KATIE SCANLAN (NEE CAHALANE)

MRS MARGARET MCCARTHY (NEE O'REGAN)
HEIR ISLAND NATIONAL SCHOOL ASSISTANT,
1923-25.

— 41 —

Lore

Island people talk a lot about the weather, not because their range of conversational topics is narrow, but because weather is a crucial factor in their lives.

In the centuries before weather forecasting on the media farmers and fishermen had to develop their own weather wisdom; they had to be weather-prophets, their judgements based on personal observation of the environment. For guidance they looked to the sky (clouds, sun, moon), to the direction of the wind, to the phases of plant life and to the behaviour of birds and animals. They quickly connected changes in nature with rhythms or patterns of weather.

The Sea

The sea is an important weather guide. If the surface of the water has a glossy appearance in early summer, sultry weather may be expected. White foam on the shoreline indicates that the sea bed is being disturbed by currents and is a sign of a 'heavy sea'. The sea breaking on the Reen, the Dún or on the off shore rocks is a sign of bad weather. Hearing the 'out-haul' or backwash of the sea on the rocks is a sign of windy weather. Particular notice was taken of this 'draw on the rocks.' In summer a heat-haze (or brone) coming in from the sea is a sign of good settled weather. Farraige chodlatach (a sleepy sea), the sea is sleepy and brooding before or after a storm.

The Sun

A glare from the sun portends rain and wind; a ring around the sun precedes rain. There is an old saying in Irish, Cosa gaoithe ar maidin, cosa cailm um thrathnóna – legs (rays) from the sun in the morning, presage wind, while in the evening they are a sign of calm weather.

The Moon

The weather often changes with a new moon for better or for worse; 'settles' the weather or 'breaks' it.

A crescent moon lying on its back which used to be called a 'she-moon' is a sign of bad weather. As somebody said, 'Dar Dia, Ellie, we have a she-moon tonight.' (moon on the flat of its back).

Beams from the rising moon is a sure sign of sharp wind.

Súil circe ré, the moon of the hen's eye: this is a circle around the moon and a certain sign of 'broken' weather.

The Sky

A gaidhsce (or sun dog) is a spot in the sky like a segment of a rainbow and is a portent of bad weather. It can be seen in the morning or evening, manifesting itself as spots on both sides of the sun.

'Mares' tails and mackerel scales, make tall ships carry low sails' is an old weather rhyme. Mares' tails are cirrus clouds, high in the atmosphere; mackerel scales are cumulus clouds. If a fisherman noticed these, he knew that within thirty six hours maximum, the weather would be too stormy to go to sea.

The followings weather rhymes, though imported from England through school text books, have proven to be trustworthy.

Red Sky in the morning
Is a sailor's warning,
Red sky at night
Is a sailor's delight

Cold is the night when the stars shine bright.

When the wind blows from the west, fish bite best.
When it blows from the east, fish bite least.

The Wind

The worst wind is the high wind that 'draws its breath' (calms temporarily) and comes in gusts.

The saotrún, or as some people call it, the say-turn, is when the wind follows the sun during the day. After sunset it goes north and becomes flat calm. This is a sign of good settled weather. However, if the wind goes against the sun, anti-clockwise, bad weather is coming.

Rain calms the wind; if the day is windy and then it starts to rain, the wind will decrease.

Landscape

When there is very good visibility and the islands appear closer, it is a sign of rain on the way. Mount Gabriel capped with white fog coming from the east, is a sign of fine weather, but covered with black fog is a sign of bad weather.

The Fastnet light was watched carefully. If it throws a broad bright flare, bad weather is sure to come. A bright blue light seen off the N.W. corner of West Skeam is a sign of an approaching storm.

Birds

Seagulls flying inland is a sign of stormy weather. The curlews cry when rain clouds begin to cover the sky. If its call is a mixture of different notes, a change in the weather is on the way. Swallows flying low is a sign of rain. Swallows are able to catch insects at high levels during periods of fine weather, but when the atmosphere is humid immediately before rain, the insects are forced to remain near ground level so that the swallows descend in pursuit.

'Black divers' (cormorants) flying south beyond the bridge, in Heir is a sign of bad weather. When they are seen flying from the south over the land – it is a portent of southerly wind and rain. When Carraig na Seagaí is covered with flocks of shags, it is a sure sign of herring or mackerel shoals in the bay. When ducks and geese go to the 'bog', the long inlet, and dive madly it is a sign of rain.

Creatures

Cows 'gadding'[1] is a sign of rain. It would seem that the gadfly is especially likely to trouble cattle when the weather is warm and the humidity is increasing, as a rain belt approaches.

It is a sign of rain if ants in a hollow place carry their eggs up from the ant hill to high ground because high ground would be less likely to be flooded. Endowed like other insects, such as crickets and grasshoppers, with a great sensitivity to atmospheric changes, the ants can anticipate rain much sooner than man can.

Mackerel 'schools' coming in close to land in July and August is a sign of good settled weather. Dolphins coming into the bay is a sign of good weather. Dogs eat grass before rain. I got the following rhymes from Willie O'Regan, Whitehall and formerly of West Skeam.

> *The dog so altered in his taste*
> *Quit mutton bones on grass to feast.*

Regarding the cricket:

> *The cricket too, how sharp he sings,*
> *'Twill surely rain, I see with sorrow.*
> *Our job it will be put off until tomorrow.*

Bad weather lies ahead if seals come in to the strand. Seals taking shelter inside Carraig na Róinte, south of Heir, was always considered a sign of a coming gale.

Weatherlore, collected by the principal teacher, Mr. Denis O'Donovan, from John McCarthy and Michael Cahalane is contained in the School Folklore Collection of 1937/38 on page 305.

Superstitions

The Heir Islanders, like all peoples and cultures had many deep seated superstitions, or piseoga, as they were called, which were part of their daily life. Some had an evident logic while others hearkened back to a darker age. People were on the watch for signs or to avoid certain occurrences. Red haired women were treated with great suspicion and if the fishermen met one in the morning they would not go fishing, a very widespread superstition. Widows were often treated with respect because of the dreaded 'widow's curse'.

Many of the islanders superstitions, naturally, were connected with the sea. Whistling on board a boat was forbidden because it might cause the wind to rise. While aboard the boat, taboo subjects of conversation were priests, foxes and pigs, indeed all four-legged animals.'

It was considered unlucky to be the third boat leaving the harbour in the morning. Sometimes a couple of boats were lashed together to prevent this. Spiders on board a boat were considered lucky and meant good prices for the fish catch. On Monday morning when the boat-owner went to his boat, usually the first job was to bail out the water which had collected in the bilge. Before bailing, the boatman always took up a couple of buckets of water and splashed it on the inside of the boat.

'A man at sea may return but not a man in a church yard.' The logic of this proverb emphasised the finality of death and also implies the very real danger of the sea for all who sail her. When turning a boat at sea, or when leaving harbour, the boat should always be steered clockwise (deiseal). It was deemed very unlucky to stick a knife in the mast. Cape Clear fishermen always had a bottle of water from St. Ciarán's well on board, while fishermen from Heir or the Skeams carried a bottle of Holy Water from Lisheen church brought home on Christmas morning.

Certain families were said to be followed by the Banshee, who was said to cry near the home of one who was about to die.

Nobody ever crossed the path of a team of donkeys or horses pulling a plough nor would anybody ever dream of stealing a plough. Stealing from a blacksmith was not just dishonest, it was considered dangerous. Walking around a card table could change a player's luck if the walking was done sunwise (deiseal). A smoker always smoked indoors for a while before leaving the house, to do otherwise was considered unlucky and bad manners.

A childless woman who stared at another's child was to be treated with great caution. The 'evil-eye' could spirit away an infant. It was thought unlucky to walk under a ladder; breaking a mirror brought seven years of bad luck. However, throwing a pinch of salt over the shoulder was an antidote for all these misfortunes.

It was considered unlucky to kill a heron or a swan as they could be embodiments of people. In old Irish folktale, the Children of Lir, an evil step-mother turned her husband's three children into swans.

Belief in fairies and spirits, the 'wee folk,' leprechauns was widespread, There was a hesitation to admit acceptance of their existence but there was always a healthy respect for that possibility.

There also was a piseog (or superstition) concerning the first hearing of the cuckoo. When the cuckoo arrived, hearing him with the right ear first was considered lucky, while, hearing with the left ear was unlucky.

Stories and Ghostly Happenings

With a whole generation growing up who cannot remember a time when there was no television, it is not surprising that many of them wonder what on earth people on the islands found to do with their time in the winter evenings long ago. They find it difficult to understand that even the longest winter evening, stretching into the small hours of the morning, was too short for the entertainment which people were able to provide for themselves, with singing, music and dancing, with cards, good talk and discussion around the fire, with folklore and storytelling.

Not, of course, that all these diversions were happening every night or in the same house. But on the islands there was always the chance of a game of cards in one house, a bit of music in another, that there were certain houses where people would gather to talk about old times and entertain the company with stories of former days, which were handed down by word of mouth from the distant past. The printed word was scarce, the *Southern Star*, a Sunday newspaper, *Old Moores Almanac* and maybe a few novels; people had to provide their own entertainment and at this they were very good.

In winter time there was much 'scoruíochting'. People gathered in different houses to chat and talk. Story-telling, ghost stories and card-playing passed the long nights. The Heir Islanders had a great love of singing and dancing. Some of the older men and women told hair-raising stories of ghosts, lights, apparitions and other supernatural phenomena. The following is a story Lizzie Minihane heard her father tell. It is called 'Cam agus Díreach' (Crooked and Straight)

The Gobán Saor [2] and his son were requested to build a castle in England. Before they crossed to England, the Gobán Saor wanted to test his son to see how clever he was. He asked him to shorten the road for them. The son didn't know how, so he returned home to ask his sister how to do it. She said, 'go back and sing a song; that will shorten the road'. Later he asked his son to build a bridge across a stream so that he wouldn't wet his feet. Again the son was baffled and again returned to his sister for advice. She told him to take off his shoes and to take his father on his back across the stream.

When the castle was almost completed, the English man, who was jealous of the Gobán Saor's remarkable ability, decided to put poison in his food when the job was completed. An Irish servant girl, who worked in the house, knew what was planned and she spoke to the Gobán in Irish. 'An dtuigeann tú Gaoluinn? (Do you understand Irish?) she asked. He replied 'Tuigim go maith, a chailín ó Éirinn' (I understand it well, my girl from Ireland). She then told him in Irish what was being planned. The Gobán Saor told his employers that he couldn't finish the work without his 'cam agus díreach' (crooked and straight). The Englishman sent his son to Ireland to get what the Gobán requested. He met the Gobán's daughter, who informed him that the 'cam agus direach' was in a large timber chest in her father's workshop. When the son put his hand into the chest she pushed him in and slammed the lid. The son was not released until the Gobán and his son returned. This is how the Gobán Saor outwitted the Englishman.

The *Thomas Joseph* was wrecked on the Catalogue Rocks in October, 1918. Denis Minihane was in North Harbour in Cape where he was fishing with Joe 'Cuais' O'Driscoll. The *Thomas Joseph* was owned by John Daly of Cape. That night the glass of a lamp in another of the Daly boats was struck three or four times by some other worldly creatures. Many people talk about seeing unexplained lights at the Catalogues where the *Thomas Joseph* was wrecked in October 1918. [3]

Near 'Leán Gamhan on the north side of Heir, there once lived a man named Ó Foghlú (Foley). One Christmas morning he slept late and missed the boats crossing to Whitehall for Mass in Lisheen. As he was about to go home, a boat with four oarsmen and a woman sitting near the stern drew near the rock. They were all dressed in black and had come very silently across the water. They offered to bring him to the Cunnamore. On the voyage not a word was spoken until one of the men said, 'will we take him now'? The woman replied that they would not take him this time. Ó Foghlú realised that he was in the company of other-worldly beings. He was landed on the mainland but was too weak to walk to Mass. He returned to the island with his neighbours. Completely shattered by his experience, he took to the bed and it took him weeks to recover. A Foley family did live here according to the Griffith Evaluation of 1852. The strand near where his house was situated is still called Foghlú.[4]

On moonlit nights the Heir Islanders sometimes drew weeds from the strands, if they had been fishing all day. One night a man was filling a basket of seaweed on the Reen. His eldest daughter was with him for company. They heard a voice telling them that the girl should be at home as she was needed there. When father and daughter returned to the house, the woman of the house was dead.[5]

One night a McCarthy man was walking up the Fásagh road after a day's fishing when he encountered a crowd of people blocking the road. When his dog came running towards him, barking, the crowd dispersed and the man went home shaken. Sadly his faithful dog died the next day. Fásagh townland is on the majnland opposite Heir Island.[6]

In one of the old houses in Paris a woman lay dying. Apparently she had hoarded quite an amount of money and had hidden it so well that nobody could find it. Before she died she whispered the words – 'faoin gcloch' (under the stone). It is said that somebody did find the money.

There is another tradition that gold bars are buried in a small garden in Paris near where John Minihane's old house was situated. I believe somebody searched the field using a metal detector but nothing of value was found.

There are various stories of inexplicable 'lights' being seen at night. A light was often seen on 'Leán Gamhan, where there was a house long ago. People claim to have seen lights on the south-west side of West Skeam, where two men were drowned while lobster fishing. Apparently the lights could be seen on the approach of a gale.

A McCarthy man, a shoemaker on the island, was mending shoes for somebody on Christmas Eve. The man needed his shoes to go to Mass on Christmas morning. The cock started to crow and flap his wings. To hear a cock crowing at any time except in the morning was considered unlucky.[7]

A legend about the curlew tells how a curlew's whistling alerted a priest saying Mass during Penal times. The story says that as a reward, the curlew was granted the privilege to make his nest in a place almost impossible to find.[8]

There are several references to a spirit being seen in the area of An Tráigh Mhor on the Reen. The spirit often took the form of a dog. One night a woman and her brother had to pass the strand on their way home and suddenly they saw the dog. The man told him to leave the road in the name of God three times. But the dog got bigger and bigger until he was as big as a cow. The man took out his pocket knife and asked the dog if he wouldn't leave in the name of God to leave in the name of the devil. The man made a drive at the dog which leaped over the ditch.

In the same strand a short time before the last incident, a man was passing by and was confronted by the spirit in the form of a man who asked him where he was going. He told the spirit that he was coming from Skibbereen and that he was going home. The spirit attacked him and he was found almost dead by his aunt, who was returning from the Northland about 10 p.m. She brought him home but he never again left the bed and died about six months later. There is a little bridge here, near the large reed bed, known as *The Dog of the Stray*.

Many stories were common among all the Celtic people of Ireland, Scotland, Wales, Cornwall, Isle of Man. These stories show common characteristics from widely separated places of the scattered Celtic people, showing their shared cultural and language traditions. One favourite story found in many parts of Ireland, including Heir Island, is the story about a man with a hump in his back. One day he was sitting near a lios, (a fairyfort). He heard the fairies chanting 'Dé Luain, Dé Máirt, Dé Céadaoin (Monday, Tuesday, Wednesday) and liking the sound, he set the words to music and struck up a tune. The queen of the fairies heard him and invited him in. She asked where he had got the song and he said that he had composed it himself. At this she was so pleased that she removed the hump from his back and the man returned home as happy as Larry. Afterwards he was telling the story to a friend of his who also had a hump. The man was interested and set off immediately for the lios and started singing, 'Dé Luain, Dé Mairt, Dé Céadaion'. Once again the fairy queen was intrigued by the song and invited the man in. She asked him where he got it and the man stated that he had composed it himself. Hearing this, the queen immediately gave him a second hump and sent him home.[9]

There are many 'strange' stories connected with Whitehall House. One Sunday a servant girl, who worked in the mansion, was asked to bring home the Communion wafer from Mass. She had been ordered to so by the Townsends and she complied as she feared she would lose her job. Tradition has it that when the Host was broken, blood flooded into the room.

Michael McCarthy of Paris loved making little rhymes which he called ditties. Here is an example.

> *'Twas Christmas time in the wester land*
> *When the lads gave a stroll to Jack,*
> *Jack being out at Mister Mick's,*
> *They stole his barm brack.*

Another saying was, 'Wild weather bound; send us a pound.' Florrie Fitzgerald of Heir Island often recited the following poem.

I have roamed in many lands
And many friends have met
Not one fair sail nor kindly smile
Can this fond heart forget.

I confess I am content,
No more I wish to roam,
Turn my boat to Heir Island
For Heir Island is my home.

CHARLES SHAW MINIHANE AND JEAN DAWE GOING TO THE SHOP.

— 42 —
The Island Today

Heir Island today has a permanent population of twenty five, of whom seven are of original Heir Island stock. Ten new houses have been built, all similar in design to the 1928 houses. Five families have settled on the island full time, and at least one other family is planning to move into the island in the near future. At weekends, especially holiday weekends, and particularly in the summer, the population swells to around one hundred.

Heir Island has been rediscovered. Its unspoilt beauty, its slow life-style has attracted many people to the island. Some of the old houses which had fallen into disrepair have been restored in the traditional manner and all new houses built on the island conform closely to the original 1928 design. East Skeam is uninhabited. A new house has been built on West Skeam and another on East Calf, but these are empty for most of the year.

The island has a new pier since 2000 and there is also a new pier at Cunnamore. A barge is available for transporting cars and lorries etc. to the island. There are two ferries servicing the island: The *Thresher*, run by John Moore and Richard Pyburn commutes five times daily between Heir Island and Cunnamore, and *Miss Josephine*, run by Danny Murphy and his son, links Heir Island with Sherkin and Baltimore as well as Cunnamore. Timetables for both ferries are well posted locally.

The infrastructure has been improved, roads resurfaced and large boulders erected near the Trá Bán to prevent erosion. The island has a new Co-op and plans are in hand for many new projects for the island.

A cross was erected in the Cillín and officially consecrated and blessed on Sunday, August, 24th 2003 by Fr. Donal Cahill, Adm. Aughadown.

There has been renewed interest in traditional boat building due to Cormac Levis' wonderful book, *Towelsail Yawls, The Lobsterboats of Heir Island and Roaringwater Bay*, which is an in-depth study of the lobster fishermen and their unique boats, telling of a way of life which is gone forever.

Hegarty's of Oldcourt is one of the few boatyards in Europe that has managed to continue an unbroken tradition of wooden boat building. Liam and John Hegarty, carrying on a legacy handed down from their father, are still building wooden boats and due to the upsurge of interest in Heir Island Yawls, four new boats have been launched, Mary Jordan and Colm Cuileannan's *Fionn*, Micheál

287

Crowley and John Colleran's *Mary Collette*, Cormac Levis' *Saoirse Muireann* and John Punch's *Rose*. Some of these boats have taken part in the Wooden Boats Festival in Baltimore and at Cruinniú na nBád in Connemara. They have also featured in many television programmes and in Classic Boats Magazine, engendering much interest in the island

There are also other boats, Heir Island Sloops, built by Gubby Williams of Heir Island. Gubby Williams came to Heir Island because he wanted to live by the sea. He was asked by Freddie Newhaus, who owns a summer house on the island, to build a small sailing boat for day sailing and possibly to race as a one design class. He came up with his own design, drawing from many influences and experiences, mostly from traditional type boats. The class name is in the hope of bringing credit to Heir Island and its traditions and he tries to get owners to name their boats after Heir Island women for the same reason. The first one was called *Theresa*, after Theresa Pyburn (nee O'Donovan), who was born in the house Freddie Newhaus now owns. The latest, also built for Freddy Newhaus, is the *Lizzie*, named after Lizzie Minihane. She was launched by Lizzie herself in June 2004. In 2004, there are six sloops in Baltimore, four in Heir Island, two in Poulnacallee and one in Crosshaven.

There is a renowned restaurant on the island, called Island Cottage, run by John Desmond and Elmary Fenton. John worked in top hotels in Paris, before settling down in Heir Island. The Restaurant has won many awards and acclaim.

John and Patricia Moore, who live in the premises formerly owned by the Burke family, are currently in the process of developing a Sailing School on the island which will be called Camp Roaringwater. The original Burke dwelling house is being extended and converted to accommodate twenty-four students and staff. The building comprises four dormitories with twin bunks, a shower block, dining room, kitchen/servery, internet café/shop, TV lounge and toilet, etc.

The island now has B. & B. accommodation, run by Kevin and Jane O'Farrell in North Pier House and there is also some splendid self catering accommodation available on the island.

The island is a haven for artists, Percy Hall, the longest established artist on Heir Island, is famous for his paintings of flowers and landscapes.

Christine Thery (Williams) came to live on the island inspired by the place and the people. Since then her work, both etchings and oil paintings, has been concerned with Heir, the surrounding islands and the lives of the islanders. She has also made a study of the local seaweeds, those traditionally eaten and other edible varieties and gives occasional workshops on these.

Ian Humphries, who has established himself as one of England's foremost younger painters, is building a house on Heir Island. Many of his paintings reflect the space, sky, tranquillity and power of the sea.

John Desmond, as well as being a famous cook, is also a well-known artist and has exhibited his work in many galleries.

Jane O'Farrell creates silk paintings and cards and her husband, Kevin, is a photographer, who also makes model boats, such as the Galway Hooker. Plans are in hand to make models of the Heir Island lobster yawls.

Liz Morris and Anglea Fewer, who have homes on Heir Island, are both well-known artists.

Heir Island was once a place of music and song; the people, despite the hardship of island life then, loved music. They danced and sang. Then the music died as the islanders left. It is great to hear music on the island again. Danny Murphy and others have revived the island set. People like the late Chris Boon, Séamus Davis and Shane O'Neill from Fásagh, Máire Bean Uí Chrualoich and her family brought the music to life again.

Photo: Carol Gilbert

DAN MCCARTHY, MÁIRE BEAN UÍ CHRUALAOI, LIAM CHAMBERS, DANNY MURPHY, MINISTER EAMON Ó CUÍV, MICHAEL JOHN HARTE, JOHN MOORE, SEAN HARTE.

BABY BURKE (NEE O'DRISCOLL), MRS BRIDGET
O'DRISCOLL (NEE O'NEILL) AND
BRIDIE AND PEGGY O'DRISCOLL.

THADY MCCARTHY HEIR ISLAND AND ARDAGH
AND JOHN CADOGAN, TURKHEAD.

DAN MURPHY, HEIR ISLAND
AND NEW YORK

PATRICK AND CATHERINE O'DRISCOLL

References

Chapter 1 – Heir Island

1. Loch Trasna: from Loch, a lake or bay and trasna, across. The name probably comes from the fact that its width is approximately commensurate with its length. Derivation could also be Bay of Destruction.
2. Carbery: from the old Irish word, cairbreach, a charioteer. Bishop John O'Brien in the 18th century wrote that, 'Cairbreacha extended from Bandon to Crookhaven and on to Kenmare'. A line drawn from Mount Owen near Dunmanway to Glandore divides Carbery into East and West. Carbery, one could say, is a more modern name for Corcalee, O'Driscoll's lands.
3. Ria, a normal drowned valley – Chambers English Dictionary.
4. Inis Arcáin: Island of the sea pig or porpoise: It has the same derivation as the Orkney Islands, from orca, the killer whale. A porpoise is a small whale. Oilean Chléire – Island of the Clergy.
5. Pleistocene: of the geological period following the Pliocene, having the greatest proportion of fossil molluscs of living species, derived from the Greek words pleistos (most numerous) and kinos (recent).
6. Akeroyd, John, Editor,*The Wild Plants of Sherkin, Cape Clear and adjacent islands of West Cork*, published by Sherkin Island Marine Station. 1996, hereinafter Akeroyd.
7. Griffiths Evaluation, 1852.
8. *Paris*: probably a corruption of palace or pallice; there were hundreds of these along the coast in the 17th to 19th centuries, where pilchards were pressed to extract "train oil". The biggest congregation of houses was in Heir Island West in *Paris* It looked like a 'city', in comparison to the smaller groups of houses elsewhere on the island, so Paris could possibly be a nickname that stuck.
9. Akeroyd.
10. Smith, Charles, *Ancient and Present State of the County and City of Cork*. 1750.
11. Podzolds: Any of a group of soils, characterized by a grayish-white, leached and infertile topsoil and a brown subsoil. (*Chambers English Dictionary*)
12. Akeroyd.
13. Dolmen: a prehistoric sepulchral chamber of erect unhewn stones, supporting a flattish stone. Chambers English Dictionary.
14. O'Leary, Paddy: Archaeology of the Mizen Area – *Mizen Journal* No 1, page 39.
15. O'Leary, Paddy: Archaeology and the Mizen Peninsula – *Mizen Journal* No 1, p. 43.
16. ibid.

Chapter 2 – O'Driscolls

1. O'Donovan, Peadar, *Irish Family Names*.
2. ibid.
3. ibid.
4. Ó Murchadha, Diarmuid: *Family Names of County Cork*.
5. Peadar O'Donovan.
6. ibid.
7. ibid.
8. Corca Laidhe (O'Driscoll territory), pronounced Corcalee, shortened and changed to Cothluighe (Colley).
9. O'Donoghue, Bruno: Parish Histories and Place Names of West Cork.
10. Ploughland: as much land as could be tilled by one plough with a proportional amount of pasture. (about 120 acres).
11. Dún na Séad: Fort of the Jewels.

12. Dún na Long: Fort of the Ships.
13. Dún an Óir: Fort of Gold; Dún na nGall, (Donegal) Fort of the Foreigners.
14. Rinn Cúl Uisce – headland of the back water, main stronghold of O'Driscoll Óg.
15. Aughadown and Ardagh, both in old Collybeg territory, are mentioned as sites of O'Driscoll strongholds, but no traces remain. In the case of Aughadown, the stones may have been used to build Aughadown House.
16. Ó Donovan, Peadar: *Irish Family Names.*
17. O'Mahony Edward: Baltimore, the O'Driscolls and the end of Gaelic Civilisation (1538-1615), *Mizen Journal* No 8, 2000, p. 110.
18. O'Mahony, Edward: The O'Driscolls and their Revenues from Fishing, *Mizen Journal* No. 8, p. 128.
19. ibid.
20. O'Mahony, Alfie: *Baltimore a Perspective.*
21 Ó Murchadha, Diarmuid: *Family Names of County Cork.*
22. ibid.
23. O'Mahony, Edward, as No. 17.
24. ibid.
25. Pickard: a large galley.
26. O'Mahony, Alfie: *Baltimore a Perspective.*
27. O'Murchadha, Diarmuid. *Family Names of County Cork.*
28. Surrender and Regrant: O'Driscoll surrendered his lands to the Queen who regrated them. O'Driscoll retained them as long as he remained loyal.
29. O'Donovan, Peadar: *Irish Family Names.*
30. ibid.
31. *Calendar of State Papers relating to Ireland of the reigns of Henry VIII. Edward VI, Mary, Elizabeth (1509-1573).*
32. O'Donovan, Peadar: *Irish Family Names.*
33. Hickey, Patrick: *Famine in West Cork,* published by Mercier Press.
34. ibid.
35. Planter: English monarchs rewarded their supporters by granting them estates in Ireland, land forfeited by Irish chieftains because of disloyalty to the crown.
36. O'Donovan, Peadar: *Irish Family Names.*

Chapter 3 – Early Christianity

1. Fintrá Cléire – the white strand of Cape Clear.
2. Lankford, E: *Naomh Ciarán, Pilgrim Islander.*
3. Informant: Micheál Ó Dálaigh, (1910-2000), Cape Clear and Turkhead.
4. Lankford, E, as 2.
5. Informant: Micheál Ó'Dálaigh, Cape Clear (1910-2000).
6. Ardnagroghery – Hangman's Height.
7. The Bernard O'Regan Story, *Mizen Journal* No. 4, page 25.
8. O'Donovan, Peadar: *Irish Family Names.*
9. O'Donoghue Bruno: *Parish Histories and Place Names of West Cork.*

Chapter 4 – Coppingers, Townsends, Beechers

1. Plowland, old spelling of ploughland.
2. Gneeve, a land measure from the Irish word, gníomh: 1/10th of a ploughland, about 12 acres.
3. Burke, J.M., Placenames of West Cork. *J.C.H.A.S.* No. 19.
4. Cadogan, Tim: *From the Ilen to Roaringwater Bay: Reminiscences from the Parish of Aughadown (Aughadown 1999)* Editors Brigid O'Brien and Mary Whooley.
5. Somerville Large, Peter, *The Coast of West Cork.* p. 95.
6 ibid.
7. Cadogan, Tim: as No. 4.
8. ibid.

Chapter 5 – The Eighteenth Century
1. Ó'Maidín, Pádraig: 'Pococke's Tour', *J.C.H.A.S.* 51, 1946.
2. Hickey, P., *Famine in West Cork*, p.18.
3. Tithe: a tax paid by Catholic landowners to support clergy of the Established Church, a tenth of the produce of land and stock, payable in kind but later in money.
4. Hickey, P., *Famine in West Cork*.
5. ibid., p. 31.

Chapter 6 – Early 19th Century Records
1. Proctor: a tithe collector.
2. Hickey, P., *Famine in West Cork*   .
3. ibid.
4. Cess: a tax, a local rate (Chambers Dictionary). It has given rise to the mild curse 'bad cess to you', said when someone or something annoys you.

Chapter 7 – Famine
1. Hickey, P. *Famine in West Cork* p.40.
2. House of Commons Report, 1824.
3. Aughadown Parish Records.
4. Hickey, P. *Famine in West Cork* p.120.
5. Aughadown Parish Records, .
6. ibid.
7. Davis, Charles: Cape Clear, a Retrospect, published in *The Month*. 1881.
8. Hickey P., *Famine in West Cork*.
9. *Dear Old Skibbereen*, edited by Cleary P. and O'Regan P.
10. Hickey P., *Famine in West Cork*.
11. ibid.
12. ibid.
13. *Skibbereen Eagle*, Jan. 5th 1849.
14. ibid.
15. ibid.

Chapter 8 – Edward Spring and the Island and Coast Society
1. Cole, J.H., *Church and Parish Records of the United Diocese of Cork, Cloyne, Ross*, Trinity College, Dublin.
2. Yearly Statement of Missionary Progress, 1848.
3. ibid. 1850.
4. Holland, W., *The History of West Cork, Diocese of Ross*. Skibbereen 1848.
5. As 2 above.
6. Missionary Tour of South of Ireland undertaken for Island Society Dublin, by Daniel Foley in 1849.
7. Yearly Statement of Missionary Progress, 1849.
8. Ibid., 1852.
9. Griffiths Evaluation, 1852. Houses leased to Spring and to Island Society shown in this area in Griffiths Evaluation Map which can be seen in Cork County Library.
10. Yearly Statement of Missionary Progress 1854.
11. *Cork Examiner*, February 2nd 1848.
12. Informant: Lizzie Minihane, Heir Island.
13. As 6 above.
14. ibid.
15. Schools Folklore Collection 1938/39, Manuscript 296, p. 20.
16. ibid.
17. *Skibbereen Eagle*, 2nd August, 1890.
18. *Skibbereen Eagle*, 9th August, 1890.
19. *Skibbereen Eagle*, 1st May, 1880.

Chapter 9 – Emigration

1. Steerage class: the cheapest berths in the ship.
2. Wiliam Justin Dealy of Bantry owned the *Dealy* brig, 400 tons, which was built in 1839 and made thirteen trips across the Atlantic, usually to St. John's, New Brunswick, bringing passengers out and timber back.
3. *Cork Constitution*, February 9th, 1847.
4. *Cork Constitution*, March 8th, 1847.
5. Papers relating to emigration to British North America (Canada), 1847–48.
6. Coombes, J., *Cork Holly Bough*, 1974.
7. Hickey, P., *Famine in West Cork*.
8. O'Donovan Rossa, *Rossa's Recollections*.
9. Harris, R.A.M. and Jacobs, D.M., *The Search for Missing Friends* (1831–1850), Boston, 1991, in four volumes.
   Harris, R.A.M. and O'Keeffe , B.E., *The Search for Missing Friends* (1851–55).
   A collection of advertisements placed in the Boston Pilot newspaper by people seeking their relatives who had gone missing.

Chapter 10 – Agrarian Trouble

1. O'Regan L. Castle Island Eviction, *Mizen Journal* No. 6, p. 116.
2. Boycott: To shut out from all social and commercial intercourse; to refuse to take part in, deal with, handle by way of trade etc., Chambers English Dictionary .
3. O'Regan L. Anna Parnell, *Southern Star*, 23rd November, 1991.
4. Fitzgerald S. *Mackerel and the Making of Baltimore, Co.Cork*. p.50.
5. ibid., p. 50.
6. O'Regan, L. Castle Island Eviction, *Mizen Journal* No. 6, p. 116.
7. *A Dictionary of Irish Biography*, Ed. Henry Boylan.
8. Informant, Willie O'Regan, Whitehall.

Chapter 11 – Fever

1. O'Mahony, A., *Baltimore, a Perspective*.
2. *Skibbereen Eagle*, March, 1880.
3. *Skibbereen Eagle*, April 3rd, 1880.
4. *Skibbereen Eagle,* August 7th 1886.
5. ibid.
6. ibid.
7. *Cork Examiner*, August 7th, 1886.
8. Mercy Congregational Archives.
9. *Skibbereen Eagle*, September 11th, 1886.
10. *Skibbereen Eagle*, August 2nd, 1890.

Chapter 12 – Timothy McCarthy Downing

1. Repeal: By the Act of Union of 1800 the Irish Parliament was voted out of existence and Ireland was ruled directly by the British Parliament in which Ireland was represented by one hundred M.P.s. The Repeal movement attempted to repeal this and have Ireland ruled by its own parliament.
2. *Eagle and Cork County Advertiser*, January 18th 1879.
3. Many landlords were heavily in debt after the Famine and attempted to regain solvency by selling parts of their estates or their estates in full. For this purpose the English Government established the Encumbered Estates Act in 1849.
4. *Cork Constitution*, 9th May, 1854.
5. Archivist, Dept. of Agriculture.
6. *Southern Star*, June 15th,1926.

Chapter 13 – 1890s in Heir and West Cork

1. Lankford, E., *Cape Clear Island, Its People and Landscape*.
2. O'Mahony, Alfie, *Baltimore, A Perspective*.

3. ibid.
4. *Skibbereen Eagle*, August 9th 1890.
5. *Skibbereen Eagle*, August 9th, 1890.
6. ibid.
7. *Skibbereen Eagle*, December 20th, 1890.
8. ibid. – supplement.
9. *Skibbereen Eagle*, February, 1891.
10. ibid.
11. Congested Districts Board, *Baseline Report* 1893 No. 83, District of Baltimore.

Chapter 14 – Shipwrecks

1. Donovan, Daniel, *Sketches in Carbery*.
2. Cadogan, Tim and O'Mahony, Colman, Shipwrecks of the South West Coast of Co.Cork to 1840, *Mizen Journal* No. 7, p. 74.
3. R.I.C. – Royal Irish Constabulary, police force prior to independence.
4. Bourke, J. *Shipwrecks of the Irish Coast*.
5. ibid.
6. *Skibbereen Eagle*, January 5th, 1849.
7. *Cork Examiner*, April 26th, 1894.
8. *Cork Examiner*, April 27th, 1894.
9. *Cork Examiner*, April 26th, 1894.
10. *Cork Examiner*, April 27th, 1894.
11. *Skibbereen Eagle*, April 28th, 1894.
12. *Skibbereen Eagle*, May 5th, 1894 check.
13. *Skibbereen Eagle*, December 22nd, 1900.
14. *Skibbereen Eagle*, December, 29th, 1900.
15. *Skibbereen Eagle*, January 19th, 1901.
16. *Skibbereen Eagle*, February 16th, 1901.
17. *Cork Examiner*, January 21st, 1909.
18. *Cork Examiner*, January 1st,1917.
19. Breeche's Buoy: a life-saving apparatus enclosing the person like a pair of breeches.
20. *Skibbereen Eagle*: January 5th, 1917.
21. ibid.
22. *Skibbereen Eagle*. February 23rd, 1917.
23. ibid., May, 1917.
24. Informants: Jack Pyburn, Neilly O'Donovan, all of Heir Island, and Bridie Fitzgerald (nee O'Driscoll).
25. *Skibbereen Eagle*, Oct 12th and 26th, 1918.
26. *Skibbereen Eagle*, May, 1920.
27. *Skibbereen Eagle*, April, 1922.

Chapter 15 – Tragedy and Heroism in Roaringwater Bay

1. Willow rods or 'withies', as they were called, were tough flexible willow branches. The old lobsterpots were made from these.
2. *Southern Star*, December, 17th, 1904.
3. Strangely, most of the fishermen of all the islands and the coast couldn't swim. Neilus Cahalane was a very strong swimmer. It is said that one of the other four made an attempt to swim ashore, but getting into difficulties, he returned to the yawl.
4. Kip: strong leather, midway between calfskin and hide.
5. Leoithín: a soft seaweed found on the seabed, which was dredged and spread on the fields as fertiliser. Because of its soft texture it was usually called 'wool'.
6. *Southern Star*, December 17th, 1904.
7. ibid., Jan 14th, 1905.
8. Perch, an old measurement, 5½ yards.
9. *Southern Star*, January 14th, 1905.
10. *Skibbereen Eagle*, January 28th, 1905.

11. Informants: Jack Pyburn, Neilly O'Donovan of Heir Island and Willie O'Regan, West Skeam and Whitehall.
12. Informant: Mary Dwyer, of East Skeam and Collatrum, niece of John Harte.

Chapter 16 – The Sea.

1. Informant: Michael Minihane, Cunnamore and Skibbereen.
2. *Skibbereen Eagle*, 1890.
3. Teamhal: a canvas cover raised on a boat to keep off rain: O'Floinn D. *Dornán Cnuais Ó Chuntaibh Chléire*, Má Nuad.
4. Boffity or baft: coarse fabric.
5. Change of light at dusk and at dawn.
6. Builg, a submerged rock: rabha, pronounced *row*, a submerged reef.
7. Dan Minihane of Heir Island and Kinsale, recorded by John Thulier, Kinsale.
8. biaste: fishing season.
9. Informant: Micheál Ó Dálaigh, Cape Clear and Turkhead .
10. Informant: George Bushe, Baltimore .
11 Informant: Seán Harte and Jack Pyburn, Heir Island.
12. Informant: Mícheál Ó Dálaigh.
13. Cutch: catechu. Dark extract of Indian plants (acacias etc), rich in tannin. *Chamber's English Dictionary*.
14. Oakum: old tarred ropes untwisted, teased out for caulking seams of boats or holes in sails.
15. to fother, to mend or repair a sail.
16. fid: a conical pin of hard wood, used by sailors and fishermen to open the strands of ropes in splicing. *Chamber's English Dictionary*.
17. Informant: Liam O'Regan, Editor *Southern Star*.
18. Smith Charles: *Ancient and Present State of the County and City of Cork*.
19. Went, E.J. – Pilchards in the South of Ireland, *J.C.H.A.S.* 51, p.174.
20. Train Oil – from the Irish word 'treighin' pronounced train: oil extracted from oily fish like pilchards and also from the livers of big fish like ling, cod, halibut, etc.
21. Pococke: Ó Maidín, P. 'Pococke's Tour of the South, and south east Ireland in 1757' *J.C.H.A.S.* 51.
22. Palace or pallice: 'houses' where pilchards were pressed to extract 'treighn oil' or where they were 'smoked' for preservation. The smoked pilchards were called fumadoes, from the Spanish.
23. Informants: James and Ted Cadogan, Ardagh, Church Cross.
24. Informants: Eddie Pyburn, Heir Island and Schull and Michael Minihane, Cunnamore and Skibbereen.

Chapter 17 – Heir Island Boatbuilders

1. Adze: A cutting tool with an arched blade which is set at right angles to the handle. *Chamber's English Dictionary*.
2. Dubbed: To dub is to smooth the wood with an adze.
3. Informant: Willie O'Regan, Whitehall.
4. Informant: Jack Pyburn and Willie O'Regan.
5. *Mizen Journal*, No. 11, 2003.

Chapter 18 – Heir Island Memories 1901–1923

1. Forty-four families lived on Heir Island in 1901.
2. Kerosene: paraffin oil obtained from shale or by distillation of petroleum. *Chamber's English Dictionary*.
3. The well referred to here is Tobar Gharraí Thaidhg: (The well of Tadhg's potato garden), probably the best well on the island.
4. Most likely 'Cos' island, marked Deadman's Rock in O.S. Map.
5. In the early part of the twentieth century, many marriages were 'arranged' by the families or with the help of a matchmaker.
6. Gentry: The inhabitants of Whitehall House, the Townsends, and their friends.

Chapter 20 – The Land

1. *Skibbereen Eagle*: June 17th, 1893.
2. Smith, Charles: *Ancient and Present State of the County and City of Cork*, 1750.
3. grafán: a strong hoe like grubber, used for breaking up the soil.
4. grafadh dóite: the top layer of grass, ferns, etc was burnt when dry.
5. sciollán: a seed potato or piece of a potato with an 'eye'. The seed potatoes were cut into two or three sciolláns.
6. súil tóin: the bottom 'eye'.
7. púca: a bag or pouch with a strap around the neck, usually made from a jute bag, which held the seed potatoes.
8. pucadóir: flat piece timber with a handle for closing the hole into which the seed potatoes were placed.
9. besom: broom, reeds tied together.
10. cos: the base of the hay rick (which was manicured to prevent rain soaking through it).
11. haggard: part of the farmyard where ricks of hay and straw were kept. (Usually pronounced haggart).
12. criathar: sieve.
13. comhar: mutual co-operation. When neighbour helped neghbour, absolutely necessary in an age when al the work was done manually.
14. meitheal: a large group of men, co-operating.
15. Riabún was made from pure hulled wheat which was first roasted in a bastable to harden the grains. It was then ground in the quern. Milk and sugar were added to make a delicious meal.
16. Collins, J.F., Influence of Local Circumstances on Land Valuation in South-West Cork in the mid 19th century. *Mizen Journal*, No. 7, p. 134.
17. Saoistín: a band made of interwoven straw.
18. Irish Schools Folklore -*School Manuscript 296*, p.9.

Chapter 24 – Captain Con Burke

1. Informants: Neilly O'Donovan and Jack Pyburn, Heir Island.

Chapter 26 – Education

1. Hickey, Patrick, *Famine in West Cork*.
2. Doucks, from Dabhacha, sandhills.
3. Dept. of Education National Schools Register, National Archives, Dublin File ED2/9, .
4. Foley, Daniel, Missionary Tour through the South of Ireland for the Irish Society, Dublin , 1849.
5. National Schools Records, ED 1/15, Folio No. 12, National Archives.
6. Informant: Jack Pyburn, Heir Island.
7. National School Records, ED 2.208, Folio 6   "   .
8. National School Records, ED2.208, Folio 6   "   .
9. As 4 above.

Chapter 27 – Religion

1. Men of Heart by Kevin F. Dwyer, O.S.A. Augustinian Publication, U.S.A.
2. Society of Jesus, N.E. Provincial Archives, Worcester, MA.
3. Archives of Archdiocese of Boston.
4. Informant: Mary Linden, Boston.
5. O'Driscoll, Tadhg, Aughadown Parish Religious Sisters, *Mizen Journal*, No. 9, 2001.

Chapter 28 – Birth, Marriage, Death

1. Keeners: from the Irish word caoineadh, meaning to cry. When the person died the corpse was lamented and cried over by the caoiners.
2. Mná Caointe: Women keeners.
3. Cillín: Graveyard for still births and children buried before Baptism. The custom of burying children in a separately designated place appears to have been practised in Ireland from at

least medieval times. Although the practice reflects in part the refusal by Church authorities to allow the burial of unbaptised infants in consecrated graveyards, it also reflects the underlying view of traditional societies that unnamed children had not attained full membership of the community into which they were born. Occasionally, adults who were considered to be outsiders or beyond salvation in some way, such as strangers, suicides and unrepentant murderers were also buried in such places.

Chapter 29 – Houses

1. Irish School Folklore Collection of 1837/38 *Manuscript 296.* p. 11.
2. mada clúir: timber cross beam.
3. treasnán: cross-piece holding planks together.
4. keeler: a small barrel. The barrel for holding fresh water on board the lobster-yawls were called keelers.
5. picture of thatching needle.
6. Súgán: woven straw chair, rope, mat, etc.
7. Kinmonth Claudia: Irish Country Furniture 1700-1950.
8. President of the Executive Council of the Irish Free State. Head of Government, now known as Taoiseach. Since Ireland became a Republic, the head of Government is known as Taoiseach.
9. *Southern Star*, February 25th, 1927.
10. Cubby hole: snug, enclosed space. *Chamber's English Dictionary*.

Chapter 30 – The Women's Role

1. firkin: an old measure, 9 gallons in brewing, 4 stone in butter, shellfish etc.
2. glugger: empty egg.

Chapter 31 – The Cycle of the Year

1. cnósach trá: strand gathering, shellfish and edible seaweed.
2. West Cork legend.
3. Wren, usually pronounced "wran" in West Cork. Hunting the "wren" and going from house to house singing the "wren" song is an old Irish custom, still practised in parts of the country. The tiny harmless wren has a loud call and he was blamed for alerting the soldiers to St. Stephen's hiding place. After being arrested he was stoned to death. There is probably a more fundamental reason. The wren came to symbolize the darkness of winter, which culminated at the winter solstice, so killing the wren symbolized the ending of darkness, the rebirth of light. Today the wren is not killed.

Chapter 32 – Social Life

1. Síbín (sheebeen). This is the Irish word for a house where illicit sports or beer is sold. The síbín on Heir was not illicit. It was connected with Deasy's brewery, Clonakilty.

Chapter 33 – Shops

1. Informant: Neilly O'Donovan, deceased.
2. Shanahan: In the Griffith Evaluation of 1852, there were six Shanahan families, all living in Heir Island Middle. The last Shanahan, John, the postman, had no family and when he retired in the 1960s, he moved to Fermoy, from where his wife had come.

Chapter 34 – Water and Electricity

1. Informant: Jack Pyburn.
2. Tobar a Lúibín. The reference to this well is taken from the School Folklore Commission of 1937-38.
3. cabhlach: a ruined house.
4. This article refers to the well just west of the school. A pump was erected on this in the early 1930s.
5. *Cork Examiner*, May 19th, 1975.

Chapter 35 – The Skeams

 1. Donovan, Daniel, *Sketches in Carbery*.
 2. *J.C.H.A.S.* 22 (1916) p.132.
 3. Informant: Willie O'Regan, West Skeam and Whitehall.
 4. Beese, Anthony, *Mizen Journal*, No. 8.
 5. Donovan, Daniel, *Sketches in Carbery*.
 6. *Mizen Journal,* No. 2.
 7. Davis, Charles: Cape Clear, a Retrospect, published in *The Month* Sept-Dec. 1881 *J.C.H.A.S.* 22 (1916) p.132.
 8. Ret: half-rot, allowed to get very wet but not to rot.
 9. Hackle. A comb for flax – *Chambers English Dictionary*. On the Skeams it consisted of a block of wood with several six inch nails driven into it. Informant Willie O'Regan.
10. Informant: Willie O'Regan, West Skeam and Whitehall.

Chapter 37 – East Calf Island

 1. Informants: Liam and Kevin O'Regan.

Chapter 38 – Connections with the Mainland

 1. Snodgrass and O'Leary, The Bernard O'Regan Story: *Mizen Journal*, No. 3.
 2. The old Lisheen Church was built in 1832 when Fr. James Mulcahy was P.P. Aughadown.
 3. Informant: Michael Minihane, Cunnamore and Skibbereen.
 4. Informant: Maureen Davis (nee Cadogan) of Poulnacallee.

Chapter 41 – Lore

 1. Gad, a blood sucking fly, Tubanus. When cattle were bit by the gad fly they ran aimlessly, usually towards the water. (gadding).
 2. Gobán Saor: an euhemerized (mythology explained as growing out of real history, its deities as merely magnified men) version of the god Goibniú, who survives in Irish Folklore, where he is depicted as a wandering architect, the builder of round towers, cathedrals and churches.
 3. Informant: Lizzie Minihane, Heir Island.
 4. Informant: Jack Pyburn, Heir Island.
 5. ibid.
 6. Informant: Lizzie Minihane, Heir Island.
 7. Informant: Jack Pyburn, Heir Island.
 8. Informant: White O'Regan, Whitehall and West Skeam.
 9. Informant: Ellen (Lou) Pyburn, my grandmother.

Appendices

Appendix 1

Irish Schools Folklore Manuscripts
1937–1938
Hare Island National School
Schools Manuscript 296

I wish to acknowledge permission to use the following material to the Head of the Department of Irish Folklore, University College, Dublin.

Local Cures – Cure for Evils

I was born on Good Friday and was baptised on Easter Sunday and when I grew up to manhood, the old people told me that I had a cure for evils. I was eventually persuaded to use my supposed power.

On six occasions, people were brought to me. They were suffering from sores, which the old people told me were a form of consumption. I blew my breath nine times on the sores, on nine successive mornings. The patients as well as myself had to be fasting. After each breath, I made the sign of the cross over the sore with the right thumb of my right hand.

The people brought to me were of both sexes, and to my knowledge, they were all cured. The sores never came back, and these people lived to be old men and women.

I have not practised this for the past 25 years for the following reason. I was lobster fishing in Ballycotton about twenty five years ago and I met a man named ..., who warned me never to use this cure again, because he told me as sure as I would, I would one day suffer from a sore myself, which could not be cured. So not for all the gold in the world would I practise this now, and I have made up my mind never again to do it.

Old Substitute for Baby Toilet Powder

When I was a little girl Baby Toilet Powder or Fuller's Earth was unknown on this Island, but I saw my own mother and the other old women using the following as baby-powder.

They used to strike the old moth-eaten beams in a rafter of the out-houses and the dry powder thus obtained used to be shaken on the babies after being washed, in the same manner as Baby Toilet Powder is used today. The old women had a very high opinion of the powder thus obtained, and held that it had wonderful healing properties.

I got this from: Mrs. Kate Burke (65 years), Hare Island Middle, Church Cross, Skibbereen, Co. Cork.

Tobar a Lúibin

This well is situated on the south side of the hill which is called 'Cnoc a trága bhain' and overlooking the strand known as the 'Tráig Bán'

I remember when I was a young man, people suffering from sore eyes used to visit this well. There was no fixed day for those visits. They used to go there three mornings – early – in succession, and on each visit they used to recite a decade of the rosary, and then bathe the eyes with the water from well.

People suffering from a pain and other sickness used also visit the well. The custom no longer prevails on Island.

From: John McCarthy (73 years), Hare Island West, Church Cross, Skibbereen.

'Food'

When I was a young boy the inhabitants of this Island used to have 'yellow-meal stir-about' for breakfast and supper. The dinner consisted of potatoes and fish. Though a lot of wheat used to be grown on the Island, it was always sold in the town of Skibbereen. The money thus obtained used to pay the rent of the holdings, and a good number of the old people were supposed to possess a lot of money at that time.

To cook the 'stir-about,' a pot of water was first boiled and then 'thickened' with yellow meal. Sufficient salt was added to taste. It was served in big deep plates. Each member of the family was given a basin of milk into which the spoon of gruel was dipped before eaten.

From: John McCarthy (73 years), Hare Island West, Church Cross, Skibbereen, Co. Cork.

Up to forty years ago, Querns were in use in every house on the Island. The grinding was usually done by night, a home made linen sheet used to be spread on the table and the Quern placed on this sheet. The wheat was first heated in a pot over the fire, and this hardened before being ground. Some of the ground flour was eaten as 'Reábúin.' Sometimes the ground flour was boiled with water and used as gruel for supper.

From: John McCarthy (73 years), Hare Island West, Church Cross, Skibbereen, Co. Cork.

N.B. Michael Driscoll – now residing in Hare Island – but born on Calfs Island which lies due west of Hare Island – told me that his family when living on the Calfs Island were often forced to live for weeks – during stormy weather when they could not venture to the mainland for food supplies – on the flour thus ground from wheat.

Michael Driscoll is now 65 years.

The Old Houses

When I was a young boy all the houses on this Island were thatched with wheaten straw. The cupboard and dresser were usually placed as a partition between kitchen and little room.

The fire place was always at the gable-end, and at that time turf was used in every house. There was no chimney or flue in these houses, and the only escape for the smoke was through a hole in the thatch by the gable end. On a calm day the house used to be filled with smoke, and often the smoke was so thick that we failed to see one another in the house.

I remember some time after this to see flues built in the old houses. A strong beam was fixed across the house from one side-wall to the other. This beam was about four to five feet from the floor and from three to four feet from gable. Strong sticks were driven into the gable. The lower sticks were driven at level of cross-beam, and as they reached the top of gable they became shorter, so that the top sticks were only about a foot long. Then through these sticks – on sides of front – briars and twigs were woven and this closed up the flue. I saw twigs and briars plastered with 'cow-dung' in my father's house. Bottom cross beam was called 'mada clúir' afterwards this type of flue was replaced by a stone and mortar one.

The space on each side of flue was called the 'Cutoir'. This was planked from the cross-beam to gable, and cured dried fish was stored in the cutoir. Every house used to have the two 'cutoir' filled with fish for the winter.

The loft over the kitchen was called the main loft. In this loft the beds were on the ground. The loft over the room was about a foot or so lower than the main loft, and here a 'standing bed' was kept.

About sixty years ago there were no 'standing' tables on the Island. The tables then in use consisted of two nine inch planks about three feet long nailed together with 'treas-náins' They had ledges about an inch and a half high to prevent potatoes from rolling off. When in use they were placed on top of boxes or Keelers. After every meal they were scrubbed and placed against the side wall of the house. Afterward, the tables were hinged to the back of the 'settle', and when not in use were held upright against the wall by a clamp.

I got this description of the old houses from: Michael Neill (73 years), Hare Island Middle, Church Cross, Skibbereen, Co. Cork.

'Lights'

When I was about ten years old, bog deal splinters were used as lights on the Island. They were sold in the town of Skibbereen and usually on Saturdays the people used to go to town and bring home a weeks' or a fortnight's supply.

The sticks of bog-deal used to be split into splinters which were about the thickness of wheaten straw. The splinters used to be stuck in the gable wall near the fire. They used to be lit while the supper was being prepared and eaten.

When I was about fifteen or sixteen years of age I saw the old people melting the livers of skate, or codfish or ling, and the oil thus obtained used to be kept in an old jar or handy vessel. They used to buy shallow vessels – (sligte) – in Skibbereen at that time. These vessels were filled with fish oil and a strip of calico or an old rag soaked in the oil was placed in the 'sligte.' One end hung out over top of the 'sligte', and this end was lighted.

Sometimes rushes were used instead of calico. The outer skin was pealed off, and the soft spongy inside used as a wick. Instead of the 'sligte' pieces of broken pots were often used. The oil was called 'geataire caol treanach'

This account was given to me by: John McCarthy, (age 73), Hare Island West, Church Cross, Skibbereen, Co. Cork.

'Funerals'

Up to sixty years ago no Priest used to visit a wake-house on the Island. An old man named Stephen Neill used to say certain prayers over the corpse to on the day of the funeral. He was called on at all deaths on the island to perform these 'rites.'

N.B. 'No one on the Island could repeat the prayer or prayers said by him.'

Three sticks – usually spade handles – were lashed underneath the coffin, and the protruding ends of the sticks were gripped by the six men who carried the coffin. Coffins were not borne on the shoulders at the time, because it was impossible to do so, as there were no roads then on the Island, and so it had to be carried over rough paths. Six men of the same name were the first to carry coffin, and the same six men used to bear the coffin into the graveyard.

This account was given by: John McCarthy, Hare Island West.

Re Funerals:

There is no graveyard on the Island. On day of Funeral the coffin is borne (now on shoulders) to 'Cuaisin na gCorp' which is situated at eastern end of the Island. Here the coffin is laid on the ground before it is put on board a boat. Here on the exact spot on which coffin is laid a clump of rushes – roughly about the length and breadth of coffin – grows. The ground around is quite clear of rushes, and during the life time of the oldest inhabitants corpses have been rested on the clump of rushes.

Though there is a fine slip at eastern end of Island and within twenty yards of ' Cuaisin na gCorp', under no circumstances would the inhabitants dream of boarding a coffin at the slip.

The boat carrying the coffin leads, all other boats following – one tied to the other by 'painter'. The corpse is landed at a point on the mainland called the 'Tobacco Point'.

I took down the following story as 'twas told to me.

About ninety years ago the people of this Island were very very poor. A good number of families were also almost starving. At the time a 'Minister' by the name of Spring came to the Island. He was a Kerryman and he had plenty of money. He built a school on the Island – 'no trace of this building today, but the site on which 'twas built is still pointed out by the old people'. – He also built a house which he used as a Church.

He went around among the people, and offered them money and food, if they would send their children to his school, and attend service in his church on Sundays. Most of the inhabitants were forced through poverty to accept the money and food. Those who attended his church got plenty money and food and clothes. Others would not take either food or money and many of them died of hunger.

He gave employment too to those who were willing to work and a rough road on the Midland is still known as 'Bóithrín Spring' There was a song made about him, but I have only a couple of verses of it.

'Spring was a Kerryman born
He took his departure of late;
He steered his course for Baltimore Harbour,
And bid adieu to his old mother Kate.

Tis there he met Carthy the Pracher,
Michael Donovan, Jerry Shea then also,
Young Harry and old Harry Casey
And a man who they call him Joe.'

'Twas hard to blame the old people for turning with him, as God only knows how badly off they were, and 'twas hunger and nothing else made them do it. But plenty food came after to them.

During Spring's time a ship laden with wheat ran ashore on the Rinn Point – southern point of Island. It was on Christmas night and at the dawn on Christmas morning the people went towards the wreck, and drew home the corn in strong home-made linen sheets. They ground the corn with Querns, and so they had plenty to eat then. Every one of them, except the family of _____ turned away from Spring and so he left the Island in disgust.

This _____ died a Protestant, and one of his sons too remained a Protestant, and afterwards joined the Police Force. I met this same man afterwards when he was in the Force. His family are Protestants to this day.

This story was told to me by: Michael McCarthy (74 years), Hare Island West, Church Cross, Skibbereen.

'Lutharagans'

I was about eleven years of age and I was one day minding the cow in a field called the Gort Bráthair which is in the western end of the Island.

About twelve o'clock I was looking towards the southern ditch of the field, and there resting on the ditch I saw a 'lutharagan'. He wore claw hammer jackets, long black trousers and a black beaver hat. He looked at me, and I got afraid. I ran home and I didn't go back to the field again that day. This was the only occasion on which I saw a 'lutharagan'.

I often heard the old people saying that this field was full of lutharagans. I heard my grandmother saying that a man named Charles McCarthy followed a lutharagan one day in the same field. He had his hand just over the lutharagan's shoulders to catch him, when the lutharagan said to him 'feach ar na caoirig sa ghort' – Look at the sheep in the field. Charles looked east but he saw no sheep and when he turned again, the lutharagan was gone.

I often heard the old people saying that the lutharagan had a purse, and that if you could get this purse you would have a shilling every time you opened it. They used to call this purse 'Sparán na scillinge'

There was a big flat stone in the middle of Gort Bráthair and the old people said that lutharagans used to live under this stone. The old people wouldn't touch this stone because they believed the lutharagans would harm them if they interfered with the stone in any way.

A neighbor and myself lifted this stone about 33 years ago, and we found a heap of different shells under it. The shells were all empty and the under side of the stone was as black as soot, just like a hob stone.

No harm came to me or my neighbour.

Signs of Weather

1. When rooks fly high 'tis a sign of bad weather.
2. When 'black divers' go south beyond the bridge, 'tis a sign of bad weather.
3. When they are seen flying from the south over land – a sign of southerly wind and rain.
4. When they fly from the north – a sign of breezy strong northerly wind.
5. When Mount Gabriel is 'capped' with white fog coming from the east, 'tis a sign of fine weather.
6. When covered with black fog 'tis a sign of bad weather.
7. When there are beams from the rising moon 'tis a sure sign of a gale or strong wind.
8. A ring around the moon portends bad weather. But if the ring is open 'tis sure to get a breeze from that point (opening).
9. When ducks and geese go to the bog and dive madly, 'tis a sign of rain.
10. When the sun goes down glaring and red-out – wind and rain.
11. Seagulls well in on the land a sign of bad weather.
12. Legs from the sun in the evening – a sign of good weather, but legs from sun in the morning sign of bad weather.

Collected from: John McCarthy (73 years), Hare Island West and Michael Cahalane (71 years), Hare Island South.

Story of a Spirit

My mother told me that she and her brother Peter Cotter were going home one night from a neighbour's house. They had to pass by a big strand, and a spirit in the form of a dog used to be seen here sometimes. Just as they were passing the strand they saw the dog. Peter Cotter stood and told him to leave the road in the name of God three times. But the dog got bigger and bigger until he was as big as a cow. Peter then put his hand in his pocket and took out his pocket knife. So he asked the dog if he wouldn't leave in the name of God to leave in the name of the Devil and Peter at the same time made a drive of the knife at the dog and as he did the dog leaped west over the ditch. They then went home and as soon as my mother went inside the door she fell in a weakness.

The told their experience to the Parish Priest, Fr. Sullivan, Aughadown, and he was supposed to have banished the Spirit. He told them that 'Spirit' would not be seen again for 60 years. The incident happened about 40 years ago.

From:_____ (28 years), Hare Island Middle

Just in the same strand and a short while before the above story, a man by the name _____ was coming home from Skibbereen. As he was passing the strand, about nine o'clock that night the spirit – in the form of a man stood before him and asked him where he was going. He told the Spirit that he was coming from Skibbereen and that he was going home. The Spirit then attacked him, and he was found almost dead by his aunt – _____ – who was going home from the 'Northland' about 10 p.m. She brought him home, but he never again left the bed, and he died about six months after.

This story was given to me by: Daniel Murphy (77 years), Hare Island Middle, Church Cross, Skibbereen, County Cork

N.B. The strand mentioned herein is situated on Southern side of the Island and is known as Traig Mor'.

The people here believe that Fr. Sullivan banished the spirit, as it has not been seen since. Fr. Sullivan was P.P. of Aughadown in the Diocese of Ross. He died about 10 years ago and is buried in Kilcoe Churchyard. He was close on 90 years when he died.

Permission to reproduce the School Manuscript Collection for Heir Island (SMC No) is acknowledged to the Head of the Department of Irish Folklore, University College, Dublin.

Appendix 2

Old Names for Heir Island

James M. Burke in an article in J.C.H.A.S. – 'Some West Cork Placenames' states that Aughadown Parish was coterminous with the O'Driscoll Óg's territory of Cothluighe Beag (Collybeg). In the Carew Papers, 1599, we read 'Collibeg is O'Driscoll Oge's: 34 plowlands, whereof 13 are spiritual'. (owned by Bishop of Ross)

The Coppinger Grant c. 1615 had 'Colhibeg (Collybeg) including Rinecoolcusky (Rincolisky), Inishdriskell, East Inishcame (Heir and East Skeam).

In the McCarthy Reagh Inquisition of 1636 we read that Collybeg was divided into Slught Fahy (Sliocht, race and faiche – exercise green), containing Eynane (Inane), Torcke (Turkhead), Poulnycally (Poulnacalee) Rinenysynnagh, Curybeg (Currabeg), Inishyduskots (O'Driscoll's Island, Heir) and Innyskaine (Skeams).

A Coppinger Will of 1665 has Rinecowluskie, (Rincollisky), Inishdriscoll (Heir) and Inishcame (Skeam)

Burke continues: 'There are two large islands in the parish viz Hare Island (Smith calls it Whitehare Island), the natives call it Inishdriscoll (O'Driscoll's Island). There are no hares as a matter of face, in the island. Perhaps it should be called Heir Island, as it may have been the patrimony of the Tánaiste of Collybeg. The East Skeam Island (the name is written Inishcame, as above, but also the Schemes, St. Kames, etc).

There are a graveyard and a ruined church in the West Skeam. The traditional account is that it is called after St. Keam, but he seems to have been forgotten in all the calendars'

By an Indenture of 20th March 1698, John Leslie demised Hare Island, otherwise Mutton Island or Gortnahorna together with other lands to James Coppinger for 999 years at a rent of £145 per annum. (Title Document – page 69)

1750 – Hare Island – From 'Ancient and Present State of the County and City of Cork, volume 2, by Charles Smith.
Hare Island   Tithe Composition also Ordnance Survey Name book.
Enniseeedriscol or Hare Islande
Hare Island: Tithe Ledger (1828)
Inis Uí Eidirsgeoil, Driscoll's Island,
Enisdriscol, alias Hare Island.

1840	Innishodriscol or Hare Island
1876	Hare Island, formerly called Innis-driscoll
1904	Inisodriscol ie. Inis Uí Eidirsceoil, now Hare Island.
1975	Hare Island, Inis O-driscoll
1975	Hare Island – Inis Úi Drisceoil.

The post mark for the island was Inis Úi Eidirsceoil until 1977. The Post Office was closed the following year 1978. Officially the island's name since 1977 is Inis Uí Drisceoil, Drisceoil being a shortened version of Eidersceoil.

In the Encumbered Estates Court Indenture of 1st July 1854, registered at Registry of Deeds Dublin 3rd July 1854 17/20, the Judges transferred the town and lands of Hare island or Mutton Island, containing 393 Acres Statute Measure, to T McCarthy Downing, his Heirs, Administrators and Assigns for the term of 999 years, subject, with other land, to the head rent of £145 and indemnified as therein.

Old Names for Skeams

1655	West Inis Came (Down Survey)
1665	Inishcame
1829	West Skeam: Tithe Composition
1837	Skeme : Lease of land in West Skeam.
1841	Skene: Receipts of land.

East Skeam

1615	East Inishcame : Coppinger Grant.
1829	East Skeam: Tithe Composition.

On Ordnance survey maps it was called East Skeam usually, but also Inis Céime and St. Kames. The two islands are often jointly called Inis Céim, Inis Cáim or the Skeams. The O'Regans of West Skeam had a mackerel boat called the *St. Kéim*. In Irish, the name Inis Cáim usually refers to the two Skeam Islands.

Inis Cáim Thiar: West Skeam
Inis Cáim Thoir: East Skeam

East Calf Island – Lao Oirtheach
1655   East Calfe (Down Survey)
1841   East Calf Island

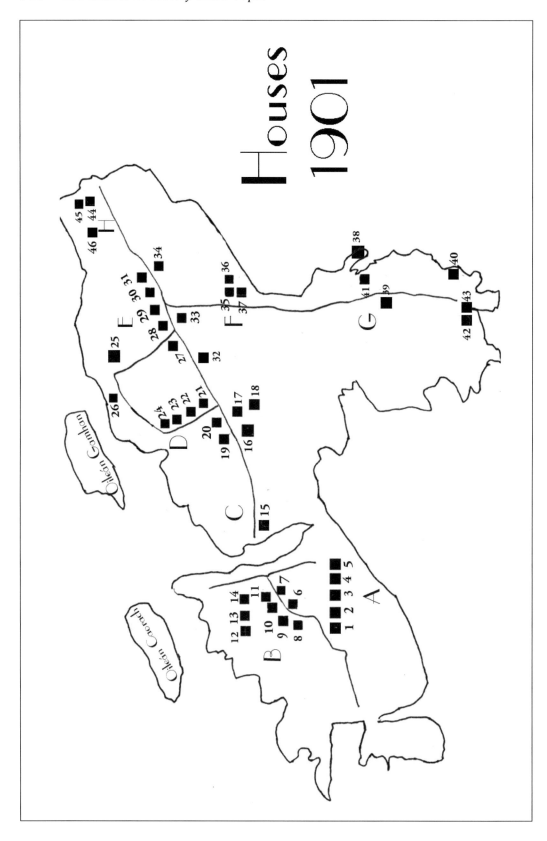

Houses 1901

Appendix 3

Map and List of Householders in 1901

Section	No.	Head of Family residing in house
A	1	Jeremiah C. McCarthy
	2	Jeremiah J. McCarthy
	3	Christopher Pyburn
	4	Unoccupied – Landowner, Denis McCarthy.
	5	Michael J. McCarthy
B	6	Michael Cadogan
	7	Michael Harte
	8	John Minihane
	9	Ellen McCarthy
	10	Ellen Minihane
	11	Daniel Murphy
	12	Jeremiah M McCarthy
	13	John M. McCarthy
	14	Jeremiah O'Donovan
C	15	Patrick Cadogan
D	16	Michael Minihane
	17	Ellen J. McCarthy
	18	John O'Donovan
	19	Catherine Murphy
	20	Patrick Murphy
	21	Michael Shanahan
	22	Patrick Shanahan
	23	Patrick Minihane
	24	John J. McCarthy
E	25	Patrick Burke
	26	Ellen J. McCarthy
	27	Florence Fitzgerald
	28	Denis O'Neill
	29	Daniel O'Neill
	30	Daniel McCarthy
	31	Florence O'Neill
	32	John O'Regan – Landowner, Ellen M. McCarthy.
	33	Michael O'Neill
	34	Michael P. O'Driscoll
F	35	Michael T. O'Driscoll
	36	Cornelius Cahalane
	37	John Cahalane
G	38	Peter Cotter
	39	Mary Harte
	40	Cornelius Harte
	41	Cornelius J. Harte
	42	Richard Cotter
	43	Cornelius C. Harte
H	44	Patrick O'Neill
	45	Mary O'Neill
	46	Unoccupied – Landowner, Ellen J. McCarthy

Appendix 4

1911 Census of Ireland

Heads of Household

Patrick Cadogan	Cornelius Burke
Michael Harte	Michael Neill
Michael Cadogan	Richard Kelly
Michael McCarthy	Michael F. O'Neill
Daniel McCarthy	Daniel McCarthy
John McCarthy	Florence Neill
Norah McCarthy	Florence Fitzgerald
Christopher Pyburn	Catherine Neill
John Minihane	MaryAnn McCarthy
Ellen McCarthy	Michael Shanahan
Ellen Minihane	Patrick Shanahan
Catherine Murphy	Cornelius Cahalane
Annie McCarthy	Michael Cahalane
Michael J. McCarthy	Michael O'Driscoll
Jeremiah Donovan	Michael P. O'Driscoll
Michael Minihane	Peter Cotter
Patrick McCarthy	Mary Ann Harte
John Donovan	Cornelius Harte
Daniel Murphy	Ellen Harte
Patrick Murphy	Annie Harte
Patrick Minihane	Richard Cotter
Michael McCarthy	Michael O'Neill
John McCarthy	Daniel O'Neill

Appendix 5

Inland Placenames

1   Páircín: little pasture field.
2   Latrach: rough marshy ground.
3   Curraichín Beag: little marsh, from currach, a marsh, pronounced 'crock'.
4   Bán North: lea ground, uncultivated.
5   Bán South: as above – where the Pyburns built their boats.
6   Clais a Phoirt: low ground of the harbour.
7   Garraí Dubh: black garden – with black fertile soil. Garraí, a potato and vegetable garden near dwelling house.
8   Conairt: from conair, a road, path.
9   Con aitinn: sloping field of the furze, possibly.
10   Barley field.
11   Fitz's Fán: sloping field belonging to Fitzgerald's; fán, a slope.
12   Lizzie's Fán: sloping field belonging to Lizzie Minihane.
13   Danny Murphy's Fán: sloping field belonging to Danny Murphy.
14   Clais a Chapaill: low lying field of the horse.
15   Clais an Óir: low lying field of gold (flowers of furze probably).
16   Sliabh: hill – higher than a cnoc.
17   Gort na Luinseachán: the cultivated field of the leprechauns.
18   Cac na bFaoilean: Seagulls' droppings (or guano).

19   Leagacs: flat stony place.
20   Gort Fiannach: cultivated field with a slope, or field of coarse mountain grass, possible.
21   Gort Brághaid, the cultivated field adjoining Cúas a Brághaid.
22   Crock (Currach): a marsh.
23   Píosa Mór: the big piece (of land).
24   Bóithrín Cabhlach: the little road to the ruined house. There was a well here, the Cabh-lach well.
25   Thunder Hole – caused by sea erosion.
26   Coinín Beag: possible cúinne beag, the little corner or conair, a path.
27   Páircín: the little field.
28   The Lough (Loch): a little lake; a stream flows eastwards into the Góilín inlet.
29   Sliabh: high field – Lizzie Minihane's.
30   Oileáinín: little island – a piece of land jutting out into the sea, a small peninsula.
31   Tobar na mBannaí:
32   Toban na mBan, well of the women. The women used to congregate here to draw wa-ter from the little well at the edge of the strand in Paris. The water only trickled out so that the women would have to wait their turn.
33   Tobar a Lúibín: well of the little bend or corner. Once considered a holy well.
34   Cabhlach well: well of the ruined house.
35   Cnoc an Trá Bhán: the hill of the Trá Bán.
36   Garraí Thaidhg: Tadhg's garden. The island's best well is located here – was used by the O'Driscoll and Cahalane families and other families in South Reen.
37   Craoibhín: little branch.
38   Gort na Giollaí: field of the servants.
39   Sliabh na bPalpa:
40   The Lic: lic or leac, place of flat stones.
41   Gort na nGallán: field of the standing stones.
42   Páircín: little field.
43   Tobar Faill a Bhrághaid: the well near Faill a Bhrághaid.
44   Gort na Cille: field of the burial ground.
45   The Cill: burial ground of young children and still births.
46   Bóithrín Spring: Spring's little road – here the Rev. Spring used to go for a stroll.
47   Leacain: sloping land.
48   Tobair Charnáin: wells of the cairn (pile of stones). There are three wells adjacent to each other here.
49   Carraig an Aifrinn: Mass Rock.
50   Cnocán Ruis: little hill of the linseed (possibly).
51   Béilic: overhanging rock, under which a person could shelter from bad weather.
52   Póna: a pound, where stray cattle were impounded.
53   Gort na gClann: field of the families.
54   Páirc: field.
55   Garraí Glas: green cultivated field. There was a well here.
56   Garraí Bán:.
57   Garraí a n'eo: field of the echoes?.
58   Gort Fada: the long cultivated field.
59   Goirtín Bearna Barla: field of the dandelions, possibly, or field of the gap.
60   Gort na Claise: field of the low ground.
61   Croí an aitinn: the heart of the furze.
62   The Big Piece (of land).
63   Upper Páircín.
64   Lower Páircín.
65   The Concaca: the hills, from cnoc, a hill.
66   Sliabh: hill, (higher than a cnoc).

67   Sparán na Scillinge: the purse of the shilling.
68   Cúilín Átha: back strand of the ford – a little stream enters the sea here.
69   Garrai Ó Mór – Big garden.
70   Barley Field.
71   Fán: slope.
72   Páirc an Chabhlaigh: field of the ruined house.
73   Father's field: from a Cadogan man, whose nickname was Father. Near here is Father's Hill east of the Bridge.
74   Minihane's Garden.
75   Páirc Trá na Gannaí: the field of the strand of the sand.
76   Claisín Airgid: little low field of silver.
77   Lúibín: field with bends, angles, not regular in shape.
78   Bodhan field.
79   Garrai Mór: big garden.
80   Coinicéar: path.
81   Hill of the Clothes: In olden times housewives spread clothes on bushes to dry here.
82   Long Field.
83   Lug: a hollow, low land.
84   Goirtín Doimhin Mór: big, deep fertile field.
85   Goirtín Doimhín Beag: little deep field.
86   Cnocán na stacaí (or Eastern Hill): little hill of the stacks.
87   Gort Mór: big cultivated field.
88   Cróins: from cró, outhouse for pigs, hens, etc.
89   Tobar Gharraí Thaidhg – the well of Tadhg's garden.
90   Garraí na Páirce.
91   Garraí Mór, big cultivated field.
92   Horseshoe field.
93   Gort na nGiollaí: cultivated field of the servants.
94   Sliabh na Palpa.
95   Breacain Mhór: big speckled field.
96   Breacain Bheag: little speckled field.
97   Gort Meánach: middle field.
98   Páirc Thobair Siofra: the field of the fairy well.
99   Tobar Siofra: the fairy well.
100 Briseadh Fraoigh: the 'break' of heather, pronounced Brishee Free.
101 Mullach: summit, the highest point in the Reen.
102 Jackeen's Field.
103 Liúire Báine: shining white – there is a little lake here.
104 The Cabhlach field: field of ruined house.
105 The Old School (1845-1900).
106 Drománach: ridged, a long backbone of hill.
107 Cuas na gCapall: cove of the horses.
108 Clais an Óir: low field of the gold (furze blossom).
109 An Chlais Dhubh: the cultivated field with black earth.
110 Goirtín Doimhín: deep little field.
111 Clais Dubh: low black earthed field.
112 Clais a Bhaicín: low field of the little twist or bend.
113 The Doucks: Na Dabhacha, the sand banks, in North Reen. The first island school was here. Near here is an extensive reed bed.
114 Botháinín: little house – name of field where there was a little house.
115 Garraí Graf: the graffed or grubbed garden.

Appendix 6

List of Lobster Boats of Heir Island and Skeams

Name of Boat	Builder	Owners
Aileen S.726	Pyburns, Toormore	Various; Johnny O'Neill, Sherkin, Michael O'Neill, Church Cross, Clayton Love (worked for him by Con Minihane, Heir and Garrettstown, John Fitzgerald, Heir, and Patsy Murphy, Heir. Now owned by Gubby Williams of Heir Island Boat Works, who plans to restore her.
Annie	Unknown	Corneilus Cahalane, Reen, Heir Isl. Won the lobsterboat race at Baltimore Regatta in 1896.
Brittania	"	Michael O'Driscoll, Heir Isl. Competed in lobsterboat race at Baltimore Regatta in 1896.
Eleanor	Richard Pyburn, Heir	Minihanes of Paris, Heir Island.
Ellen S.969	"	Michael Cadogan, Heir Island.
Fear Not	Richard Pyburn Heir	Mike Cahalane, The Reen, Heir Island. Won third prize at Baltimore Regatta 1929, second prize in second class section of lobsterboat race at Baltimore Regatta 1930 Timothy John Cadogan bought her from Cahalane and used her as a sandboat on the Ilen River in the 1940s. Like many of the yawls, she ended her days as a roof on an outhouse.
Flower of May S.350	Richard Pyburn	Ricky O'Regan, West Skeam; later, Timmy O'Driscoll, Schull; she was known in West Skeam as the *Green Yawl*.
Hannah	Unknown	Cornelius Cahalane, The Reen, Heir Island. Came second in the lobsterboat race at Baltimore Regatta in 1924, when owner was given as Ml. Cahalane.
Hanorah S.463	Richard Pyburn, Heir	Con Harte, The Reen, Heir Island.
Irish Leader S.411	Flor O'Neill, Baltimore	Denis Minihane, Midland, Heir Island. First prize for First Class Boats in lobsterboat race at Baltimore Regatta 1930 First prize at Baltimore Regatta 1939; First Prize " " 1940; Third Prize " " 1941.
Laveneer S.1055	Willie Skinner (probably)	Michael O'Neill, Heir Island. Picture page 109.
Lily S.125	Richard Pyburn, Heir	Ricky O'Regan, West Skeam; Known as the White Yawl.
Maria S.909	Unknown	John Fitzgerald, Heir Isl; Second prize Kinsale Regatta 1927; Second prize at Baltimore Regatta 1931.
Mary Ellen S.1016		John Minihane, Heir Island.
Mary Hannah S.896.	Richard Pyburn, Heir	Michael McCarthy, Paris, Heir Island.
Mary Hannah	Unknown	Michael O'Neill, Heir Island, first owner; John

S.1055 (S.258 when owned by John O'Donovan)		O'Donovan, Heir Island was her second owner; Third prize in lobsterboat race at Baltimore Regatta 1930 with Michael O'Neill.
Mary Kate S.391	Flor O'Neill, Baltimore	Michael McCarthy, Paris, Heir Island.; Second prize at Kinsale Regatta 1930
Nonpareil S.1022	"	Michael J. O'Driscoll (Merchant) Heir Island.
Othello S.495 (Sage)	"	Pat Burke, Heir Island.; Better known as the Sage. Later owned by Timmy McCarthy, Paris, Heir Island.
The Pride S.124	Unknown	Jeremiah McCarthy, Heir Island.
Pride of Toe Head S.894	Henry Skinner,	Timothy O'Donovan, Heir Island. First prize at Kinsale 1927; First Prize in lobsterboat race in Kinsale Regatta, 1930; First prize at Baltimore Regatta 1931; Third prize at Schull – first class section – 1932; Second prize at Baltimore 1933; First prize at Baltimore 1941; Third prize at Baltimore 1944; Owned for a while by Patrick Whooley of Lisheen. She was a good sailer as evidenced by the numerous prizes won at Regattas.
Safe Return S.198	Henry Skinner	Con Minihane, Heir Island.
Safe Return	Flor O'Neill, Baltimore	Jim Barry, East Skeam; Later owned by John Hosford, see picture page 125.
St. Anna S.136	Pyburns, Heir Island	Patrick O'Neill, Heir Island.
St. Helena S.19	Unknown	Michael O'Neill, Heir Island.
St. Margaret S.47	Willie Skinner,	Johnny Harte, The Reen, Heir Island. First Prize at Baltimore Regatta 1929.
St. Patrick and Mary S.249	Unknown	John Harte, Heir Island and Laheratanavally.
Swan S.121	Unknown	Richard Cotter, The Reen, Heir Island; First prize Schull Regatta 1935 with J. O'Donoghue, Cape Clear. Traditionally she was last boat built by Richard Pyburn, Heir Island.
Two Fishes S722 (originally Mary Ellen)	Richard Pyburn, Heir	Michael O'Neill, Heir Island.
Valetta S852	"	Dan Murphy, Heir Isl First owner; John O'Donovan, Heir Isl, Second owner; Second Prize in first class section of lobster boat race at Baltimore Regatta in 1930.
Village Maid S889	Unknown	John Harte, Heir Island.
Water Lily S186	Unknown	Michael McCarthy, Heir Island.

The *Luas* was the lobster boat owned by Timmy O'Donovan before he bought the *Pride of Toe Head*. Regatta results are not complete. A few are printed to give an idea of how important the yawl racing was.

Towelsail yawls of Aughadown South.

1. *Atlanta* S.193. Built by Henry Skinner of Baltimore for Philip (Phil) Dwyer of Marsh.
2. *Catherine of Baltimore* S.611. Built by Willie Skinner, Rathmore, Baltimore for Cornelius Cadogan of Poulnacalee.
3   *Chance* S.352 owned by Will Morgan of Fásagh. Built in Dunmanus in 1885. She was

24.7 feet in length, 7.5 feet wide, 4 feet deep and had a tonnage of 5.08 tons.
4. *Eliza* S750 was owned by Daniel Dwyer, Collatrum.
5. *Mary Ellen* S.1013. Built by Flor O'Neill, Baltimore for Denis Minihane, Cunnamore.
6. *Safe Return* S.12 and S.141. Built by Richard Pyburn, Heir Island for John Dwyer, Collatrum, Aughadown.
7. *St. Patrick and Mary* S.249. Owned by John Harte of Laheratanavally, Aughadown.
8. *Shamrock* S1100. Built in Baltimore for Phil Dwyer and John O'Mahony of Lake Marsh, Aughadown.
9. *St. Paul* S.426, owned by Timothy O'Donovan, Whitehall. Built in Courtmacsherry. She was 24.7 feet long, 6.8 feet wide, 3.6 feet deep, with a tonnage of 3.67.
10. The *Daisy* S.588 owned by Jer Minihane of Kilcoe. Built in 1908, builder unknown. She was 24.3 feet in length, 7.6 feet wide and 3.5 feet in depth.
11. *Victory* II S.14. Built in Baltimore for Michael Coughlan, Kilkilleen, Aughadown

Appendix 7
Boats owned by Con Burke

	Builder	
Barker S.113	Pyburns, Toormore	Cornelius Burke 30/9/1944. Cornelius Harte 1950. Charlie O'Neill. 1951. Also called *Southern Hope* on change of ownership; Length: 23.8 ft.; Tonnage: 1.78.
Horizon. S.261	Unknown	Cornelius Burke. Ex ship's lifeboat; Skippered by John Burke; Broken up 19/11/1948; Length: 30 ft.; Tonnage: 4.18.
St. Kaileen S687	Unknown	Cornelius Burke, 1908. Registered 1908; Length: 30.2 ft; Tonnage: 9.18; Sailing nobby, lug, jib, mizzen sails; Broken up 1925.
Marion S.109629	Joseph Thulier, Kinsale	Con Burke, Heir Island, 1899; Length – 53 ft.; Gross tonnage 42.79; Two masts, dandy-rigged, carvel built; Oak sailing fishing vessel.
Mary Ann S.20	Unknown	Con Burke (1901 Census); Tonnage: 25; Crew of 8
Réalt na Maidne S.309	Joseph Thulier, Kinsale	Con Burke; Length: 61 ft.; Tonnage: 37.75; Sailing lugger, main sail; Mizzen Mast, jibsail; Broken up 1943.
Siubhan S.338	1878, Peel, Isle of Man	Con Burke, Heir Island; Registered 8/7/1919; Length: 51 ft.; Tonnage: 34.36. Formerly the *Mary Hannah* (S.992), when owned by Patrick Cadogan, Turkhead.
St. Margaret S.133479	1901, Plymouth	Con Burke; Length 40.7 ft.; Tonnage 14.95; Two masted nobby, carvel built. Oak fishing vessel. Engine; Installed 1906. Broken up 1929.

Surf S.69	Probably Pyburns, Heir Island	Con Burke; Length: 28 ft.; Tonnage: 4.08; Sailing yawl, standing lug and fore-sail. Sold 1940.
St. Finbarr S.369	Unknown	Con Burke; Registered 1917; Burnt at sea 2/4/1920 off Mizen Head without loss of life; It is said that he also owned the *Erin's Hope*.

Appendix 8

List of Miscellaneous Heir Island Registered Boats

	Builder	**Owner**
Mary Joseph S.162	Wm. Skinner, Rath.	Jack Pyburn, Heir Island; previously owned by Terence O'Regan, Sherkin; Length: 28.7 ft.
Sally Browne S.69	1913 Southampton.	Cornelius Harte; Registered 1951; Length: 31.5 ft.; Tonnage: 2.41; Sold 1961.
Heber S.144737	Baltimore Fishing School 1915	Michael O'Driscoll, Heir Island, 1920; Length: 33 ft.; Tonnage 7.31; Two masted nobby, sailing fishing boat; Auxiliary engine fitted 1920; Sold in 1948 to Kieran Cotter, Cape Clear; Jim Pyburn of Heir died on board in May 1953, while mackerel fishing near the Fastnet.
Coleen S.687	Unknown	John Harte, Heir Island 1959; Bought from John Beamish, Sherkin; Sailing yawl with auxiliary motor; Fore, main and jib topsail; Length: 30.2 ft.; Tonnage: 9.18.
Naomh Nicholas S.142545	Henry Skinner 1918	Michael Cahalane. 1919; Length: 38 ft.; Tonnage: 9.69; Sailing dandy, two-masted; Parsons motor installed 1922.
Wild Wave	Skinners, Rath	Timmy Cahalane, Heir Island and Sherkin; Length: 30.5 ft.; Tonnage: 5.31; Motor installed.
Primrose CT 84	Isle of Man	Michael O'Neill, Mike the 'Cloud', Heir; Mackerel yawl.
St. Anthony S.544	Sherkin 1925	Denis Nolan, Union Hall 1931; Michael Casey, Marsh 1931; Corns. Harte, Heir Is. & Cloughboola, Skibbereen 1965; Patrick Crowley, Hollyhill, 1973; Length: 28 ft.; Tonnage: 5.06; Sailing yawl with auxiliary motor; Lug and foresail.

The Dalys of Fásagh, Aughadown, had a mackerel boat called the *Swan* on which some Heir Islanders worked. A song was written about her and one verse of it goes like this.
'Tim Daly of Fásagh, ye all know the man,
The owner and skipper of a boat called the Swan'.
Tim Daly was drowned near Sandy Island early in the 20th century.
Informant: Tadhg Cadogan, Lissaree

Appendix 9
1901 Census
Shipping Return for the townlands of Hare Island & Collatrim

Reg.No. Vessel	Type of Boat.	Ton-nage	Name	Employ-ment	Country	Port	Owner	Crew Men	Boys
S.7	Fishing Boat	27	*Sarah Jane*	Fishing	Ireland	Turkhead & Baltimore	C. Cadogan	6	1
S.20	Fishing Boat	25	*Mary Anne*	Fishing	Ireland	Hare Island & Baltimore	C. Burke.	7	0
S.102	Fishing Boat	32	*St. Bernard*	Fishing	Ireland	Collatrim & Baltimore	D. Dwyer Snr.	6	1
S.109	Fishing Boat	32	*St. Anna*	Fishing	Ireland	Collatrim & Baltimore	D. Dwyer Jnr.	6	1
S.376	Fishing Boat	25	*The Heorine*	Fishing	Ireland	Collatrim & Baltimore	Tim Dwyer	6	1
S.421	Fishing Boat	27	*Ripple*	Fishing	Ireland	Turkhead & Baltimore	Tim Cadogan	6	1
S.992	Fishing Boat	27	*Mary Hanna*	Fishing	Ireland	Turkhead & Baltimore	Pat. Cadogan	6	1
C.T.20	Fishing Boat	33	*Excel*	Fishing	Isle of Man	Isle of Man	Jerome Desmond	7	0
C.T.84	Fishing Boat	33	*Primrose*	Fishing	Isle of Man	Isle of Man	Michael Neill	6	1
CT.89	Fishing Boat	32	*Majestic*	Fishing	Isle of Man	Isle of Man	John Murphy	6	1
PL355	Fishing Boat	30	*Leader*	Fishing	Ireland	Kinsale	Daniel Neill	6	1

Also listed in the Baltimore Shipping Returns in the 1901 Census was the *The Flying Cloud*, which was captained by Patrick O'Neill (25) Heir Island. The crew members listed are Cornelius Minihane (29), Jerry McCarthy (21), Michael O'Neill (36) Patrick Minihane (35) and John O'Driscoll (17), all of Heir Island. This boat was usually known as *The Cloud* and her owner, Michael O'Neill, was known as Mike the Cloud. He also owned the *Primrose* (C.T. 84).

The *St. Keams* (or Kearns)
Captain: Timothy O'Regan (30). Crew: James Leahy (18), Florence Whooley (21), Patrick Nugent (34), Timothy O'Driscoll (20), Florence O'Sullivan (18). The Captain, Timothy O'Regan was from West Skeam. Brother of Tom O'Regan, he emigrated to the U.S.A. The crew members were from Long Island and Castle Island.

Appendix 10
A sample of Heir Island Flora.

Name of Flower In English	Botanical Name	Irish Name
Primrose	Primula vulgaris	Sabhaircín
Lesser Celandine	Rannunculus ficaria	Grán arcáin
Violet	Viola Riviniana	Fanaigse
Thrift	Armeria maritime	Rabhán
Irish Spurge	Euphorbia hyberna	Bainne caoin na n-eán
Ox-eye daisy	Leucanthemum vulgare (Called bull-daisies in Heir)	Nóinín Mór
Poppy	Papaver dabium	Cailleach dhearg

Orchids:

Early Marsh Orchid	Dactylorhiza incarnata	Magairlín mór
Western Marsh Orchid	Dactylorhiza majalis	Magairlín gaelach
Heath Spotted Orchid	” maculate	Magairlín circíní
Autumn Lady's Tresses	Spiranthes	Cúilín Muire.
Kidney Vetch	Anthyllis vulneraria	Méara Muire
Foxglove	Digitalis purpures	An Lus Mór
Ragged Robin	Lychnis flos-cuculi	An Lus Síoda
Honeysuckle	Lonicera perielymenum	Taithfhéithleann
Yellow flag iris	Iris	Feileastram (liostrum)
Camomile	Chamaemelum nolile	Camán meall
Meadowsweet	Filipendula ulmaria	Airgead Luachra
Dog Rose	Rose canina	Feirdris
Bird's Foot Trefoil	Lotus corniculatus	Crobh éin
Self heal	Prunella vulgaris	Duán ceannchosach
Yarrow	achillea millefolium	Athair thalún
Pale Butterwort	Pinguicula lusitanica	Leith uisce bheag
Brookweed	Samolus valerandi,	Falcaire uisce
Heath Bedstraw	Galium saxatile	Luibh na bhfear gonta
Yellow centaury	Cicendia filiformis	Deagha buí
Common centaury	Centaurium erythracea	Dréimire Mhuire
Vetch (tufted)	Cicia craca	Peasair na luch
Tormentil (yellow)	Potentilla erects	Néalfartach
Milkwood	Polygals serpyllifolia	Na Deirfiúiríní (the little sisters)
Sun Spurge	Euphorbia helioscopia,	Lus na bhfaithní
Petty Spurge	Euphorbia peplus,	Gearr nimhe
Bluebell	Hyacinthoices non scripta	Coinnle Corra
Pink Lousewort	Pedicularis sylvatica	Lus an ghiolla
Lady's smock	Cardamine pratensis	Biolar gréagáin
Bladder Campion	Silene vulgaris	Coireán na gcuach
Sea Campion	Silene uniflora	Coireán mara
Bog Pimpernel	Anagallis tenella	Falcaire corraigh
Goden Rod	Solidago virgaurea	Slat óir
Devils bit Scabious	Succisa pratensis Moench	Odhrach bhallach
Common Milkwort		Lus an bhainne
Field Scabious	Knautia arvensis	Cab an ghásaín.
Knapweed	Centaurea nigra	Mínscoth.
St. John's Worth	Hypericum.	

Heather, heath:

Cross leaved heath	Erica tetralix	Fraoch naoscaí.
Bell Heather	Erica cineria	Fraoch cloigíneach.
Ling	Calluna Vulgaris	Fraoch Mór.

Ferns:

Royal Fern	Osmunda regalis	Raithneach ríúil.
Polypody ferns	Polypodium interjectum	Scim mheánach.
Hart's-tongue Fern,	Asplenium scolopendrium	Creamh na muice fia.
Rustyback Fern	Asplenium ceterach	Raithneach rua.
Wall spleenwort	Aspleniumruta-muraria	Luibh na seacht ngábh.

Appendix 11: Songs

The Memphis

The Memphis she left Montreal,
The weather it was so fine
Said the captain to his officers,
We'll have a jolly time.

She reached the Irish Coast
And met with a heavy fog
The Captain lost his reckoning
By an error in the log.

On the 17th of November
At eight o clock that night
The lookout man on the fo'csle hand
He thought he saw a light.

He took it to be the Fastnet Rock.
But sorry am I to say
That by a fatal error
We were wrecked in Dunlough Bay.

The starboard boats being quickly lowered
And getting fully manned
But before they reached the water
The aft took the land.

The forehead one went by
The boat she swung around
The crew got in the water
And nine of them were drowned.

The other boat being safely lowered
And the painter was made fast
The crew, was getting into her
The captain was the last.

When a heavy sea came rolling in
And swept the boat away
And left our captain to his fate
That night in Dunlough Bay.

But Providence proved kind to him
There was luck for him in store
He jumped upon a bullock's back
And safely swam ashore.

There he was treated well
By the people of that place
It is time for me to end my story
Of the wreck in Dunlough Bay.

The Memphis was wrecked in Dunlough Bay on the 17th Nov. in 1896

The Sailor's Alphabet

A is for the anchor, of course you all know,
B is for the bo'sun that stands on the bow,
C is for the capstan that we all heave around,
D is for the deck where our sailors are found,
     Chorus: so merry, so merry, so merry are we,
     Give the sailors their grog boys

And we'll' never go wrong.
No mortal on earth like a sailor at sea.
E is for the engine that makes our gallant ship go,
F if for the foc'sle where you will find all the crew,
G is for the gunwhale at which you will stand,
H is for the hawser that seldom does strand
    Chorus: so merry, so merry, so merry are we,
    Give the sailors their grog boys
    And we'll' never go wrong.
    No mortal on earth like a sailor at sea.
I is for the iron, so stout and so strong,
J is for the jib-boom that often does slip,
K is for the keelson away down below
L is for the lanyards that always will hold
    Chorus: so merry, so merry, so merry are we,
    Give the sailors their grog boys
    And we'll' never go wrong.
    No mortal on earth like a sailor at sea.
M is for the mainmast so stout and so strong,
N is for the needle that never points wrong,
O is for the oars of our gallant ship's crew,
P is for the pennant that was never reefed in.
    Chorus: so merry, so merry, so merry are we,
    Give the sailors their grog boys
    And we'll' never go wrong.
    No mortal on earth like a sailor at sea.
Q is for the quarter deck where our Captain oft stood,
R is for the rigging that often doth shake,
S is for the Starboard of our bold ship,
T is for the topsail we seldom embrace.
    Chorus: so merry, so merry, so merry are we,
    Give the sailors their grog boys
    And we'll' never go wrong.
    No mortal on earth like a sailor at sea.
U is for the ugliest old Captain of all,
V are for the vapours that come with the squall,
W is the windlass on which we do wind and
X, Y and Z, well I can't put in rhyme.
    Chorus: so merry, so merry, so merry are we,
    Give the sailors their grog boys
    And we'll' never go wrong.
    No mortal on earth like a sailor at sea.

The Ballad of Sweet Nonie Nance

On a wee bit of greenery, off the coast of south Ireland,
A sweet little colleen was born there one day
Her father, Cornelius, and Mother named Ellen,
They lived on Heir Island in Roaringwater Bay.

Though their darling young daughter was baptised as Nora,
She was known across the island as sweet Nonie Nance
And the joy that she brought to her family and friends
She would lighten their spirits when ere she'd a chance.
O Sweet Nonie,
Little sweet Nonie fair,
With eyes of blue and ringlets of brown,
A babe from the Isle of Heir.

Her lobsterman father, he sailed the rough waters,
His freshly caught treasures at the market did sell,
And Nonie and Mother, they'd wait along the shore's edge,
For his safe journey home with the stories he'd tell.
Now this sweet little angel, she's say to her father,
O Daddy my dearest, would you sing me a song
She's climb on his knee for his tales about the sea
And his sail around Cape Clear with the winds blowing strong.

O Sweet Nonie,
He loved his sweet Nonie Nance
When he'd whistle a seafaring melody
She'd slip to her feet with a dance.

Along with sister and brother and neighbour and kin
This lovely sweet child, on the shores she did play.
But with age came demands for the caring of land
And it was out to the fields for the saving of hay.
With school by the day, then on with her chores,
Nonie Nance Cahalane desired much more
And her eyes they would beam as she'd often daydream
Of a new world awaiting at its beckoning shore.

O sweet Nonie,
Lovely sweet Nonie Fair,
With eyes of blue and ringlets of brown
The girl from the Isle of Heir.

By boat they did travel for to the mainland for fancies,
And frolic or prayer at the parish nearby,
But as she grew older, her dreams became bolder
And Nonie then knew like a bird she must fly

But at twenty-two years, her eyes filled with tears
She cried as she buried her sweet mother dear
The saddened young maiden, her heart overladen,
Left home on Heir Island for life's new frontiers.

O sweet Nonie, lovely sweet Nonie Fair,
With eyes of blue and ringlets of brown,
Always from the Isle of Heir.
Yes she left her home for the seas to roam.
But she is still from the Isle of Heir.

Composed by Alan Hembrough.

*Alan Hembrough was a personal friend of Nonie Nance
and was so entranced with her stories of Heir Island
that he composed the Ballad of Sweet Nonie Nance
in her honour.*

Significant Dates

1839	Night of the Big Wind.
1845	Potato blight strikes for the first time. First primary school opened.
1847	'Black 47' the worst year of the Famine.
	Wreck of *Stephen Whitney* on West Calf.
1848	Island and Coast Society establish school and prayer house on Heir Island.
1848	*Susan,* of Milford, with cargo of wheat, wrecked on Reen; Heir Islandman shot by coastguards.
1878	Fr. Davis has private audience with Queen Victoria. Three Cape Clear fishermen on deputation with him.
1881	Small slip built on Heir Island East.
1885	Slip improved.
1887	Baroness Burdett Coutts sails into Baltimore to officially open Baltimore Fishery School.
1890	William O'Brien, M.P. advocate of 'Plan of Campaign' addressed tenants in Middle Calf Island.
1891	Congested Districts Board set up to improve facilities in poor areas on the south and west coast.
1891/92	Construction of road through island.
1894	Night of Big Wind.
	Rescue of sailors of *Christian Wilhelm* by Heir Island Fishermen
1900	Ailsawald goes on rock in Sherkin. Repaired on Giornan Point in 1901
	New School opened
1904	Drowning Tragedy in Roaringwater Bay; three Heir Islandmen drowned.
1908-09	Causeway (bridge) constructed.
1909	*Savonia* wrecked in Middle Calf.
1916	*Alondra* on Kedge. Heir Island lobstermen assist in rescue.
1917	Hartes and Cahalanes assist the *Saurnaut* on rocks at Toe Head.
1918	*Thomas Joseph* wrecked on Catalogue Rocks; five rescued by Heir Island fishermen, John Harte, Timothy Murphy and Jerry McCarthy.
1920	Burning of *St. Finbarr*, owned by Con Burke, off the Mizen.
1922	*St. Brigid*, of Baltimore, goes on Taylor's Rock.
1927/28	'New' houses built on Heir Island.
1930s	Pump erected over well near school.
1932	Subsidy scheme for sea sand.
1936	Island bought by Land Commission.
1940	Last family leaves West Skeam (Tom O'Regan).
1941	Wireless telephone system installed on Heir Island connecting the island with the mainland.
1958	Last families leave East Skeam (Cadogans and Hartes).
1950s	Pump erected over well in Paris
1962-66	Béal Boats bought by Jack Pyburn, Seán Harte and John Harte.
1976	E.S.B. – Electricity comes to Heir Island; school closed.
1983	Piped water scheme.
1988	Post Office closed.
2000	New Pier completed.
2003	Blessing of Cross and consecration of Cillín.

Bibliography

Akeroyd, John.	The Wild Plants of Sherkin, Cape Clear and Adjacent Islands of West Cork. Sherkin Island Marine Station, 1996
Brady, W. Mazier.	Clerical and Parochial Records of Cork, Cloyne & Ross, Dublin, 1864
Cleary P. and O'Regan P.	
	Dear Old Skibbereen, Skibbereen, 1991
Cole, J.H.	Church and Parish Records of the United Diocese of Cork, Cloyne and Ross
Corkery, Daniel.	*The Hidden Ireland*, Dublin, 1975
Crowley, Flor	*In West Cork Long Ago*, Mercier Press, 1979
Danagher, Kevin	*Irish Country Households*, Mercier Press, 1985
Danagher, Kevin	*In Ireland Long Ago*, Mercier Press, 1972
Danagher, Kevin.	*The Year in Ireland*, Mercier Press, 1972
Danagher, Kevin.	*Irish Country People*
Donovan, Daniel	*Sketches in Carbery*
Donnelly, James S	*The Land and the People of Nineteenth Century Cork*. Routledge and Keegan Paul, London, 1975
Donnelly, James S	*The Great Irish Potato Famine*, Sutton Publishing, 2001
Dowling P.J.	*The Hedge Schools of Ireland*, Cork, 1968
Durell, Penelope	*Discover Dursey*, 1996
Evans, E. Estyn	*Irish Folkways*, London 1957
Fitzgerald, Seámus	*Mackerel and the Making of Baltimore, Co.Cork*. Irish Academic Press, 1999
Flanagan, Deirdre and Laurence.	*Irish Place Names*.
Harris, R.A.M. and Jacobs D.M.	*The Search for Missing Friends*, Boston, 1991
Harrison, Richard S.	*Four Hundred Years of Drimoleague*
Healy, James N.	*The Castles of County Cork*, Mercier Press, 2002
Henderson John	*Early Murphy Descendants of Mary Hurley and James McCarthy: From Roaringwater Bay, Cork, Ireland to The Falls of the Androscoggin, Maine, U.S.A.* Hindsight Historical Publishing, Maine, U.S.A.
Hickey P	*Famine in West Cork*, Mercier Press, 2002
Holland W.	*The History of West Cork and the Diocese of Ross*, Southern Star, Ltd., Skibbereen, 1949
Kingston W.J.	*The Story of West Carbery*. The Friendly Press, Waterford, 1985
Kinmonth, Claudia	*Irish Country Furniture 1700–1950*, Yale University Press, New Haven and London, 1993
Lankford, Éamon,	*Cape Clear Island, Its People and Landscape*, Cape Clear, 1999
	Naomh Ciarán, Pilgrim Islander, Cape Clear Museum.
Levis, Cormac	*Towelsail Yawls, The Lobsterboats of Heir Island and Roaringwater Bay*, Galley Head Press, 2002
Lewis Samuel	*Topographical Dictionary of Ireland*, London 1837
McCarthy P. and Hawkes R.	*Northside of the Mizen*, Dublin 1999
Moody, T.W. & Martin F.X.	*The Course of Irish History*, Mercier Press, 1967

Nolan, P.	*When We Were Young: Life in West Cork*, Impact Printing, Ballycastle, Coleraine, 1998
O'Brien, Brigid and Whooley, Mary	*From Ilen to Roaringwater Bay, Reminiscences from the Parish of Aughadown*
Ó Cróinín, S and D	*Seanchas O Chairbre*, 1985
O'Donoghue, Bruno	*Parish Histories and Place Names of West Cork*
O'Mahony, J.	*West Cork and its story*
Ó Murchadha Diarmuid	*Family Names of County Cork*, The Collins Press, Cork, 1996
Ó Síocháin, Conchúr	*Seanchas Chléire*
O'Sullivan, Donal J.	*The History of Caheragh Parish*
Sharkey, Olive,	*Old Days, Old Ways*, O'Brien Press, 1985
Somerville-Large, Peter	*The Coast of West Cork*, London 1972
	The Irish Country House
Smith, Charles	*Ancient and Present State of the County and City of Cork* Second edition, Cork 1815
Townsend, Horatio	A General & Statistical Survey of the City and County of Cork
O'Reilly, Dolly	Sherkin Island

Journals

Mizen Journal, Volume 1 – 12
Journal of the Cork Historical and Archaeological Society
Rosscarbery Past and Present, Volumes 1-5
Ardfield and Rathbarry Journal